CAN
THESE
BONES
LIVE?

CAN THESE BONES LIVE?

A Catholic Baptist Engagement with Ecclesiology, Hermeneutics, and Social Theory

BARRY HARVEY

BrazosPress

a division of Baker Publishing Group
Grand Rapids, Michigan

© 2008 by Barry Harvey

Published by Brazos Press
a division of Baker Publishing Group
P.O. Box 6287, Grand Rapids, MI 49516-6287
www.brazospress.com

Printed in the United States of America

Library of Congress Cataloging-in-Publication Data
Harvey, Barry, 1954–
    Can these bones live? : a Catholic Baptist engagement with ecclesiology, hermeneutics, and social theory / Barry Harvey.
       p. cm.
    Includes bibliographical references and index.
    ISBN 978-1-58743-081-7 (pbk.)
    1. Church. 2. Christian sociology. I. Title.
BV600.3.H445 2008
262—dc22   2008011655

To Sarah
for her grace, courage, and beauty

Contents

Acknowledgments

The writing of any book, and especially of this book, is never the achievement of an isolated individual. Family, mentors, colleagues, friends, and students all make important contributions, in many and varied ways, to what an author finally produces. Simply mentioning them here does not repay the debts that I owe them, but perhaps it will suffice as a token of my appreciation. Scott Moore, Ralph Wood, and Douglas Henry in particular have been wonderful friends and critics, as have Curtis Freeman, Beth Newman, Mike Broadway, and Philip Thompson. And I must not forget to mention the late James McClendon, whose encouragement and gentle wisdom and wit were invaluable to me. Discussions with these and others over the years have helped immeasurably to refine the proposals I put forward in this book, though of course they bear no responsibility for the use I have made of their insights.

I am also grateful for my colleagues, past and present, at Baylor University. I cannot imagine a more supportive dean than Thomas Hibbs, or provost than Randall O'Brien. Included among the many mentors and conversation partners through the years are Donald Schmeltekopf, Robert Miner, Philip Donnelly, Robert Sloan, Peter Candler, David Jeffrey, Michael Hanby, Mikeal Parsons, Susan Colon, Michael Foley, Glenn Hilburn, C. W. Christian, Daniel Williams, Bob Patterson, Sarah-Jane Murray, Daniel McGee, William H. Bellinger, Jr., John Wood, Jonathan Tran, Paul Martens, Michael Beaty, Robert Kruschwitz, Todd Buras, Victor Hinojosa, Margaret Tate, Francis Beckwith, Amy Vail, Daniel Payne, and the late A. J. Conyers. I trust that I shall be forgiven if I have omitted someone who should have been mentioned here.

Friends that I have found in connection with the Ekklesia Project, whose love for the church is manifest in all they do and say, have blessed my life. They include Michael Budde, Trecy Lysaught, Kyle Childress, Steve Long, Jon Stock, James Lewis, Brent Laytham, Mike Cartwright, Stan Wilson, B. J. Heyboer, Phil Kenneson, Kelly Johnson, William Cavanaugh, Joel Shuman, Stanley Hauerwas, and Michael Bowling. I have also been gifted with students—graduate and under-graduate, past and present—who consistently provide both the enthusiasm and the rationale for undertaking a project such as this. What I have accomplished in this book would not have been possible save for all that I have learned from and with them.

I am also indebted to Rodney Clapp and all those at Brazos Press who helped to make this book a reality. Rodney has been a friend for some time now, and the opportunity to work with him on a book project was something that I have long sought to do. As a mutual friend put it, Rodney's vision for the integrity of theology led him to establish Brazos Press, so that those of us who are unapologetic about doing theology, locate ourselves within the church's intellectual and moral tradi-tion, and seek to bear critical and charitable witness to the wider world about us would have a place to publish.

My daughter, Rachel, and son, John, are my constant joy and delight. More than anyone else, they continue to teach me the importance of patience and loving-kindness.

I dedicate this book to my wife, Sarah. I could not imagine my life without her wisdom, delightful humor, enthusiasm, wit, and encouragement. To her and to all, and always to a gracious and merciful God, I give thanks.

Introduction:
Where, Then, Do We Stand?

Toward an Ecclesially Based Theological Hermeneutics

Theology is a laborious attempt to explain the joke about this ordinary physical, political world.

Herbert McCabe, *God Matters*

The desire to ask about the beginning, writes Dietrich Bonhoeffer, is the innermost passion of our thinking as creaturely beings, imparting reality to every genuine question we ask. And yet no sooner is the question of the beginning put before us than our thinking is thrown back on itself, spending its strength like huge breakers crashing upon a rocky shore. In its desire to reach back to the beginning, human reasoning cannot help but pound itself to pieces. We are intractably located in the middle, knowing neither the end nor the beginning.[1]

In contrast to those who are perennially tempted by the Gnostic illusion that there is "a spark of breath" in each of us going back "to before the Creation,"[2] the church has taught that we always find ourselves somewhere, that our patterns of speaking and acting take shape within a context formed by the time, place, and people of which we are a part. Indeed, if others are to take what we say or do seriously, we must take up and consistently maintain some standpoint, and they must

1. The knowledge that we find ourselves in the middle of things, Bonhoeffer adds, also deprives human beings of self-determination (Dietrich Bonhoeffer, *Dietrich Bonhoeffer Works*, vol. 3, *Creation and Fall: A Theological Exposition of Genesis 1–3*, trans. Martin Rüter and Ilse Tödt [Minneapolis: Fortress, 1997], 25–28).

2. Harold Bloom, *The American Religion: The Emergence of the Post-Christian Nation* (New York: Simon & Schuster, 1992), 22.

11

do likewise.[3] The theological task facing the church, then, is not to try to find an unsullied point of departure, a method, impulse, or insight that can lift us out of our time and place so that we might see all the kingdoms of the world in a moment. It is instead to help a fallen world take its bearings here in the middle, to understand something of what went before, to learn about the ways things developed in the past that led to the way they are now. Instead of asking where do we begin, a more fruitful question would be, "Where, then, do we stand?"[4]

This question can, of course, be parsed in several different ways. It can be taken in an epistemic sense: what are the warrants for our claims to know something significant about ourselves? It also suggests a historical referent: it is commonplace to say that we now live in a "postmodern" era, whatever that means. Though these are important considerations that we shall ponder in what follows, for Christians the question of where we stand has above all an eschatological trajectory. As citizens of another city that is to come (Heb. 13:14), we have no permanent standpoint or proper place in the present time. We are on pilgrimage through history, looking with anticipation for the coming of the commonwealth whose architect and builder is the Triune God (Heb. 11:10; cf. Phil. 3:20). When we ask where we now stand, we do so as a people seeking to go on and go further toward that future which summons all of God's creatures, and especially humankind.

In what follows I contend that the church, by being what it is—the earthly-historical body of Christ—constitutes an interpretive surmise about creaturely life as lived in relation to God. The existence of this people is grounded in a distinctive practice of life and language that is a socially embodied, historically extended interpretation of the world in general, and of human life in particular. The answer to the question of what is signified by the word *God* cannot finally be ascertained by the kind of conceptual clarification practiced by analytic philosophers (though that might be helpful at certain points), but only by observing how this community orders its life together through its worship, teaching, witness and work.[5] This hermeneutical dimension is implicit in the understanding of the church as a sacrament, that is, as "a sign and instrument . . . of communion with God and of unity among men."[6]

Another way to put this is to say with John Milbank that theology in a postmodern setting can be practiced only by way of explicating Christian practice: "The Christian God can no longer be thought of as a God first seen, but rather as a God first prayed to, first imagined, first inspiring certain actions, first put into words, and always already thought about, objectified, even if this objectification

3. James Wm. McClendon Jr., *Systematic Theology*, vol. 2, *Doctrine* (Nashville: Abingdon, 1994), 172.

4. Nicholas Lash, *Believing Three Ways in One God: A Reading of the Apostles' Creed* (Notre Dame, IN: University of Notre Dame Press, 1993), 2.

5. Rowan Williams, *On Christian Theology* (Malden, MA: Blackwell, 2000), xii, 135.

6. *Lumen Gentium*, in Austin Flannery, OP, ed., *Vatican Council II: The Conciliar and Post Conciliar Documents*, new rev. ed. (Northport, NY: Costello Publishing Company, 1992), 68–69.

is recognised as inevitably inadequate."[7] The dependence of theory on practice is not limited to theology or religion more generally. From literary theory to the physics laboratory, all attempts at interpretation or explanation are at bottom forms of explication of already existing practices.

This book can be classified as an exercise in theological hermeneutics, though not in the narrow sense of formulating a general theory of meaning that establishes normative rules, procedures, and standards for the interpretation of written texts (though it does involve, among other things, the careful reading of scripture and other writings). Stephen Fowl contends, rightly in my view, that all efforts to produce a general theory of meaning, also known as a general hermeneutics, are necessarily question-begging and should be avoided. Interpretation, he argues, should be underdetermined, that is, it should be free to use a variety of interpretive practices and results without granting epistemic priority to any of them.[8]

In the sense I will use it here, hermeneutics is heir to the Aristotelian tradition of practical reasoning, *phronesis,* about the possibilities of human action, fulfillment and happiness, encompassing ethics, politics, poetics, rhetoric, cosmology, and metaphysics.[9] Theology has a vested interest in all these areas of investigation and thus qualifies as a hermeneutical enterprise, but it attends to these matters, says Robert Jenson, in the course of asking how to carry on with a specified message at that point in life "where past hearing turns to new speaking. . . . Theology is an act of interpretation; it begins with a received word and issues in a new word essentially related to the old word."[10]

A theological hermeneutics thus attends to the question, What does the life, death, and resurrection of the man Jesus of Nazareth have to do with this life that we now live? If we are to grasp the significance of Christ and his earthly-historical body for our lives, living as we do in a different time and place, in circumstances that are marked by their own particularity and contingency, it is necessary that we learn how to narrate our lives both as distinct from his story and, at the same time, as a continuation of it. To this end theologians engage in a threefold hermeneutical activity: first, with respect to the scriptures as the book of the church; second,

7. John Milbank, "'Postmodern Critical Augustinianism': A Short *Summa* in Forty-two Responses to Unasked Questions," *Modern Theology* 7 (April 1991): 226–27. In chapter 5 I shall return to this question of how the church deals with the inadequacy of its objectifications of God.

8. Stephen E. Fowl, *Engaging Scripture: A Model for Theological Interpretation* (Malden, MA: Blackwell, 1998), 33.

9. See in this regard Hans-Georg Gadamer, "Hermeneutics and Social Science," *Cultural Hermeneutics* 2 (1975): 316, cited by Richard J. Bernstein, *Beyond Objectivism and Relativism* (Philadelphia: University of Pennsylvania Press, 1983), 40, and Paul Ricoeur, "Life in Quest of Narrative," in *On Paul Ricoeur: Narrative and Interpretation,* ed. David Wood (New York: Routledge, 1991), 20–33.

10. Robert W. Jenson, *Systematic Theology,* vol. 1, *The Triune God* (New York: Oxford University Press, 1997), 14. Peter Hodgson states in similar fashion that theology is a form of hermeneutics that involves "a construal of the meaning of Christian faith in light of a particular set of cultural exigencies and on the basis of a particular reading of texts and traditions." Peter C. Hodgson, *Winds of the Spirit: A Constructive Christian Theology* (Louisville: Westminster/John Knox Press, 1994), 7.

with respect to the practices of the church (which are themselves interpretive actions in that they have to do with possibilities of human flourishing); and third, with respect to the political and economic regimes, cultural norms, and forms of knowledge that distinguish our particular time and place in history.[11]

This "venture of an overall view"[12] consists principally of the intellectual, moral, and spiritual convictions, dispositions, and activities that have been handed on to us within the Christian community by our mothers and fathers in the faith. This heritage is now ours to take up and develop, not only so that we might learn how to conduct ourselves truthfully and faithfully in our own circumstances, but also that we might hand it on in good working order to our spiritual offspring.[13] This book is therefore also a work in ecclesiology, with an emphasis on the constitutive practices of the church: scriptural reasoning, doctrine, baptism and Eucharist, and spiritual formation. I refer to these practices as constitutive because all Christians must engage in them in some fashion if we are to cultivate and sustain the distinctive form of life that characterizes the body of Christ in the world. In this respect the church is not unique. In virtually every society there are set practices that specify the nature and hierarchy of goods that order its common life, determine who belongs to the community and who is an outsider, facilitate the production and distribution of material goods among its members and guests, assign social roles and responsibilities to each man, woman, and child, and maintain just and orderly relations among its members and between members and those on the outside.

My proposal to outline a theological hermeneutics grounded in the life and language of the church immediately encounters a serious problem in the fact of a divided church, or, as I shall describe it, the dismembered body of Christ. Indeed, these divisions may make theology impossible, since the proper agent of such a hermeneutics does not exist, unless one simply declares that one particular branch of the church catholic totally comprehends that reality. If we are to go on and go further as the pilgrim people of God in the context of a divided church (if this can happen at all), writes Jenson, then we must confess that "we live in radical self-contradiction and that by every churchly act we contradict that contradiction. Also theology must make this double contradiction at and by every step of its way."[14] This need not be a pessimistic assessment, since the members of Christ's body live by hope in the coming kingdom of God. And so we wait in the knowledge that it is a blessing to theology that we need not wait for the church to be "re-membered" to do our work.

11. See Graham Ward, *Cultural Transformation and Religious Practice* (New York: Cambridge University Press, 2005), 14.

12. Dietrich Ritschl, *The Logic of Theology: A Brief Account of the Relationship between Basic Concepts in Theology* (Philadelphia: Fortress, 1987), 202.

13. See Dietrich Bonhoeffer, *Dietrich Bonhoeffer Works*, vol. 6, *Ethics*, trans. Reinhard Krauss, Charles C. West, and Douglas W. Stott (Minneapolis: Fortress, 2005), 128.

14. Jenson, *Triune God*, vii.

Some may object at this point that proceeding from the standpoint of the church community and its interpretive tradition will mean that we must suppress the critical and speculative side of our rational nature, but these fears are ultimately unfounded. When inquiring after knowledge generally, writes John Henry Newman, "we must assume something to prove anything, and can gain nothing without a venture."[15] Human beings must therefore make a hermeneutical surmise of one sort or another to know or do anything at all, from the most mundane tasks to the most elaborate research programs in science, and such ventures are always subject to subtle reworking, substantive revision, or outright rejection. The church is not exempt from this principle, and it is the work of theology to test the convictions of its interpretive venture, to criticize and transform them when warranted, and to take account of the differences and disputes that exist between the church and other human associations.[16]

What theologians must refuse, however, is the illusory notion that there is an unsullied beginning point, a "mid-air" position that we can occupy through the application of some sort of critical method, allowing us—without getting our feet wet, so to speak—to judge which claims are true and which are not. We should not confuse what William of St. Thierry refers to as the hesitations of thought (*haesitationes cogitationum*) that invariably accompany the thoughts of faith (*fidei cogitationes*) with the sort of dishonest rationality (*rationalitas improba*) that adopts an antagonistic attitude to faith.[17] The skepticism that arises from this kind of antagonism necessarily leads to either despair or cynicism, or to both in alternation.[18]

Dismembering the Body of Christ

So then, where *do* we stand? Though I shall deal with this question in more detail throughout the book, a preliminary statement is in order. Suffice it to say that we do not stand where our mothers and fathers in the faith once stood. They saw the world as followable, a "book," as it were, authored by God, with the events of history unfolding in the manner of a dramatic narrative. The complex plot and many subplots of this story were detailed for the faithful in God's other work, the Bible, according to which all things ultimately find their significance in their being either receptive to or closed off from the work of God in Christ's life, passion, and resurrection.

15. John Henry Newman, "The Nature of Faith in Relation to Reason," in *Fifteen Sermons Preached before the University of Oxford between A.D. 1826 and 1843,* intro. Mary Katherine Tillmann (Notre Dame, IN: University of Notre Dame Press, 1997), 215.

16. James Wm. McClendon Jr. and James M. Smith, *Convictions: Defusing Religious Relativism,* rev. ed. (Valley Forge, PA: Trinity Press International, 1994), 9.

17. William of St. Thierry, *Speculum Fidei* (*PL,* 180, 388 D, 378 AB), *The Mirror of Faith,* trans. Thomas X. Davis (Kalamazoo, MI: Cistercian, 1979), 38, 65; cf. Henri de Lubac, SJ, *The Mystery of the Supernatural,* trans. Rosemary Sheed (New York: Crossroad, 1998), 170.

18. Paul Tillich, *Dynamics of Faith* (New York: Harper & Row, 1957), 19.

The church's venture of an overall view of things was not confined to the privatized realm of religion, there sequestered from the everyday world, that is, the workings of politics, economics, and the like. It was interwoven with a complex social space that was comprised of intersecting associations—church practices and institutions, civil authorities, clans, monasteries, guilds, and towns. The obligations, immunities, and entitlements that men and women owed to one another within these *societates* were not conferred by an omnicompetent, centralized state but subsisted within these overlapping associations of which they were members. Each person and association was regarded as an integral whole that also constituted a part of a larger whole, generating a complex conception of space that was conceived on the Pauline theology of the body of Christ.[19]

Over the last several centuries, however, radically new configurations of world and self have been instituted to train those who formed the heart of Christendom in Western Europe and North America to think, feel, and act quite differently in every sphere of life. A vast technical and institutional apparatus—the emergence of the state as the normative form of political community, the commodification of property, goods and labor, the development of complex monetary systems, the rise to social prominence of managerial expertise, and radical changes in political and moral discourse—has uprooted the social relationships and personal identities that were previously embedded in local associations. In place of these encumbrances, modern institutions sought to establish a direct and unmediated relationship between the sovereign power of the state and the unencumbered individual whose only necessary identity was as a unit of production and consumption, and for whom other individuals were only variables in the calculation of self-interest.

The peoples of Christendom were thus divested of the practices, dispositions, and institutions that had enabled them to follow the world as an ensemble of signs uttered and intended by God. The accumulated social capital—the moral habits and conceptions about human community and the good—was reinvested in a series of political, economic, and cultural projects that stipulated that the social mediation of transcendence was no longer needed to ascend to truth, goodness, and beauty. People were set free from the constraints of shared past and the claim of others on their lives to fashion their own stories (save, of course, from the authority of the state, which promised to ensure that freedom in exchange for unquestioned political sovereignty). Progress would be measured solely by the degree to which individuals realized independence from any relationship or authority outside themselves.[20]

---

19. John Milbank, *The Word Made Strange: Theology, Language, Culture* (Cambridge, MA: Blackwell, 1997), 268–92; Otto Gierke, *Associations and Law: The Classical and Early Christian Stages*, trans. George Heiman (Toronto: University of Toronto Press, 1977), 143–60; William T. Cavanaugh, *Theopolitical Imagination: Discovering the Liturgy as a Political Act in an Age of Global Consumerism* (New York: T & T Clark, 2002), 99–100.

20. For a more detailed account of this project, see Michael J. Sandel, *Democracy's Discontent: America in Search of a Public Philosophy* (Cambridge, MA: Belknap, 1996).

Of all the relationships that needed to be dismantled for the modern project to go forward, none was more crucial than those once located within the church. The political and economic regime that separated the day-to-day lives of women and men from the social ligatures of family, clan, guild, estate and village also severed the ecclesial sinews that bound them to the risen Christ and to each other. Working gradually and methodically, the new order of things dismembered the body of Christ by abating its common life and vitiating its witness to the Triune God. The substance of Christian faith was separated from the constitutive practices that made it possible for women and men, in the power of the Spirit, to participate in the economy of God's redemptive work in the world, with the capacity to imagine, reason, desire, feel, and act as members of Christ's true body.

Apart from these practices and the habits they cultivated, Christians were increasingly subject to the political whims and machinations of the modern state, with little sense of the difference between the obligations they owed to God and those owed to the state. They also became caught up in habits of consumption that no longer served any higher purpose but became ends in themselves, to be desired for their own sake. Ensnared by stunted imaginations and unfettered appetites, we still routinely confuse having a plethora of choices with being free.[21] These desires and habits not only are out of proportion to what men and women need to flourish as creatures made in the image of God, but radically transform the character of their relations with others, not only within the body of Christ, but also with those outside the fellowship of the church.

The dismembering of the body of Christ thus had a significant impact on the earthly commonwealth as well, for the institutions that for centuries constituted the social fabric of Western Europe and North America were largely fostered by the church. However deficient we might finally judge this arrangement to be theologically, it provided a measure of moral coherence and direction to a succession of temporal regimes that helped to preserve a fallen world for the gathering together of all things in Christ at the end of the age. People can only go about their business on the tacit assumption that error, deception, self-deception, irony, and ambiguity, though everywhere present in these interactions, will not finally render reliable reasoning and coherent action impossible.[22] These assumptions are formed and sustained by the stock of activities, stories, habits, and institutions that foster a common life and language within a society. These practices and habits provide the conventions that enable the members of a community to engage one another in meaningful transactions by making inferences about future behavior and present intentions from premises about past behavior.

21. For further insight into the difference between Christian and liberal conceptions of freedom, see David Burrell, *Faith and Freedom: An Interfaith Perspective* (Malden, MA: Blackwell, 2004); and Reinhard Hütter, *Bound to Be Free: Evangelical Catholic Engagements in Ecclesiology, Ethics, and Ecumenism* (Grand Rapids: Eerdmans, 2004).

22. Alasdair MacIntyre, "Epistemological Crises, Dramatic Narrative, and the Philosophy of Science," in *Why Narrative?* eds. Stanley Hauerwas and L. Gregory Jones (Grand Rapids: Eerdmans, 1989), 139.

When these shared practices and dispositions begin to lose their authority over the habits of body and mind that bind men and women together into a community, and mutually incompatible accounts of what is going on around them begin to multiply seemingly exponentially, but with none achieving a "critical mass," the result is the kind of social fragmentation that we see with the demise of the social project of Christendom. As a consequence, writes Rowan Williams, there is an ever-widening gap or wound in the secular body politic, "which neither conventional right nor conventional left are currently doing much to recognise or repair." In place of shared patterns of judging human behavior and relationship that allow people to determine what they can reasonably do and say together to foster a just and equitable common life and language, the ruling regime of nation-states and global markets offers political discourse that is dominated by the marketing of slogans and sound bites, and the calculation of short-term advantages, which are incapable of sustained deliberations about the basic conditions of our humanity.[23]

Christians cannot lay the blame for this state of affairs solely on the advent of modernity. The *corpus Christianum* had been sagging under its own accumulated weight for several centuries, and the final supports are now giving way to the stress of a rapidly secularizing world. With its collapse, its patterns of relating to the world are rapidly deteriorating as well. The nations of Europe and North America delayed for a time the dehumanizing effects of this process by selectively drawing on a residual stock of practices, convictions and dispositions held over from the traditions of medieval Christendom. But as the contents of this reserve were disconnected from the ecclesial practices and institutions that had nurtured them over the centuries, their intelligibility and credibility began to unravel, somewhat slowly at first, and then more rapidly as the era of "enlightenment" and "progress" unfolded.

The compliment typically paid to this "postmodern" situation, cobbled together from the debris left by the ancien régime, is that it is pluralistic and multicultural, but this is hollow praise indeed. In the end these are but names for the reduction of all values to those that can be marketed as commodities in the global market. In place of a stock of images and ideas, inscribed in a shared body of texts, that foster a rich common life, the ruling consortium seeks merely to secure a pragmatic minimum of coexistence between unencumbered individuals and their mutually tangential projects by means of a combination of managerial skills and economic policies.[24] The euphemisms of *pluralism* and *multiculturalism* serve as a facade to hide the incoherence and antagonism that afflict all. Many people now wonder whether there is anything at all genuinely and intrinsically human beyond their

---

23. Rowan Williams, *Lost Icons: Reflections on Cultural Bereavement* (Edinburgh: T & T Clark, 2000), 2–3, 9.

24. Rowan Williams, "Between Politics and Metaphysics: Reflections in the Wake of Gillian Rose," in *Rethinking Metaphysics*, ed. L. Gregory Jones and Stephen E. Fowl (Oxford: Blackwell, 1995), 4; Rowan D. Williams, "Postmodern Theology and the Judgement of the World," in *Postmodern Theology*, ed. Frederic B. Burnham (San Francisco: Harper & Row, 1989), 99.

momentary appetites and desires, and any identity they might share in common resides not in a positive good that commands their assent, but in suspicion of and hatred for their enemies, both real and imagined.

The dismembering of Christ's body, if it is to be adequately understood, must therefore be conceived diachronically as well as synchronically. It did not happen overnight, nor can it be simply laid at the doorstep of the Protestant Reformation or the Enlightenment. The logic of separation that emerged in the sixteenth and seventeenth centuries and gained momentum in the modern era has its origins much earlier, when the church joined forces with the rulers and authorities of the present age to govern the *saeculum*.[25] The division of the church must therefore be examined in conjunction with the emergence, development, and demise of the social project of Christendom. In addition to being a work in hermeneutics and ecclesiology, then, this book must also engage the much-contested domain of social theory.

Re-embarking on Pilgrimage

As we prepare, then, to take our bearings for the future from what went before us, what lessons should we learn from our present circumstances? First, we need to be careful, lest we romanticize the past and find ourselves caught up in nostalgic longing for what has been. Though nostalgia can be a potent form of social criticism, the church cannot simply rebel against the modern in an effort to return to the simplicity and pristine faithfulness supposedly proffered by the premodern era. We cannot return, moreover, because modernity was shaped by the deliberate rejection of the past, and modernity is part of our past.[26] Rebellion against rebellion imprisons us within an insidious antithetical bondage. Indeed, part of the modern world's genius was its ability to conscript its adversaries into its modes of regulating behavior, which rely not so much on explicit coercion as on widely diffused modes of regulation that train us how to think, feel, and act in ways appropriate to its basic modes of governance and accumulation.

Nostalgia also clouds the fact that the social arrangements of Christendom failed to a significant degree because, as Vigen Guroian expresses it, the church "endeavored to be not what it is but what it is not." These arrangements failed not only the church, in that it lost sight of itself as "the sacrament of the Kingdom, a holy community, God's eschatological vehicle of passage for this world through time into the world to come," but also the world to which it was sent as sign and instrument. According to Guroian, the failure was twofold. First, in its efforts to

25. In the original sense of that term, both church and world are secular realities. The Latin *saeculum* did not designate a space or realm separate from the religious or sacred, but a time. Early Christian writers used the term to refer to the temporal period between fall and *eschaton*, and after the coming of Christ to the overlap of the two ages in the here and now.

26. Joseph Bottum, "Christians and Postmoderns," *First Things* 40 (February 1994): 28–29.

redeem and sanctify the existing social order, the church forgot its earlier understanding of the world as both created and therefore good, and fallen and therefore
a mortally sick order. Second, when the church accepted its status as a juridical
and hierarchical institution within the established order, it forfeited its calling as
a free community of faith whose very presence in the world is both a judgment on
and a boundary to the claims of every worldly authority and power.[27]

The collapse of Christendom is thus a timely opportunity for the church to
recover its missional status as another city making its way toward the age to come.
The laments and prophetic rebukes in scripture remind us that among the remnants
of the failed kingdoms of Israel and Judah, there was a struggle to understand what
had happened, and out of their humiliation they revised their own history, seeing
it as "a story of unceasing resistance to and rebellion against God." They nonetheless concluded that God had not utterly abandoned them, but in his faithfulness
had instead folded the destruction of the northern kingdom, the fall of Jerusalem,
the exile to Babylon, and the dispersion of the chosen people among the nations
of the world back into the saving history of Israel. In their affliction they learned
to "recognize their guilt and turn back to God, thus correcting the direction they
[were] going. The very crisis of the people of God would then be one of the reasons
why God's cause does not fail, but instead goes forward as a history of salvation."
The end of the monarchy in Israel did not spell Israel's end but led instead "to a
rebirth of the people of God," thus making the event of the exile part of "a *saving
history and a step into the future*."[28]

Unfortunately, the church, particularly in North America, seems more oblivious
to its precarious situation than were the exiles in Babylon. One must look long and
hard for similar retrospectives on the part of the church with respect to its own
history. "On the contrary," writes Gerhard Lohfink, "[t]he faith for which Israel
still struggled and over which it wrangled is dissolving in the current decades . . .
almost without resistance, and unnoticed by a great many, into religion: a religion
that permits everything, that surrenders to everything, that has countless gods
but no longer a history with the biblical God."[29] In our feeble efforts to hold on to
the remnants of the ancien régime, too many Christians willingly accommodate
the substance of the faith to the demands of a world that no longer is interested
in what the church has to say.

Nevertheless, we have the opportunity as members of the body of Christ to
reconsider our own history with the biblical God, to acknowledge our failures
and guilt, and to return to our first love, so that we too might learn to see what has

---

27. Vigen Guroian, *Incarnate Love: Essays in Orthodox Ethics*, 2nd ed. (Notre Dame, IN: University
of Notre Dame Press, 2002), 146–47. For a more detailed discussion of the failure of Christendom, see
my *Another City: An Ecclesiological Primer for a Post-Christian World* (Valley Forge, PA: Trinity Press
International, 1999).

28. Gerhard Lohfink, *Does God Need the Church? Toward a Theology of the People of God*, trans. Linda
M. Maloney (Collegeville, MN: Liturgical Press, 1999), 96, 105.

29. Ibid., 96–97.

happened over the past few centuries as part of God's redemptive history and thus as a way forward. The turn of fortune that has thrust the church back outside the city gate (Heb. 13:12), no longer having a portfolio in the ruling regime, is an occasion for Christians once again to take our cues from the story of God's revelation in Jesus Christ, and to reclaim our identity as an eschatological commonwealth whose interests are ultimately vested not in institutions that are condemned to pass away, but in the world to come.

Organization

The book is divided into two parts. In part 1, I endeavor, first, to describe briefly what it means for the body of Christ to have been dismembered and to set forth what the church must do to recover its status as the earthly-historical form of Christ in the world; second, to locate the hermeneutical surmise of the church in the *apocalypse* of the reign of God in Christ's life, death, and resurrection; and third, to narrate the events and the changes that dismantled the church's traditional regime of life and language that extended the apocalyptic action of God to every time and place, leaving the scattered members of Christ's body at the mercy of the powers and authorities of this present age.

In chapter 1, I contrast the general understanding of nature and history proposed by the patristic and medieval church, according to which all created things are also signs that refer to their beginning and end in God, with new configurations that arose with the modern world, and which contend that the intelligibility of nature, the meaningfulness of history, and the purposefulness of human existence no longer require these sorts of references. I then provide an initial sketch of the interpretive art that allows us to follow God's critical, decisive, and final action and purpose for the world in the apocalypse of the long-awaited reign of God in Jesus Christ.

Chapter 2 takes up and develops further the apocalyptic motif that is at the heart of the church's interpretive art. The first group of disciples who followed the way of Jesus found themselves caught up in a set of allegiances, convictions, dispositions, and loves that put them in the middle of the divine struggle with, and triumph over, temporal powers and principalities that sought to usurp divine sovereignty over creation. God's intrusion into a world enslaved to sin and death did not, however, appear out of a social or historical vacuum but marked the continuation of the story of Abraham and Sarah's offspring under new and distinct circumstances. The early church understood itself to be the first fruits of messianic Israel united with the risen Lord, recapitulating the sorts of trials and temptations that the chosen people had faced for centuries, only now under the figure of Jesus's cross, resurrection, and return.

In the third chapter I discuss in more detail how the church was dismembered as the body of Christ. It began when the Christian community exchanged its distinctive way of life as a company of fellow pilgrims garnered from every tribe and language, every people and nation, to serve the nations a sign and instrument of God's eternal commonwealth, for a power-sharing arrangement with the rulers and authorities of the earthly city. As a result, the body of Christ was gradually caught up in an unfolding series of disciplinary regimes that effectively domesticated, marginalized, and exploited the church's life and language. Special care must be taken on this point. It is easy to issue a blanket condemnation of "Constantinianism," and though that might allow some to give voice to their dissatisfaction with the present situation, it would not address what is basically at stake in this matter. As Oliver O'Donovan reminds us, the *corpus Christianum* of the medieval and early modern worlds was "the womb in which our late-modernity came to birth. Even our refusal of Christendom has been learned from Christendom. Its insights and errors have fashioned, sometimes by repetition and sometimes by reaction, the insights and errors which comprise the platitudes of our own era."[30] At the same time the concern with the momentous changes that took place beginning in the fourth century must be accounted for.

In part 2, I turn our attention to the question of how the church might by God's grace be gathered together once again and re-membered by the power of the Spirit as the body of Christ. I say "might," for we can never ensure the presence of Christ by means of a formal institution that connects the present with the past, as though it were an expression of an immanent historical process. We cannot compel the grace of God through some sort of procedural or ritualistic alchemy. God's messianic reign only comes to gather the church *epicletically*, that is to say, "in the constantly renewed pleading of the faithful that the Holy Spirit enact the Kingdom in their midst. Historical continuity never determines the presence of Christ; the eschaton rules history, but is also enacted *in* history."[31]

A people cannot set out on a journey and reasonably expect to survive, much less make progress, without being properly trained and provisioned. We must constantly be gathered together so that we will not scatter along the way; we must learn how to take our bearings, so that we know where we are, where we are headed, and how to get from the one to the other; we must be disciplined so that we keep our eyes trained on what lies before us and not be tempted to return to the fleshpots of Egypt; and we must learn how to distinguish among the wide range of regimes we shall encounter in the earthly city along the way.

The convictions and skills that make up the art of surviving and prospering as a community whose homeland lies in the future are not easily or quickly acquired but must be carefully cultivated over extended periods of time. The assumption of some that though specific features of the church may vary according to time,

---

30. Oliver O'Donovan, *The Desire of the Nations: Rediscovering the Roots of Political Theology* (Cambridge: Cambridge University Press, 1996), 194.

31. William T. Cavanaugh, *Torture and Eucharist: Theology, Politics, and the Body of Christ* (Malden, MA: Blackwell, 1998), 270; cf. John D. Zizioulas, *Being as Communion* (Crestwood, NY: St. Vladimir's Seminary Press, 1985), 204–8.

place, and circumstance, its existence and basic character will always be relatively unproblematic has proven to be false. We cannot take it for granted that
there will continue to be a church that more or less resembles the one we have
inherited.[32]

Re-membering the church as Christ's body involves, among other things,
recreating a universe of theological discourse that has grown stagnant from mis-
construal and neglect.[33] In the first two chapters of part 2, I attempt to spell out
in some detail the relationship between imagination and intellect in terms of
the practices of scriptural reasoning and church doctrine. I contend in chapter
4 that imagination is the crucial point of exchange between the senses and the
intellect, and that it gives rise to the convictions and dispositions that allow us
to reason truthfully about the inscrutable mystery that is the reality and activity
of the Triune God. The wellspring of the Christian imagination is the generative
memory of the Bible, and thus the practice of reading the scriptures as a narrative that directs our steps toward the future constitutes the church's basic mode
of reasoning.

Scriptural reasoning, though it is basic to the life of discipleship, cannot by itself
sustain the body of Christ over the long term. As the members of this body seek
to testify truthfully to the triune God, interpretive questions about God, Christ,
and the world arise that cannot be resolved strictly within the scope of biblical
imagery and narration, no matter how winsome these images and stories may be.
Imagination and abstraction, metaphor and concept, figure and analogy, story
and doctrine are "undivided and yet distinct," to borrow from the Chalcedonian
definition of Christ's divine and human natures. In chapter 5, then, I examine the
development of doctrines by the church over the course of centuries that address
these questions. The principal function of doctrine is to explicate the church's convictions about the significance of Christ and his earthly-historical body, through
which the peoples, powers, and principalities of this world are confronted time
and again with the Word of God made flesh.

Theology by itself, even when it is rightly situated as a practice of the church,
is limited in what it can do. Milbank offers a sad yet insightful commentary on
the current state of the church when he observes that theology is tragically too
important today, with many feeling as though it falls to the theologian to resuscitate true Christian practice.[34] Some go so far as to state that it is the unique task
of theology to open as many windows on the infinite as it can, "and thus to make
a view of God once again possible in our culture."[35] But when our speech about

32. Michael Budde, *The (Magic) Kingdom of God: Christianity and Global Culture Industries* (Boulder,
CO: Westview, 1997), 13.

33. Hans Frei thusly describes a principal contribution of Karl Barth's *Church Dogmatics* (Hans W. Frei,
Types of Christian Theology, ed. George Hunsinger and William C. Placher [New Haven: Yale University
Press, 1992], 159).

34. Milbank, *The Word Made Strange*, 1.

35. Anton Houtepen, *God: An Open Question*, trans. John Bowden (New York: Continuum, 2002), 30.

God rests on theological performance for its vitality and verisimilitude, we shall likely be talking about a deity other than the God of Israel.[36]

Attempts by theologians to make a view of God possible in isolation from the other practices of the church trade in a fundamental misconception—that Christian faith subsists in a worldview, that is, a set of beliefs that can be understood and embraced by virtually anyone apart from the other practices and habits of God's pilgrim people.[37] Disembodied concepts and propositions will not reunite us to Christ or to one another as members of his body; neither will they cultivate the requisite dispositions and desires. The mind does not move spontaneously to truth, goodness, and beauty but requires power of a certain sort to create the conditions for telling the truth (in both senses of "tell"), delighting in the beautiful, and striving after the good. This power, which is mediated to us as the effect of an entire network of dedicated practices, is not the antithesis of what is good, true, and beautiful.[38] It is a question, rather, of *whose* power and *which* practices suitably frame their pursuit.[39] For Christians, then, this is a question that brings us to the third person of the Trinity, the Holy Spirit.

Christians encounter the Spirit whose power binds us to Christ and to one another, sanctifying and sustaining his earthly-historical body in its work and witness, principally through the sacraments of baptism and Eucharist. As I suggest in chapter 6, these sacramental signs constitute the material point of entry of God's apocalyptic regime into the day-to-day life of this world, creating in the body of Christ an alternative social idiom for creaturely existence. Baptism and Eucharist, by incorporating us into the mystery of God's redemptive presence and activity in the world, propel us beyond the boundaries within which state and market seek to confine us, gathering us together in a new political body through which the age to come confronts the powers of this age.

With its intrusion into the disordered loves of a fallen world, the apocalypse of God in the midst of history requires a radical restructuring of our life together. In order for the members of Christ's body to make this alternative social idiom our own, however, we must undergo an extended process of spiritual formation, in which we give ourselves daily to God as we live "unreservedly in life's duties, problems, successes and failures, experiences and perplexities."[40] In chapter 7, then, I examine some of the ways that practices generally associated with spiritual formation—prayer, confession, fasting, hospitality, the giving and receiving of counsel,

36. Mark A. McIntosh, *Mystical Theology: The Integrity of Spirituality and Theology* (Malden, MA: Blackwell, 1998), 15.

37. See John Milbank, *Theology and Social Theory: Beyond Secular Reason* (Cambridge, MA: Blackwell, 1990), 386.

38. Talal Asad, *Genealogies of Religion: Discipline and Reasons of Power in Christianity and Islam* (Baltimore: Johns Hopkins University Press, 1993), 35.

39. See Steven Lukes, ed., *Power* (New York: New York University Press, 1986); and Stewart R. Clegg, *Frameworks of Power* (London: Sage, 1989).

40. Dietrich Bonhoeffer, *Letters and Papers from Prison*, enlarged ed., trans. R. H. Fuller, J. Bowden, et al. (New York: Macmillan, 1971), 370.

rites of forgiveness and reconciliation, and the works of mercy—incorporate the habits and skills of the church's interpretive art into our bodies. The *telos* of these practices is unselfing, being unmade so that we can be remade. Unselfing interrupts the solidifying of our identities as disembodied consumers and faceless producers promoted by the state and the global market, in order to cultivate a new selfhood within the politics of the Spirit, one that is not confined by humankind's "Adamic" past, but liberated for its future in the messianic kingdom.

In the concluding chapter I examine some of the recurring tendencies in the social idiom of the present age that set the context in which the members of Christ's body must practice the art of pilgrimage. In one way or another these tendencies are linked to what Augustine calls the *libido dominandi*, the lust for mastery that is predicated on the possession, threat, and use of coercive force, and thus on death and the fear of death. The desire to control our world manifests itself most destructively in war, but it also finds its way into activities overseen by the state and the market that are connected to the needed goods of daily life. The church needs to develop habits of discernment regarding the use of these goods, so that we might discriminate between those that are open to God's apocalyptic activity in Christ, and should therefore be thought of as natural, and those that are closed to Christ, and must be regarded as unnatural.

Discernment by its very character involves the use of reason, which belongs to the natural realm, and so Christians must become discriminating artisans of our ability to reason, particularly to the extent that our powers of rationality are developed within the structures of the liberal state and the global market. In the next chapter I attempt to say why this task, which is challenging under the best of circumstances, is now much more difficult because we have been separated from each other and from the interpretive art that allows us to be attentive to the ways of Christ in a world that is fallen but nonetheless still cherished by its Creator.

PART
One

1

Can These Bones Live?

But the incarnate Son of God needs not only ears or even hearts; he needs actual, living human beings who follow him. That is why he called his disciples into following him bodily. His community with them was something everyone could see.

Dietrich Bonhoeffer, *Discipleship*

It was a gruesome scene envisioned by the prophet Ezekiel: a valley littered with human skeletons bleached dry by the sun. "Mortal," said God, "these bones are the whole house of Israel. They say, 'Our bones are dried up, and our hope is lost; we are cut off completely.'" Very little remained of the tribes of the Lord after their defeat at the hands of Assyria and Babylon. A remnant had survived the carnage, but of these many had been scattered to the four winds. Those left behind in the small towns and villages that dotted the countryside, the so-called people of the land, struggled as always to eke out a meager subsistence, but now they did so under foreign domination. As Ezekiel surveyed the disturbing panorama, God asked him, "Can these bones live?" Seemingly at a loss for an answer, the prophet could only respond, "O Lord GOD, you know" (Ezek. 37:1–3, 11).

A people that once had come upon the scene with such promise had apparently met a tragic end. Many years before, their ancestors had left home, family, and friends to go to a land far away. For centuries they struggled with their neighbors and among themselves to survive and flourish in what could be a harsh and unforgiving land, and—perhaps unknowingly—to realize a fragment of that promise. During that time Israel had weathered famines and withstood marauders, witnessed the rise of powerful kings and faced threats from foreign invaders, enduring much suffering and no little bloodshed in the process. Now some found themselves refugees and exiles, carted off to a strange land where they were compelled to "serve other gods made by human hands, objects of wood and stone that neither see, nor hear, nor eat, nor smell" (Deut. 4:28). Those who remained in the land bore the brunt of occupation. The possibility that these two groups would ever be brought back together again to live as one people in their own land must have seemed remote.

And yet the Jewish people did not disappear from the pages of history. They persevered against incredible odds, sustained in exile, occupation, and dispersion by their memory of the land their ancestors once possessed and a hope that God would at some point in the future gather them together and return the scattered tribes to their true homeland. As they struggled to understand not only what had happened to them, but what their ongoing existence signified for themselves and the world, they developed a distinctive way of communal life that often made them suspect in the eyes of their Gentile neighbors. It was this life together that constituted a socially embodied, historically extended interpretation of the world as lived in relation to God, such that the answer to the question, What is the meaning of this word *God*? could be ascertained only by observing the way they worshipped and ordered their life together.[1]

The church presently finds itself in circumstances similar to those suffered by the Jews in Ezekiel's day. It was not war, however, that was responsible for the fragmentation of its life and witness. Instead, powerful political structures, economic forces, and social movements have severed the sinews that bound the members of the risen Christ's earthly-historical body to one another and to the crucified and risen Lord. Stripped of its status as the body of Christ in the world, the Christian community has been reconstituted as a *collegium pietatis*, a social club for the cultivation of a privatized spirituality.[2] Faith has likewise been reconfigured from its biblical specifications encompassing the whole of bodily life and concerns into a purely private, inward, and "spiritual" matter, and the community of word, sacrament, and discipleship into a vendor of spiritual goods and services. The dry bones of the church are now beholden to "spirits" to which, ironically, Christians helped give birth, and which now exercise a usurped authority over them that God had reserved for the work of the Holy Spirit. The question that left the prophet perplexed, "Can these bones live?" is thus one that is posed to us as well.

Christians can find a measure of hope in the response of God to the question put to the prophet. In spite of Israel's disobedience and punishment, Ezekiel insisted that God would remain faithful to this people and to the mission for which they had

---

1. Williams, *On Christian Theology*, xii, 135. According to Michael Wyschogrod, the truth that arises out of the covenant between God and Israel is nothing apart from the ongoing existence of the Jewish people: "Only this people can bring this truth off, almost like a joke that a particular performer can bring to life but when told by others falls flat" (Michael Wyschogrod, *The Body of Faith: God in the People Israel* [San Francisco: Harper & Row, 1983], 28).

2. Dietrich Bonhoeffer, *Dietrich Bonhoeffer Works*, vol. 5, *Life Together and Prayerbook of the Bible*, trans. Daniel W. Blosch and James H. Burtness (Minneapolis: Fortress, 1996), 45.

been called. After viewing the valley of dry bones, he states that God commanded him to prophesy to these bones, and say to them: "O dry bones, hear the word of the LORD. Thus says the Lord GOD to these bones: I will cause breath to enter you, and you shall live. I will lay sinews on you, and will cause flesh to come upon you, and cover you with skin, and put breath in you, and you shall live; and you shall know that I am the LORD" (Ezek. 37:4–6). Ezekiel obeyed the injunction to prophesy, and in his vision he saw these bones—this people—joined together by sinew, covered with flesh, reanimated by the breath of God, and thus made to live again.

Dry bones being brought back to life by the breath of God afford an apt figure around which to develop a theological account of the constitutive practices that are necessary to re-member the scattered followers of Jesus as the earthly-historical form of the crucified and risen Christ. If by means of these activities the church reclaims convictions and dispositions that allow it to strip off the practices of the old humanity and clothe itself with the new humanity, "which is being renewed in knowledge according the image of its creator" (Col. 3:10), the world may yet see communities of faith, hope, and charity reanimated by the Spirit and made to live again. The church may once again become a people able to interpret the persons, structures, and institutions that constitute the present world by comparing them to its own social practice that manifests (imperfectly to be sure) the form of community that alone truly deserves the title of peace: the City of God.[3]

If this is to happen, however, we will need to reckon with political, economic, and cultural developments that have relegated matters of the "spirit" to what has to do with the soul as opposed to the body, divorcing them from issues related to the production and reproduction of life in all its dimensions.[4] By contrast, the doctrine of the incarnation, God made flesh, authorizes the followers of Christ to live unreservedly in the material world without fear of being unfaithful to God.[5] The significance of this one man's existence for everyday life, in all of its diversity, is reconstituted time and again within the earthly-historical body of Christ. This community, gathered together by the Spirit from every tribe and nation, offers to all peoples a social idiom in terms of which the beauty, goodness, and truth of the world can be followed.

A Glimpse of the Beauty of Truth

As I mentioned in the introduction, our mothers and fathers in the faith regarded the world as a book authored by God, with the events of nature and history

3. Augustine, The City of God against the Pagans, XIX, 17, ed. R. W. Dyson (New York: Cambridge University Press, 1998).

4. Bernard McGinn, "The Letter and the Spirit: Spirituality as an Academic Discipline," Christian Spirituality Bulletin 1 (Fall 1993): 3.

5. D. Stephen Long, The Divine Economy: Theology and the Market (New York: Routledge, 2000), 101.

unfolding in the manner of a dramatic story.[6] People, objects, and events had their own integrity and relative independence, but they were also seen as signs of God and his intentions for creation. The transactions and relationships that comprised nature and history were linked together within this narrative frame of reference, constituting either anticipations or rejections of the gathering-up of all things, both in heaven and on earth, in Christ. And as in all good stories, the role played by the exchanges and associations in this drama would not be fully revealed until the ending. Historical judgments were provisional in nature, typically cast in terms of a figural contrast between the present age and the age to come, the flesh and the Spirit, the earthly city and the City of God.[7] All this was predicated on the conviction that the form of this world was passing away, and that they, the pilgrim people of God, were to make wise use of its goods and to endure patiently its hardships as they made their way to the world to come.

The complex plot and many subplots of this story were detailed for the faithful in God's other text, the Bible, according to which all things ultimately find their significance in their convergence upon or divergence from the person and work of Christ. Were it not for sin, writes Henri de Lubac, "the symbol of the world, in its unspoiled transparency, would have sufficed." But after the fall, humans needed the help of scripture to decipher it.[8] "The whole created world is now covered in a veil," writes Dietrich Bonhoeffer; "it is silent and lacking explanation, opaque and enigmatic."[9] In the words of John Scotus Erigena, "the surface of the Scriptures" and "the sensible forms of the world" now comprised the two garments of Christ. They were like two veils that filtered the overwhelmingly brilliant light of his divinity. But they were also signs that, through their "reason" or "spirit," allowed women and men to catch a glimpse of the beauty of truth itself.[10]

The church thus taught that the persons, places, events, and objects of the world were traces of the beginning and end of all things, and of rational beings in particular. On their own, however, human beings were too weak to find the truth by pure reason and "needed the authority of the sacred scriptures."[11] With the help of the Bible, all creatures could truthfully be seen as "signs of the possibility of communion, covenanted trust and the recognition of shared need and shared hope."[12] Catherine of Siena states, for example, that God desires that we love him in the same way God loves us, but then concedes that this is not possible, for God loves us gratuitously, but

6. On the danger of pantextualism, see Asad, *Genealogies of Religion*, 173–88, and Ward, *Cultural Transformation and Religious Practice*, 6.

7. See David Lyle Jeffrey, *People of the Book: Christian Identity and Literary Culture* (Grand Rapids: Eerdmans, 1996), 151.

8. Henri de Lubac, *Medieval Exegesis: The Four Senses of Scripture*, vol. 1, trans. Mark Sebanc (Grand Rapids: Eerdmans, 1998), 77.

9. Bonhoeffer, *Creation and Fall*, 126.

10. John Scotus Erigena, *De Divisione Naturae*, bk. 3, cited by Lubac, *Medieval Exegesis*, 77.

11. Augustine, *The Confessions*, VI.5.8, trans. Maria Boulding (Hyde Park, NY: New City, 1997), 142.

12. Williams, *On Christian Theology*, 218.

we love him out of duty. This is why God put us among our neighbors, she writes, so that we can do for them what we cannot do for God: "love them without any concern for thanks and without looking for any profit for [ourselves]."[13]

Augustine set forth the details of this hermeneutical surmise in *De Doctrina Christiana,* where he states that all reality should be provisionally classified as either *res* (thing) or *signum* (sign), and that each *res* that human beings encounter acts upon their willing in one of two ways. A thing may be regarded as complete in itself and thus it could be enjoyed (*frui*) for its own sake, or it may be used (*uti*) as a means to a greater and more proper satisfaction, and thus as intending more than itself. The people, places, and things that human beings encountered in their daily comings and goings were thus also signs that direct their attention to God, who alone is to be enjoyed for his own sake.[14]

God alone was therefore truly *res,* and yet not actually some thing or some body, but that which is beyond all specification. As Anselm would finally conclude, "that than which nothing greater can be thought" is in actuality "greater than can be thought."[15] (This is what makes it so very difficult to use "God" intelligibly, for it is not the name of some person or object that makes itself available for our inspection.) Nevertheless, by God's own initiative there was a *signum* of the divine reality in the Word made flesh that not only referred to God but was God's own self-communication. Because of the embodiment of the divine utterance, God could be truly and truthfully named and enjoyed by women and men as the one true end of desire. The incarnation thus decisively disclosed the nature of the world as "sign" or trace of its Creator.

According to Rowan Williams, the Word made flesh "instructs us once and for all that we have our identity within the shifting, mobile realm of representation, non-finality, growing and learning, because it reveals what the spiritual eye ought to perceive generally—that the whole creation is uttered and 'meant' by God, and therefore has no meaning in itself." But apart from this imaginative venture generated by scripture and tradition, humans invariably seek or fashion finalities within the created order that would block off the processes of learning about and desiring God. It is only when we know that we live in a world of signs that we are "set free for the restlessness that is our destiny as rational creatures."[16] The distinctive use

13. Catherine of Siena, *Dialogue,* 64, trans. Suzanne Noffke, OP (New York: Paulist, 1980).

14. Augustine, *Teaching Christianity: De Doctrina Christiana,* I.1–40, trans. Edmund Hill, OP (Hyde Park, NY: New City, 1996). Christians were not the only people at this time to propose such a reading of this world. The noted medieval Muslim scholar Averroës argues for the forms of reasoning that allow believers to consider existing things "and the indication of artfulness in them . . . for one who is not cognizant of the artfulness is not cognizant of what has been artfully made, and one who is not cognizant of what has been artfully made is not cognizant of the Artisan" (Averroës, *Decisive Treatise and Epistle Dedicatory,* 8, trans. Charles E. Butterworth [Provo, UT: Brigham Young University Press, 2001], 5).

15. Anselm, *Proslogion, with the Replies of Gaunilo and Anselm,* II, XV, trans. Thomas Williams (Indianapolis: Hackett, 1995).

16. Rowan Williams, "Language, Reality and Desire in Augustine's *De Doctrina,*" *Literature and Theology* 3 (July 1989): 141. I am deeply indebted to Williams's analysis of Augustine's theory of signs.

of things by Christians was thus a part of and contributed to the church's ongoing interpretation of human existence lived in relation to the Triune God.

The literary work that in the Middle Ages exemplified this figure for the world as a book authored by God was Dante Alighieri's *Divine Comedy*. All things that took place on earth, under the earth, and in heaven, past, present, and future, were mysteriously ordered toward the beatific vision; and the story of the poet's journey through the punishments of the Inferno, up the penitential path of Mount Purgatory, and into the celestial rose of Paradise recapitulated in poetic form the pilgrimage of the soul to its beginning and end in God. Along the way the political intrigues and personal animosities, the friendships and the rivalries that character-ized Dante's rough-and-tumble world were vividly displayed in their orientation either away from or toward "the Love that moves the sun and the other stars."[17]

The church thus engaged the world of time and space in the context of divine mystery and providence, and more precisely, as the issue of God's "speech." Were it not for the fall, creation's testimony to God's "eternal power and divine na-ture" (Rom. 1:20) would be followable to all (I shall say more about this crucial property of followability below). As it now stood, however, the "text" of God's speech had been effaced by our usurpations of power, making it unintelligible to humankind's natural abilities. In a postlapsarian world, men and women needed the Bible to make sense of it and of themselves. The church's contemplative activ-ity, which began and ended with the mystery of the Triune God, originated from, and was sustained by the practice of scriptural reasoning—the continuation and extension of the imaginative process of figuring and refiguring the world that gave rise to the Bible—carried out in the context of eucharistic worship.[18] The figural interpretation of the Bible that informed this practice, and which was a key contributor to the intellectual and moral capital of the Christian tradition,[19] enabled exegetes to locate the whole sweep of history within the providential scope of divine rule.

The beauty of truth (and of goodness) manifested in a world uttered and meant by God was eternal, but the church did not think the ability to trace it to its source and consummation in God was commonly available to all. The eucharistic com-munion that constituted the body of Christ in its earthly-historical or ecclesial form comprised the "site on which universal truth was produced, and it was clear to them that truth was not produced universally."[20] The practices and institutions of

---

17. Dante Alighieri, *Paradise*, XXXIII.145, trans. Anthony Esolen (New York: Modern Library, 2004).

18. See Steven Kepnes, "A Handbook for Scriptural Reasoning," *Modern Theology* 22 (July 2006): 367–83. Though I have been a participant in the Society for Scriptural Reasoning and have benefited greatly from its work, my use of the term in this book is my own and should in no way be taken as representative of this or any other similar group.

19. Henri de Lubac, SJ, *Scripture in the Tradition*, trans. Luke O'Neill (New York: Herder & Herder, 1968, 2000), 6.

20. Asad, *Genealogies of Religion*, 45n29; cf. 35. Formally, the judgment that truth was not produced universally would have been affirmed by Jews and Muslims as well.

the body of Christ were therefore needed if men and women were to participate as fully as the mind of a rational animal was able in the triune life of the One who had created the world. Only those who had achieved a sufficient level of competence in the skills and virtues of the ecclesial household would be capable of truthfully following the movements and motifs of history as elements of a dramatic story. "Whoever enters Jesus' house is his true disciple," writes Origen. "He comes in by thinking with the Church, by living according to the Church."[21]

Christians thus did not regard the patterns and rhythms of history as givens, a sort of universally accessible text that anyone with a modicum of intelligence could use to decode the meaning of human existence. The practices, virtues, and skills of the ecclesial body of Christ, through which beauty, truth, and goodness were mediated to a fallen yet cherished world, were required if human beings were to respond truthfully to the Love who is the author of all things, who both moves the sun and the other stars, and who cherishes the creature specially made in Love's image. This ascent of the mind to the divine Love ultimately depended on God's prior act of gathering together the commonwealth of Israel, from which came the Messiah, and into which his Gentile followers have been grafted to form the church (Eph. 2:12, Rom. 11:17).[22] Apart from this community and tradition the nations would continue in the futility of their minds and remain alienated from the life of God (Eph. 4:17–18).

A New Configuration

The assertion that human beings must be apprenticed within a particular community and tradition in order to follow the truth, goodness, and beauty of this world was deeply offensive to modern sensibilities. Increasingly it was thought that humans unencumbered by such impediments could in actuality get to the bottom of things, that the only limits that mattered were the limits of being itself, which were identical to the limits of human reason.[23] They thus sought a vantage point that would transport men and women beyond the limits of mere creatureliness to see all the kingdoms of the world in an instant. These epistemic moves were accompanied by a pronounced shift in how determination and contingency were depicted, with human choices, natural causes, and random chance replacing cosmologies such as one finds in the *Divine Comedy*.

In making what we now recognize as hermeneutical moves, the chief architects of modernity continued to assume that the intelligibility of nature, the meaningfulness

---

21. Origen, "Dialogue of Origen with Heraclides and His Fellow Bishops on the Father, the Son, and the Soul," trans. Robert J. Daly, SJ, *Ancient Christian Writers: The Works of the Fathers in Translation*, no. 54, ed. Walter J. Burghardt, Thomas Comerford Lawler, and John J. Dillon (New York: Paulist, 1992), 69.

22. In the words of Wyschogrod, "To be *Judenfrei* ('free of Jews') is to be abandoned by God" (Wyschogrod, *Body of Faith*, 214).

23. Lubac, *The Mystery of the Supernatural*, 171.

of history, and the purposefulness of human existence would not be seriously disturbed. They did think, however, that the world was the real text on which God's writing was inscribed, regarding the Bible as simply the republication of "Natural Religion." The book of nature had its own independent intelligibility, invested with indisputable authority for interpreting the meaning and truthfulness of all sacred texts, written as they were in merely human language.[24] The church and its practices were no longer needed to see what was true, good, or beautiful.

There was a great deal of disagreement among these pioneers, to be sure, over the precise nature of the plot and the identity of the author of the book of nature, but until recently relatively few seriously doubted whether it finally made sense. In a provocative essay that appeared in the fall of 1989, for example, Francis Fukuyama argues that the collapse of the Soviet Union and its sphere of influence, symbolized by the dismantling of the Berlin Wall, represented the "unabashed victory of economic and political liberalism" in its ideological struggle with Marxism, signaling "the end of history as such . . . the end point of mankind's ideological evolution and the universalization of Western liberal democracy as the final form of human government."[25]

According to Nicholas Boyle, Fukuyama takes these events as evidence that G.W.F. Hegel was right and Karl Marx was wrong, that ideas rather than economics are in fact the driving force of human history (evidently it never occurs to Fukuyama that there might yet be other possibilities). The cold war between the United States and the Soviet Union was fundamentally a competition over ideology, a contest over which ideas, which narratives rational human beings should prefer. Liberal capitalism is thus "a kind of ideology in practice, something that people choose to impose on themselves because they are convinced on rational grounds that it is right."[26] In Fukuyama's picture of the social universe, the principles of liberalism comprise the ultimate goal of history, and with the collapse of Soviet-style communism, they are now being extended to every part of the globe. Although things would obviously continue to happen, the world would now witness the culmination of ideological conflict and development, and in this sense it now stands at the end of history.[27]

In actuality the formal features of Fukuyama's faith in a book of nature that is followable were bequeathed to him by modernity's Christian (and ultimately Jewish) forebears, who cultivated their stories about creation with care over the centuries. In addition to these precedents, however, there are yet other traditions of thought that

24. Asad, *Genealogies of Religion*, 41.

25. Francis Fukuyama, "The End of History?" *The National Interest* 16 (Summer 1989): 3–4; cf. Francis Fukuyama, *The End of History and the Last Man* (New York: Free Press, 1992).

26. Nicholas Boyle, *Who Are We Now? Christian Humanism and the Global Market from Hegel to Heaney* (Notre Dame, IN: University of Notre Dame Press, 1998), 69. Max Stackhouse shares this ideological understanding of the competition between liberal capitalism and socialism. See his *Public Theology and Political Economy: Christian Stewardship in Modern Society* (Grand Rapids: Eerdmans, 1987), 84–85.

27. Boyle, *Who Are We Now?* 76.

are at least as significant. In North America, for example, a powerful proposal for a meaningful history was put forward when elements of the Christian hope for the future were detached from their ecclesial context and their material specifications in scriptures, and grafted onto another narrative to form what is often referred to as the American dream. According to John Howard Yoder, one of those alien lines of thought was the ill-defined yet potent idea of progress, which came into the American psyche from many sources: German idealism (Hegel and Marx), Darwinian social theory,[28] and other transmutations and reformulations of hopefulness "which seem similar to the Christian hope for history yet are founded on other kinds of warrants." Progress becomes a kind of cosmic imperative, the necessity of which can be asserted with certainty even if we do not presently see evidence of it.[29]

The theme of progress merges seamlessly with the apparent success of the continental takeover by Western European immigrants, "the first and most successful specimen of the worldwide colonial expansion of European travel and technology." The seemingly inexhaustible supply of natural resources (once "liberated" from the control of the previous inhabitants of this continent, who did not "choose to develop" them as they "should" have), the ability and the willingness of the immigrants to exploit them as they sought to fashion a powerful civilization from a "wilderness" (again, those who once lived here do not count) "reinforced still further the ethnocentric self-confidence which European culture had enough of to begin with and gave to the notion of a religiously founded civilizing mission the powerful amplification of several generations of impressive success."[30]

The development of the idea of nature as followable *etsi deus non daretur*, as if God does not exist, does not occur all at once and certainly did not happen according to some grand conspiracy. Galileo Galilei, René Descartes, and Isaac Newton did not want to dispense with what they regarded as the unquestioned "given" of morality that seemed to be jeopardized by their new scientific accounts of nature. Their intellectual heirs—Jean-Jacques Rousseau, Immanuel Kant, and Hegel—attempted to do this by seeking a way of discriminating between the human world of freedom and purpose and the "natural" world of seemingly blind cause and effect, and they settled on the notion of history. George Grant writes in this regard:

It was indeed in this intellectual crisis (the attempt to understand the modern, scientific conception of nature that excluded any idea of final purpose, and to relate

28. Contrary to many modern defenses of Darwin that assert that such social theories represent an illicit extension of Darwin's strictly biological research, Michael Hanby demonstrates that many key concepts in Darwin's work are borrowed directly from the social science of the time, especially the political economy of the eighteenth and nineteenth centuries (Michael Hanby, "Creation without Creationism: Toward a Theological Critique of Darwinism," *Communio* 30 [Winter 2003], 654–94).

29. John Howard Yoder, *For the Nations: Essays Public and Evangelical* (Grand Rapids: Eerdmans, 1997), 128–29.

30. Ibid.

that conception to human purposiveness) that the modern conception of history first made its appearance. . . . "History" was used to describe the particular human situation in which we are not only made but make. In this way of speaking, history was not a term to be applied to the development of the earth and animals, but a term to distinguish the collective life of man (that unique being who is subject to cause and effect as defined in modern science, but also a member of the world of freedom).[31]

This modern concept of history as a sphere of activity over which humanity would gain strategic sovereignty as their permanent dwelling came about as a result of a series of interrelated developments, many of which predate the Enlightenment by several centuries. A partial list would include nominalism's depiction of an undifferentiated deity;[32] the demise of traditional forms of biblical exegesis, particularly figural interpretation;[33] the diremption of the concept of the literal, giving birth both to the heretofore unheard-of notion that the literal sense stands over against metaphor, analogy, and the like, and eventually to the idea that the mind is an incorporeal mirror that merely represents reality;[34] the world as a stock of resources that exist solely for our enjoyment; the introduction of the concept of "pure nature," which regards the world as "a closed and self-sufficient whole," created with an end that is proportionate to humankind's natural powers;[35] the invention of "religion" as a discrete and essentially private aspect of human life; and the emergence of the state as the sole legitimate bearer of political authority.[36]
Different narratives were invoked to track the plot of a history reconfigured around the institutions of the state and a capitalist market—social contract, manifest destiny, the inevitable triumph of science, liberal democracy, world socialism or global capitalism, etc.—all of which sought to reinforce the conviction that we inhabited a world possessing the properties of a unitary story. But with the

31. George Grant, *Time as History* (Toronto: University of Toronto Press, 1995), 11–12. The restriction of the concept of nature to the nonhuman world is a departure from its use in the medieval world, where it was used to distinguish the operations of the created order in its own integrity from those of grace. See David B. Burrell, CSC, *Freedom and Creation in Three Traditions* (Notre Dame, IN: University of Notre Dame Press, 1993), 3–4.
32. See Michael Allen Gillespie, *Nihilism before Nietzsche* (Chicago: University of Chicago Press, 1995), 12–32.
33. See Hans Frei, *The Eclipse of Biblical Narrative: A Study in Eighteenth and Nineteenth Century Hermeneutics* (New Haven: Yale University Press, 1974).
34. See Gerard Loughlin, *Telling God's Story: Bible, Church and Narrative Theology* (New York: Cambridge University Press, 1996), 120–38.
35. Lubac, *Mystery of the Supernatural*, 145; cf. Henri de Lubac, *Augustinianism and Modern Theology*, trans. Lancelot Sheppard (New York: Crossroad, 2000), 105–83. See also David Schindler's introduction to *Mystery of the Supernatural*, xvii–xviii.
36. See William T. Cavanaugh, "'A Fire Strong Enough to Consume the House': The Wars of Religion and the Rise of the State," *Modern Theology* 11 (October 1995): 397–420; and William T. Cavanaugh, "The City: Beyond Secular Parodies," in *Radical Orthodoxy: A New Theology*, ed. John Milbank, Catherine Pickstock, and Graham Ward (New York: Routledge, 1999), 182–200.

passing of time this belief became increasingly difficult to sustain in a credible manner. Each attempt to identify a convincing replacement for God in the narrative progress of history contributed another chapter to the chronicle of modernity's increasingly frantic effort to hold on to its inherited faith in a followable world. The very forms of reasoning that distinguished the modern era from all that had gone before it proved to be a powerful corrosive, eating away at the assumption that human beings could, at least in principle, become like gods and distinguish between universal rationality and local acculturation, between the permanent truths of reason and temporary truths of facts, and between religion, myth, and tradition and something ahistorical, common to all human beings qua human. Humans, it turns out, possess no ahistorical essence; we are "historical contingency all the way through."[37]

The Church and the Modern World

These new configurations of human life, which were conceived in Europe but first executed in America, sought to maintain an abiding faith in an underlying order to the book of nature, and especially to the purposefulness of human history, while gradually disassociating themselves from the God who had been its beginning and end, and from the practices and traditions of the church that bore witness to God.[38] According to Richard Rorty, notables such as Walt Whitman and John Dewey (whom one pundit calls the chief apostles of American civil religion[39]) "hoped to separate the fraternity and loving kindness urged by the Christian scriptures from the ideas of supernatural parentage, immortality, and providence, and—most important—sin. They wanted Americans to take pride in what America might, all by itself and by its own lights, make of itself, rather than in America's obedience to any authority—even the authority of God."[40]

Though they obviously did not wish to separate fraternity and lovingkindness from the Christian tradition, many Protestant groups in the United States increasingly relied on the coherence and intelligibility of these new social configurations as they made themselves at home in this new social order. They embraced the promise and possibility of a new and more perfect Christendom, a conviction that was exemplified in the title of a book by Walter Rauschenbusch, *Christianizing the Social Order*. The preeminent voice in the social gospel movement in the first

37. Richard Rorty, "The Priority of Democracy to Philosophy," *The Virginia Statute for Religious Freedom*, ed. Merrill D. Peterson and Robert C. Vaughan (New York: Cambridge University Press, 1988), 267.

38. Robert Jenson, "How the World Lost Its Story," *First Things* 36 (October 1993): 21.

39. Richard John Neuhaus, "Three Constellations of American Religion," in *First Things* 111 (March 2001): 72. Neuhaus reminds us that Rorty's civil religion is the continuation of the social vision of Walter Rauschenbusch (who is his maternal grandfather), "except it is stripped of God and, if one may put it this way, the attendant theological baggage."

40. Richard Rorty, *Achieving Our Country: Leftist Thought in Twentieth-Century America* (Cambridge: Harvard University Press, 1998), 15–16.

half of the twentieth century, Rauschenbusch declares that social progress—by which he meant the spread of democracy—"is more than natural. It is divine." He commends Baptists, Congregationalists, Disciples, Unitarians, and Universalists in particular, stating that they "represent the principles of pure democracy in church life. That is their spiritual charisma and their qualification for leadership in the democratization of the social order."[41]

A contemporary of Rauschenbusch, E. Y. Mullins, makes the connection between Christian faith and democratic habits and institutions more explicit. He likens the "fundamental principles of true religion" to a stalactite descending from heaven to earth. The most important of these axioms is "soul competency," which asserts that individuals unencumbered by any social practice or convention possess a timeless inner source of spiritual insight that makes them competent to judge for themselves the state of their relationship to God. American political society, in turn, is the stalagmite, with its base upon the earth rising to meet the stalactite. Both the stalactite and the stalagmite are formed from the same life-giving stream of water that flows from the throne of God down to humankind. "When the two shall meet," he writes, "then heaven and earth will be joined together and the kingdom of God will have come among men. *This is the process that runs through the ages*."[42] History is approaching its true *telos* in the convergence of these principles of religion and the institutions of procedural democracy. When this process is concluded it would mark nothing less than the presence of God's reign on earth.

Rauschenbusch and Mullins, together with countless others, perpetuate the ancient Stoic assumption that the "natural" and the "social" orders form a single entity,[43] and thus there exists at present one all-encompassing cosmopolis, one universal community made up of all human beings, within which the church properly functions as one of a number of secondary subsystems. When the church feels relatively at home in the world as it is, it becomes easier to assume that everyone is Christian, or at least shares essentially the same set of moral ends and virtues. When one asks what Christians should do, one also asks what society as a whole

41. Walter Rauschenbusch, *Christianizing the Social Order* (New York: Macmillan, 1912), 23, 30.

42. E. Y. Mullins, *The Axioms of Religion: A New Interpretation of the Baptist Faith* (Philadelphia: American Baptist Publication Society, 1908), 274, my emphasis. Rauschenbusch and Mullins were not the first Baptists to link the American democratic experiment with divine providence. A century earlier John Leland was making similar claims for America and for certain of its founders: "what wonders has nature's God been doing in America, in the course of twenty-five years. . . . heaven above looked down, and awakened the American genius, which has arisen, like a lion, from the swelling of Jordon, and roared like thunder in the states. . . . What may we not expect, under the auspices of heaven, while [Thomas] Jefferson presides, with [James] Madison in state by his side. Now the greatest orbit in America is occupied by the brightest orb: but, sirs, expect to see religious bigots, like cashiered officers, and displaced statesmen, growl and gnaw their galling bands, and, like a yelping mastiff, bark at the moon, whose rising they cannot prevent" (John Leland, "A Blow at the Root," in *The Writings of John Leland*, ed. L. F. Greene [New York: Arno, 1969], 255).

43. See Stephen Toulmin, *Cosmopolis: The Hidden Agenda of Modernity* (Chicago: University of Chicago Press, 1990), 67–69; and Martha C. Nussbaum, *Cultivating Humanity: A Classical Defense of Reform in Liberal Education* (Cambridge: Harvard University Press, 1997), 58–59.

should do. The moral expectations of the church for its own members must then be consistent with what is required of those who maintain society's principles and directives: the diplomat, the investment banker, the soldier, the chairman of the board, the social worker, the factory manager. Ethical obligations are aligned with what is needed to maintain the given order of things, not by what might be entailed in the apocalyptic intrusion of God into that order. Not surprisingly, over the centuries the outlines of the body of Christ become less distinct, and the day-to-day existence of Christians becomes coextensive with, and thus indistinguishable from, that of any other citizen.

Though the kinds of assumptions we can credibly make about history are very different from those that Rauschenbusch and Mullins thought they could make in the first half of the twentieth century when they spoke confidently about a fundamental harmony between Christian identity and American society, there are still some who continue to make similar claims about the convergence of Christianity and the secular regime. Max Stackhouse, a theologian influenced by Rauschenbusch, has argued that the Old Testament's prophetic vision of a single created realm where all peoples live under a divine law and toward a divine end is being realized in the economic process of globalization. He declares unequivocally that "God is in globalization."[44] For the most part, however, we live in a world that rarely bothers to feign allegiance to the God whom Rauschenbusch and Mullins worshiped in all sincerity; neither does it believe that the bits and pieces that remain from Christendom's breakup are still needed to keep the wheels of unconstrained commerce and conspicuous consumption turning. The so-called mainline churches that once dominated the American social landscape have been pushed to the periphery of a culture of aimless production and narcissistic consumption, where they continue to make periodic pronouncements, as if they still enjoyed a monopoly in American religious life, while at the same time constantly adapting themselves to a world they still think they control.[45]

The gradual diremption of the book of nature from the plot, setting, and characters of the Bible, dramatically reenacted time and again by the people of God, thus may have for a time retained a residual sense of the coming to be and passing away of history that seemed coherent and convincing, but it has become progressively thinner and less persuasive as the years have gone by.[46] As a result, the assertion that we are at the end of history may not signify that there is a meaningful plot to human existence, provided we are clever enough to know where to look for it. On the contrary, it could mean that the world is unfollowable, and thus our hopes for an enduring meaning and purpose may in the end be illusory. As Frank Kermode puts it, both world and book may be "hopelessly plural, endlessly disappointing;

44. Max L. Stackhouse, "Public Theology and Political Theology in a Globalizing Era," in *Public Theology for the 21st Century*, ed. William F. Storrar and Andrew R. Morton (New York: T & T Clark, 2004), 179.

45. Martin B. Copenhaver, Anthony B. Robinson, and William H. Willimon, *Good News in Exile: Three Pastors Offer a Hopeful Vision for the Church* (Grand Rapids: Eerdmans, 1999), 31–32.

46. See Loughlin, *Telling God's Story*, 127–38.

we stand alone before them, aware that they may be narratives only because of our impudent intervention, and susceptible of interpretation only by our hermetic tricks." If this is the case, our sole hope and pleasure "is in the perception of a momentary radiance, before the door of disappointment is finally shut on us."[47] What we call "history" could well be a mere succession of happenings without connection, purpose, or goal other than the interpretations we impose on them, the arbitrary nature of which only serves to mock us with the capriciousness of our existence.

Learning Again to Take Our Bearings

For all their differences, the divergent interpretations of the modern world offered by Fukuyama and Kermode put different versions of the question posed in the introduction: Where, then, do we stand? At the end of history, either triumphant, confident, and in control, able to see all the worlds in an instant, as Fukuyama claims? Or alone, helpless, and disoriented, mired in our parochial particularities, as Kermode suspects? Our attempt to answer this question will be conditioned by the fact that, as the poet Wallace Stevens observes, "we live in the description of a place and not in the place itself."[48] In other words, all human beings inhabit the world in terms of some sort of imaginative depiction of how that world is ordered and how they are related to it. By itself the end of history, narrated so differently by Fukuyama and Kermode, does not point unambiguously in one direction or the other but is susceptible of rival interpretations that seem to be little more than expressions of taste and personal preference, having no compelling connection to the world of time and space.

The conclusion that human beings are historical all the way through cannot help but be a counsel of despair for those who had placed their faith in the projects of the modern world. This despair, expressed in the absolute relativism and romantic nihilism of some forms of postmodern thought, is but the inverted image of modernity's arrogance. The apparently unanticipated possibility that human beings may not be gods after all is a discovery that weighs heavy upon many, for once the picture of an eternal, ahistorical truth has been exposed as a chimera, they still assess the everyday world "from the perspective of eternity—static and changeless as the printed word is when compared with the spoken. So we think of ourselves as being left with 'only' the realities and Being that are disclosed in time, and left 'only' with history."[49] Indeed, for far too many in our world of aimless

47. Frank Kermode, *The Genesis of Secrecy: On the Interpretation of Narrative* (Cambridge: Harvard University Press, 1979), 145. Nicholas Lash rightly calls Kermode's conclusions an example of sober and clear-sighted atheism (Nicholas Lash, *Theology on the Way to Emmaus* [London: SCM, 1986], 73).

48. Wallace Stevens, April 4, 1945, letter to Henry Church, *Letters*, ed. Holly Stevens (New York: A. A. Knopf, 1966), 494.

49. William H. Poteat, *A Philosophical Daybook: Post-Critical Investigations* (Columbia: University of Missouri Press, 1990), 65.

production and conspicuous consumption, there is finally no history, no memory, no past or future, only the nothingness from which we can try to rescue the present moment and perhaps hope to snatch the next moment as well.[50] Dietrich Bonhoeffer concludes, perhaps with a touch of sad irony, "Nothingness binds itself to us and nothingness puts us in its debt."[51]

Christians need not be paralyzed by this false dichotomy. There are no good reasons (only residual habits of mind and their associated neuroses) to be forced into choosing between the illusion of being able to comprehend the whole in one glance or the despair of stumbling blindly along in the encircling gloom. Instead we may transcend the circumstances and preoccupations of the present by discovering something of how we came to be the way we are. We do this by examining where we have come from and where we think we are headed. Though we cannot get "outside" our time, we can take our bearings within history and seek to discern the shape of its temporal horizons.[52] There are no theories that can supply the necessary perspective, though they may assist us along the way. As Augustine understood when he sat down to compose *The City of God*, only the writing of a certain kind of narrative history can provide the church with what it needs to follow the course of events that led to its current state.[53]

As I have already indicated, there was a time when Christians took their interpretive bearings from the practices cultivated by and constitutive of the church as the body of Christ, which also proclaimed the end of history. These practices embodied a specific shared way of interpreting human life as it is lived in relation to God and to the world about them. And the church did this not for itself alone, but for the sake of the nations, for the diverse meanings of this peculiar term *God* are far from self-evident. They could be learned only by observing what this community did, not only when it was involved in explicit theological reflection (though this was important), but also when it gathered to worship, teach, and exchange gifts, and then disperse so that it could offer itself as a living sacrifice, sharing in and bearing witness to the irruption of God's regime in the world.[54] Such sacrifice involved the particular ways they use the same range of goods and endure the same sorts of hardships that all suffer in this age.

These Christians knew that the kingdom of God consists not in talk, but in power (1 Cor. 4:20), and that the divine presence and activity are principally manifested not in words or ideas (though these do have an important role to play), but

---

50. Bonhoeffer, *Ethics*, 128.

51. "Nichts haftet and nichts behaftet" (Dietrich Bonhoeffer, *Dietrich Bonhoeffer Werke*, vol. 6, *Ethik*, ed. Ilse Tödt, Eduard Tödt, Ernst Feil, and Clifford Green [Munich: Chr. Kaiser, 1992], 120, my translation). The most recent English translation of Bonhoeffer's *Ethics* renders it, "Nothing is fixed, and nothing holds us" (Bonhoeffer, *Ethics*, 129).

52. Lash, *Theology on the Way to Emmaus*, 65.

53. See Alasdair MacIntyre, *After Virtue*, 2d ed. (Notre Dame, IN: University of Notre Dame Press, 1984), 113; and Milbank, *Theology and Social Theory*, 71.

54. Williams, *On Christian Theology*, xii.

in and through a social regime of power, that is, a communal discipline consisting of activities, habits, and relationships that over time bound women and men to Christ and thus to each other in much the same way as a person's extremities are attached to her or his body. In this context faith is not primarily a matter of what goes on "inside" isolated individuals but has everything to do with what happens to our bodies and what we do with our bodies—eating and drinking, enjoying the company of friends, marrying and giving in marriage, having children and burying parents, making and using signs, acquiring and disposing of property, producing and exchanging goods, enduring the normal hardships of human life and suffering at the hands of enemies, and above all, bearing witness before the fallen powers of this age to the wisdom of God in its richness and diversity (Eph. 3:10).

Christians in an earlier era knew, then, that the world happens to us—addresses us, summoning us to respond—only as bodily beings. The body is integral to Christian life, language, and witness, constituting the site where temporal events, the making and use of signs (both linguistic and liturgical), and a social idiom of communications, production, and exchange intersect to form the irreducible sinews of human existence. From this standpoint the world that happens to bodies does not consist of lumps of inert "stuff" waiting for us to impose our self-selected valuations on it. We inhabit the world, understand it, are affected by, and act upon it only as an embodied complex of signs, the meaning of which is never self-evident. In the constantly shifting interactions between events, signs, and networks of communication, individual action and social situation can never be isolated from each other; their respective contributions to this complex are thoroughly contingent (without, however, being arbitrary) and constantly modifying each other.[55]

With the dismemberment of the church, however, Christian bodies are at the mercy of secular regimes of power. Faith is no longer intrinsically related to the social exchanges that occur only between physical bodies, or to the mediation of signs and texts that have their material origin in these same bodies.[56] Abstract notions such as "conscience," "individual belief," and "sensibility" now fill the role once played by ecclesial practices.[57] All talk of redemption, forgiveness, and reconciliation is confined to the interior life of the individual, with no intrinsic connection to the unfolding of history, the sacramental life and theological language of the church, or the social and political structures of this world. As a result, Christians regularly embrace a range of moral positions and live lives that are increasingly indistinguishable from those of non-Christians.[58]

55. Milbank, *Theology and Social Theory*, 71; cf. Michel de Certeau, *The Mystic Fable*, vol. 1, *The Sixteenth and Seventeenth Centuries*, trans. Michael B. Smith (Chicago: University of Chicago Press, 1992), 80–81; Boyle, *Who Are We Now?* 59–60, 155, 226, 228, 241.

56. Rodney Clapp, "At the Intersection of Eucharist and Capital: On the Future of Liturgical Worship," in *Border Crossings: Christian Trespasses on Popular Culture and Public Affairs* (Grand Rapids: Brazos, 2000), 97.

57. Asad, *Genealogies of Religion*, 39.

58. Ibid., 79.

In its present condition the church has little to offer for the healing of the nations. Indeed, it can barely help itself, ensnared in what I call the Schlesinger Bind.
In his insightful biography of Reinhold Niebuhr, Richard Fox observes that many
of those who admired Niebuhr's work nonetheless wondered with Harvard professor and presidential advisor Arthur Schlesinger, Jr., whether "the part about God
and sin was really necessary."[59] Niebuhr no doubt would have answered with an
emphatic and unequivocal yes, but the ambivalence surrounding the theological
underpinnings of his thought is a byproduct of a general tendency on the part of
many churches, particularly in North America,[60] to see the gospel as essentially
the capstone of human experience, capable of being translated virtually without
remainder into terminology that is not explicitly Christian or even theological.
As one astute observer puts it, this tendency is nicely expressed in the conclusion
to many a sermon, "And perhaps Jesus said it best . . ."[61]

The challenge confronting the church in these circumstances is analogous
to the epistemological crises that have occupied the attention of philosophers
of science for several decades now. Such a crisis occurs when anomalies arise
within a basic research project that resist all attempts to deal with them. The
problem, says Joseph Rouse, "is not that scientists do not know what to believe;
scientists are professionally accustomed to uncertainty of *that* sort. It is that
they are no longer quite sure how to proceed: What investigations are worth
undertaking, which supposed facts are unreliable artifacts, what concepts or
models are useful guides for their theoretical or experimental manipulations?"[62]
While crises of this sort seldom if ever collapse completely the intelligibility
of a field of activities and achievements, they do blur its shape and direction,
such that practitioners become disoriented, unable to place their own work
within it. They recognize the need to try a different approach, another set of
techniques or new instrumentation, but what sense these things would make
is no longer clear.

In like manner the problem for the body of Christ is not that we do not know
precisely what to believe, say, or do when confronted with new or puzzling circumstances. Men and women down through the centuries have known that human
beings must deal with such ambiguity countless times throughout their lives.
Indeed it is a perennial aspect of Christian life and thought as well. "The Christian
engaged at the frontier with politics, art or science," writes Williams, "will frequently
find that he or she *will not know what to say.*" This is a time of real testing for the
viability and flexibility of the church's tradition, as Christians struggle to discover

59. Richard Wightman Fox, *Reinhold Niebuhr: A Biography* (San Francisco: Harper, 1987), 225.
60. The situation of the church in Latin America, Asia, and Africa obviously requires independent
assessment. In *The Next Christendom: The Rise of Global Christianity* (New York: Oxford University Press,
2002), Philip Jenkins suggests that Christians in these areas of the world may in fact be reinventing the
Christendom model.
61. Copenhaver, Robinson, and Willimon, *Good News in Exile*, 9.
62. Joseph Rouse, *Knowledge and Power* (Ithaca, NY: Cornell University Press, 1987), 33–34.

whether there is any sense in which the other languages we are working with can be faithfully incorporated in our theology.[63]

The difficulty is rather that the shared practices, judgments, and institutions that once allowed Christians to interact with the world about them and engage in meaningful transactions with one another have eroded to the point that we no longer know how to proceed. The uncertainty, however, is not limited to a single field or enterprise, as with an epistemological crisis in science. It affects virtually every aspect of Christ's body; its members, sundered from one another, are disoriented, unable to locate the coherence and meaning of their lives within a common frame of reference that lends significance to their shared existence. In such circumstances Kermode's contention that world and book may be hopelessly plural, and history endlessly disappointing, appears to many to be increasingly plausible.

Though we might be tempted, Christians would be foolish to follow the lead of self-described postmodernists who discern nothing in the universe but chaos and call it carnival. The holophobia that feeds such tendencies reflects the pessimism of a generation of intellectuals whose hopes in the triumph of the institutions of modernity—cultural, social, political, scientific, and economic—over the ills of humankind proved ill-founded.[64] As Cornel West has observed, the postmodern disclosing and debunking of the binary oppositions in the Western philosophical tradition are "interesting yet impotent bourgeois attacks on the forms of thought and categories of a 'dead' tradition, a tradition that stipulates the lineage and sustains the very life of these deconstructions." These attacks are symbiotic with their very object of criticism, remaining alive only as long as they give life to their enemy.[65] According to Boyle, such behavior is a form of neurosis, and those who suffer from it exhibit a characteristically neurotic compulsion to repeat a particular emotional stimulus, in this case, the parricidal act of shattering bourgeois identity. They are unable to accept the loss of their past, namely, the emancipatory project of modernity, and thus subscribe to a view of the present—as an endlessly repeated moment of consumption—that excuses them from having to consider time at all.[66] They too greedily devour what past generations have produced but produce little or nothing to sustain future generations.

Boyle traces the postmodern compulsion to the writings of Martin Heidegger, whom he calls the first systematic philosopher of the post-bourgeois age. Heidegger failed in the task he set himself, to construct a philosophy of historical time, because he did not take adequate account of the process of consumption, which takes place in the form of the reception of a historical tradition.[67] In particular, says

63. Williams, *On Christian Theology*, 38–39 (emphasis original).

64. Terry Eagleton, *The Illusions of Postmodernism* (Cambridge, MA: Blackwell, 1996), 4–5.

65. Cornel West, "Ethics and Action in Fredric Jameson's Marxist Hermeneutic," in *Postmodernism and Politics*, ed. Jonathan Arac (Minneapolis: University of Minnesota Press, 1986), 138.

66. Boyle, *Who Are We Now?* 318.

67. Ibid.

Boyle, he cut his links to the most extensive corpus of thought on the relation of Being and historicity that the Western world has to offer: Catholic Christology and ecclesiology. Inherent in both of these doctrines is a theme neglected throughout Heidegger's thought: bodies, that is, "the natural and risen body of the incarnate Lord, and the bodies of the faithful, sexually generated, destined to die, and sustained in life by their participation in the economic nexus. How these bodies have become or are to become the Mystical Body, the temples of the Spirit, is the question in theological anthropology Heidegger decided in 1919 not to answer."[68]

Neurotic postmodernists, by contrast, fail to take adequate account of the process of production, by which we hand convictions and virtues on to the next generation. Their respective accounts detach the activities of thinking and writing, and the formation of identity, from the socioeconomic reality of purposive work, and so in the end from a followable history. Once we learn how to see ourselves as both consumers and producers existing in the world in bodily form, however, "thought and writing and identity can again be related to historical time. To produce for others is to make a future, and to consume what others have produced for us is to receive a past."[69]

Though Boyle's astute observations about Heidegger and postmodernism are intriguing, I am particularly interested in his claim that the activities of production and making, reception and consumption, constitute the substance of our bodily relationship to past and future. In other words, who we are and what we are to be about in the world become concrete and visible to us in an act of historical interpretation, "in the words by which a past given to us is related to a future of our own making." The church's interpretive art opens the way for our participation in the unfolding of time as history.[70]

At the heart of the these practices is memory, which is the wellspring of both personal and communal identity, and the means by which we constitute ourselves as identifiable subjects with a coherent and continuing personal narrative. It is only through memory that we learn that character *and* situation, self *and* other, are made and therefore not immutable. The concepts of person and community are but abstract indices denoting actual lived continuities that *are* memory, capable of generating at any particular point in time an almost infinite range of moves. Because of this power, men and women are not trapped and confined in the present moment but can locate it as the invention of temporal processes and actions, which gives them the wherewithal to transcend the limitations to which the here and now would restrict us.

68. Ibid., 226.

69. Ibid., 318. This is not to say that we do not have to attend to all that travels under the banner of postmodernism. David Harvey rightly states, "Whatever else we do with the concept, we should not read postmodernism as some autonomous artistic current. Its rootedness in daily life is one of its most patently transparent features" (David Harvey, *The Condition of Postmodernity: An Enquiry into the Origins of Cultural Change* [Cambridge, MA: Blackwell, 1990], 63).

70. Boyle, *Who Are We Now?* 318.

Following as Interpretive Activity

Linking interpretation to memory does not mean that what was said and done in the past provides formulas that can decipher an infinite variety of historical and social contexts through the application of deductive logic. As heir to the Aristotelian tradition of practical reasoning, it falls to hermeneutics to unravel the complex and confusing contingencies of human existence, and to account for the ever-changing nature of social regimes and their distinctive ways of regulating bodies. In our present circumstances our interpretive efforts must come to terms with a world that is fashioned around, on the one hand, the state's claim to exclusive political sovereignty, a claim that is grounded principally on the possession and use of coercive force,[71] and on the other, evolving patterns of capital accumulation and modes of social regulation that have reconstituted production and consumption as a series of discrete functions with no principle of continuity save that which is exercised solely in accordance with the global market.[72] The challenge to theology as a hermeneutical endeavor, then, is to show how the church's interpretive venture, grounded in its generative memory, enables us to say in these circumstances that the world is followable, that it can be truthfully narrated as having been spoken into existence by God, provided that our habits of mind have been properly trained and provisioned.

To understand something of what it means to claim that the happenings of the world are followable, consider what is involved in following the action in a game of skill and chance such as baseball.[73] The skills that are needed to keep track of the game at any given moment, to see which moves in certain situations would most likely lead to a good outcome, to know how each pitch, hit, out, and inning contributes to the final outcome, cannot be reduced to knowing the rules. Someone who has never seen a baseball game could obtain a copy of the rulebook and memorize it and still not have the slightest notion of how to follow the action on the field. We must first be attentive to the teleological character of baseball if we are to track the progressions of the game as it moves inexorably toward its mandated though as yet unresolved conclusion. In the sense I am using here, then, following is a form of attentiveness that is ordered to a *telos*, an end.

There are, of course, various levels of skill in following a baseball game, from the casual fan who knows the difference between balls and strikes, ground-outs and homeruns, but not much more, to the expert who can explain to less knowledgeable spectators the ins and outs of tactics and strategies—the placement of players in

71. In the words of Max Weber, "the state is a relation of men dominating men, a relation supported by means of legitimate . . . violence" (Max Weber, *Politics as Vocation* [Philadelphia: Fortress, 1965], 1).

72. Boyle, *Who Are We Now?* 28.

73. Other activities, such as following a piece of Western tonal music, could be examined with equal insight. Much of what follows is from W. B. Gallie, *Philosophy and the Historical Understanding* (New York: Schocken, 1964), 38. Gallie uses the game of cricket in his discussion, but following James McClendon, I shall change the game to baseball (James Wm. McClendon Jr., *Systematic Theology*, vol. 3, *Witness* [Nashville: Abingdon, 2000], 351–53).

the field, why one reliever rather than another was brought in from the bullpen—and even predict which team is more likely to win the game. Explanations of this sort are best made not in the abstract, but while viewing an actual game, making clear to novices not only why the manager pinch-hit for this player, or intentionally walked that one, but also pointing out what could have been done differently in this situation and why it might have made more sense. One thus cultivates a grasp of the point and purpose of the game, what counts as winning or losing, whether a particular game was played well or poorly, and a host of other considerations.

Following a baseball game also demands that one have an intrinsic interest in the way the game develops "play by play." Unlike a gambler, for example, who need not know how to follow in detail the game on which he bets, since his interest rests solely in the final score, followers have a stake in the outcome—in the case of a ballgame, which team wins or loses. The stakes are raised when those who are following the action are also participants in the game. The attentiveness that is cultivated by players immediately engages their action on the field, and as such it constitutes the game in ways that not even the most knowledgeable spectators in the stands are able to do. "Only followers are in a position to judge the truth about the game," writes James McClendon, "and part of that truth is whether one is a player or only a spectator."[74]

Though one may be a skillful spectator, there will always be a difference between those who sit along the baselines and those who are "doers of the word, and not merely hearers" (James 1:22). With reference to the mission of the church, this level of following is called discipleship, which, beginning with conversion, consists of taking the way of Jesus as one's own.[75] We must take care, however, not to take the analogy too far on this point, for in the matter of whether life or death has the final word, there are ultimately no spectators. The church learns how to "follow the game" to serve the world as sacrament of God's will and wisdom for the whole of creation. The members of Christ's body thus are summoned to learn how to attend to the work of God in Jesus's life, death, and resurrection for the sake of a world that can see but not understand, hear but not comprehend. Through the admittedly imperfect activity and communion of these disciples, men and women are confronted time and again with the words and works of Jesus and thus are given the opportunity to discover, first, who and what they have become in the economy of this fallen age, and second, to reclaim who and what they are called to be in the household of God's creative and redemptive activity.

Following the Apocalypse

The activity of following the action on a ball field begins with the obvious yet necessary assumption that it is in fact a baseball game that is being played and not

74. McClendon, *Witness*, 356.
75. Ibid.

some other sport. The interpretive art of Christian pilgrimage that provides the church with the ability to follow the rhythms and progressions of a world that is fallen and yet cherished by its Creator also begins with certain assumptions, starting with the hermeneutical stance narrated in New Testament texts and spelled out in the early church's *regula fidei*, or rule of faith,[76] and its historic creeds. This interpretive surmise both emerges from and leads back to the church's constitutive practices as a distinctive way of interpreting the world, both as it has been and now is, and as it will be in the end. The point of engagement between these two times intruded into the world in and through one Jewish man, an itinerant rabbi who spent his days pursuing a way of life that moved inexorably toward confrontation and violence. His life was cut short by a peculiar alliance between the mightiest and most efficient empire the world had ever known and those whom this imperial power had selected to administer the affairs of his own people.

The execution of Jesus did not, however, bring his story to an end. His followers testified to his mysterious triumph over death, signaling the divine vindication of all that he had said and accomplished during his lifetime. His resurrection from the dead decisively established him as the center from which all things on earth and under heaven move and toward which they return. Creation had crossed a threshold that signaled the advent of a state of affairs that is regularly interpreted in the New Testament with apocalyptic motifs and concepts. The imagery of the sun being darkened and stars falling from the heavens accentuates the divine presence and activity, in particular its conflict with powers that enslave the whole of creation. The divine activity in this conflict is decisive, displaying for all to see "the grain of the universe."[77]

As Douglas Harink points out, apocalyptic discourse is language about a "disclosure" or "revelation," but these terms should be heard "in the sense of the timely and effective disclosure of God's critical, decisive, and final action and purpose for the cosmos, and not as the unveiling of a previously hidden state of affairs immanent within human nature or the cosmos." The *apokalypsis* of the God of Israel is not the extraordinary delivery of a truth about the way things are (though it is most extraordinary and has everything to do with what is eternally true, good, and beautiful), but an action that brings about what is disclosed.[78] For those with eyes trained to see and ears to hear what was happening in their midst, the times between the present age and the age to come had contracted, and the last things (*eschata*) were near at hand, pressing upon the ways and means of this world. The people, places, and things of this age were immediately confronted with God's critical, decisive, and final action for all of creation, an action that continues through the life, worship, and witness of the church.

76. See Paul M. Blowers, "The *Regula Fidei* and the Narrative Character of Early Christian Faith," *Pro Ecclesia* 6 (Spring 1997): 199–228.

77. John Howard Yoder, "Armaments and Eschatology," *Studies in Christian Ethics* 1 (1988): 58.

78. Douglas Harink, *Paul among the Postliberals: Pauline Theology beyond Christendom and Modernity* (Grand Rapids: Brazos, 2003), 68–69.

As a consequence of the apocalyptic action of God in Jesus Christ, the church audaciously claims that the meaning of every human action and affection, the significance of every movement of history, the veracity of every assertion, the wisdom of every construal of human experience, the reasonableness of every assumption of how human beings should relate to each other and the world of which they are inextricably a part, yea, even the movement of the sun and other stars, can in the final analysis be truthfully assessed only in connection with the brief but intense flurry of events that swirled around this one Jewish man and the band of followers he gathered around him.[79] Through the living sacrifice of his disciples down through the centuries, the risen Christ continues to call into question the dominant practices, relations, and habits of the age, and thus the reworking of life and language is a never-ending task for the church.[80] The church can therefore never be truly "at home" in a fallen world but exists in this time between the two ages as a pilgrim city.

Few have unpacked this interpretive stance better than James McClendon in his discussion of the "baptist vision,"[81] which he defines as "shared awareness of the present Christian community as the primitive community and the eschatological community. In a motto, the church now is the primitive church and the church on judgment day; the obedience and liberty of the followers of Jesus of Nazareth is our liberty, our obedience, till time's end." To clarify the sense of the copulative "is" in these phrases, McClendon draws an analogy to the Catholic doctrine of the Eucharist: "There the bread (and wine) upon the altar, when consecrated, *is* the body (and blood) of Christ. Not 'represents' or 'symbolizes,' but *is*. No lesser word will do. In the force of that 'is' lies the power, the distinctive emphasis, of the Catholic doctrine.... Now compare the claim made by the baptist vision: The church now *is* the primitive church; *we* are Jesus' followers; the commands are addressed directly to *us*." The "is" in the baptist vision "is mystical and immediate; it might be better understood by the artist and poet than by the metaphysician or dogmatist."[82]

McClendon is surely right when he says that the sort of imagination typically cultivated by artists and poets is needed to attend truthfully to the intersection of

79. This is not to insist that every utterance we make must be directly and explicitly related in some fashion to Christ, for the Christian concern with truth finally has to do "with the need to preserve the possibility of the kind of encounter with the truth-telling Christ that stands at the source of the Church's identity" (Williams, *On Christian Theology*, 82).

80. Rowan Williams, *The Wound of Knowledge*, 2nd ed. (Boston: Cowley, 1990), 1.

81. This idea of the baptist vision encompasses more than those groups that explicitly claim the title of Baptist (hence, the lowercase "b"). Under this category McClendon includes Disciples of Christ and Churches of Christ, Mennonites, Plymouth Brethren, Adventists, Russian evangelicals, Baptists of African American descent, the Church of God, the Church of the Brethren, plus perhaps some Methodists, Assemblies of God, Quakers, and assorted other Christian communities. The term is a concession to the fact that at present "Christianity itself is not one congruent whole," but does not capitulate to a divided church (James Wm. McClendon Jr., *Systematic Theology*, vol. 1, *Ethics*, rev. ed. [Nashville: Abingdon Press, 2002], 18–19, 33).

82. McClendon, *Ethics*, 30–31.

past and future (a point to which I shall return in chapter 4). That said, his account fails to describe adequately the imaginative surmise that ties together the various constitutive practices of the church into an interpretation of human life lived in relation to God.[83] Its chief liabilities lie in part with the univocal force he attributes to the "is" in the proposition "the church now is the primitive church and the church on judgment day," and also with his claim that the "is" articulated by this herme-neutical principle is "mystical and immediate." The challenge of following Christ in our time and place is a question that cannot be resolved simply by identifying ourselves directly with those called by Jesus during his lifetime. To begin with, our situation is not identical to that of the first disciples, and we must attend to the dif-ference between the two times if we are to be faithful to the commands of Christ. Moreover, those who were in the company of the Lord during the days of his earthly existence "belong to the word of God and thus to the proclamation of the word. In preaching we hear not only Jesus' answer to a disciple's question, which could also be our own question. Rather, question and answer together must be proclaimed as the word of scripture." At the same time, says Bonhoeffer, eliminating obedience to Christ's commands would wrongly annul a straightforward understanding of the commandments. We are therefore presented with a real dilemma: simple obedi-ence to the word of scripture is necessary for the followers of Christ if cheap grace is to be avoided, but it is misconstrued "if we were to act and follow as if we were contemporaries of the biblical disciples."[84]

In spite of his missteps, McClendon gives us our best clue for how to deal with this part of the problem in his appeal to the real presence in the Catholic understanding of the Eucharist.[85] First, Christ's real presence in the eucharistic feast is indeed mystical, but it is not immediate, for the sign of bread and wine mediates his presence, his self-communication, to the church now. Indeed, given our fallen, failing, as-yet-unresurrected bodies and our current powers of bodily communication, the presence of the risen Lord, the communication of his resur-rected body, requires sacramental mediation. The reality of the resurrection and the world to come can only appear in this age in the form of a sign. If the future were ontologically commensurate with present history, it would no longer be future, and Christ's presence with us would no longer be sacramental, for we could then see him "face to face" (1 Cor. 13:12).

Considered in this context, the Eucharist is the presence of Jesus of Nazareth's raised body insofar as it can communicate with, and be communicated to, our mor-tal bodies. This understanding of the real presence is predicated on the conviction that the resurrection radicalized and intensified Jesus's bodiliness. In his *premortem* existence Jesus's presence, his ability to communicate, to interact intelligibly with

---

83. See Williams, *On Christian Theology*, xii.

84. Dietrich Bonhoeffer, *Dietrich Bonhoeffer Works*, vol. 4, *Discipleship*, trans. Martin Kuske and Ilse Tödt (Minneapolis: Fortress, 2001), 82.

85. In what follows I am indebted to Denys Turner, *Faith, Reason and the Existence of God* (Cambridge: Cambridge University Press, 2004), 63–67.

others, was limited by his mortality. When he was raised from the dead, he was released from those limitations, and thus when he ate fish with his disciples in the upper room, he was more present to them, not less. The resurrection freed him from the constraints of mortal existence while at the same time allowing him to be involved in that existence.[86] In this sense he is thus more bodily present to us now in the sign of the Eucharist than before his death. But this presence also involves a real absence, because as he was, we are. In short, Christ both "is" and "is not" present in the Eucharist.

This leads us to a second point. Christ is not locally present in the same sense that the bread and wine, the material sign of Christ's presence, are. According to Thomas Aquinas, "Christ's body is not in this sacrament in the same way as a body is in a place, which by its dimensions is commensurate with the place; but in a special manner which is proper to this sacrament. Hence we say that Christ's body is upon many altars, not as in different places, but 'sacramentally': and thereby we do not understand that Christ is there only as in a sign, although a sacrament is a kind of sign; but that Christ's body is here after a fashion proper to this sacrament." It is important not to confuse the material reality of the signifier and the formal character of the sign in its function as signifying. The force of the qualifier "real" is therefore not that of being materially in that place (*localiter*), because in its formal character the sign signifies Christ's body and blood precisely insofar as they are also "absent," the latter term defined by contrast to the material presence of the sign itself. Only the material sign is locally present, not the risen Christ, who, after all, is in heaven, seated at the right hand of the Father.[87]

On this much Thomas and those who reject the real bodily presence of Christ in the eucharistic celebration agree. Ulrich Zwingli, for example, writes, "Observe, therefore, what a monstrosity of speech this is: I believe that I eat the sensible and bodily flesh. For it is bodily, there is no need of faith, for it is perceived by sense; and things perceived by sense have no need of faith, for by sense they are perceived to be perfectly sure."[88] The difference comes when Thomas asserts that the locally present sign *becomes* the body and blood of Christ, whereas for Zwingli he is present only in our commemoration of him, not in reality. This means, ironically, that the bread and wine become for Zwingli the unequivocal sign of Christ's real absence, such that the sign completely displaces what is signified, whereas for Thomas they form the "sesquiguous" sign of both his real presence and his eschatological absence.[89] The same one who walked along the shores of the Sea of Galilee and is

86. Rowan Williams, *Resurrection: Interpreting the Easter Gospel* (New York: Pilgrim, 1984), 106.

87. Saint Thomas Aquinas, *Summa Theologica*, IIIa.75.2; cf. IIIa.58.1., rev. ed., trans. Fathers of the English Dominican Province (New York: Benziger, 1948).

88. Ulrich Zwingli, *Commentary on True and False Religion*, ed. Samuel Macauley Jackson and Clarence Nevin Heller (Durham, NC: Labyrinth, 1981), 213–14.

89. A "sesquiguous" sign or utterance is one, writes Herbert McCabe, that "lies between the *ambiguous* and the *plonking* or flat statement." More specifically, it is "one in which the speaker both commits himself to a position and is simultaneously aware of the inadequacy of what he is saying, and of his own position

now at the right hand of the Father is truly, really, bodily "there" in the Eucharist, but not as he was in Galilee two thousand years ago, nor as he is now and will be seen by us in the kingdom, "face to face." He is "there," instead, sacramentally.

The sesquiguous meaning of the copulative "is" in the eucharistic liturgy applies also to the church's interpretive surmise. Because the world to come has intruded into the middle of history in the life and passion of Jesus, the past now lives on, and the future is already present. At the same time, the incursion of the new creation in the life, death, and resurrection of Jesus of Nazareth, extending through the bodies of those who are united to one another in him, remains to be consummated. Christ's followers have thus had to do with a unique and unanticipated set of circumstances, because they exist at the point of intersection between these two ages. Past and future are at hand in the only way that the biblical past (which apart from the sovereign act of God is irretrievable) and the apocalyptic future (appearing in the midst of the regularities by which the fallen world holds together) can be present—in the form of a sign, namely, the church itself, which is the mysterious sign of union with God and of unity among humankind.[90]

We can therefore say that there is a sense in which the church now *is* the primitive disciple band and the church on judgment day, but we must also say *pace* McClendon that the time we now inhabit is *not* that of Jesus and the twelve, and because we still pursue a modus vivendi with a world living under the sentence of sin and death, it is also *not* that of the messianic age. This dialectic of "is" and "is not," in which neither the affirmation nor the negation has preeminence, gives rise to the hermeneutical challenge with which the church must always contend. Like those first disciples, we find ourselves hard-pressed between competing allegiances. Jesus claims our total faithfulness as the one who reveals the Father, and will tolerate no competitors or rivals for the requirements of the kingdom. He summons us to the freedom of obedience, however, in the midst of a world over which rebellion and death still exert their power. We still await the day of the Lord, and the members of his body must continue to proclaim the reality of the cross until he comes in glory.[91]

Unlike for Jesus's first followers, the world with which we have to contend is not identical to that of first-century Galilee, Samaria, and Judea. Given the contingencies of creaturely existence, simple obedience cannot be reduced to identifying ourselves directly with those called by Jesus during his lifetime, or with any other point in history.[92] As with each generation of Christians seeking to obey the sum-

---

in saying it" (Herbert McCabe, *God Matters* [London: Geoffrey Chapman, 1987], 176). I deal in more detail about the nature of these kinds of utterances in chapter 5.

90. Dogmatic Constitution on the Church (*Lumen Gentium*), 1, in Flannery (ed.), *Vatican Council II*, 68–69.

91. Mark 13:26; 1 Cor. 11:26.

92. According to Michael Hollerich, Protestants in particular have tended to privilege, indeed to canonize, the sixteenth century "with unique normative significance in a peculiarly definitive way— not tradition as *norma normata* but actually another *norma normans* alongside of Scripture" (Michael J.

mons of Jesus to follow him, we must take up the question of how we best narrate the intrusion of the age to come into the distinctive circumstances of our own time and place. To do this we must take into account the dismembering of the church as that set of bodily practices that allows human beings to live truthfully and faithfully in the world before God, a process that must be examined in conjunction with the emergence, development, and demise of the social project of Christendom.

Some will no doubt disagree, insisting instead that a cultural or institutional synthesis between the body of Christ and society analogous to the one that once distinguished the *corpus christianum* can and should be salvaged.[93] Others recognize the futility of such a salvage operation and look for ways to translate the Christian hope of salvation into a social idiom that is acceptable to the regime composed of state and global market.[94] Scripture and tradition point us in a different direction. As the followers of he who "suffered outside the city gate in order to sanctify the people by his own blood," the members of Christ's earthly-historical body are citizens of another city, on pilgrimage to the messianic kingdom. We linger for a time in the circumstances in which we find ourselves, making a home for ourselves "as in a foreign land, living in tents" (Heb. 11:9). Under the figure of living in tents, then, we look to the form of life the Jews developed in exile and Diaspora for our initial understanding of the church's interpretive practices. Before we can examine the dismembering of Christ's ecclesial body, then, we must first explore the historical currents that caught up the early followers of Jesus in the apocalyptic action of the God of Israel.

Hollerich, "Retrieving a Neglected Critique of Church, Theology and Secularization in Weimar Germany," *Pro Ecclesia* 2 [Summer 1993]: 329).

93. See Max L. Stackhouse, *Covenant and Commitments: Faith, Family, and Economic Life* (Louisville: Westminster/John Knox, 1997).

94. See Houtepen, *God: An Open Question.*

2

Caught Up in the Apocalypse

There was a time when the church was very powerful—in the time when the early Christians rejoiced at being deemed worthy to suffer for what they believed. . . . Whenever the early Christians entered a town, the people in power became disturbed and immediately sought to convict the Christians for being "disturbers of the peace" and "outside agitators." But the Christians pressed on, in the conviction that they were "a colony of heaven," called on to obey God rather than man.

Martin Luther King Jr., *Letter from Birmingham Jail*

I n Graham Greene's novel *The Power and the Glory*, a nameless "whiskey priest" does not immediately flee to safety in the aftermath of an anticlerical revolution in Mexico, as others had done, but stays behind performing the duties of his office. He finally tries to escape but is arrested after delaying one more time to hear the confession of a dying man. Once in custody he gently debates the police lieutenant who had pursued him for months, telling him that he is not fighting against a dissolute cleric unworthy of the martyrdom that was about to be his fate, but God. The officer, looking to shift the focus of the conversation, asks him why he, "of all people," remained behind when the others fled. The priest replies, "Once I asked myself that. The fact is, a man isn't presented suddenly with two courses to follow: one good and the other bad. He gets caught up."[1]

---

1. Graham Greene, *The Power and the Glory* (New York: Viking, 1946; New York: Penguin, 1991), 190–95.

Greene's whiskey priest reminds us that our normal modes of engaging the world are not formed by choosing beliefs and dispositions for which we have good evidence or rational warrants, but by getting caught up in activities and judgments that provide the basic constraints on what human beings in a particular time and place can reasonably do and say together. The allegiance we pledge to God, country, or kin, our settled habits of acting and speaking, our imaginative grasp on the world, the modes of reasoning we employ, and especially the loves that shape and direct our lives, are never the product of autonomous individuals choosing a worldview in response to some sort of disengaged study of reality. These begin to develop as we are, quite literally, born into sets of relationships and historical events. Though it would be manifestly false to say that our convictions, habits, and affections can never change, such change occurs only when certain relationships and events catch and hold us within their nets. When that happens, we typically say that we have undergone a conversion of some sort.[2]

Getting caught up in a peculiar way of living and thinking accurately describes the process that has constituted the body of Christ from its inception. A group of Galilean Jewish peasants unexpectedly found themselves, as Dietrich Bonhoeffer puts it, "caught up into the way of Jesus Christ, into the messianic event."[3] This event was the *apocalypse* of the long-awaited eschatological reign of God, decisively setting "the sign of God's justice on earth" before the rulers and authorities of this age.[4] Christ's life, death, and resurrection plunged these unsuspecting women and men into the midst of the divine struggle with, and triumph over, temporal powers and principalities that have long sought to usurp God's sovereign authority over creation. A new and distinctive set of allegiances, beliefs, dispositions, and loves had irrupted in the middle of a world subject to the rule of death and sin, proclaiming the good news to all creatures that, in the end as in the beginning, God will be all in all, and creation will be liberated from its bondage to decay, for life rather than death will have the final word.

The apocalyptic incursion of God into the world, however, did not appear out of a social or historical vacuum. The early followers of Jesus regularly described themselves as "the first-fruits of restored Israel and ... heir of all those confessions by which Israel had classically defined itself."[5] Gentile believers, engrafted by their baptism into the covenants and commonwealth of Israel by Christ's passion and resurrection, shared in God's blessing of Abraham and Sarah and in Israel's calling to be a priestly kingdom, to bless all the families of the earth (Eph. 2:11–14; Gen. 12:1–3; Exod. 19:6). Caught up in a reconfigured Jewish story, the early Christian

2. D. Stephen Long, *The Goodness of God: Theology, the Church, and Social Order* (Grand Rapids: Brazos, 2001), 37. My thanks to Long for bringing Greene's story and observations to my attention.

3. Dietrich Bonhoeffer, *Letters and Papers from Prison*, 361–62.

4. André Trocmé, *Jesus and the Nonviolent Revolution*, trans. Michael H. Shank and Marlin E. Martin (Scottdale, PA: Herald, 1973), 52.

5. Ben F. Meyer, *The Early Christians: Their World Mission and Self-Discovery* (Wilmington, DE: Michael Glazier, 1986), 43.

community recapitulated the nomadic life of the people Israel, with the same kinds of trials and temptations, only now under the apocalyptic shadow of the cross.

Jesus's ministry was decisively shaped by his reading of the scriptures, and that reading was performatively set within Jewish practices and institutions of first-century Galilee and Judea. Everything that he said, did, and suffered in connection with his company of followers not only summed up Israel's history and experience with God but also anticipated what the chosen people would become in the future through God's apocalyptic action. The biblical events and ideas that decisively shaped Jesus's self-understanding and ministry can therefore not be described as mere "husks" that can be discarded once the kernel has been extracted.[6] Though it is certainly the case, as Henri de Lubac so eloquently puts it, that "Jesus causes them to burst forth or, if you prefer, sublimates them and unifies them by making them converge upon himself," these ideas and images do so only insofar as they retain their original references to historical facts and realities. "These realities, in the context of which Jesus places himself and which he thereby transforms, are sown all through the history of Israel and constitute the very object of Israel's expectations."[7]

The apocalyptic activity of God thus intrudes into the world through events that constitute Israel as a particular people or nation. Human beings learn about God, not first of all through an abstract set of divine attributes, but by the fact that "he is the God of a people who live 'thus-and-not-otherwise' . . . the God of *this* community with its particular, socially distinctive features."[8] The unutterable name of the God of Israel is revealed "as part of the process whereby a community takes cognizance of its own distinctive identity." It cultivates an understanding of who this God is "by asking what it is that constitutes *itself*."[9] A truthful understanding of God is fashioned in and through the existence of this people who supply tangible signs of God's redemptive activity in the world. "The circumcised body of Israel is," writes Michael Wyschogrod, "the dark, carnal presence through which the redemption makes its way in history. Salvation is of the Jews because the flesh of Israel is the abode of the divine presence in the world. It is the carnal anchor that God has sunk into the soil of creation."[10] The story of the apocalypse of God in Jesus Christ and his pilgrim people can be truthfully narrated only in connection with the story of Israel as God's chosen people.[11]

---

6. The dubious image of kernel and husk is taken from Adolf von Harnack, *Das Wesen des Christentums*, translated into English as *What Is Christianity?* by Thomas Bailey Saunders (New York: Harper & Brothers, 1957).

7. Lubac, *Scripture in the Tradition*, 7–8.

8. Williams, *On Christian Theology*, 134. As I argue in chapter 5, the doctrinal task of parsing out the divine attributes is of critical importance, but the meaning of these attributes ultimately depends on the naming of God by and with this people who live "thus-and-not-otherwise."

9. Ibid., 135.

10. Wyschogrod, *Body of Faith*, 256.

11. I do not pretend to offer here a narration of the biblical story that Jews would want to claim as their own. Recognition of their common heritage by Jews and Christians does not translate into a generalized

Reading the New Testament in Light of the Old

When Jesus came onto the scene announcing the drawing near of God's apocalyptic reign (Mark 1:14–15), the Jewish people had been laboring for centuries to make sense of what had happened to them following their expulsion from the Promised Land in the sixth century BCE. The covenants that God had made with their ancestors seemed remote, their promises largely unfulfilled. And yet, surprisingly, they did not abandon the ways of their forebears. Instead, they reconfigured old practices and institutions and devised new ones that would at the same time allow them to cope with the harsh realities of exile and dispersion while remaining faithful to the God of Abraham and Sarah, Moses and Miriam, Deborah and David, Jeremiah and Huldah.

Jewish life in the first century CE was permeated with tensions and ambiguities. In their synagogues and the temple in Jerusalem they worshiped the God of their ancestors, professing with the psalmist that "the LORD, the Most High, is awesome, a great king over all the earth. . . . Sing praises to God, sing praises; sing praises to our King, sing praises. For God is the king of all the earth; sing praises with a psalm" (Ps. 47:2, 6–7). There is no king but God, they declared, whose dominion over the creation admits no rivals and no partners. And yet everywhere they looked in their daily lives, they saw something very different. A vast array of

---

understanding that could yield a common account of our shared inheritance. For a very different take on this material, see David Klinghoffer, *Why the Jews Rejected Jesus: The Turning Point in Western History* (New York: Doubleday, 2005). On the other hand, it is possible for Christians to tell faithfully their story in ways that avoid the anti-Semitism and virulent supersessionism that for centuries distorted Christian relations with their Jewish neighbors. See in this regard R. Kendall Soulen, *The God of Israel and Christian Theology* (Minneapolis: Fortress, 1996); Scott Bader-Saye, *Church and Israel after Christendom: The Politics of Election* (Boulder, CO: Westview, 1999); John David Dawson, *Christian Figural Reading and the Fashioning of Identity* (Berkeley: University of California Press, 2002); and Michael G. Cartwright and Peter Ochs, "Editors' Introduction," *The Jewish-Christian Schism Revisited*, by John Howard Yoder (Grand Rapids: Eerdmans, 2003), 1–29.

That said, it is not clear that Christians can escape every implication of the charge of supersessionism, nor that they should. We cannot simply ignore the New Testament claim that God has chosen to lead human beings into radically new modes of living that require that Jews either dispense with or regard as no longer constitutive "beliefs and practices once held or practiced." The traditional Christian practice of reading scripture "extends without supplanting the former Jewish meanings—that the spirit does not undermine but instead draws out the fullest meaning of the letter; the letter must remain in the spirit because the spirit is the letter fully realized" (Dawson, *Christian Figural Reading*, 217). Jewish theologian David Novak rightly notes, "Supersessionism is the subject of deep theological debate today. Many Jews have seen it as the core of Christian anti-Judaism. Many Christians are embarrassed by it, seeing it as part of the anti-Judaism that was so easily appropriated by modern anti-Semitism. Yet Christian supersessionism need not denigrate Judaism. It can look to the Jewish origins of Christianity happily and still learn of those origins from living Jews, whom Pope John Paul II likes to call 'elder brothers.' Christian supersessionism can still affirm that God has not annulled his everlasting covenant with the Jewish people, neither past nor present nor future. Jews can expect no more than that from Christians, and Christians probably cannot concede any more to Judaism. For if Christianity does not regard itself as going beyond Judaism, why should Christians not become Jews?" (David Novak, "Edith Stein, Apostate Saint," in *First Things* 96 [October 1999]: 17).

worldly powers and authorities claimed privileges and prerogatives they reserved for God and God's rule alone. According to the poet Virgil, for example, the gods had "set no limits, space or time" to the Romans, granting them "empire without end."[12] These principalities challenged divine sovereignty at virtually every turn, claiming that the constellation of institutions, events and peoples over which they presided was the true, real, and rational order of things, and there was no choice but to act in accordance with it.

Jews, whether in foreign lands or in the occupied land of their ancestors, thus found themselves hard-pressed between competing demands on their allegiance. There was the exclusive and all-encompassing claim of the God of Abraham, the God of Isaac, and the God of Jacob on them: "Hear, O Israel: The LORD is our God, the LORD alone. You shall love the LORD your God with all your heart, and with all your soul, and with all your might" (Deut. 6:4–5). This confession was not an abstract idea about what God was like, but "always a polemical statement directed outwards against the pagan nations."[13] Jewish teachings about monotheism, election, covenant, holiness, idolatry, and the ways they presupposed one another were "a shorthand way of articulating the points of pressure, tension and conflict between different actual communities, specifically, Jews and pagans."[14] Beliefs were not incidental to their common life, but like threads in a finely woven garment, which once removed from that piece of cloth, soon lose all pattern and texture.

Loyalty to the God of their ancestors thus took the precarious form of following a way of living that distinguished them from the ways of the peoples in whose midst they lived, affecting every aspect of life. But Jews were not only faced with the daily necessities of building houses, planting gardens, marrying and giving in marriage, and raising sons and daughters, for most had to go about these matters while dwelling as aliens in foreign lands. Moreover, they not only had to attend to the task of securing their own well-being but were also charged by God to work for the common good of the place where they lived, for as Jeremiah had written to exiles in Babylon, they were to seek the peace of the city where God had sent them, praying to the Lord on its behalf, for in its welfare they would find their welfare (Jer. 29:7).

Over the centuries, then, Diaspora Jewish communities large and small culti-vated the difficult and precarious art of living between competing interests and demands on their loyalty. They worked diligently to forge forms of life befitting their status as the people chosen by God to serve the peoples of the earth as "a priestly kingdom and a holy nation," while at the same time formulating a viable modus vivendi with the established ways of their hosts. The practices, habits, convictions, and institutions that they developed as the constitutive elements of this art of diasporic politics gave shape and direction to their lives and enabled them to remain faithful to God while they dwelt in foreign lands.

12. Virgil, *The Aeneid*, I.333–34, trans. Robert Fagles (New York: Viking, 2006).
13. N. T. Wright, *Who Was Jesus?* (Grand Rapids: Eerdmans, 1993), 49.
14. N. T. Wright, *The Climax of the Covenant* (Minneapolis: Fortress, 1992), 122.

At the foundation of their art was the practice of attending to their present circumstances under the sign of their past, in terms of an ongoing history with God that they were convinced was not over and done with. Gathering together on the Sabbath in local synagogues, and whenever possible on festival days in Jerusalem, the Jewish people developed modes of reasoning about the world on the basis of a common set of texts that had grown out of their ancestors' experience with God. It was largely this need to learn time and again in new circumstances what it meant to be God's in-between people that the biblical canon gradually took shape. And these lessons were painful on more than a few occasions, as they were compelled to suffer, as Wyschogrod puts it, "for the sanctification of God's name."[15] And suffer all too often they did, like "a tempest-battered ship lurching to windward first and then to lee."[16] *Israel* was thus a fitting name for them, for throughout their history they were compelled to strive with God and other human beings, and only in the striving did they flourish (Gen. 32:28).

This story began when a man and a woman, without so much as a single heir, left their ancestral home to journey toward an unknown place and an uncertain future. By all appearances Abraham and Sarah were destined for a life of anonymity as nomads in the land of Canaan. One would never have guessed that they would be the forebears of that people through whom all the other families of the earth would be blessed. And yet, writes Gerhard Lohfink, this is the way the God of Israel works, beginning "in a small way, at one single place in the world. There must be a place, visible, tangible, where the salvation of the world can begin: that is, where the world becomes what it is supposed to be according to God's plan. Beginning at that place, the new thing can spread abroad, but not through persuasion, not through indoctrination, not through violence. Everyone must have the opportunity to come and see. All must have the chance to behold and test this new thing."[17]

More was afoot, then, than just the beginning of yet one more people group. The structure and vocabulary of Genesis suggest that in Abraham, Sarah, and their progeny, God begins the work of re-creating the *imago Dei* in humanity. When the Lord summons Abraham and says that in him and his descendents all the families of the earth shall be blessed (Gen. 12:3; cf. 26:2–5; 28:13–15), the rebellion and resulting curse that holds all creation in its sway begin to be reversed. The blessing of Adam and Eve at creation, and the divine command to "be fruitful and multiply, and fill the earth and subdue it; and have dominion over the fish of the sea and over the birds of the air and over every living thing that moves upon the earth" (1:28), reappears in connection with the promise made to Abraham, Sarah, and their offspring. At major turning points in their story—the initial summons, the making of the covenant, and the sacrifice of Isaac (12:2–3; 17:2, 6, 8; 22:16–18)—the

---

15. Wyschogrod, *Body of Faith*, 24. Cf. Aquinas, *Summa Theologica*, Ia.13.8 ad.1.

16. Dante Alighieri, *Purgatory*, XXXII.116–17, trans. Anthony Esolen (New York: Modern Library, 2004).

17. Lohfink, *Does God Need the Church?* 27.

language of blessing, of multiplying and being fruitful, is transferred to them and their descendents, albeit with two significant changes. The command ("be fruit-ful . . .") becomes a promise ("I shall make you fruitful . . ."), and possession of the land of Canaan takes the place of Adam's dominion over all the earth.[18]

From the faithfulness of this couple, fragile and fallible though it was, a small group of people emerged over the course of several generations. As the life-giving breath of God animating this people encountered the sweltering winds of human rebellion and death, storm clouds began to boil up on the horizon. The first faint rumbling of thunder came wafting across the arid wasteland of a fallen world when their descendants, now a small group of prospering herdsmen, suffered under the brutal hand of oppression and slavery in Egypt. But the God who had made a covenant with their ancestors heard their cries and delivered them from their bondage "with a mighty hand and an outstretched arm, with a terrifying display of power, and with signs and wonders" (Deut. 26:8). Once they were out of Egypt, this God led them to a mountain where he identified himself by a strange name, which, following Gregory of Nyssa, we may render as "he who is sought,"[19] or which we shall paraphrase as "he who is known only on the journey."[20]

There is no fact in Jewish teaching more significant, writes Wyschogrod, than the recognition that the God of Israel has a proper name. Tradition thus surrounded this name with endless mystery, "so that it became an ineffable name because it celebrated the most terrible of all recognitions, the personality of God."[21] This and other forms of address for God are not generic concepts that refer in the first instance to a sublime species displaying a specific set of esoteric metaphysical properties,[22] but personal names that allowed them to attend truthfully to the One who rescued them from their captivity in Egypt. With these names they

18. N. T. Wright, *The New Testament and the People of God*, vol. 1, *Christian Origins and the Question of God* (Minneapolis: Fortress, 1992), 262–63.

19. Gregory of Nyssa, *Commentary on the Song of Songs*, hom. 6, cited by Lubac, *The Mystery of the Supernatural*, 200. I shall honor the Jewish practice of not writing God's name. Save for those places where I am citing another author, I shall follow the standard practice of using the euphemism *Adonai*, "the LORD" (rendered in upper case letters) whenever *Hashem*, "the Name," appears in the biblical text.

20. See McClendon, *Systematic Theology*, vol. 1, *Ethics*, vol. 2, *Doctrine*, 285.

21. Wyschogrod, *Body of Faith*, 91.

22. This is the basic affirmation of philosophical theism, which should never be equated with the Christian confession of the Triune God. In its most pernicious form, so-called classical theism, God is supposedly static, aloof, indifferent to the world, "an external ruler who pushes, thrusts, twists, moves his subjects at will, with little or no regard for their own self-realization . . . a dictator" (Norman Pittenger, "Process Thought: A Contemporary Trend in Theology," in *Process Theology*, ed. Ewert H. Cousins [New York: Newman, 1971], 26–28).

Thomas Weinandy observes: "This is indeed a devastating array of criticisms. The only problem is finding someone or some position to whom or to which they refer. One knows to whom they are meant to refer—the Fathers and scholastic theologians, especially Aquinas—but as [Langdon] Gilkey states: "What process philosophers of religion call 'classical theism' is a strange hodgepodge that bears little historical scrutiny" (Thomas G. Weinandy, OFM Cap., *Does God Change? The Word's Becoming in the Incarnation* [Still River, MA: St. Bede's, 1985], 126–27).

recognized that God had freely and truly identified himself *by* and *with* them.[23] The creator of the heavens and the earth had thus bound himself to one particular portion of his handiwork, not for its own sake alone, but for the sake of all the nations of the earth.

Under Moses's leadership, the people went into the wilderness of Sinai to enter into covenant with their deliverer. They gathered at the foot of the mountain of God to receive the Torah, a life-conferring gift of salvation closely aligned with their deliverance from bondage. Indeed, it was essential, since no society can long exist without a determinate social order articulated by a network of laws that direct human actions and relationships to their proper, just ends.[24] The Torah specified the political form that the community was to take once they reached the Promised Land, orchestrated around the command to worship the LORD alone, with every aspect of life oriented to the God of Abraham, the God of Isaac, and the God of Jacob.

Following the travails that occurred in connection with this assembly, the people resumed their journey toward an uncertain future and an unknown place, with only the judgments, witnesses, and decrees of the nascent Torah to hold their fragile band together. At the culmination of their prolonged trek through the wilderness, the tribes of the LORD finally entered the land promised to the offspring of Abraham and Sarah. This aspect of the story is crucial, for the existence of Israel as God's peculiar people was originally and fundamentally mediated, not only by the Torah, but through the land as well. Possessing the land was necessary if they were to follow the order of life God had established in the Torah; possessing Torah was necessary if they were to flourish on the land that was God's gift to them and to their descendants forever. The Promised Land, Oliver O'Donovan contends, was the material cause of the LORD's kingly rule over Israel,[25] forming together with Torah and the people of Israel an indissoluble triad.

Situated at the junction of Europe, Asia, and Africa, this particular piece of real estate, like the people themselves, occupied an in-between place. From the rise of the great ancient civilizations in Egypt, Asia, Asia Minor, and Europe until today, most of the great empires of the world have fought for control of this land. Hittites, Egyptians, Philistines, Assyrians, Babylonians, Persians, Greeks, Romans, Muslims, Crusaders, Europeans, Americans, and others have sought to control this tiny corridor between three continents. There are few places on this planet more suitable for a people whose raison d'être demanded that they come into contact with the nations of the world.

In the early years of their existence in the Promised Land, the tribes of Israel eschewed any sort of central ruling authority. The absence of a king or similar figure represents a significant development. Monarchs whose sovereignty was

---

23. See Jenson, *Triune God*, 46–50, 59–60.

24. Lohfink, *Does God Need the Church?* 74–88.

25. O'Donovan, *Desire of the Nations*, 41; cf. Walter Brueggemann, *The Land: Place as Gift, Promise, and Challenge in Biblical Faith*, 2nd ed. (Minneapolis: Fortress, 2002).

secured by divine decree ruled the nations all around them. In Mesopotamia, Egypt, and Canaan, the institutions of kingship and centralized rule were woven by sacred epic into the fabric of reality from the beginning of time. Obedience to the gods and obedience to the king were inextricably related. The tribes of the LORD, however, were to be the exception to this rule. The distinctiveness of early Israel's regime is set forth in exemplary fashion in the story of Gideon, an early charismatic figure who led a small band of warriors to victory against one of their perennial enemies, the Midianites. Elders from a handful of tribes, impressed with Gideon's courage and ingenuity in battle, saw him as someone who could provide stability and security to a loose-knit collection of peoples struggling to survive in a harsh and unforgiving land. And so, in keeping with the practice of the nations and peoples around them, the "men of Israel" offered him the opportunity to establish a dynastic monarchy for himself and his sons. But Gideon emphatically declined their offer, declaring instead that neither he nor his sons, but only the LORD, would rule over Israel (Judg. 6:11–8:23).

Though the notion of divine kingship does not by itself explicitly *denote* a specific political realm, it does by *connotation* suggest the existence of a people who profess allegiance as subjects of that king. The reality of God's reign can gain traction in the political world of tribes, monarchies, and empires only through the actual gathering together of a people that give their allegiance to him as his loyal subjects, and through whom the world would be confronted by his exclusive claim upon it.[26] God's claim to sovereign rule over all creation thus found historical expression as a distinct *regime* in the covenant concluded at Sinai between Israel and the God of their ancestors, who would forever be their king ruling over a kingdom (*malkuth*) unlike that of any earthly king (Exod.19:6).

The reality of God's kingship thus engaged the characters and events of history through a people whose life together displayed, albeit imperfectly, the significant political features of divine sovereignty. The tribes of Israel—in their actions and relationships, their memories and expectations, their achievements and failures— constituted both the enduring form and content of this regime. As a result, though the events of the exodus took place before the Sinai assembly was convened, they derived their lasting significance from what subsequently took place in the wilderness and then in the land promised to Abraham and Sarah. Deliverance from slavery, Lohfink notes, "does not happen for its own sake; it is not solipsistic. A departure simply for the sake of departure would be absurd. The Exodus brought the people out of Egypt in order to bring them into a new society."[27] Israel's liberation, writes John Howard Yoder, was "*from* bondage and *for* covenant, and *what for* matters more than *what from*."[28]

26. Wright, *The New Testament and the People of God*, 307.

27. Lohfink, *Does God Need the Church?* 74–75.

28. John H. Yoder, "Withdrawal and Diaspora: The Two Faces of Liberation," in *Freedom and Discipleship: Liberation Theology in Anabaptist Perspective*, ed. Daniel S. Schipani (Maryknoll, NY: Orbis, 1989), 81 (emphasis original).

Over time, however, Israel eventually gave in to the temptation that to survive they must become like the other nations. According to 1 Samuel, the elders of the various tribes implored the prophet Samuel to appoint for them a king, a request that he greeted with dismay. In a subsequent prayer he was told by God, "Listen to the voice of the people in all that they say to you; for they have not rejected you, but they have rejected me from being king over them. Just as they have done to me, from the day I brought them up out of Egypt to this day, forsaking me and serving other gods, so also they are doing to you" (8:4–8). Thus began a turbulent and tragic experiment with the ways and means of ancient monarchies: "warrior and soldier, judge and prophet, diviner and elder, captain of fifty and dignitary, counselor and skillful magician and expert enchanter" (Isa. 3:2–3).

The covenant is thus handed over to a regime that had formerly been regarded as antithetical to its constitution at Sinai, perhaps under the belief that the institutions, offices, and practices of human kingship could be accommodated while remaining true to Israel's identity as God's priestly people. During this period the prophets played a key role, serving as the advocates and interpreters of God's sovereignty over against the pretensions of the royal and priestly families in the kingdoms of Israel and Judah. They were not solitary religious geniuses who set themselves over against the institutionalized power of canonical texts, dogmatic traditions, priestly hierarchies, and rote liturgies. Instead they kept alive in Israel the constitutive memory of divine kingship, and also helped to refine the picture of the God they served and of their own status as the chosen people. "Thus says the LORD," they repeated time and again, preserving the identity of Israel's only true sovereign, who demands justice from those in power, acts on behalf of the poor and oppressed, and invites all to make their way toward that future country where all shall "sit under their own vines and under their own fig trees, and no one shall make them afraid; for the mouth of the LORD of hosts has spoken" (Micah 4:4).

The experiment in monarchy, though it lasted in one form or another for more than four centuries, was ultimately a failure, the work of the prophets notwithstanding. The kingdoms of Israel and Judah fell to Assyria and Babylon, their populations slaughtered, deported, or left destitute while outsiders from all over the region poured into the social vacuum that was created. Virtually all the significant markers of Israel's covenant relationship with God—possession of the land, the Davidic dynasty, the temple in Jerusalem—disappeared, trampled underfoot by imperial armies that proclaimed their sovereignty over all the earth. And yet, remarkably, though the God of their ancestors had abandoned them to their enemies, he did not dissolve the covenant with them, and their existence as a people, with their self-identity in the most important respects intact, did not come to an end. The chosen people survived against all odds, and at times they even flourished. Why this happened demands an explanation of some sort, particularly if the status of the church as the pilgrim city of God is connected in some significant way to these events.

Following the Rhythms of History and Creation

What could possibly have persuaded the "dry bones" of Israel to continue to believe in the reality of God and their covenant relation? Were their hopes anything more than an exercise in collective self-deception? According to Friedrich Nietzsche, it was only during the time of its kings that Israel stood in a right and natural relationship to all things. Its depiction of God "was the expression of a consciousness of power, of joy in oneself, of hope for oneself: through him victory and welfare were expected; through him nature was trusted to give what the people expected—above all, rain." The people, in their cultic festivals, expressed this affirmation of themselves, of their power and nobility, through offerings of gratitude "for the great destinies which raised them to the top" and for "the annual cycle of the seasons and to all good fortune in stock farming and agriculture." But with their eviction from the land, says Nietzsche, these expressions of vitality, confidence and joy were taken away. "The old god was no longer able to do what he once could do," Nietzsche concludes. "They should have let him go."[29]

Nietzsche's reading of the situation cannot be dismissed out of hand. The exilic and postexilic prophets repeatedly promised the faithful that "when you call upon me and come and pray to me, I will hear you. When you search for me, you will find me; if you seek me with all your heart, I will let you find me, says the LORD, and I will restore your fortunes and gather you from all the nations and all the places where I have driven you, says the LORD, and I will bring you back to the place from which I sent you into exile" (Jer. 29:12–14).[30] But as the years, decades, and centuries went by, the long-awaited "return of the LORD to Zion" in power did not occur (Isa. 52:8). Yet the Jews did not abandon their ancestral heritage, as so many clans, tribes, peoples, and nations in similar circumstances had done, and as we might expect. They would not let the God of their ancestors go.

The exiles did not do as Nietzsche suggests but continued to affirm that God had plans for their welfare, to give them a future with hope (Jer. 29:11), in large part because of the way they learned to narrate their journey through time *as* history, that is, as a followable story with a beginning, a middle, and an end.[31] Drawing on the writings of their ancestors they developed a form of attentiveness to the constantly shifting interrelation of bodies, both human and nonhuman, that constitute

29. Friedrich Nietzsche, *The Antichrist*, in *The Portable Nietzsche*, trans. Walter Kaufmann (New York: Penguin, 1954), 594.

30. Cf. Isa. 11:12; 14:1–2; 40:10–11; 43:5–6; 49:5; 56:8; Jer. 23:1–4; 31:7–9; 32:36–41; 33:1–11; Ezek. 11:17–20; 20:33–39; 28:25–26; 34:11–16; 36:22–25; 39:25–29; Mich. 2:12–13; 4:6–8; Hag. 2:6–9; Zech. 10:6–12.

31. There are many, of course, who will quickly protest that to inhabitants of a postmodern world these sorts of grand interpretive schemes are no longer credible. The proclamation of the end of all metadiscourses, narrated in Nietzsche's famous story of the murder of God, makes a far more grand, far more totalizing claim than any of the stories that have supposedly been unthroned ever made. Like an unwelcome houseguest, metanarrative may have been tossed out the front door, but it almost immediately slipped in the back (Friedrich Nietzsche, *The Gay Science*, trans. Walter Kaufmann [New York: Vintage, 1974], 181).

history.[32] They learned to see human life as embedded within multiple and overlapping temporal layers that were moving incessantly toward some sort of resolution, that is to say, an *eschaton*. Of these temporal strata, the most obvious are the regular and reliable patterns of the physical world: sunrise and sunset, new moon and full moon, wet, hot seasons and dry, cool seasons, times to sow and to harvest, and so on. The psalmist thus writes:

> You have made the moon to mark the seasons;
>   the sun knows its time for setting.
> You make darkness, and it is night,
>   when all the animals of the forest come creeping out.
> The young lions roar for their prey,
>   seeking their food from God.
> When the sun rises, they withdraw
>   and lie down in their dens.
> People go out to their work
>   and to their labor until the evening (Ps. 104:19–23).

Note that the author does not regard human existence as essentially separate from the world around it, but as immersed in its recurring patterns.

Of course, Israel's Canaanite, Egyptian, and Mesopotamian neighbors also had forms of attentiveness to these regularities of "nature," as we are now wont to label the nonhuman world. They typically regarded them as deities who guaranteed the established order and stability of the world. Their veneration as the guarantors of continuity and return against the ever-present threat to the fragility of the established regime served as the social basis for regulating day-to-day life within these ancient kingdoms. Indeed, says Robert Jenson, the gods "*are* Continuity and Return," their identity and authority vested in the persistence of a beginning whose continuing stability needed to be protected against the vagaries of time and fortune.[33] The modes of power and knowledge fostered around the worship of these gods served to organize both time and space as a predictable field of operations subject to the institutions of monarchy and priesthood, palace and temple. As such, these deities that are inhabitants of the world and of history became for Israel figures of alienation, dependency, and oppression.[34]

In Israel, by contrast, a distinctive temporal rhythm for dealing with these patterns developed, orchestrated around the number seven. This rhythm of life and work wove together the regularities of the material world, cultic observance, and the social order around an institution unique to Israel: the Sabbath. Through this day of rest that cuts at regular intervals into life, writes Lohfink, "God draws the

32. Boyle, *Who Are We Now?* 226.
33. Jenson, *Triune God*, 67.
34. McCabe, *God Matters*, 42.

people out of its work every week anew, so that it cannot lose itself in the world and work. It is to shape the world through its work, of course, but not to enslave itself to the world and its gods."[35] When observed in exile and Diaspora, this aspect of the art of living between competing claims provided the Jewish people with the means to live faithfully both within and above a world that routinely succumbs to the process and products of its own labor. Without such a practice, writes Abraham Heschel, women and men eventually fall victim to the works of their hands, "as if the forces we had conquered have conquered us."[36]

The major agricultural festivals were also structured around this pattern of seven, again with the aim of setting the Israelites apart from their Canaanite neighbors. The Feast of Unleavened Bread was to last for seven days, followed by seven weeks of seven days, leading up to the Festival of Weeks (Exod. 24:18–22). "The purpose of this is clear," writes Lohfink, "precisely where the Canaanite world of the gods held its strongest position—in the fruitfulness of the fields, in rain and harvest—Israel set itself apart, giving itself a different festival rhythm and thus also in this field, so sensitive for an agricultural people, giving all honor to YHWH."[37] Through these festivals God reconfigured a social world that was originally set up to perpetuate what had always been.

The markers that these recurring patterns of seven introduced into the unfolding of time as history were not limited to clearly demarcated "cultic" observances and rituals but played a significant role in organizing the type of social relations that should exist among members. As Lohfink points out, it was not just the single year that was subjected to God's rule by being divided into weeks, each ending with the Sabbath. The passing of years was also divided up into sabbatical intervals. Every seventh year the social world was to be reconstituted, as debts were forgiven and slaves set free. And in the year of jubilee, which came after seven sets of seven years, any land sold to pay debts was to be returned to its original owner (Deut. 15:1–5, 12–15, 17; Lev. 25:1–55).[38]

Through these practices and habits, the regularities of nature interacted with other, more irregular and complex, rhythms—in particular, the physical and psychological development of human beings from birth to old age and then death, and the social sinews that comprised the political, economic and cultural structures and relationships that existed within and between nations and peoples. Situated like all other peoples in the middle of these complex rhythms, exilic Jews discovered a coherence and purposefulness in things that moved toward a kind of closure or completion in the form of a "gathering together" of the created

35. Lohfink, *Does God Need the Church?* 82.

36. "How proud we often are of our victories in the war with nature, proud of the multitude of instruments we have succeeded in inventing, of the abundance of commodities we have been able to produce. Yet our victories have come to resemble defeats" (Abraham Heschel, *Sabbath: Its Meaning for Modern Man* [New York: Farrar, Straus, 1952], 27).

37. Lohfink, *Does God Need the Church?* 81.

38. See Lohfink, *Does God Need the Church?* 82.

order.[39] They discerned that the rhythms and progressions of human history, the constantly transforming social positions and political hierarchies, closed down certain possibilities and opened up others, the realization of which may or may not take place in the manner they anticipated. Once these possibilities unfolded, the whole process moved on to pose new progressions. Only by taking account of time in this manner, then, did they learn who they were, how things came to be way they were, and the range of possibilities that might still lie "behind" them in the future.[40]

From Israel's vantage point, then, history was not cyclical or, strictly speaking, linear. The coming to be and passing away of time was instead marked by a dynamic field of equilibrium and tension, repetition and innovation, recapitulation and resolution embodied within and between these overlapping natural and social strata. The "tensed" quality of temporal interrelations between natural and human bodies, arising out of antagonism or a state of incompleteness, meant that matters would not be left as they were at any given moment. They found themselves drawn toward the future, with an expectation that the various possibilities for completion—for example, the establishment of harmonious and just relations between parties formerly involved in conflict—would somehow be resolved and the truth of their existence would be disclosed, but also with the understanding that the particulars of any resolution, closure, and disclosure would generate in turn further tensions, progressions, and possibilities.[41]

To speak of history as followable, therefore, is to invoke a particular metanarrative about time. Israel's story (which took form in the developing canon of the Bible) was ordered around God's mighty acts and righteous judgments, coalescing over time into a complex pattern of expectation, tension, delay, and resolution. This pattern was traced back to the beginning of things, when God's peaceable intentions for creation were disrupted by humankind's desire for mastery over themselves and the garden in which they lived. The natural unity of the human race, grounded in the image of God, was torn asunder by the attempt to usurp God's prerogative as Creator and Sovereign. "Whereas God is working continually in the world to the effect that all should come together into unity," writes Lubac, "by this sin which is the work of man, 'the one nature was shattered into a thousand pieces' and humanity which ought to constitute a harmonious whole, in which 'mine' and 'thine' would be no contradiction, is turned into a multitude of

---

39. In what follows I am deeply indebted to the work of Jeremy Begbie in his insightful book *Theology, Music and Time* (Cambridge: Cambridge University Press, 2000), especially 37–68.

40. Lohfink reminds us that, unlike in modern habits of speaking, the ancient Israelites did not "look forward" to the future. The Hebrew word for *future* is "behind," and thus its movement into the future was not guided by abstract speculations about the things to come, "but by reflection on what had already occurred. Because the past appeared like a coherent trace in which right and wrong steps, detours and false ways were reflected, the next step was possible" (Lohfink, *Does God Need the Church?* 105).

41. See Paul S. Fiddes, "Story and Possibility: Reflections on the Last Scenes of the Fourth Gospel and Shakespeare's *The Tempest*," in *Revelation and Story: Narrative Theology and the Centrality of Story*, ed. Gerhard Sauter and John Barton (Burlington, VT: Ashgate, 2000), 31.

individuals, as numerous as the sands of the seashore, all of whom show violently discordant inclinations."[42] This shattering of primal unity, depicted so powerfully by Adam and Eve's effort to blame someone or something else for their disobedience, gives rise to division and death, fratricide and idolatry, filling the earth with violence (Gen. 1:26–28; 3:4–6, 12; 6:11). As Fyodor Dostoevsky puts it in "The Dream of a Ridiculous Man,"

> Oh, I don't know, I can't remember, but soon, very soon the first blood was shed: they were shocked and horrified, and they began to separate and to shun one another. They formed alliances, but it was one against another. Recriminations began, reproaches. They came to know shame, and they made shame into a virtue. The conception of honor was born, and every alliance raised its own standard. . . . A struggle began for separation, for isolation, for personality, for mine and thine.[43]

In short, history had become "a complex network of human denial and deceit."[44]

The disruption of God's intended end for creation resulted in the dispersal of the nations (Gen. 11:1–9). But God did not abdicate divine sovereignty over a fragmented and antagonistic world or abandon it to utter futility. Time and again God intruded into humankind's self-devised plans and strategies, with the chosen people as the principal point of divine incursion.[45] The blessing of Abraham and Sarah, and the summons to follow God to a new land, where they would become the progenitors of a people through whom God would bless all the families of the earth, thus sounded the first notes of the divine counterpoint to humankind's unconstrained lust for mastery and usurpation of power.[46]

The recurring pattern of equilibrium, dissonance, recapitulation, innovation, and resolution, ever giving rise to new waves of temporal development, is deeply embedded in Israel's metanarration of history. Called to be a "peculiar people,"[47] whose blessing at the hands of God would be extended to all the families of the earth, Israel nonetheless wanted to serve their God the way other nations served

42. Henri de Lubac, *Catholicism: Christ and the Common Destiny of Man*, trans. Lancelot C. Sheppard and Elizabeth Englund, OCD (San Francisco: Ignatius, 1988), 33–34. The embedded quotations are from Maximus the Confessor, *Quaestiones ad Thalassium*, covering letter and q. 64.

43. Fyodor Dostoyevsky, "The Dream of a Ridiculous Man," in *The Best Short Stories of Dostoevsky*, trans. David Magarshack (New York: Modern Library, 1955), 316–17.

44. David Burrell, CSC, and Elena Malits, CSC, *Original Peace: Restoring God's Creation* (New York: Paulist, 1997), 15.

45. Wyschogrod states that the existence of the Jewish people is the earthly abode of God, "among or in whom God dwells." It is vital, therefore, that this people live ethically, and when they do not, God severely punishes them. Nevertheless, sin does not drive God out of the world completely, for that would happen only with "the destruction of the Jewish people." Wyschogrod then makes the surprising claim that Hitler understood this: "He knew that it was insufficient to cancel the teachings of Jewish morality and to substitute for it the new moral order of the superman. It was not only Jewish values that needed to be eradicated but Jews had to be murdered" (Wyschogrod, *Body of Faith*, 223).

46. On the lust for mastery, *libido dominandi*, see Augustine, *City of God*, I.Pref., 30; XIV.28; XIX.14.

47. Deut. 14:2 (KJV); cf. Deut. 26:18; Titus 2:14; 1 Pet. 2:9.

theirs. This motif recurs throughout scripture: the complaints of the Hebrews as they left Egypt and made their way to Sinai; their initial refusal to enter the Promised Land following the making of the covenant out of fear of giants and fortified cities; the constant worship of idols during the period of the judges, which left them perpetually subject to the rule of Canaanite kings; the request to have their own king during the time of the prophet Samuel, so that they might be like all the other nations; the seductive trap of trusting in the horses and chariots of unreliable allies during the time of the divided monarchy. Time and again Israel did evil in the sight of the LORD, repeatedly exchanging their birthright as God's chosen people for the tepid and idolatrous pottage of temporal security and welfare.

As a result of their disobedience (which is consistently linked in scripture with the worship of idols), Israel was caught up in habits and institutions that led to its expulsion from the land of promise and dispersion among the nations.[48] But even then the frenzied nature of their existence in exile did not come to an end. Those who returned to the land in the days of King Cyrus of Persia continued to languish under the oppressive rule of foreign powers, thus perpetuating the exile of slavery. Their God had not yet returned triumphantly to Zion to redeem Israel as promised by the prophets.[49] With Joel they cried out: "Have pity, O LORD, upon your people! Do not hand over your possession to shame, that foreign nations should rule over them."[50]

The Rise of Apocalyptic

In spite of the disappointment and hardship of exilic life, the Jewish people were still by and large persuaded that God's redemptive work had not been arrested by their hardheartedness. When in the past they cried out to God in repentance, the LORD had heard their cry and acted in their behalf. Manna was provided in the wilderness; judges were raised up to deliver the people from their enemies; a man after God's own heart was anointed as king; Jerusalem was graciously spared when threatened with seemingly overwhelming force. With each provisional fulfillment the original promise was elaborated or augmented, often in surprising and yet consistent ways. Each partial resolution created an expectation and hope for something more, thus expanding the content and range of the original promise. "As successive hopes find fulfillment," writes Anthony Thiselton, "a tradition of

48. Lohfink, *Does God Need the Church?* 90.

49. Isa. 52:7–8, 10; Ezek. 43:1–9.

50. Joel 2:17, based on a translation by Hans Walter Wolff, *Joel and Amos: A Commentary on the Books of the Prophets Joel and Amos*, trans. Waldemar Janzen, S. Dean McBride Jr., and Charles A. Muenchow (Philadelphia: Fortress, 1977), 39. O'Donovan notes: "Corresponding to the notion that the land as a whole is Israel's possession as a whole is an assertion that Israel itself is [the LORD's] possession. Possessing the gift, she is possessed by the giver; and this is something that is either to be true of the whole nation or not to be true at all" (O'Donovan, *Desire of the Nations*, 41).

'effective history,' or 'history of effects' . . . emerges in which horizons of promise become enlarged and filled with new content."[51]

The gradual return of Jews to the Promised Land, fragmentary and under the dominion of foreign rulers though it may have been, was regarded by some as just such a partial fulfillment of the promised ingathering of Israel. But it was evident that a complete return had not occurred, and that the dispersion continued. In these circumstances the dry bones of Israel and Judah were compelled to make a critical hermeneutical judgment. In the minds of many, "the promise of a nation righteous and true and peaceful had eventually either to be spoken as an *eschatological* promise or to be forgotten."[52] The God of their ancestors either had utterly abandoned them, or, in the course of handing them over to their enemies, had begun "a new thing" in their midst (Isa. 43:19), a work that eluded human planning and calculation, and would culminate in the rescue and restoration of Israel and the consummation of God's blessing to all nations as well.

Later biblical authors settled on the second option, reconfiguring the story of God's presence and activity (once vested in the reality of this world in Davidic palace and Solomonic temple) in apocalyptic terms. They envisioned the realization of God's promises within a radical transposition of the rhythms and hierarchies that ordered creaturely life.[53] A new covenant with the chosen people was in the works, which would not be "like the covenant that I made with their ancestors when I took them by the hand to bring them out of the land of Egypt—a covenant that they broke, though I was their husband, says the LORD" (Jer. 31:32). This new thing would not merely add new works to old ones, enlarging and expanding upon the prophetic motifs that formerly distinguished the historical vectors of their life with God, but would transcend the old works' modes of continuity.[54]

Many Jews thus began, over a period of centuries, to look for signs of the radical restructuring of the patterns around which nature and history unfold and cohere.[55] The initial strains of this hope were sounded during the seventh century BCE, as a new intensity in the eschatological visions of judgment and restoration began to emerge within the ranks of the prophets. Jeremiah tells the inhabitants of Jerusalem and Judah that he had "looked on the earth, and lo, it was waste and void, and to the heavens, and they had no light. . . . I looked, and lo, the fruitful land was a desert, and all its cities were laid in ruins before the LORD, before his fierce anger. For thus says the LORD: The whole land shall be a desolation; yet I will not make a full end" (4:23, 26–7). The whole cosmos, and not just the people of Israel and their immediate enemies, now stood beneath God's sovereign gaze. "For the day of the LORD is near against all the nations," says Obadiah. "As you have done, it

---

51. Anthony C. Thiselton, *Interpreting God and the Postmodern Self: On Meaning, Manipulation and Promise* (Edinburgh: T & T Clark, 1995), 150–51.

52. Jenson, *Trinune God*, 69.

53. Ibid., 70.

54. Ibid., 69.

55. Ibid.

shall be done to you; your deeds shall return on your own head. . . . But on Mount Zion there shall be those that escape, and it shall be holy; and the house of Jacob shall take possession of those who dispossessed them" (1:15, 17).[56]

Protoapocalyptic redactors of the prophetic books then elaborated upon this theme of a radical transfiguration of the continuities by which time and space are ordered. In the book of Isaiah we read that though presently the "earth lies polluted under its inhabitants . . . [who] have transgressed laws, violated the statues, broken the everlasting covenant," the time was coming when God would "create a new heavens and a new earth; the former things shall not be remembered or come to mind." On that day the powers in heaven and rulers on earth would "be gathered together like prisoners in a pit; they will be shut up in a prison, and after many days they will be punished," while the peoples of the earth who would be invited to a feast dwell on God's mountain, where they would find rich food filled with marrow, and well-aged wines strained clear. At that time the LORD would destroy "the shroud that is cast over all peoples, the sheet that is spread over all nations; he will swallow up death forever" (24:5; 65:17; 24:21–22; 25:6–8; cf. Ezek. 38–9).

In the books of Zechariah and Daniel the earlier prophetic oracles and literary redactions that speak of cosmic judgment and redemption coalesce into fully developed apocalypses depicting a world that is commensurate with the hope of God's promise to Israel. For that reason, the world to come appears in this age only in image and figure, not as event. In Zechariah's "night visions," a patrol sent by God reports that the world remains unchanged, and that any prospect for the redemption of Jerusalem depends on God's intervention. The prophet then sees that the powers or "horns" that scattered Judah and Israel will be struck down, allowing Jerusalem to be reestablished, protected by a wall of fire that is the glory of God's own presence in the city. Two "anointed ones" unite those who have returned to the city in anticipation of God's Spirit filling the earth. As a result of God's action, "Many nations shall join themselves to the LORD on that day, and shall be my people; and I will dwell in your midst" (1:7–21; 2:11; 4:1–4, 10b–14; 6:1–8). In Daniel it is the opposition of these nations to Israel and Israel's God that is detailed, with their fate decided by the coming of "one like a son of man." Following the decisive battle between the forces aligned against God and those powers who fight for the LORD, the defeat of death implied in other portions of scripture is explicitly described in terms of resurrection (12:1–3).[57]

Since the present order of the world cannot contain the promise and prospect of these events, apocalypses announce that it would at some point come to an end, thus making time and space for a new heaven and a new earth to appear. The time

56. See also the prophet Joel, in which a locust plague serves as a portent of cosmic judgment, depicting a cosmic judgment culminating with an enemy horde threatening to destroy Jerusalem until God intervenes to save the city. See Brevard S. Childs, *Biblical Theology of the Old and New Testaments: Theological Reflection on the Christian Bible* (Minneapolis: Fortress, 1992), 184.

57. See Jenson, *Triune God*, 70–71.

of creation is therefore subdivided into the exile of the present age (*ha-'olam hazeh*), when the wicked flourish and God's people suffer the rule of idolatrous powers that claim for themselves what belongs to God alone, and the age to come (*ha-'olam haba'*), when all creatures would witness the restoration of God's sovereignty, the defeat of sin and death, and the vindication of Israel and righteous Gentiles. Extraordinary phenomena—eclipses, earthquakes, and floods—are used as portents of this transposition, for only such language could do justice to the dreadful events that would accompany such momentous events.[58]

Many people have a strong aversion to apocalyptic imagery, in part for its supposedly "otherworldly" character and for advocating withdrawal from the everyday world where people deal with the necessities of eating, drinking, marrying and giving in marriage, having children, burying parents, acquiring and disposing of property, and exchanging goods. Associations of apocalyptic thought with otherworldliness can be traced to an erroneous assumption, which is that apocalyptically minded Jews in the years leading up to the first century CE expected the imminent collapse of the domain of time and space, and with it all sense of history. This misperception is due to some degree to an inherent ambiguity in the English word *end*, which can signify either a termination of some kind or the goal of an act, and often it can refer to both. In apocalyptic thought there is an intrinsic relationship between purpose and finality, speaking both of the aim and the limits of life, the course that creation is taking in history and the consummation that awaits it. The "*eschaton*" marks that toward which everything tends, giving shape and direction to history, indeed, marking the passage of time *as* history.

Far from predicting the imminent destruction of time and space, of "history" itself, then, the apocalyptic imagination both preserves and intensifies the sense of expectation, delay, tension, and eventual resolution that pervades Israel's attentive following of history. The biblical writers hold in generative tension the motifs of the nearness *and* the deferment of God's reign and regime, that is, the "is" and "is not" of apocalyptic thought. We thus find throughout these writings a pronounced sense of exigency and longing for the day of the LORD compounded by exhortations to patience that tacitly acknowledge that God does delay. "There is, in other words," writes Begbie, "an appeal both to God's righteousness—God's justice will eventually prevail—and to God's sovereignty—his righteousness will prevail at his own appointed time. Neither element need be suppressed in favour of the other."[59]

The Promised Land continued to figure prominently within the apocalyptic transposition of the rhythms that order the world. Pledged by God to Abraham, Sarah, and their descendants (Gen. 12:7), the land—signified by the temple— formed an indissoluble triad with the Torah and Israel's status as God's chosen people. Israel had possessed the "Holy Land," in whole or in part, from Joshua to

---

58. Wright, *The New Testament and the People of God*, 299.
59. Begbie, *Theology, Music and Time*, 2000, 119.

Josiah, a time span of more than five hundred years. It is therefore not surprising that in exile the desire to return to the land was the cornerstone of Jewish hopes:

> By the rivers of Babylon—
>> there we sat down and wept
>> when we remembered Zion
> On the willows there
>> we hung up our harps.
> For there our captors asked us for song
>> and our tormentors asked for mirth, saying,
>> "Sing us one of the songs of Zion!"
> How could we sing the LORD's song
>> in a foreign land?
> If I forget you, O Jerusalem,
>> let my right hand wither!
> Let my tongue cling to the roof of my mouth,
>> if I do not remember you,
> If I do not set Jerusalem
>> above my highest joy (Ps. 137:2–6).

In the early years of the exile Jews were sustained by this powerful memory and by the hope that God would soon gather the exiles and return them to this land.[60] As the months and years turned into decades and centuries, however, the land continued to languish under the domination of foreign rulers. Its rich yield, its fruit and its good gifts, went to foreign kings whom God had set over them (Neh. 9:36–7; cf. Isa. 62:8–9). In addition, pagan institutions were established, often in or around Jerusalem, which had become the focal point of the land of promise. And though there is disagreement among scholars regarding the amount of taxation levied by the Gentile rulers on Jews that had returned to Judea and Galilee, virtually all agree that making a living from the land was at best extremely difficult.[61]

With the memory of shared space growing ever more remote and the hope of return seemingly infinitely deferred, many believed that only a radical reordering of the regularities by which the world coheres could possibly vindicate this memory and hope. Jewish apocalyptic writings were in part a response to the shared memory of life together in the holy land and to the hope that one day they would return and live there once again "under their own vines and under their own fig trees, and no one shall make them afraid" (Micah 4:4). In his prayer for the people, the figure of Daniel cries out: "Incline your ear, O my God, and hear. Open your eyes and look at our desolation and the city that bears your name. We do not present our supplication before you on the ground of our righteousness,

---

60. See Daniel Boyarin, *A Radical Jew: Paul and the Politics of Identity* (Berkeley: University of California Press, 1994), 245.

61. See E. P. Sanders, *Judaism: Practice and Belief, 63 BCE–66 CE* (Philadelphia: Trinity Press International, 1992), 168–69.

but on the ground of your great mercies. O Lord, hear; O Lord, forgive; O Lord, listen and act and do not delay! For your own sake, O my God, because your city and your people bear your name!" (Dan. 9:18–19; cf. Ezek. 36:16–28). And when God would finally act to redeem his people, he would restore the land and cleanse the temple, the rule of the kings of this world would be shattered, the mountain of the LORD's house would fill the whole earth, and God's rule would encompass all peoples (Dan. 2:35; 7:14; cf. Micah 4:1).

Another development within postexilic Judaism's metanarrative reading of time as history, appearing in close proximity with the rise of apocalyptic forms of reasoning, was a host of vaguely defined and often conflicting messianic expectations. Though there was no one accepted understanding of the Messiah, the various movements that spoke in these terms did tend to share an expectation that Israel's long history and suffering would finally reach its goal. The coming king who would be the agent through whom God would accomplish the great restoration of Israel would also cleanse the Holy Land promised to their ancestors. The messianic ruler thus became for some " the focal point of the dream of national liberty."[62]

The initial impetus for the messianic idea had been the struggle between the proponents of monarchical unification of the tribes of Israel and those who continued to represent the case for divine kingship. This crisis led eventually to the prophetic designation of the human king of Israel, the one who follows the LORD (cf. 1 Sam. 12:14), as the anointed of the LORD, *meshiach YHWH*.[63] Heightened expectations were invested in a new king from the line of David who would be "Wonderful Counselor, Mighty God, Everlasting Father, Prince of Peace," establishing justice and righteousness forever, such that even nature's own predatory predilections would be pacified (Isa. 9:6; 11:6–9). Jenson notes: "Whether . . . such predications were simply the demanded encomium of a new heir or expressed expectations that were in a more self-aware way eschatological makes little difference; they burden the coming one with expectations this age cannot accommodate."[64]

There is one final and inescapable step in this radical transposition of the temporal patterns that presently order heaven and earth. "Everlasting and universally encompassing righteousness and peace, eternal and universal love, and these as characters of a reality transcendent to 'this age,'" says Jenson, "can only be predicates of God himself." The content of Israel's apocalyptic hope is only possible through a participation in God's own reality, described by the Greek fathers as "deification." But such a conclusion is not possible strictly within the context of the Old Testament, for without a resurrection "hope for deification would be intolerable hubris."[65]

---

62. N. T. Wright, *Jesus and the Victory of God*, vol. 2, *Christian Origins and the Question of God* (Minneapolis: Fortress, 1996), 483.

63. Martin Buber, *Kingship of God*, 3rd. ed., trans. Richard Scheimann (New York: Harper & Row, 1967; Atlantic Highlands, NJ: Humanities Press International, 1990), 162.

64. Jenson, *Triune God*, 84.

65. Ibid., 71. And yet, Jenson argues, elements within postcanonical Judaism did affirm deification materially if not formally in its description of the life of the blessed in the age to come, when "the righteous

Jesus and the Apocalypse of God

According to developing apocalyptic sensibilities, God does not leave the world to its brokenness and violence but intrudes upon the immanent causal sequences of history with portents of judgment and redemption. The Jewish people found themselves time and again in between a God intent on judging a wayward world, and a rebellious creation. As the psalmist puts it, "Our God comes and does not keep silence, before him is a devouring fire, and a mighty tempest all around him. He calls to the heavens above and to the earth, that he may judge his people: 'Gather to me my faithful ones, who made a covenant with me by sacrifice!'" (Ps. 50:3–5). As they had been for centuries, the people of Israel were to be the chosen "body" through which the decisive divine activity would take place and reclaim God's rightful dominion over a world presently ruled by death and sin.

It is from this communal and historical soil that Jesus of Nazareth emerged, proclaiming to his fellow Israelites, "The time is fulfilled, and the kingdom of God has come near; repent, and believe in the good news" (Mark 1:15; cf. Matt. 4:17). Through his life, death, and resurrection, God's messianic rule promised to Abraham and Sarah's offspring becomes a present reality in connection with the day-to-day concerns and celebrations of life. Over against the forces and powers that had governed the course and content of life in the ancient world virtually uncontested, Jesus introduces an alternative pattern of communal life, a distinctive set of personal habits and relations, and a different story in terms of which to make sense of all things on earth and under heaven. The meaning of all other figures, events, and institutions no longer resides in themselves. They are now derivative signs, the significance of which can be followed only in their relationship to this one Jewish man and the body politic of the church, over which he rules as head.

The New Testament witness to the messianic event is by no means uniform, as evidenced by its literary and theological diversity, but the distinctive motifs of apocalyptic thought nonetheless figure prominently in virtually every book. Owing to what God accomplishes in Christ, the world had crossed a decisive threshold with the triumph of God over death and sin. At the same time, however, all creation awaits the final transfiguration of heaven and earth. The necessities of eating, drinking, marrying and giving in marriage, having children, burying parents, acquiring and disposing of property, and producing and exchanging goods, continue as before. The biblical writers thus locate the whole of creation in a period of time in which two ages and two social orders overlap. There is the present age over which the authorities and powers exercise dominion, but which will ultimately pass away, and the age of God's everlasting reign, when all creatures will witness God's triumph over sin and death, and the vindication of the righteous in Israel and among the nations.

[will] sit with their crowns on their heads enjoying the effulgence of the *Shekinah*" (*Bab. Barakot* 17a, cited by Jenson, 71n55).

To follow the coming of God's everlasting rule in connection with events in the present, the gospel authors refined the literary technique of foreshortening introduced in the Old Testament by the Book of Daniel. Foreshortening compresses the time between what is near at hand and the last things, putting them into immediate juxtaposition. In chapter 7, for example, the author, writing sometime in the middle of the second century BCE during the Maccabean revolt, adopts the sixth-century perspective of the character of Daniel to describe events that had already occurred (the conquests of Alexander the Great and the rise of Hellenistic kingdoms in the Middle East in the fourth century, culminating with the rule of the tyrant Antiochus IV in the second) in connection with God's immanent judgment on these kingdoms (the "present" of Daniel's readers) and the establishment of the everlasting kingdom of the Son of Man (the eschatological backdrop against which all these events are depicted).

Through skillful use of foreshortening, the things that had already occurred, the things that would occur shortly, and the things that will be revealed at the end of the age are blended together with the "present" of the author, not in an effort to deceive his readers by surreptitiously claiming the *ex eventu* authority of a past hero of Israel, but to fashion what McClendon calls a trioptic awareness: (1) the memory of Daniel and his friends struggling to survive in Babylon during the exile, providing the narrative standpoint for the passage, (2) a depiction of how everything on earth and under heaven would eventually end up with the coming of the Son of Man, whose reign would be everlasting, and (3) how both of these impinged upon the times and tasks of the Jews during the Maccabean revolt (the "present" of the book's intended readers).[66]

The same procedure is used in the thirteenth chapter of the Gospel of Mark, the so-called Little Apocalypse. In this extended discourse (which is rare in Mark), Jesus warns about the impending destruction of the temple in Jerusalem. When questioned about the timing of these events by his inner circle of disciples, Jesus gives what appears to be a confusing answer. He begins by stating that there is coming a time of persecution for his followers leading up to the consummation of this age, as they will be brought before governors, kings, and synagogues to testify about him. Jesus then ties these tribulations to allusions about the coming destruction of Jerusalem, which will bring with its terrible suffering and give rise to false messiahs and prophets (vv. 5–23). He then speaks in explicitly apocalyptic terms about the sun being darkened and the stars falling from the heavens, which are harbingers of the final coming of the Son of Man in clouds of glory (an image drawn from Daniel 7) to gather the elect from the four corners of the earth (vv. 24–27). Finally, he counsels his disciples to learn the lesson of the fig tree, and to recognize from the signs that "all these things" will occur within this generation, but that no one but the Father knows the day or hour these things will occur. Jesus concludes with a short parable summoning his disciples to stay awake, to remain alert (vv. 28–37).

66. McClendon, *Doctrine*, 94.

If the author of Mark wrote these verses sometime between 60 and 70 CE (or even later), then it would seem that Jesus was mistaken about the timing of these events, if not completely incoherent. The end of the age had not occurred during the generation of Jesus's listeners, and the fall of Jerusalem had either already taken place or was imminent. And yet the evangelist sets these words down with no apparent discomfort. This fact leads McClendon to argue that Mark had skillfully adopted the standpoint of the pre-Easter disciples for his narrative. All the events depicted in this chapter, "the spread of the gospel, the suffering of the missionaries, the destruction of Jerusalem, the coming of false Messiahs, and the apocalyptic last coming of the Son of man were from the time standpoint of the first disciples' future events." Through the technique of foreshortening, Mark has fashioned attentive awareness to "(1) what Jesus had once said and done (the 'present' of Mark's narrative), (2) how everything would end up (the long future), and (3) how both of these impinged upon the 'present' needs and tasks of the Marcan church (the 'present' of Mark's readers)."[67]

These disciples served the world as a tangible sign that God had not left it to its own futility, but invited all to share now in the well-being of the city that is to come (Heb. 13:14). The innumerable transactions that constituted the common life of the these early Christians were caught up in the exchange that God in the incarnation made with the *oikonomia* of the world, a term derived from "house" (*oikos*) and "law" (*nomos*), and which in its most comprehensive sense denoted the regulation of the household that is creation itself. In the words of St. Athanasius, the Word of God assumed a body capable of death so that it, "through belonging to the Word Who is above all, might become in dying a sufficient exchange for all, and, itself remaining incorruptible through His indwelling, might thereafter put an end to corruption for all others as well, by the grace of the resurrection." This exchange was accomplished, not through some sort of legal or monetary transaction, but through the union of the immortal Son with human nature, clothing it with incorruption in the promise of the resurrection: "For the solidarity of mankind is such that, by virtue of the Word's indwelling in a single human body, the corruption which goes with death has lost its power over all."[68]

The Eucharist was the *res et sacramentum,* the reality and the sign performed by the church that, more than any other, made present this exchange of charity between God and humankind whenever and wherever Jesus's followers were gathered together in his name. Paul declares, "Because there is one bread, we who are many are one body, for we all partake of the one bread" (1 Cor. 10:17). Time and again the eucharistic liturgy made the church what it is, *re-membered* it as Christ's true body, with each participant connected not only to Christ who is the head of the body, but to one another as in a natural body. Every time believers gathered

---

67. Ibid.

68. St. Athanasius, *On the Incarnation: The Treatise De incarnatione Verbi Dei*, §9, trans. and ed. a religious of the CSMV (Crestwood, NY: St. Vladimir's Seminary Press, 2000).

around the table of their Lord, the things of this world—including its modes of accumulating, consuming, and exchanging material goods and services—were turned toward God. This meal positioned all other realities, because it made a present reality "the moment of *ultimate exchange* between God and humanity that Christians cannot but claim to be the basis for all other exchanges."[69] The Eucharist thus became the paradigm for all other exchanges between human beings.

The life that Jesus lived with his followers thus marked the beginning of the re-capitulation of all things, setting before a rebellious cosmos the decisive sign in terms of which all other relationships and exchanges that comprise humankind's common life were to be parsed. As a consequence of this one Jewish man's life, the prevailing order of time and space was turned upside down in classic apocalyptic fashion, including the normal distribution of material goods. The Gospel of Luke thus proclaims in Mary's song of praise and thanksgiving that

> [God] has shown strength with his arm;
> he has scattered the proud in the thoughts of their hearts.
> He has brought down the powerful from their thrones,
> and lifted up the lowly;
> he has filled the hungry with good things,
> and sent the rich away empty. (Luke 1:51–53)

Though no one economic regime can claim to be adequate for every time and place, Jesus cultivated with his band of disciples a very distinct and concrete mode of life together. The inaugural sermon of Jesus, recorded in the fourth chapter of the Gospel of Luke, is a case in point. Instead of using the phrase "the kingdom of God is at hand; repent and believe in the good news" to introduce the period of Jesus's public ministry, as Matthew and Mark do, Luke places Jesus in the syna-gogue in his hometown of Nazareth, where he reads a passage from Isaiah 61 that he then turns upon himself and his forthcoming ministry:

> The Spirit of the Lord is upon me,
> because he has anointed me
> to bring good news to the poor.
> He has sent me to proclaim release to the captives,
> and recovery of sight to the blind,
> to let the oppressed go free,
> to proclaim the year of the Lord's favor. (Luke 4:18–19)

After reading, he sits down and declares that this scripture had that very day been fulfilled in their hearing. John Howard Yoder notes that this passage not only is explicitly messianic but also conceives of that expectation in expressly social terms. Jesus's first-century Jewish audience would have heard this passage as a reference

69. Long, *Goodness of God*, 236.

to the fulfillment of the year of Jubilee, and in the context of his ministry suggested that the coming of the kingdom would, as a part of the restoration of Israel, bring about a new regime of accumulation and exchange among the elect in lines with Jubilee provisions for releasing slaves, forgiving debts, and redistributing land to those who had lost it due to economic exigencies.[70]

Yoder's reading of Jesus's proclamation frames in sharp relief other texts in the Lukan corpus. In Luke's version of the Beatitudes, Jesus says, "Blessed are you who are poor.... Blessed are you who are hungry now," emphasizing the beneficence of God's apocalyptic reign for those who suffer from want, in a way that the Matthean version does not (6:20–21).[71] Later in the same Gospel, at the conclusion of a crucial passage in which Jesus tells the crowds that they must take up the cross and follow him to be his disciples, he says to them, "none of you can become my disciple if you do not give up all your possessions" (14:33). And following the exchange with the rich ruler in Jerusalem, Jesus tells his followers that those who left house and family for the sake of the kingdom will receive back much more in this age; and in the age to come, eternal life (18:29–30).

Similar practices are detailed in the Acts of the Apostles. Following Peter's Pentecost sermon and the release of Peter and John, for example, we read that the believers had all things in common (en autois panta koina), and that they would sell their possessions and goods and distribute the proceeds "as any had need" (2:44–5; 4:32, 34–5). In 1 Corinthians 11 Paul argues that believers were dying because they had failed to "discern the body," each going ahead with his own meal (to idion deipnon). Paul's choice of words here explicitly parallels that of a statement in Acts 4, where Luke writes that "no one claimed private ownership of any possessions, but everything owned was held in common," in Greek, oude eis ti ton hyparchonton auto elegen idion einaialla en autois panta koina (4:32). The contrast is that of the faithful life, where all things are held in common, with the life they had left behind, in which one could treat his or her possessions as private.[72]

Paul's observations in 1 Corinthians are supported by the story of Ananias and Sapphira in Acts 5. The couple sought to participate in the new messianic community but deceptively withheld a portion of the proceeds gained from the sale of property. As Stephen Long notes, "they were not forced to participate in this restoration, and thus by withholding their goods and seeking to deceive others

70. John Howard Yoder, The Politics of Jesus: Vicit Agnus Noster, 2nd ed. (Grand Rapids: Eerdmans, 1994), 11, 29.

71. Matthew's version of these Beatitudes reads: "Blessed are the poor in spirit.... Blessed are those who hunger and thirst for righteousness" (5:3, 6). It would be a mistake, however, to conclude that one version emphasizes "material" poverty while the other focuses strictly on "spiritual" matters, which would be an unhappy and anachronistic reading. George Beasley-Murray rightly observes in this regard that the same Jubilee passage in Isaiah 61 that informs Jesus's Nazareth sermon in Luke also informs the Matthean Beatitudes, addressed as they are to "the Lord's poor, broken-hearted, grief-stricken people, for whom he has planned his 'day of recompense'" (George R. Beasley-Murray, Jesus and the Kingdom of God [Grand Rapids: Eerdmans, 1986], 161 [emphasis original]).

72. Long, Goodness of God, 237.

about it, they place themselves outside the community of faith. They die. Peter's response to Ananias and Sapphira was not a Stalinist purge that forced them to part with their property, for not an enforced justice but a gifted charity is the basis for this restoration."[73] Apart from divine charity, death exerts its dominion unchallenged.

The first Christians attended to this radical restructuring of human existence, which at its heart involved a transfer of allegiances and a transformation of conduct, with great seriousness. The author of the epistle to the Colossians, in an exhortation to his readers not to lie to one another, reminds them that they "have stripped off the old humanity with its practices, and have clothed [themselves] with the new humanity, which is being renewed in knowledge according to the image of its creator. In that renewal there is no longer Greek and Jew, circumcised and uncircumcised, barbarian, Scythian, slave and free; but Christ is all and in all!"[74] The transition from the old society (exemplified by Rome) into the vanguard community of the new creation involved "a change of rulers, a turning away from the gods and demons of Gentile society and an entry into the Church as the space of Christ's lordship." To guide this transition, says Lohfink,

> probably as early as the second century the candidates for baptism each had to produce a guarantor who would attest the sincerity of their conversion. They had to take part in a three-year baptismal catechesis that carefully educated them in Jewish-Christian discernment and the form of life demanded by faith. The ancient Church took it for granted that the Christian life of the baptismal candidates would not come of itself, but had to be learned. It was also assumed that evil is powerful and that every inch of the reign of God had to be fought for.[75]

Caught Up in the Spirit

The inauguration of God's apocalyptic reign in the ministry, passion, and triumph of Jesus proved to be so disruptive to established regimes that the reorganization of human existence became a never-ending task for his followers. It took centuries to develop relatively adequate ways of saying what needed to be said about the sense and direction of his life, death, and resurrection. They discovered, for example, new uses had to be put to the word *God*. Without jeopardizing the mystery and simplicity of God, they determined after years of deliberation that the only way to do justice to all that Jesus did and suffered was to speak of him as the incarnate Word of God. In the words of Ignatius of Antioch, Christ "is the mouth . . . by which the Father has truly spoken."[76] In the person of Jesus, God joined the divine nature to the day-to-day realities of human existence in order to recreate its shattered bone and

73. Ibid., 236.

74. Col 3:9–10, my revision of the New Revised Standard translation.

75. Lohfink, *Does God Need the Church?* 211.

76. Ignatius of Antioch, *Epistle to the Romans* 8 (*ANF* 1:77). Williams paraphrases Ignatius's statement here as "he is himself 'what the Father says.'" (Williams, *Wound of Knowledge*, 19).

severed sinew. Without effacing the difference between the speaker and the word spoken, the church was convinced that it was *God* who appeared in the particular events and circumstances of this man's life and worked to gather together what had been dispersed by humankind's disobedience.

The church's conviction that God's address and agency took flesh in a particular person who lived at a certain time and place, and said and did and suffered certain things, did not cancel or set aside the particularities of Jesus's own history. On the contrary, so crucial were the events of his life, the only appropriate form in which the truth about him could ultimately be told was that of a story. But as pivotal as his personal story was, it was not sufficient to confess that the Son entered fully into time and history, and in so doing perfectly fulfilled the will of the Father. The mere fact of God's self-identification with humanity through the incarnation made no particular difference to the lives of others. Hans Urs von Balthasar observes, "In that light his life is still only one existence among others; and if it is no more it can only be, even in its highest perfection, a (perhaps unattainable) moral example for others living before and after him."[77]

By itself, then, the story of this one man's life, as remarkable as it was, remains extrinsically related to the lives of those who came after his earthly ministry. The question is, therefore, what does *that* life of faithfulness to God, *that* death willingly accepted, *that* triumph over death, have to do with *this* life that each man and woman must now live? And so when the church down through the centuries struggled with what to make of this continuously unfolding drama, they concluded that they could not stop with the confession of Jesus as God's own utterance, for to do so would reduce his story "to the status of an *anecdote:* a tale without enduring or universal significance."[78] If all those who live in a different time and place, who do and endure things in circumstances that are marked by their own distinctive particularity and contingency, are to grasp the significance of Jesus, they must learn how to narrate their own lives as both distinct from and, yet at the same time, a continuation of his story. This happens only as the universal efficacy attributed to Christ's concrete historical existence is performatively extended to and displayed in every time and place, so that it becomes the immediate norm of every human being's singular existence.

It is the work of the Holy Spirit to orchestrate time and again in the ever-changing circumstances of creaturely existence the divine polyphony of life,[79] which takes form in what St. Augustine calls the whole Christ, *totus Christus*, consisting of both head and body,[80] mediated through gathered Christian communities throughout the globe. The Spirit's labor is an ongoing, never-ending endeavor, because times

77. Hans Urs von Balthasar, *A Theology of History* (San Francisco: Ignatius, 1994), 79.

78. Nicholas Lash, *Easter in Ordinary: Reflections on Human Experience and the Knowledge of God* (Charlottesville: University Press of Virginia, 1988), 282.

79. See Bonhoeffer, *Letters and Papers*, 303.

80. St. Augustine, "First Homily on First John," *Augustine: Later Works*, ed. John Burnaby (Philadelphia: Fortress, 1955), 261.

and circumstances change. New characters, social settings, and historical events are constantly being incorporated within the ebb and flow of time around its center. The meaning of this process is therefore never fixed but continues to unfold in the style of a historical drama that is never over and done with.[81] The unity of this drama's story line resides not in the sameness of its performance, but in timely and faithful transpositions of the rhythms and progressions of human acting and relating that God had decisively set in motion with the call of Abraham and Sarah, which reached its decisive moment in the suffering and resurrection of Jesus.

This connection between Israel and Jesus needs to be constantly reiterated, because the church is perpetually tempted to see Jesus and his followers as having left completely behind all the crucial elements of Israel's story—the Torah, the land, the temple, the rites, and the holy days. There is, to be sure, a good deal of ambivalence in the New Testament with respect to these things, as witnessed in the tension in some of Paul's statements about the works of the Law (Rom. 3:28; Gal. 3:11) and Jesus's proclamation that not one letter or letter stroke will pass away from the Torah until "all is accomplished" (Matt. 5:18).[82] Another prominent example is found in the various ways the temple figures into the story of Jesus and the early church. On the one hand, the announcement of the birth of John the Baptist occurs in the temple (Luke 1:8–20). Jesus's parents present him in the temple soon after his birth "according to the law of Moses" (Luke 2:22). The only story about Jesus between his birth and the beginning of his public ministry occurs in the temple (Luke 2:41–50). Jesus sees to it that the temple tax is paid (Matt. 17:25), and refers to it as God's house that needed to be cleansed of the money-changers (Matt. 21:12–13; John 2:14–17). And the conclusion to Luke's Gospel states that after the resurrection and ascension of Jesus, the disciples returned to Jerusalem and "were continually in the temple blessing God" (24:53). On the other hand, Jesus states that something greater than the temple is in the world, with the implication that it is inextricably associated with him (Matt. 12:6), that the temple complex would in the not-too-distant future be laid waste (Mark 13:2), and that his body would be the new temple that would be destroyed and then raised in three days (John 2:19).

A similar ambiguity regarding the temple, and Jerusalem and the Promised Land more generally, can be discerned in other New Testament writings. In the Acts of the Apostles, for example, the disciples continue to worship in the temple on

81. For example, the ways that Christ's body gathers in those of African descent in the United States will differ in certain respects from the ways it interacts with other persons and groups. The dissonance involved in the struggle of African American Christians finds no more poignant expression than in the poem by Harlem Renaissance poet Countee Cullen, "The Black Christ" (C. Cullen, *The Black Christ and Other Poems* [New York: Harper & Brothers, 1929], 67–110).

82. An ambivalence, notes Frederick Bauerschmidt, that is already present in first-century Judaism, as seen, for example, in the tension between the ideals of the exodus tent of presence and the Jerusalem temple (Frederick Christian Bauerschmidt, "Walking in the Pilgrim City," *New Blackfriars* 77 [November 1996]: 517n4).

a regular basis (2:46). At the same time, however, the Promised Land functions in the narrative as a point of dispersion for the gospel, that it might reach "to the ends of the earth" (1:8). In the Epistles it is the body of Christ that is described as God's temple (1 Cor. 3:16; 2 Cor. 6:16; Eph. 2:21–22; 1 Pet. 2:11), "a dwelling place for God as visible as the Temple in Jerusalem, but nomadic, on pilgrimage."[83] Hebrews alludes to the temple in Jerusalem as a "parable" (*parabola*) of the present age and a "mere copy" of the heavenly sanctuary or age to come (9:8–9, 24). And in the final vision in the Revelation of John, the New Jerusalem, whose dimensions seem to encompass the whole earth, has no temple, "for its temple is the Lord God the Almighty and the Lamb" (21:22; cf. 21:16).

It is clear that these markers of Jewish identity no longer serve the same function that they did within Second Commonwealth Judaism. The Torah is reinterpreted christologically, attesting to the disclosure of the righteousness of God in the faithfulness of Christ (Rom. 3:21). National, ethnic, and geographical boundaries are also radically reconfigured by the advent of the messianic age. As Frederick Bauerschmidt puts it, the "Spirit-filled community, dispersed throughout the world, enacting again the story of Jesus in a multitude of places, telling his story in alien tongues, creates sacred 'spaces' in which the land of promise appears not as 'this soil' but as 'this people.'"[84] Or as N. T. Wright characterizes the change, "Jesus and the church together are the new Temple; the world . . . is the new Land."[85]

At the same time, however, these pivotal aspects of Jewish life and language are not discarded as useless husks by the intrusion of God's apocalyptic economy into the world, but as Paul states in Romans 9–11, they continue to stand, in all their particularity, as permanent figures and types within it, without which the story of Jesus and the church cannot be truthfully narrated.[86] As noted above, the blessing of Adam and Eve at creation and the divine command to be fruitful and multiply, and to have dominion over the earth, are recapitulated in the promise of offspring and land made to Abraham. But just as the world was not abandoned when God entered into covenant with Israel, neither are Israel and its key symbols left behind with the fulfillment of that covenant in the life, death, and resurrection of Christ and the creation of the church.

Caught Up in the Messianic Suffering

In continuity, then, with all that God had accomplished in and through Israel, the Spirit gathers together a people from every tribe and nation, language, and culture (Rev. 5:9) to be the living members of the body of Christ. This community exists not for its own sake, but for the sake of a world that even in its violence

---

83. Ibid., 506.
84. Ibid., 507.
85. Wright, *The New Testament and the People of God*, 366n31.
86. Bauerschmidt, "Walking in the Pilgrim City," 507.

and rebellion God has never stopped cherishing. The followers of Jesus are constituted, as the tribes of Israel had been before them, as an in-between people, this time as the vanguard of the messianic age in the midst of the present world. This constitution puts this fragile and fallible community squarely at the meeting point between the two ages, where life is never boring, frequently precarious, and at times positively dangerous. "For while we live," Paul writes to the saints in Corinth, "we are always being given up to death for Jesus' sake, so that the life of Jesus may be made visible in our mortal flesh" (2 Cor. 4:11). The members of the body of Christ thus do not simply find themselves passive bystanders to the events of a fallen world. The Spirit receives the offering of their bodies (Rom. 12:2) as a living sacrifice to extend that pivotal point of exchange—fashioned initially by Jesus's life, death and, resurrection—between a world destined to pass away and one that will endure forever.

The New Testament authors use a variety of apocalyptic images to drive this point home. As we have already seen, Paul regularly divides the time of creation into two ages. There is the present age, when the wicked flourish and God's people languish under the rule of idolatrous powers that claim for themselves what belongs to God alone. And there is the age to come, when all creation will witness the restoration of God's sovereignty, see the vindication of Israel and the righteous among the Gentiles, and celebrate the blessings of a new heaven and a new earth, where death will have been vanquished, and neither the sound of weeping nor the cry of distress will be heard. In Christ, Paul argues, this new creation has already been manifested: "So if anyone is in Christ, there is *a new creation*: everything old has passed away; see, everything has become new" (2 Cor. 5:17, my emphasis).

Apocalyptic imagery of this sort is not confined to the Pauline correspondence but can be found in Jesus's own teaching and preaching as well. In Mark's Gospel, for example, Jesus tells his disciples, "Truly I tell you, there is no one who has left house or brothers or sisters or mother or father or children or fields, for my sake and for the sake of the good news, who will not receive a hundredfold now in this age—houses, brothers and sisters, mothers and children, and fields *with persecutions*—and in the age to come eternal life" (Mark 10:29–30, my emphasis). Not only does the image of two ages appear prominently in this passage, but also the recognition that belonging to Christ's circle of friends brings with it two things: a foretaste of the blessings of the messianic age in the form of shared practices and resources, *and* the sort of trouble that comes with belonging to a group that refuses to play by the established rules of the game.

As Jesus's words clearly indicate, the members of Christ's body could expect to bear the enmity that the present age harbors for the ways of the world to come. "Blessed are those who are persecuted for righteousness' sake," says Jesus, "for theirs is the kingdom of heaven. Blessed are you when people revile you and persecute you and utter all kinds of evil against you falsely on my account" (Matt. 5:10–11). Paul likewise commends the saints in Thessalonica, because they "became imitators of us and of the Lord, for in spite of persecution you received the word with joy inspired by the Holy Spirit, so that you became an example to all the believers in Macedonia and in Achaia" (1 Thess. 1:6–7). And in 1 Thessalonians Paul also reminds his readers, "For you, brothers and sisters, became imitators of the churches of God in Christ Jesus that are in Judea, for you suffered the same things from your own compatriots as they did from the Jews" (2:14).

The conflict of God's rule with the established authorities and powers that culminated in Jesus's crucifixion at the hands of the Jewish and Roman authorities is thus recapitulated time and again by his followers, for all the world to see. In the New Testament the cross is not an abstract symbol of the ambiguity of history or of humankind's finite freedom. It signifies instead the concrete and decisive contraction of time between the two ages, and as such it entails several interwoven layers of meaning. The cross was, first of all, a free act of sacrifice offered by Jesus to God for the sake of God's people, and ultimately for the sake of all creation. Paul thus writes in the salutation of his letter to the Galatians that the Lord Jesus Christ "gave himself for our sins to set us free from the present evil age, according to the will of our God and Father" (Gal. 1:3–4). But even at this basic level the cross did not stand by itself but was seen as the culmination of a life lived wholly out of obedience to God. As Paul reminds us in the great christological hymn recorded in his letter to the Philippians, Jesus "humbled himself and became obedient to the point of death—even death on a cross" (Phil. 2:8).

In a variety of ways, then, scripture describes Jesus's crucifixion as necessary. In the story of the two disciples making their way to Emmaus, for example, the risen Lord appears to them and says to them, "Was it not necessary that the Messiah should suffer these things and then enter into his glory?" (Luke 24:26). The necessity of his death had nothing to do with satisfying some sense of penal justice on God's part. Nowhere in the New Testament do we find depicted a courtroom scene in which God the Father is the righteous judge, Christ the defendant, and his suffering and death a penalty paid. The cross is necessary because of the kind of world we have made for ourselves, a world bent not toward God but toward violence and death. Crucifixion is what happens when human beings are faithful to God rather than the rulers of the present age. Atonement occurs in turn because of God's faithfulness to Jesus. Paul thus regards the cross as a triumph over the rulers and powers of this present age (Col. 2:15; cf. 2 Cor. 2:14). By accepting his death, Jesus demonstrated that he was free from the rebellious deceptions of a world that thinks that the creature rather than the creator determines the order and end of all things.

In this aspect the cross was a unique and unrepeatable event, for with Christ "everything—absolute everything—had, of course, been already given."[87] It was not merely a heroic example of how we ought to live and perhaps die for our fellow human beings, but the decisive moment in time where God's life-and-death struggle for the destiny of creation was decisively joined. But the cross is also the central figure for our participation in the life of Christ, which is a communal life

---

87. Lubac, *Scripture in the Tradition,* 6

of faithfulness to the God who breaks into the humanly contrived order of things with the peace of the city that is to come. It is in this sense that Paul introduces the great christological hymn in Philippians with the admonition, "Let the same mind be in you that was in Christ Jesus" (2:5). The Epistle to the Hebrews declares in like manner that is was fitting that

> God, for whom and through whom all things exist, in bringing many children to glory, should make the pioneer of their salvation perfect through sufferings. . . . Since, therefore, the children share flesh and blood, [Christ] himself likewise shared the same things, so that through death he might destroy the one who has the power of death, that is, the devil, and free those who all their lives were held in slavery by the fear of death. . . . Therefore Jesus also suffered outside the city gate in order to sanctify the people by his own blood. Let us then go to him outside the camp and bear the abuse he endured. (2:10, 14–15; 13:12–13)

The cross thus serves as a synecdoche in early Christian writings, signifying a life lived wholly out of obedience to God, and in that capacity names a pattern of atonement to be repeated by the communal body of Christ. As Paul asserts in Romans, the righteousness of God is revealed through the faith of Christ for our own life of faith (Rom. 1:17; 3:26). The apocalyptic fault line formed by the meeting of the two ages, decisively established by the events of Jesus's life, now cuts straight through each and every member of Christ's body. His followers constitute the temporal intersection between Pentecost and parousia within which all creation is now set. In this "tensed" interval, Christians become in Christ the righteousness of God (2 Cor. 5:21), embodying sacramentally the healing of the whole of creation.

And since in God life, not death, has the final word for creation, God's vindication of the way of Christ signified by the cross was disclosed in the resurrection. With the ascension of the risen Lord to the right hand of God, the early Christians declared that the world was no longer the same, having definitively crossed the threshold into the age to come. The rulers and authorities of this present age, though not directly acknowledging Christ's lordship, had been decisively defeated and brought under his sovereignty, and thus they were the unwitting servants of God's final (though still future) triumph. The practices and habits that bound together this motley mob of misfits and malcontents in a new style of life were a tangible sign to the world that God's everlasting reign, which had drawn near in all that Jesus did and suffered, was now making its way to the ends of the earth in the power of the Holy Spirit. "The church is God's new will and purpose for humanity," says Bonhoeffer. "God's will is always directed toward the concrete, historical human being. But this means that it begins to be implemented *in history*. God's will must become visible and comprehensible at some point in history."[88]

---

88. Dietrich Bonhoeffer, Dietrich Bonhoeffer Works, vol. 1, *Sanctorum Communio: A Theological Study of the Church*, trans. Reinhard Kraus and Nancy Lukens (Minneapolis: Fortress, 1998), 141 (emphasis original).

The visibility of this fellowship was crucial, for though the triumph of God over death signaled that this new era was at hand, they also quickly discovered that the "end" was not yet. Paul's description of the church as living between the times typifies the struggle of the New Testament authors to find appropriate ways to depict this overlap between two ages and two social orders, for in appearance most things went on pretty much as they had before. Babies were born and parents buried, goods were bought and sold, the priests and scribes continued to gather at the Temple, the Romans looked to expand their empire, and death still exercised its terrible dominion over the created order. The summons of Jesus in the Sermon on the Mount for his followers to be salt and light (Matt. 5:13–16) draws metaphorically upon two different senses of the body to drive home the same point: that they were to manifest the coming reign and regime of God to a world that had not completely disappeared but was destined to wither away.

The church, caught up in the apocalyptic action of God (a fact celebrated in eucharistic gatherings and lived out in a life of communal solidarity and hospitality to the stranger), thus bore witness to the world that the end toward which all creation is moving is not determined by those whom this age calls powerful, but by the one who gathers together all things in heaven and on earth in the crucified Messiah of Israel (Eph. 1:10). God's messianic rule established the goal toward which all things tend, and it also set the limits for the exercise of power by all worldly authorities. In and through this small group of people everything in the created order, all life, was "immediately confronted with a claim that is non-negotiable in the sense that in the end God will irrefutably be—God."[89] The mission of the church was not merely to communicate information about him to anyone who would listen, but to put the bodies of its members on the line between the two ages on behalf of him who lived and died for the sake of the world.

The Fading of Apocalyptic Attentiveness and the Re-expansion of Time

The New Testament's emphasis on the imminence of the apocalyptic day of the Lord was preserved to varying degrees well into the patristic era, as seen, for example, in the fathers' understanding of all that is involved in Christ's cosmic triumph over death, the devil, and sin.[90] Augustine, to cite but one example, cautions his readers against those who said that there would be no more persecutions of the church until the time of the Antichrist.[91] But as the centuries wore on, the apocalyptic compression of time that captivated the imagination of the early church gradually faded into the background, and the vivid sense of expectation generated by this view of things was relaxed. History "re-expanded," and the *eschaton* was

---

89. McClendon, *Systematic Theology*, vol. 2, *Doctrine*, 66.

90. See The Very Rev. Georges Florovsky, "Empire and Desert: Antinomies of Christian History," *The Greek Orthodox Theological Review* 3 (Winter 1957): 133–59.

91. Augustine, *City of God*, XVIII.52.

projected further and further into the future "and thus into insignificance."[92] The keen awareness of living in the tension between the "is" and the "is not" gradually faded, and the demarcation between church and world (and the corresponding line that passes through the soul of each Christian[93]) grew more and more opaque.

With the fading of the apocalyptic tension that so characterized the life and witness of the early church, Christians increasingly made themselves "at home" in the present world. As Martin Buber puts it, the "Christian cosmos arises; and this was so real for every mediæval Christian that all who read [Dante's] *Divina Commedia* made in spirit the journey to the nethermost spiral of hell and stepped over Lucifer's back, through purgatory, to the heaven of the Trinity, not as an expedition into lands as yet unknown, but as a crossing of regions already fully mapped."[94] Buber paints here with too broad a brush, but the portrait he creates rightly directs our attention to momentous changes in the ways Christians came to be caught up in the world that have become visible only in retrospect. It is to the story of these changes we now turn.

92. McClendon, *Doctrine*, 90.

93. McClendon, *Ethics*, 17.

94. Martin Buber, "What Is Man?" in *Between Man and Man*, trans. Ronald Gregor-Smith (New York: Routledge, 2002), 153.

3

Let Us Be like the Nations

Caught Up in the Powers and Principalities of the Present Age

The children of the world are consistent too—so I say they will soak up everything you can offer, take your job away from you, and then denounce you as a decrepit wreck. Finally, they'll ignore you entirely. It's your own fault. The Book I gave you should have been enough for you. Now you'll just have to take the consequences for your meddling.

Walter M. Miller Jr., *A Canticle for Leibowitz*

In her book *Bystanders: Conscience and Complicity during the Holocaust,* Victoria Barnett identifies some of the factors that "fostered passivity and complicity in Nazi Germany and in other countries"[1] in the lives of ordinary people during this most odious of episodes in human history. By "ordinary people" she is referring not to prominent members of the Nazi Party or to the soldiers of the *Waffen-SS* (*Schutzstaffel*) who operated the concentration and death camps. Instead, she has in mind those people who sought to go about their daily lives while one of the most sinister regimes the world has ever known committed unspeakable atroci-

1. Victoria J. Barnett, *Bystanders: Conscience and Complicity during the Holocaust* (Westport, CT: Praeger, 1999), xvi.

93

ties all about them. They might have been ordinary people, but their behavior was anything but ordinary. It was instead grotesque and freakish.[2]

Barnett compares and contrasts these bystanders to the handful of people who worked to rescue the victims of the Nazi regime. She notes in particular that the differences between the rescuers and those who went about their daily lives without attending to the great evil taking place all around them were not noticeable prior to 1933, the year that Adolf Hitler came to power in Germany. "In social and historical circumstances that demanded little of them personally," she writes, "the two groups were indistinguishable from one another. After 1933, however, these good citizens begin to move in opposite directions."[3] The question, therefore, is what factors led bystanders and rescuers to take such diametrically opposed paths.

According to Barnett, studies show that strongly held religious feelings and beliefs were *not* significant factors for distinguishing bystanders from most rescuers. When interviewed, less than 30 percent of Polish rescuers cited religious conviction as a motive, and in Italy and Denmark, where there was significant activity against Hitler's "Final Solution," religious factors evidently did not play a major role.[4] The principal difference was that rescuers found it difficult "to remain passively on the sidelines under a system like Nazism. Their natural tendency was to help its victims and resist the dictatorship's demands upon them." Barnett contends in particular that those who worked to rescue the victims of the Third Reich were preeminently distinguished from bystanders by a certain type of *vision*. This vision was of a different kind of society and of themselves as citizens of that alternative society. It compelled them to be attentive, to see that they had "a personal stake in what was happening around them."[5]

Bystanders by contrast were generally people who were principally concerned about themselves. Those who averted their gaze from the evil going on around them were those whose lives had always been centered around their own needs: "Even those who had qualms about what was happening under Nazism chose to remain silent. They evaded the intentionality that is the prerequisite for rescue or resistance. . . . They denied any connection between their own lives and what was taking place around them." They accepted the persecution of the Jews as an unpleasant but unchangeable reality, and arranged their lives, psyches, and ethics accordingly, so that they did not have to deal with what was going on there. When asked after the war about these events, the good citizens of these towns claimed that they were *machtlos*, powerless to do anything about their situation, paralyzed by fear and the threat of retribution (though relatively little harm typically came to those in villages who did refuse to comply with Nazi policies).[6]

2. See Flannery O'Connor, "Some Aspects of the Grotesque in Southern Fiction," in *Collected Works* (New York: The Library of America, 1988), 813–21.

3. Barnett, *Bystanders*, 159.

4. Ibid., 30, 158.

5. Ibid., 159, 172.

6. Ibid., 5–8, 159.

Two of the factors cited by Barnett to account for the inaction of the bystanders, when taken together, shed light on our inquiry into the dismembering of the church as the body of Christ. The first has to do with her observation that in social and historical circumstances that demanded little of them personally, the two groups were indistinguishable from one another. The existence of the Christian had become coextensive with, and thus indistinguishable from, that of the typical citizen of the nation-state. The second is the claim of bystanders, including many Christians, that they were powerless to resist the evil in their midst. They literally knew no other power, no other disciplined form of life, than that regulated by the rulers and authorities of this age.

As I noted in the last chapter, the early followers of Jesus, having been caught up in the apocalypse of God, embodied before the world a distinctive pattern of life together, constituted by an alternative set of habits and relations, and a different story in terms of which to follow the rhythms and progressions of history. God fashioned from the resources of diverse times and places a transformative social idiom for catching a glimpse of truth's beauty. Through their participation in the body of Christ, these women and men bore witness that the meaning of all other figures, events, and institutions could be discerned only in relationship to the one in whom God's own speech took flesh. The reorganization of human life and language inaugurated by the life and passion of Jesus, a project embodied in and mediated by the practices and institutions of the church, including modes of material exchange, became a never-ending task.

The mission of the early Christian community was, therefore, as Alexander Schmemann puts it, "not to exist 'in itself' but to be the 'sacrament,' the *epiphany*, of the new creation." Its shared practices established the performative links between, on the one hand, day-to-day life in a world where people eat and drink, marry and give in marriage, have children and bury parents, acquire and dispose of property, exchange goods, and the like, and on the other, the resurrection and the world to come. The body of Christ embodied this new social dimension into the world, its practices not just the *means* but also the *media* of grace. In and through these activities the church learned of its calling, received the power of the Spirit to fulfill it, and became "the sacrament, in Christ, of the new creation; the sacrament, in Christ, of the Kingdom."[7]

The process of getting caught up in new or different forms of life and thought, however, can and does work the other way as well. The tribes of Israel had been gathered from among the nations to be a "peculiar" people,[8] that the world might know the will, wisdom, and blessing of God. They did not relish their peculiarity, however, but wanted to serve their God the way other nations served theirs. "Let us be like the nations," they declared to the prophets, and thus they found

---

7. Alexander Schmemann, *Church, World, Mission: Reflections on Orthodoxy in the West* (Crestwood, NY: St. Vladimir's Seminary Press, 1979), 136–37, Schmemann's emphasis.

8. Deut. 14:2; 26:18 KJV; cf. Titus 2:14; 1 Pet. 2:9.

themselves entangled in a series of events that led eventually to their exile and dispersion (Ezek. 20:21; cf. 1 Sam. 8:5, 20). The story of God's chosen people, who repeatedly responded to the divine summons by reproducing the disobedience and rebellion of the fall, is in important respects one of being caught up in the worship of necessity that is idolatry. The catastrophe of the fall of the monarchy, the destruction of Jerusalem, and the exile did not, however, spell the end of the covenant relationship. A faithful God instead folded this event back into the saving history of the chosen people, allowing them in their affliction to "recognize their guilt and turn back to God, thus correcting the direction they [were] going. The very crisis of the people of God would then be one of the reasons why God's cause does not fail, but instead goes forward as a history of salvation." The end of David's monarchic regime led "to a rebirth of the people of God," thus making the exile and Diaspora parts of "a *saving* history and a step into the future."[9]

Like Israel before it, the church became ensnared in a similar pattern of divine call, rebellion, and judgment. It exchanged its peculiar portion in the promises of God to Israel, bequeathed in the messianic event of Jesus Christ, for a share in a new sort of regime for the earthly city, one in which the church hierarchy shares power and authority with secular rulers. The aim of those who led the way was in many respects a noble one: to help liberate creation from the dominion of death and darkness, and make it new before God by the power of the Holy Spirit. But what they set into motion led instead to the dismemberment of the church as the bodily presence of Christ in the world, leaving its scattered members at the mercy of powers and authorities that now no longer even bother to give lip service to the God of Abraham and Sarah.

The body of Christ is now caught up in a powerful disciplinary regime that subdivides social space into discrete spheres—political, economic, civic, cultural, religious, domestic. This process of differentiation functions effectively to domesticate, marginalize, and exploit the church's traditional regime of life and language. We find ourselves, like Israel, refugees and exiles in a strange land, where we are compelled to "serve other gods made by human hands, objects of wood and stone that neither see, nor hear, nor eat, nor smell" (Deut. 4:28). If we are persuaded, as participants in the covenants of promise, that in spite of what has happened, our life with God has not come to an end, then we must once again find our bearings and discover something of how we came to be in this situation. What happened to the church, where it now stands, and what we may hope for it in the future must therefore be parsed in terms of Israel's story, for the events of Israel's history with God are types (*tupoi*) intended to instruct the church in precisely this task (1 Cor. 10:6, 11). But which is the most adequate type?

9. Lohfink, *Does God Need the Church?* 105.

Peculiarity and Conformity

In *The End of the Church: A Pneumatology of Christian Division in the West*, Ephraim Radner advances a bold and controversial claim: the post-Reformation church, governed by a separative logic that contradicts Christ's mandate that the members of Christ's body should love each other in a way that relies on the other in visible unity, has been abandoned by God. This willful refusal to maintain the bonds of ecclesial unity, especially a common eucharistic communion, has prompted God to withdraw the Spirit from the church, thus condemning it to destruction and death. Radner formulates his thesis on the basis of a typological reading of the story of divided monarchy in the Old Testament. Due to this division, Israel was eventually abandoned by God to its enemies and forced to endure war and an exile that in some respects has never ended. And as with all good figural readings of the Old Testament, Radner connects this reading to the person and work of Christ, who mediates the figure of Israel to the church, including his acceptance of complete divine abandonment on the cross.[10]

There is much to commend in Radner's figural reading of the present situation, above all his recognition that the present status of the church must be construed typologically in terms of Israel's canonical story. He is also correct in pointing out that there has been a centuries-long contradiction of ecclesial love and a separative logic at work in a willfully divided church. Among different Protestant denominations in particular there is a persistent and pervasive tendency to pit variegated aspects of Christian life and thought against one another: Bible versus tradition, personal experience versus ecclesiastical authority, feeling versus intellect, spontaneity versus liturgy, discipleship versus doctrine, evangelism versus spiritual formation, apostolic office versus apostolic teaching, and so forth. Virtually nonexistent is any confession of the sin of denominational self-sufficiency—the failure to recognize that one tradition needs the others. The sort of humility that is generous enough to accept correction from other traditions, or a generosity humble enough to accept that each tradition must recognize its place within, dependence on, and gifts to offer to the larger church catholic, is seldom in evidence.[11]

In the final analysis, however, the specific features of Radner's figural reading do not adequately account for the dismembered state of the church, particularly its diachronic dimensions. The failure of charity that currently divides the body of Christ must be traced in large part to a new love that long ago seduced it with promises that this false suitor had no intention of keeping. The seeds of the separative logic that germinated during the sixteenth and seventeenth centuries and

10. Ephraim Radner, *The End of the Church: A Pneumatology of Christian Division in the West* (Grand Rapids: Eerdmans, 1998).

11. I am indebted to Gerald Schlabach for this way of putting the matter. See Gerald W. Schlabach, "The Correction of the Augustinians: A Case Study in the Critical Appropriation of a Suspect Tradition," in *The Free Church and the Early Church: Bridging the Historical Divide*, ed. D. H. Williams (Grand Rapids: Eerdmans, 2002), 74.

blossomed with the rise of the modern world were in fact sown centuries earlier, when the church joined forces with the rulers and authorities of the present age to govern the *saeculum*. As the church became increasingly at home in the world, the task of forming the Christian body, both communal and individual (with the exception of religious communities), was ceded incrementally to the secular authorities and institutions, resulting in a minimalist ethics that effectively adapted the social mission of the church so that it could accommodate the habits and relations of the secular regime.[12] When that sphere began to fragment in the late Middle Ages, the division of the church, first into separate denominations and then into isolated monads, was for all practical purposes a foregone conclusion.

The problematic nature of Radner's spiritual reading of the Old Testament lies in his selection of the division of David and Solomon's kingdom as the principal figure for interpreting the state of the post-Reformation church. At first glance the typological resemblance between a divided kingdom and a divided church seems ready-made. But positing the division of the kingdom as the source of Israel's disobedience and failure of steadfast love (*hesed*) obscures the plain sense of the text on which sound spiritual exegesis necessarily depends. Both Torah and the Prophets link the idolatry and rebellion that led to Israel's destruction and exile not to the division of the united monarchy (an institution that certain prophets had doubts about from the outset), but to the usurpations of monarchic practices and institutions in both north and south. Hosea is thus typical when he says that

> Israel has spurned the good;
>   the enemy shall pursue him.
> They made kings, but not through me;
>   they set up princes, but without my knowledge.
> With their silver and god they made idols
>   for their own destruction (8:3–4).

And therefore, says Amos to the inhabitants of the kingdom of Israel,

> you have built houses of hewn stone,
>   but you shall not live in them;
> you have planted pleasant vineyards,
>   but you shall not drink their wine (5:11).

When the elders of the tribes of Israel first approached the prophet Samuel about appointing for them a king, it is evident that they envisioned the institution of the monarchy as a reliable locus of social stability and prosperity: "we are

---

12. In the United States, for example, the doctrinal and moral content of latter-day Christendom steadily diminishes to accommodate the expansion of civic religion that began with New England Puritanism and then to a more generic version of Protestantism, and from there to "mere Christianity," then to some strange hybrid called "Judeo-Christianity," and finally to an amorphous notion of "family values."

determined to have a king over us, so that we also may be like other nations, and that our king may govern us and go out before us and fight our battles" (1 Sam. 8:19b–20). Their desire to be like other nations was not a preference based on a carefully calculated typology of political regimes.[13] It was instead the expression of a desire for the sort of stability and security that was associated with the gods of the other nations, an idolatrous longing that, as Samuel and then Nathan sought to make clear from the beginning,[14] ran counter to the mission first set before Abraham and Sarah.

It is the shift to a monarchic regime, setting into motion the forces that ultimately led Israel into exile, and not its subsequent division along tribal lines, that offers the most instructive *tupos* in the Old Testament for figuring the dismembered state of the body of Christ in this time after Christendom. We must take care, however, not to perpetuate a caricature or promote a blanket condemnation of what is often referred to as "Constantinianism." The question of whether it is even accurate to refer to the changes that took place beginning in the first half of the fourth century CE as the Constantinian shift is widely debated. Many in the patristic era celebrated the first "Christian emperor" as a sign of divine providence, pronouncing his reign an extension of Christ's heavenly kingdom. Eusebius of Caesarea compares him favorably to Moses in the dispensation of salvation, leading his people from the captivity of persecution.[15] And closer to our own time, Charles Cochrane has called him the "architect (to a very great extent) of the Middle Ages."[16] To such minds Constantine's conversion marked the beginning of the *corpus Christianum*. Recent scholarship generally takes a more restrained approach. Sociologist Rodney Stark, for example, contends that Constantine's conversion was an expedient response to, rather than the cause of, the exponential growth of the church during the latter half of the third century.[17] Historian Averil Cameron concurs with Stark, arguing that "Constantine marks a convenient but not an all-important landmark" in the spread of Christianity within the empire.[18]

It is imprecise, moreover, in certain respects to speak of Constantinianism, as though the relations between church and secular rulers that developed during

13. Such as we find in Plato, Aristotle, and Thomas Aquinas. See Plato, *The Republic*, 544e–569c, 2nd ed., trans. Allan Bloom (New York: Basic Books, 1991); Aristotle, *Nicomachean Ethics*, VIII.10, 2nd ed., trans. Terence Irwin (Indianapolis: Hackett, 1999), and *The Politics*, III.6–8, IV.2–10, trans. Carnes Lord (Chicago: University of Chicago Press, 1984); and Aquinas, *On Kingship*, I.1–3, in *Readings in Medieval Political Theory: 1100–1400*, ed. Cary J. Nederman and Kate Langdon Forhan (Indianapolis: Hackett, 1993).

14. 1 Sam. 8:7–9; 2 Sam. 7:4–7.

15. Eusebius, *The History of the Church*, 9.9.5–6, *The Life of Constantine*, 1.12 (NPNF[2] 1:363–64, 485).

16. Charles Norris Cochrane, *Christianity and Classical Culture: A Study of Thought and Action from Augustus to Augustine* (London: Oxford University Press, 1940), 211.

17. Rodney Stark, *The Rise of Christianity: A Sociologist Reconsiders History* (Princeton: Princeton University Press, 1996), 5, 10.

18. Averil Cameron, *Christianity and the Rhetoric of Empire: The Development of Christian Discourse* (Berkeley: University of California Press, 1991), 13.

the Middle Ages, and which eventually led to the fracturing of the church as an institution in the sixteenth century, were the direct design and result of Constantine's efforts, or at the very least the essentials of which were firmly in place by the end of the fourth century. There was a series of changes following the time of Constantine that kept the situation very fluid, beginning with the collapse of the empire in the West in the fifth and sixth centuries and the rise of Germanic kingdoms that replaced the imperial regime. Moreover, there existed a line of thinking in both Jewish and Christian circles, going back to at least Philo, that accords the emperor a significant place within God's providential rule of history. According to R. A. Markus, Melito of Sardis states that the unification of the *orbis Romanus* under imperial rule was providentially geared to the propagation of the gospel.[19] And no lesser figure than Origen provides the classical formulation of this theme in his polemic against Celsus. By reducing the many nations of the earth to one rule, God was preparing the nations for Christ's teaching by easing the way of the apostles.[20]

Finally, though the many institutional arrangements of Christendom did not achieve what its first proponents set out to accomplish—liberate creation from the dominion of death and darkness, and make it new before God by the power of the Holy Spirit—neither did they completely abandon the understanding of history embodied in the life and ministry of Jesus and in the early church. As the ill-fated shift from tribal confederacy to monarchy in Israel did not take place without serving an important role in unfolding the divine ordering of creation, the history of this phase in the life of the church also served a similar purpose. The patristic and medieval church cultivated practices and principles that retained something of the early church's regulation of everyday life. John Howard Yoder notes, for example, that the "higher level of morality asked of the clergy, the international character of the hierarchy, the visibility of the hierarchy in opposition to the princes, the gradual moral education of barbarians into monogamy and legality, foreign missions, apocalypticism and mysticism . . . preserved an awareness, however distorted and polluted, of the strangeness of God's people in a rebellious world."[21]

That said, we must nonetheless recognize that though Constantine's "conversion" was not the sole or perhaps even the single most important cause of the changes that took place, the new social status subsequently enjoyed by the church, followed a few decades later by official recognition as the true *pietatis* of Rome during the reign of Theodosius I (379–395), would not have come about as it did were it not for Constantine's toleration of, and personal identification with, the church. The emperor's change of heart set into motion a series of events that would contribute materially to the dismemberment of the church as Christ's true body.

---

19. R. A. Markus, *Saeculum: History and Society in the Theology of St Augustine*, rev. ed. (Cambridge: Cambridge University Press, 1988), 47–48.

20. Origen, *Contra Celsus*, II.30 (*ANF* 4:443–44).

21. John H. Yoder, *The Royal Priesthood: Essays Ecclesiological and Ecumenical*, ed. M. G. Cartwright (Grand Rapids: Eerdmans, 1994), 58.

Those who downplay the significance of the first "Christian" emperor frequently overcompensate for past indiscretions on the part of church figures and secular historians alike. Constantine's conversion played a key role in the rapidly changing circumstances of the church with respect to its status and mission and thus with regard to its relationship to the world about it.

Citizens of Another Commonwealth

Prior to the events at the Milvian Bridge,[22] early Christians regularly referred to themselves as citizens belonging to another commonwealth, a company of fellow travelers garnered from every tribe and language, people and nation to populate a city on pilgrimage. Some might find this terminology confusing, accustomed as we are to a very different account of what constitutes the respective realms of politics and religion. In the modern world "politics" is reserved for the practice of statecraft,[23] while religion is something that individuals do in the solitude of their "inner self," an interior disposition of the soul toward that which transcends the physical world, and which thus has no direct bearing on their public lives. But in classical antiquity "city" functioned as the principal trope denoting the shared practices, habits, and relationships that enable women and men to flourish in accordance with their highest good.[24] Politics was the art of human community, the end of which was living well, and political institutions were a means to this

22. According to Eusebius, as Constantine prepared to meet his rival Maxentius in battle, he saw superimposed on the sun a cross and the words "*in hoc signo vinces*," "in this sign, conquer" (Eusebius, *Life of Constantine*, 1.28 [NPNF² 1:490]).

23. Statecraft in its most basic guise has to do with the maintenance and operation of the mechanisms of the nation-state. Liberal statecraft further stipulates that the nation-state is the only legitimate form of political association. Liberalism thus invests the state with virtually unlimited political sovereignty over society, in particular the adjudication of conflicting interests between individuals and all other social groups, thus privileging it as the fulcrum of all social and political change. Underwriting the practice and theory of liberal statecraft is the absence of any substantive conception of the common good, which effectively reduces politics to a set of procedures for protecting and promoting individuals' pursuit of self-interest in the marketplace of desire and consumption. See Daniel M. Bell Jr., *Liberation Theology after the End of History* (New York: Routledge, 2001), 13.

24. More specifically, the figure of "city" functions in scripture and the early Christian tradition as a synecdoche, by which a species stands in for the genus, "political association." Precision is important, for there are those who, either wittingly or not, misconstrue this notion by pigeonholing its use in connection with the church as a "metaphor." Not only do such renderings perpetuate a faulty conception of metaphor as essentially ornamental speech, they clearly misrepresent the semantic force on this particular figure as employed by Christian authors. Jean Bethke Elshtain, for example, tries to downplay the political significance of the church in Augustine's *City of God* in this fashion, observing that Augustine himself states at the beginning of Book 15 that he is "speaking allegorically." What she fails to see, unfortunately, is that the allegorical dimension refers to the distinction between the two orders of human life; at the beginning of Book 14 Augustine asserts in univocal language that there exists two orders of human society, *duo quaedam genera humanae societatis existerent* (Augustine, *City of God*, XIV.1; cf. XV.1). See Jean Bethke Elshtain, *Augustine and the Limits of Politics* (Notre Dame, IN: University of Notre Dame Press, 1995), 95.

end, supporting and sustaining those tasks that direct its members toward that highest good.[25]

The community of Jesus's followers deliberately cast itself as a body politic when it referred to itself as an *ekklesia*, a Hellenistic term for the assembly of those holding rights and privileges of citizenship. When the church adopted this term for their association, rather than that of the ancient guilds or civic clubs, it was claiming the status of a public assembly of the social whole. The goods and activities of this particular body politic, however, were not those of the Greek *polis* or the Roman *imperium*. On the contrary, the assembly of God's messianic regime ordered the life of its members in ways that called into question virtually every social, political, and economic convention of its time. The church thus retained the classical *telos* of politics, which is the good life, and the practices and institutions of social life were likewise understood to be means to this end.[26] But it gave the practice of politics new content, namely, "the art of achieving the common good through participation in the divine life of God."[27]

By its very existence as a political community, the church called into question the dominant political assumptions and social categories of that time and place. It regarded the builders of earthly kingdoms and empires with a wary eye, because they invariably laid claim to an authority that belonged to God alone. Rome saw itself as "*the City*, a permanent and 'eternal' City, *Urbs aeterna*, and an ultimate City also. In a sense, it claimed for itself an 'eschatological dimension.' It posed as an ultimate solution of the human problem." The empire proclaimed itself a universal commonwealth, embodying the decisive expression of "humanity" and offering to all over whom it exercised authority the only lasting and genuine peace, the *pax romana*. As such it claimed to be omnicompetent over human affairs and thus demanded the complete and unconditional allegiance of its subjects. "The Church was a challenge to the Empire," writes Georges Florovsky, "and the Empire was a stumbling block for the Christians."[28]

Church teaching prior to the fourth century, in keeping with the Old Testament and rabbinic tradition, relativized the role that the rulers and authorities of this world played in the unfolding of history. Their claim to be the determinative players on the stage of history was abrogated, and like the Persian king Cyrus (Isa. 44:28–45:4, 13), they were recast as merely supporting actors. These temporal authorities were granted the right or power of the sword (*ius* or *potestas gladii*), which they were to use to help preserve a rebellious and chaotic world until, as Paul puts it, "Christ came, so that we might be justified by

---

25. See Aristotle, *Politics*, III.9; and Cicero, *De Re Publica de Legibus*, trans. Clinton Walker Keyes (Cambridge: Harvard University Press, 1951), I.25.39.

26. See Aristotle, *Politics*, III.9.

27. Michael Baxter, "'Overall, the First Amendment Has Been Very Good for Christianity'—NOT! A Response to Dyson's Rebuke," *DePaul Law Review* 43 (Winter 1994): 441.

28. Florovsky, "Empire and Desert," 135, 137.

faith" (Gal. 3:24).[29] These authorities served this function by pursuing certain legitimate yet limited goods, e.g., restraining evil through the prudent use of coercion, facilitating the production and exchange of material goods through the institutions of private property and markets, and in general maintaining social cohesion so that the church could proclaim the gospel unhindered.

At the same time, however, the pre-Constantinian church as a rule prohibited believers from wielding the *gladius ultor*, the avenging sword. "Shall it be lawful," Tertullian asks, "to make an occupation of the sword, when the Lord proclaims that he who uses the sword shall perish by the sword?"[30] According to Hippolytus, a soldier who converted could remain in that position, but it was forbidden for him to put a person to death or take an oath. Moreover, no catechumen or baptized Christian could become a soldier, for to do so would be to despise God.[31] Christians were to use a different weapon, described in scripture as the sword of the Spirit, which is the word of God (Eph. 6:17). Clement of Alexandria, calling the *gladius spiritalis* (spiritual sword) the Christian's invulnerable weapon, writes:

> The loud trumpet, when sounded, collects the soldiers, and proclaims war. And shall not Christ, breathing a strain of peace to the ends of the earth, gather together His own soldiers, the soldiers of peace? Well, by His blood, and by the word, He has gathered the bloodless host of peace, and assigned to them the kingdom of heaven. The trumpet of Christ is His Gospel. He hath blown it, and we have heard it.[32]

It is extremely important to note that for these early fathers the two "swords" did not designate complementary offices within a unified social order, one dealing with the affairs of the material world and the other with "spiritual" matters having to do with interior dispositions of the soul, as they later became, but as mutually exclusively modes of dealing with the world's evils.[33]

Toward a Christian Empire

When in the fourth century the empire that had regularly ridiculed, and on occasion persecuted, the church sought it out so that the body of Christ might serve the imperial household, it was initially seen as a response to the Gentile mission of the church, "constituted not by the church's seizing alien power, but by alien power's becoming attentive to the church." In other words, the Christendom idea initially

---

29. See Lester L. Field Jr., *Liberty, Dominion, and the Two Swords: On the Origins of Western Political Theology (180–398)* (Notre Dame, IN: University of Notre Dame Press, 1998), 45–49.

30. Tertullian, *De Corona* XI (ANF 3:99).

31. Hippolytus, *The Treatise on the Apostolic Tradition*, II.xvi, ed. Gregory Dix and Henry Chadwick (Ridgefield, CT: Morehouse, 1937, 1968, 1992).

32. Clement of Alexandria, *Protrepticus* XI (ANF 2:204).

33. See John Courtney Murray, SJ, *We Hold These Truths: Catholic Reflections on the American Proposition* (Lanham, MD: Sheed and Ward, 2005), 79–81, 186–90.

presupposed the apocalyptic eschatology of the early church, with church and secular rule as distinct structures belonging to two distinct societies or cities: "Until the end of the patristic period this *vis-à-vis* is constantly in evidence, and the meaning of the Christian empire as a *capitulation* to the throne of Christ is not forgotten."[34]

The Constantinian and Theodosian establishment of a Christian empire was therefore in the minds of many a confirmation and continuation of the church's missional confidence in the triumph of God over the rulers and idols of this age.[35] The body of Christ set out to exorcise the world of its demonic powers, to liberate the empire from the thralldom of the "prince of the air," in short, to make "this world 'new' before God by the power of the Holy Spirit." The church of Christendom's initial configuration sought to serve the world while remaining true to its identity as the sacrament of the kingdom, "God's eschatological vehicle of passage for this world through time into the world to come." Unfortunately, it failed in the attempt, and in spite of its best intentions the blame rests largely with the church, because in the end it succumbed to the temptation to be like the other nations, and thus "endeavored to be not what it is but what it is not."[36] The body of Christ became caught up in a series of events that would lead to the dismembering of its societal fellowship and the reallocation of the dissected parts to the institutions of the modern nation-state and the globalized market.

There were some in the fourth and fifth centuries who came to see the Constantinian settlement as something other than the "fruition of the promised kingdom of God."[37] According to Robert Wilken, John Chrysostom disabused those who were under the impression that if one became a monk he would always receive honor and respect from Christian rulers. Chrysostom insisted that there might come a time that policies would change, or unbelievers regain power (a possibility that he had personally witnessed with the ascension of Julian to the imperial throne). "Unlike Eusebius," writes Wilken, "John did not celebrate the emperor as a 'mighty victor beloved of God,' a king who had 'wiped away all tears and cleansed the world of the hatred of God.'" Unlike many of his contemporaries, he "had no conception of a Christian empire. The Church, in John's view, was 'not dependent on the good will of the rulers.'" For Chrysostom the high hopes of the previous generation had been tempered by the recent memory of martyrs.[38]

For a time Augustine ascribed to the Christian emperor, and by implication to the empire itself, a central role in the history of God's redemptive work. Around

---

34. O'Donovan, *The Desire of the Nations*, 195–96.

35. Ibid., 193–199; Markus, *Saeculum*, 31. O'Donovan also notes that prior to the time of Constantine Christian apologists identified the rise of the Roman empire as a sign of the rout of demons, the plurality of nations previous to it being an aspect of polytheism (*The Desire of the Nations*, 198).

36. Guroian, *Incarnate Love*, 146.

37. Schlabach, "Correction of the Augustinians," 64.

38. Robert L. Wilken, *John Chrysostom and the Jews: Rhetoric and Reality in the Late 4th Century* (Berkeley: University of California Press, 1983), 31–32. Augustine makes a similar observation about Julian in *City of God*, XVIII.53.

the year 400, however, a radical transformation occurs in his thinking, stimulated by the Donatist theologian Tyconius.[39] Owing to God's activity in Christ, made visible to all through the church, Augustine contends, there exist in the world two distinct kinds of human society, one earthly and the other on pilgrimage to a city that is not of its own making.[40] These two societies are related eschatologically, each possessing a different faith, a different love, and a different hope.[41] While on pilgrimage in this world, calling out citizens from all nations and forming a *civitas* of aliens speaking all languages, the church is not to occupy itself with differences in the customs, laws, and institutions by which earthly peace is achieved or maintained.[42]

According to Augustine, Christians may not neglect this earthly peace, but must co-operate with the earthly city in pursuit of those things that belong to the mortal nature of human beings—what we shall eat, what we shall drink, what we shall wear. He does add one very important proviso, which is that such pursuits should "not impede the religion by which we are taught that the one supreme and true God is to be worshipped." Therein lies the problem, he writes, for it has not been possible for the church to have rules detailing its obligations to God in common with the earthly city. "It has been necessary," says Augustine, "for her to dissent from the earthly city in this regard, and to become a burden to those who think differently. Thus, she has had to bear the brunt of the anger and hatred and persecutions of her adversaries." In spite of this animosity, Christians should cultivate skills that will allow us to use prudently those earthly goods that are necessary to life in this age, directing every good act toward that alone which can truly be called peace, "a perfectly ordered and perfectly harmonious fellowship in the enjoyment of God, and of one another in God."[43]

Augustine's rejection of an *imperium Christianum* notwithstanding, the social convergence of the church and the empire continued unabated, and by the end of the fifth century it had begun to change significantly. Pope Gelasius reconfigured Augustine's *temporal* demarcation between the two cities as a *functional* distinction

39. See Markus, *Saeculum*, 115–22. I am venturing into the highly contested field of Augustinian studies, wherein few topics are more disputed than Augustine's conception of the political. In what follows in this chapter I am indebted to Rowan Williams's insightful discussion "Politics and the Soul: A Reading of the *City of God*," *Milltown Studies* 19/20 (1987): 55–72. Over against Hannah Arendt, Markus, and others, Williams contends—persuasively, I would argue—that Augustine does not repudiate the public realm in this work. "Rather he is engaged in a *redefinition* of the public itself, designed to show that it is life outside the Christian community which fails to be truly public, authentically political" (Williams, "Politics and the Soul," 58). For a different understanding of Augustine on matters political, see John von Heyking, *Augustine and Politics as Longing in the World* (Columbia: University of Missouri Press, 2001). For extended debate on this question see Dorothy F. Donnelly, ed., *The City of God: A Collection of Critical Essays* (New York: Peter Lang, 1995).

40. *[D]uo quaedam genera humanae societatis existerent* (Augustine, *City of God*, XIV.1).

41. Ibid., XVIII.54.

42. Ibid., XIX.17; see also V.17.

43. Ibid.

between royal power (*potestas*) and priestly authority. These two would rule jointly, each according to their proper office, with the weight of authority oriented toward sacerdotal *auctoritas*, because as the pope put it in a famous letter to the emperor Anastasius, "they must answer for kings at the divine judgment. Indeed, you know, most clement Son, that though you have received the power to govern mankind, nonetheless you must bow your head to those who have charge of divine affairs and must seek from them the means of your salvation."[44] In place of the two types of society that Augustine describes allegorically as Jerusalem and Babylon,[45] sacred and civil officials were now to rule conjointly within one social order. The duality of cities, which had distinguished the present age from the age to come, became a duality of government function or office. Sacred and secular officials were now to rule cooperatively within society, with the priestly office recognized as supreme.

A second transformation occurred during the years between Charlemagne and Pope Gregory VII, the so-called Carolingian period. Gelasius's two "swords" were themselves redefined in terms of the two natures of Chalcedonian Christology. Christendom as such, and not just the church, was now the one body of Christ, with the dual offices of king and bishop corresponding to the two natures—human and divine, neither confused nor separated—of Christ. Whereas in Gelasius's schema the *potestas* of king and emperor was outside the church, and all true authority resided solely within the church,[46] now kingship and empire were fused together with the church, with the temporal ruler endowed with titles such as "Vicar of Christ" and "King and Priest." The anointing of a king acquired a sacramental significance comparable to that of baptism and ordination.[47] In this configuration the king "exercised his office of ruling wholly within the church, as a kind of lay ministry or charism." With this "change from 'world' to 'church,'" writes O'Donovan, "the last consciousness of a notional distinction between the two societies had disappeared; one could no longer say that the ruler ruled Christians *qua* civil society but not *qua* heavenly city."[48]

The nearly total erasure of the eschatological demarcation between the two cities and the expansion of the concept of Christ's body to include temporal regimes significantly altered the mission of the church as an ongoing interpretation of creaturely existence lived in relation to the Triune God. The contraction of the two ages that characterized the apocalyptic motifs of the New Testament and early church faded into the background. The rhythms and progressions of history once again re-expanded as the *eschaton* was projected further and further into the future. The Christian hope gradually shifted from the renewal of all things in Christ

---

44. Pope Gelasius, "Letter Twelve to Emperor Anastasius," in Hugo Rahner, SJ, *Church and State in Early Christianity*, trans. Leo Donald Davis, SJ (San Francisco: Ignatius, 1992), 174.

45. Augustine, *City of God*, XV.1.

46. Milbank, *Theology and Social Theory*, 96.

47. Ernst H. Kantorowicz, *The King's Two Bodies: A Study in Mediaeval Political Theology* (Princeton, NJ: Princeton University Press, 1957, 1985), 42–61, 318–19.

48. O'Donovan, *Desire of the Nations*, 204, 212.

to a concern with the fate of the individual after death. In keeping with this shift of temporal focus, patristic descriptions of Christ's cosmic triumph over death, sin, and the devil were supplanted by a preoccupation with the pains of Christ in his passion, and spiritual discipline became increasingly focused on dealing with the multiplicity of affections and appetites that mark the spiritual progress of the individual believer.[49]

The Invention of the "State"

In the eleventh and twelfth centuries, yet another shift took place, this one in connection with the Investiture Controversy. According to Gerhart Ladner, Pope Gregory VII (1073–1085) recognized that the Carolingian arrangement between prince and bishop was unwieldy and unworkable, in large part because the line of demarcation between the two powers was in practice almost impossible to define: "Even though the superiority of the spiritual over the temporal was undisputed on principle, the right order between the two was not easy to maintain in the contingencies of history."[50] The result was a gradual separation of the offices of civic and ecclesiastical authorities, with kingship increasingly divested of its sacerdotal connotations. In this arrangement the popes reserved the title of Vicar of Christ for themselves, while kingship was reconceived along the lines of what was to become the dominant conception of God's sovereignty over the earth: "as opposed to the earlier 'liturgical' kingship, the late-mediaeval kingship by 'divine right' was modeled after the Father in Heaven rather than after the Son on the Altar, and focused in a philosophy of Law rather than in the . . . physiology of the two-natured Mediator." To reinforce this separation of civil rule from the body of Christ, Innocent III decreed in "On Holy Unction" that there was a separate anointment for bishops and kings, and that the royal anointing did not confer in sacramental mode the Holy Spirit.[51]

Taken cumulatively, these changes significantly modified once again the way that church and civil authorities were related in time. With the diremption of the crown from the human nature of Christ, a new form of political association emerged in the fifteenth century, with roots reaching back as far as the twelfth century.[52] This new political artifact was the state, a centralized form of public power that was conceived in abstraction both from those who rule and those who are ruled, and exercising

49. Colin Morris, *The Discovery of the Individual, 1050–1200* (New York: Harper & Row, 1972), 70–79, 139–52.

50. Gerhart B. Ladner, "Aspects of Medieval Thought on Church and State," *Review of Politics* 9 (1947): 409; see also Joseph R. Strayer, *On the Medieval Origins of the Modern State* (Princeton, NJ: Princeton University Press, 1970), 21–24.

51. Kantorowicz, *The King's Two Bodies*, 93, 319–21; Strayer, *On the Medieval Origins of the Modern State*, 23–26.

52. Strayer, *On the Medieval Origins of the Modern State*, 15–27; Hendrik Spruyt, *The Sovereign State and Its Competitors* (Princeton, NJ: Princeton University Press, 1994), 79.

supreme authority within a geographically defined space.[53] The nascent state, which was centered on a formal and abstract concept of law, claimed a sempiternity or quasi-eternal character of its own in imitation of the pilgrim city of God. The idea of the "'temporal,' which had previously indicated that the coercive force of kingship was 'temporarily' necessary while awaiting the second coming of Christ," came to signify "an autonomous sphere which pursues its own perpetuity."[54]

The embryonic state, in a bid to establish its status as an independent and sacred "body" over against and yet parallel to that of the church as Christ's mystical body, quickly adopted ecclesial symbols and sacramental images to secure that standing. "The new territorial and proto-national state," writes Kantorowicz, "self-sufficient according to its claims and independent of the Church and the Papacy, quarried the wealth of ecclesiastical notions, which were so convenient to handle, and finally proceeded to assert itself by placing its own temporariness on a level with the sempiternity of the militant Church."[55] One vestige of this move on the part of kings to mimic the trappings of ecclesiastical authority was commandeering the language of sanctification and sacrifice, such that the theological idea of martyrdom came to be applied to dying in behalf of one's nation-state as one's earthly *patria*.[56]

In its struggle to maintain its temporal authority in light of the fragmentation of the social unity of Christendom in the West, the church responded in kind, modifying its own self-understanding through a similar conception of law. A distinction began to appear in canon law in the thirteenth century between the sacramental power (*potestas ordinis*) conferred on priests with their ordination, giving them the ability to transubstantiate the host and thereby produce the true body (the *corpus verum*) of Christ, and the power of ecclesiastical jurisdiction (*potestas jurisdictionis*) vested in the bishop. According to this distinction, the consecration of a new bishop added nothing to his priestly authority. Instead, he received jurisdictional powers to govern the mystical body of the church. Imitating these new territorial sovereignties, the church located its source, not as it once did, in the sacrament of the Lord's body, but in formal legal concepts. Canon lawyers adopted the term *corpus mysticum* in their efforts to establish the character of the church as a legal corporation.[57] "What mattered about the term was its organic

---

53. Quentin Skinner, *The Foundations of Modern Political Thought*, vol. 2, *The Age of Reformation* (London: Cambridge University Press, 1978), 353; Bruce D. Porter, *War and the Rise of the State: The Military Foundations of Modern Politics* (New York: Free Press, 1994), 6. Those who claim with Charles Curran that the state is "natural and necessary" and "based on creation" have turned a blind eye to the radically changing nature of political community since antiquity (Charles E. Curran, *Catholic Social Teaching, 1891–Present: A Historical, Theological, and Ethical Analysis* [Washington, DC: Georgetown University Press, 2002], 138–39).

54. Cavanaugh, *Torture and Eucharist*, 216.

55. Kantorowicz, *King's Two Bodies*, 207.

56. Cavanaugh, *Torture and Eucharist*, 217. As the etymological connection makes evident, the modern concept of patriotism derives from this extension of martyrdom.

57. Kantorowicz, *King's Two Bodies*, 200–206.

connotations and not any connection with the sacramental body of Christ. In that process . . . corporational doctrines developed by the Church were to be of major importance."[58]

The use of the term *corpus mysticum* was a legal strategy, devised to stress the juridical bonds between the church and its head, the pope. Canon lawyers, at the behest of the pontiff, appropriated the concept of the right of property as set forth in Roman and feudal law and developed it in connection with the late medieval doctrine of the church as Christ's mystical body into the theory of "the absolute and universal jurisdiction of the supreme authority, and developed it into the doctrine of the *plenitudo potestatis* of the Pope."[59] On the basis of the doctrine, the popes tried to re-establish political unity under their authority, and to do so in a world where "secular control was rapidly on the rise and the political unity of Christendom was being fragmented into sovereign nation-states."[60] The doctrine of the *corpus mysticum* did increase the authority and prestige of the Roman pontiff within the Catholic church, but when Boniface VIII attempted to rein in the political power of Philip the Fair of France by asserting his authority over all Christians, his capture and humiliation by Philip's troops demonstrated that it was now the lay ruler, not the pope, who could count on the primary allegiance of the people.[61]

With these changes the social bodies of the church and the developing territorial states were increasingly separated into two independent and parallel jurisdictions. Church authorities sought to meet the rising power and independence of the state by declaring their own legal and corporate power.[62] Cavanaugh observes that, "The first treatises on the church as an organization were written only in the early fourteenth century, with the purpose of establishing the church as an 'ecclesiastical kingdom' parallel to the secular polity." Though the process of transforming the church into a "spiritual" body concerned solely with an individual's private, interior life would take several more centuries to develop fully, "it was clear at this point the construction of a separate and sempiternal political space outside the church was

58. Cavanaugh, *Torture and Eucharist*, 217.

59. John Neville Figgis, *Studies of Political Thought from Gerson to Grotius, 1414–1625* (Cambridge: University Press, 1956), 4; cf. O'Donovan, *Desire of the Nations*, 206.

60. Cavanaugh, *Torture and Eucharist*, 218.

61. Jospeh R. Strayer, "The Laicization of French and English Society in the Thirteenth Century," *Speculum* 15 (1940): 76.

62. Nicholas Boyle notes that "the Church has always, and of necessity, taken much of its institutional character from the political world of its day. The popes have been feudal lords in a feudal era, absolute monarchs in the age of absolutism, in the nineteenth century they became something like presidents-for-life of a kind of international nation-state within the nation-states. . . . The First Vatican Council was a very necessary battening-down of the hatches to face the totalitarian pretensions of the state in the era of unrestrained nationalism: in order to face down the dictators, from [Prussian leader Otto von] Bismarck to [Polish communist leader Wojciech] Jaruzelski, the Church had to turn itself into something very like the militarized dictatorships it was opposing—Orwell was right to see the Catholicism of his day as a variant of the nationalism he deplored, though he was wrong to imagine that it was the whole, or even a large part, of the Catholic Church" (Boyle, *Who Are We Now?* 91).

underway."[63] When John Calvin writes two and a half centuries later that "whoever knows how to distinguish between body and soul, between this present fleeting life and that future eternal life, will without difficulty know that Christ's spiritual Kingdom and the civil jurisdiction are things completely distinct,"[64] he unwittingly reproduces late medieval conceptions that were originally aimed at maintaining the waning authority of the pope over temporal powers.

These modifications to the Carolingian arrangement between the church and civil authorities in the West remained in place until shortly before the time of the Reformation, when social changes further undercut the ability of ecclesiastical authorities to limit secular power. The dominance once exercised by the hierarchy over the civil rulers in medieval society was sharply inverted, as the church either gave up its separate jurisdictional authority voluntarily or was relieved of it, and was redefined as a purely suasive body. Its withdrawal from the political field allowed the state to become the absolute and unquestioned authority within the (often arbitrary) boundaries that defined its territory. With the loss of its independent political authority that allowed it to demand that civil rulers account for their actions, the ability of the church to influence its social context began to erode as well. Secular rulers maneuvering to gain control of these new political entities, by contrast, proved to be far more adept at manipulating doctrinal disputes and confessional loyalties in their ascent to power.[65]

The Magisterial Reformers, for all of their insights into the fallen nature of the medieval church, did not question the division of labor between ecclesiastical and civic authorities in the latter Middle Ages. To the contrary, by aligning their movements with particular states' claims to absolute sovereignty over the political realm, as Martin Luther did in Germany, they not only shredded further the visible unity of the body of Christ (particularly in its transnational and ecumenical expression) but also effectively (though unwittingly) provided ideological props for modern politics, especially its nationalistic fervor. The immediate effect of this novel alliance of Christian piety and national allegiance was to fan the flames of national and ethnic hatred that burned out of control in what are mistakenly called the Wars of Religion.[66]

The Invention of "Religion"

Structural changes in the ever-changing social regime of Christendom were accompanied by new modes of regulating the relationship between the pilgrim city of God and the earthly city, the most significant of which was the invention

63. Cavanaugh, *Torture and Eucharist*, 219.
64. John Calvin, *Institutes of the Christian Religion*, IV. 20. trans. Ford Lewis Battles (Philadelphia: Westminster, 1960).
65. See Cavanaugh, "'A Fire Strong Enough to Consume the House,'" 397–420.
66. See Cavanaugh, *Theopolitical Imagination*, 20–31.

of "religion." As odd as it may sound, prior to the fifteenth century no one used this idea in its distinctively modern sense, having to do with the private beliefs of an individual that have little or no direct bearing on public life. When *religio* does occur in medieval writings (which is rare), it refers either to the rule or discipline of monastic life,[67] or to an acquired virtue similar to that of sanctity, a habit that, in concert with other virtues, directs the faithful to know and love God: "the activity by which man gives the proper reverence to God through actions which specifically pertain to divine worship, such as sacrifice, oblations, and the like."[68] In either sense the term presupposed a context of practices embodied in the communal life of the church. As Cavanaugh puts it, "virtuous actions do not proceed from rational principles separable from the agent's particular history; virtuous persons instead are embedded in communal practices of habituation of body and soul that give their lives direction to the good."[69]

Beginning in the fifteenth century, however, the doctrinal and moral convictions that had been fostered by church teaching were gradually separated from the life and language of Christ's ecclesial body, and reconfigured as abstract systems of beliefs that could be embraced voluntarily by individuals about what is ultimately true and important in their lives, but without the need to participate in the worship and witness of the church. According to Peter Harrison, Nicholas of Cusa laid much of the groundwork for this transition in the first half of the fifteenth century by attributing different modes of faith as the result of epistemic limitations of finite human beings, with a single, infinite reality standing behind the heterogeneous expressions. He thus speaks of "one religion in the multiplicity of rites." According to Harrison, it is clear that

> Cusanus does not mean one "religion" in the modern sense, for that would imply an end to the "diversity of rites." Yet neither is he using the term in the limited sense of "monastic rule." Instead, he seeks to promote the view that diverse religious customs (the accidents of "religion," if you will) conceal a true or ideal "religion." This *"una religio"* is the unattainable truth about God—the Platonic ideal of which all existing belief systems are but shadowy expressions. The faithful of all nations and creeds should persevere in their particular expressions of piety in the firm belief that the one true "religion" is the basis of them all.[70]

According to Wilfred Cantwell Smith, Marsilio Ficino builds on Cusanus's Platonic speculations in his 1474 book *De Christiana Religione*, positing *religio* as a human impulse or propensity common to all women and men, "the fundamental distinguishing human characteristic, innate, natural, and primary." For Ficino,

---

67. Richard William Southern, *Western Society and the Church in the Middle Ages* (Harmondsworth, UK: Penguin, 1985), 214; Asad, *Genealogies of Religion*, 39n22.

68. Thomas Aquinas, *Summa Theologica*, IIa.IIae.81.2.

69. Cavanaugh, *Theopolitical Imagination*, 32.

70. Peter Harrison, *"Religion" and the Religion in the English Enlightenment* (New York: Cambridge University Press, 1990), 12.

religio names the Platonic ideal of genuine perception and worship of God, which Smith translates as "religiousness." The various historical manifestations of this predisposition, the varieties of pieties and rites that we now call religions, are all just more or less true approximations of the one true *religio* divinely implanted in the human heart.[71] That which directs us to know and love God is thus interiorized and naturalized, made a matter of an inward awareness or affection orienting individuals toward the transcendent, an innate disposition essentially unrelated to any particular ecclesial context.[72]

According to Quentin Skinner, humanists in the sixteenth century provide a theoretical basis for the reconfiguration of Christian faith around this new concept of religion. Seeking to secure religious liberty, Guillaume Postel contends that Christianity is the name of a set of demonstrable moral truths (what we now call a worldview) rather than theological claims and practices that are conjoined to a particular social regime called the church. Christian truth is based on universal axioms that underlie all particular expressions of "religious belief," and he is confident that they commend themselves to all rational women and men, even the infidel, once they learn of them.[73]

The concept of religion thus comes to be identified with a set of propositions rather than a virtue or set of virtues embodied in the church, gaining wide currency in Protestant circles through the writings of Ulrich Zwingli and John Calvin, both of whom use it in the titles of two of the most widely circulated books of the sixteenth century: Zwingli's *Commentary on True and False Religion* and Calvin's *Institutes of the Christian Religion*. In the early seventeenth century, writes Smith, Hugo Grotius writes in *De Veritate Religionis Christianae* that the Christian religion teaches, rather than simply being the true worship of God.[74] According to Harrison, Edward Brerwood in like fashion uses this concept to distinguish between "four sorts of Sects of Religion"—Christianity, Mahometanism (i.e., Islam), Judaism, and paganism.[75] The plural "religions," a theoretical construct that would have been incomprehensible according to medieval usage, first appears in the writings of this period, with each tradition so designated thereby related to the others as a species of a common genus.[76]

The effect of these developments is hard to deny. Though we may disagree with the contention that there is a common, universal set of truths accessible to reason apart from the Bible or the church that informs and legitimates all particular or "positive" religious beliefs, most people routinely speak of religion as a worldview or system of belief embraced by individuals. We simply

71. Ibid., 12–13; Wilfred Cantwell Smith, *The Meaning and End of Religion: A New Approach to the Religious Traditions of Mankind* (New York: Macmillan, 1962), 32–34.

72. Cavanaugh, *Theopolitical Imagination*, 33.

73. See Skinner, *Age of Reformation*, 244–46.

74. Smith, *Meaning and End of Religion*, 39–40.

75. Harrison, *"Religion" and the Religion in the English Enlightenment*, 39.

76. Cavanaugh, *Theopolitical Imagination*, 33.

assume that, for example, the notion of Christianity, mere or otherwise,[77] refers to something actual. We habitually speak of the life and faith of the church as "Christianity," and we do not see that this is an abstraction that did not exist prior to the fifteenth century.[78]

There are, of course, those who will argue that the transformation of an ecclesially formed faith into a religious worldview unencumbered by the untidiness of the material and social world properly lets "the spiritual be the spiritual, without public interference, and the public be the secular, without private prejudice."[79] It was initially thought that, for the sake of the unity of the state, there had to be one religion, just as there was one ruler, or at least there should be no public dispute over such matters, lest good order and the authority of God's appointed governors be disturbed. King Charles I of England, for example, declares in 1628,

> Being by God's ordinance . . . Defender of the Faith and Supreme Governor of the Church within these our dominions, we hold it most agreeable to this our kingly office and our own religious zeal, to conserve and maintain the Church committed to our charge in unity of true religion and the bond of peace; and not to suffer unnecessary disputations, altercations or questions to be raised which may nourish factionalism both in the Church and commonwealth.[80]

However, once "the Business of Civil Government" is clearly distinguished "from that of Religion,"[81] and Christians can be persuaded that the biblical chant "We have no king but Caesar" is no longer blameworthy, then it becomes a matter of indifference, at least in the short term, whether there be one religion or many.

What *is* essential in this concept of religion to the rise of the territorial state is the invention of the autonomous individual. According to Robert Nisbet, the state developed as a political institution through "the gradual absorption of powers and responsibilities formerly resident in other associations and by an increasing directness of relation between the sovereign authority of the State and the

---

77. I allude, of course, to C. S. Lewis's famous book *Mere Christianity* (New York: Macmillan, 1952, 1960). My point is not to denigrate Lewis's work, or to promote the modern notion that convictions have little or nothing to do with "real Christianity," but to draw attention to the sorts of assumptions that Christians typically and in all innocence make but which unwittingly perpetuate the dismemberment of the church as Christ's true body.

78. What exists are churches and everything associated with them, which of course is what the concept of "Christianity" is designed to marginalize. See Carl Braaten, *Mother Church: Ecclesiology and Ecumenism* (Minneapolis: Fortress, 1998), 5–6.

79. See Milbank, *Theology and Social Theory*, 10.

80. "The King's Declaration," in *Documents of the English Reformation*, ed. Gerald Bray (Minneapolis: Fortress, 1994), 481.

81. John Locke, *A Letter concerning Toleration*, ed. James H. Tully (Indianapolis: Hackett, 1983), 26. Religious tolerance was not absolute in Locke's opinion: "Those are not at all to be tolerated who deny the Being of a God. Promises, Covenants, and Oaths, which are the Bonds of Humane Society, can have no hold upon an Atheist" (Locke, *A Letter concerning Toleration*, 51).

individual citizen."[82] The aim of this process was to free people from the authority of other forms of association, to make their lives dependent on the state alone, unencumbered by medieval guilds or moral strictures regarding economic matters. As Cavanaugh so ably phrases it, the "realization of a single, unquestioned political centre would make equivalent and equal each individual before the law, thereby freeing the individual from the caprice of local custom and subloyalties which would divide them from their fellow-citizens."[83] Freed from such "caprice," one's allegiance to the state becomes the sole political association that necessarily binds the individual. When Christian faith is transvalued into "religion," it no longer is embedded within the communal life and thought of the church, and thus poses no intrinsic threat to the authority of the state.

Empty Time

The demise of Christendom, the emergence of the state, and the invention of religion were not the only forces working to dismember Christ's body in the post-Reformation era, leaving behind bits and pieces no longer capable of exercising discipline over the bodies of its members. The last 450 years have also seen the development of new regimes of accumulation, production, exchange, and consumption, accompanied by new modes of regulating human behavior to promote and perpetuate these regimes. These economic forces work in concert with the state, replacing ecclesiastical and civil authorities as the two "swords" that jointly govern the course of the body politic, though at times, like their predecessors, they vie for supremacy. Together they have accelerated the rupture of the social ligatures that bound Christians to God, to each other, and to their own physical bodies.

The exchange of material goods in Christendom prior to the rise of capitalism was situated within a social structure that sought to order such matters to certain ends, that is, to a substantive good to which all human transactions, in their capacity as signs, were to bear witness. Jesus's appropriation of the Jubilee provisions to order the day-to-day life of his followers and the holding of all things in common described in the Acts of the Apostles, though they did not become the standard for economic activity down through the centuries, served as types for the church's teaching regarding the accumulation and use of property. (The practice of holding property in common did not disappear but was kept alive by the many religious orders.[84]) It was widely understood that "the sharing of possessions was both a sign

82. Robert A. Nisbet, *The Quest for Community: A Study in the Ethics of Order and Freedom* (New York: Oxford University Press, 1953), 104. Included among the institutions that facilitated this transfer of political authority were the development of law courts that allowed the king to mediate disputes between noble lords, and the creation of mechanisms that enabled the crown to collect tax revenue directly from the populace (Strayer, *On the Medieval Origins of the Modern State*, 26–33, 61, 69).

83. Cavanaugh, *Theopolitical Imagination*, 74.

84. This is a legacy that Protestants in particular dismiss all too quickly, in part because we are heirs of a theological debate whose problematic terms were bequeathed to us by late medieval nominalism, and

of the Christian community's faithfulness and a form of witness to the world."[85] Getting caught up in the apocalypse of Jesus Christ invariably involved some form of the just distribution of the things needed for this life. The church could not be the church without embodying this witness in its life, and thus practices and principles were developed that retained something of the biblical life and witness with respect to use of material goods and the means of exchange (i.e., money) for that use.

For those not called to a religious life, with its renunciation of private property, it was still understood that one's rights over the use of property was not absolute. According to Catherine of Siena, God did not concentrate the temporal goods necessary for mortal life in the hands of a few but divided them "indifferently," so that "man should, perforce, have material for love of his fellow ... that one should have need of the other."[86] Three principles emerged as guidelines for the faithful in this regard. First, all property is a gift from God, and since it is impossible for that which is finite to make an adequate return to the One who is eternal and infinite, all creatures are, quite literally, eternally and infinitely indebted. Owners of private property were to hold it as a kind of patrimony to be used for the common good, especially for the poor and needy. Such an understanding, of course, conflicts with the virtually absolute right of private property that prevails in capitalist markets. Second, there was the much-maligned and poorly understood prohibition against usury. This prohibition did not forbid all charging of interest, only that which is contrary to the charity owed to one's neighbor. Third, a just wage should be paid to workers sufficient not only to support them and their families, but also to contribute to the common good.[87]

In a market-driven society, however, the formal equivalence or exchange value of a good or service prevails over a use value that can only be determined according to shared judgments promulgated by a community structured around a common good. The result is a paradoxical situation of a heterogeneity of ends (i.e., pluralism), determined solely by consumer preference, which is imposed by and secured within an increasingly homogeneous economy. The bifurcation of fact from value quickly becomes one of the most important principles of the regulatory scheme orchestrating a global marketplace (another being the credo of the "maximization of self-interest"). "Fact" is reserved for matters that belong to the public sphere as determined by "objective" (i.e., instrumental) and "rational" (self-interested) methods, that is to say, the sphere where "people eat bread and pursue debtors, hope for power and execute subversives."[88] The concept of values denotes what has

---

in part because many tend to view all mention of common property through the lens of the twentieth-century struggle between capitalism and scientific socialism.

85. Long, *Goodness of God*, 243.

86. Catherine of Siena, "A Treatise of Divine Providence," in *Late Medieval Mysticism*, ed. Ray C. Petry (Philadelphia: Westminster, 1957), 282.

87. See Long, *Goodness of God*, 243–46.

88. John Howard Yoder, *Priestly Kingdom: Social Ethics as Gospel* (Notre Dame, IN: University of Notre Dame Press, 1984), 62.

been assigned to the ephemeral sphere of private concerns, matters of choice, and personal preference and thus are irrational or at best arational. As such they come into the picture only after the facts of the matter have been determined.

Religious belief is "protected" as one species of value within this mode of regulation, to be sure, but at the cost of being effectively excluded from any kind of meaningful involvement in the concerns of everyday life. In the famous words of Thomas Jefferson, "it does me no injury for my neighbour to say that there are twenty gods, or no god."[89] Such matters are shunted to the "margins," where things are no longer intrinsically good, where their public "value" is determined solely by market exchanges governed by the principles of formal equivalence and substitutability. In our socially scripted role as consumers, we are thus free to stroll among the virtual shelves of the moral and religious shopping mall and pick out whatever marginal value "takes our fancy—Buddhism, scientology, environmentalism, feminism, gay liberation, animal rights, Jehovah's Witnesses . . ."[90]

The regulatory apparatus of liberal capitalism stipulates that a substantive understanding of what constitutes a good life must be excluded from the public sphere from the start, supposedly because teleological notions are too wedded to particular beliefs and histories to be useful in the determination of what is objective and thus universal for a multicultural society.[91] Alan Gewirth, for example, contends that if we are to regard a moral principle as rationally warranted, it must be analytic, and that any conclusions that follow from the premises of such reasoning must be necessarily entailed by those premises.[92] Thick accounts of the good such as one finds in the ancient traditions of the world are therefore deemed incapable of accommodating the vast diversity of "comprehensive doctrines"[93] that human beings have embraced at one time or another. If adherents to these doctrines cannot in good conscience restrict them to the realm of the private, neither they nor their views can be permitted within a democratic social order.

There is more at work in this exclusion of comprehensive doctrines, however, than initially meets the eye. Ruling out-of-bounds all questions about what might claim our allegiance as moral agents other than the two swords of state and market effectively opens up a space over which human beings, unencumbered by such distractions, can exert their own sovereignty against the vagaries of fortune. This

89. Thomas Jefferson, *Notes on the State of Virginia*, Query XVII, "Religion," in *The Writings of Thomas Jefferson*, ed. William Peden (Chapel Hill: University of North Carolina Press, 1954), 159.

90. Boyle, *Who Are We Now?* 80–81.

91. See Long, *Divine Economy*, 3–4.

92. Alan Gewirth, *Reason and Morality* (Chicago: University of Chicago Press, 1978), and *The Community of Rights* (Chicago: University of Chicago Press, 1996).

93. According to John Rawls, a viewpoint or set of beliefs is comprehensive if "it includes conceptions of what is of value in human life, and ideals of personal character, as well as ideals of friendship and of familial and associational relationships, and much else that is to inform our conduct, and in the limit to our life as a whole. A conception is fully comprehensive if it covers all recognized values and virtues within one rather precisely articulated system" (John Rawls, *Political Liberalism* [New York: Columbia University Press, 1993], 13; see also175).

autonomous domain of human sovereignty comes complete with its own epic metanarrative,[94] the comprehensive scope of which, as I noted previously, was pretentiously demonstrated by Francis Fukuyama's declaration that with the triumph of capitalism over Soviet-style communism, history had come to an end. A chief feature of the modern myth is that this sphere of the purely human and rational had always been accessible to rational (i.e., calculative) thought, though for much of history access to it lay dormant, hidden under a "sacred canopy" of ancient superstition, medieval metaphysics, and ecclesiastical tyranny.[95] Max Weber was perhaps the first to renarrate this leitmotif in the world of economics, stating that the medieval church imposed an irrational form of exchange upon an uneducated and gullible populace by means of superstition, ritual, and coercion. Thankfully, the Calvinists came along to move us toward a more rational form of economics.[96]

According to the modern epic, then, "irrational religion" had for centuries hidden the true nature of the world from humanity, and only in this, the age of science, have we been able to poke holes in this canopy and see what the universe is "really" like. Like Aeneas in Virgil's classic epic, humankind had to leave behind the pious sagas and obtuse speculations that science has reduced to ruins (Troy), and resist the seduction of a socialist utopia (Carthage), to find its true destiny and homeland (Rome), where an empire waits to be won. Some even argue that this desacralizing tendency could be located at the origins of Christianity, but it was suppressed by the imperial aspirations of priests, bishops, cardinals, and popes during the first fifteen centuries of the church's existence. Fortunately, the Reformation started a process that would reverse that corrupt trend, and then in the nineteenth and twentieth centuries Protestant theologians, in collaboration with the new science of sociology, finally succeeded in stripping away the irrational husk of ecclesial restrictions to reveal the purity of humankind's spiritual kernel.[97] And they did indeed free spirituality from any public interference, precisely by denying it any meaningful, that is to say, critical, posture vis-à-vis the public sphere.

94. According to noted classicist Stanley Lombardo, epic is that genre that recounts events with far-reaching historical consequences, and sums up the fullness and variety of the world in such a way that nothing further that is truly essential needs to be done or known (Stanley Lombardo, Introduction to Homer, *Iliad* [Indianapolis: Hackett, 1997], xxi).

95. Peter L. Berger, *The Sacred Canopy: Elements of a Sociological Theory of Religion* (Garden City, NY: Doubleday, 1967).

96. Max Weber, *The Protestant Ethic and the Spirit of Capitalism*, trans. Talcott Parsons (London: Unwin, 1930), 118–19. Perhaps predictably, in telling the story Weber horribly distorts the nature of both medieval Catholicism and post-Reformation Calvinism. The slight differences between Calvin and Aquinas have been grossly exaggerated by Protestant political economists, and some theologians have accepted Weber's reading and have declared Calvinism a superior rationality over against Catholicism because it is able to accommodate itself to capitalism. "But," says Long, "neither Calvin nor Aquinas was interested in such a social order, and one cannot help but think that both would be utterly scandalized by the dominance of a utilitarian ethic in such a social order rather than a social order that seeks to instill into its members the life of charity" (Long, *Goodness of God*, 248).

97. The classic example is, of course, von Harnack, *Das Wesen des Christentums*.

Just as the Israelites, through their distinctive way of life, narrated the coming to be and passing away of persons, peoples, and places as history, the ongoing performance of the modern epic, with state and market cast as the leading players on the world's stage, projects a mythical scene against which that performance is permanently set.[98] This picture is not the traditional Christian understanding, which is shaped by figural relationships that invoke a simultaneity of past and future in the present, such that the great personages of the Christian tradition are not regarded as alien, separated by a gulf of ever-advancing time, but as contemporaries, linked to the present time by divine providence.[99] The modern epic, by contrast, imagines a linear temporal sequence of cause and effect that occurs within what Walter Benjamin has labeled homogeneous, empty time,[100] which is measured by the precise, immutable units of calendar and clock. In this mythical setting the past, if rightly narrated, is the guarantor of both present and future, "hence the importance of locating distant founding fathers and founding wars (even where their antiquity must be invented)."[101]

The aim of the modern metanarrative is to fashion a synchronic sense of time so that citizen-consumers imagine themselves as contemporaries, not with the great cloud of witnesses of God's chosen people down through the centuries (Heb. 12:1; cf. 11:1–40), but with all those living simultaneously within the typically arbitrary boundaries of a particular nation-state, even though none of them will ever know more than a handful over the course of their lives. This story seeks to cultivate the picture of a stable community moving perpetually out of a heroic past, through the difficulties of the present, and into an unbounded future.[102] It is not mere coincidence, moreover, that the preoccupation with founding fathers and wars, venerated as the guarantors of continuity and return against the ever-present threat to the fragility of the established order, bears the same marks of idolatry as do the ancients' worship of their gods.

The same epic that underwrites the categorical division of facts and values tacitly posits a certain metaphysical stance stipulating that the actual is the real and the rational, in short, a realism of appearances.[103] What truly is—a commercial and consumerist oligopoly—begins with the choices of individuals.[104] This social

98. See Milbank, *Theology and Social Theory*, 383.

99. Benedict Anderson, *Imagined Communities: Reflections on the Origin and Spread of Nationalism*, rev. ed. (New York: Verso, 1991), 22–24; Cavanaugh, *Torture and Eucharist*, 222. I return to this question in chapter 4.

100. Walter Benjamin, *Illuminations*, trans. Harry Zohn (New York: Schocken, 1969), 262.

101. Cavanaugh, *Torture and Eucharist*, 223.

102. Ibid.; Anderson, *Imagined Communities*, 24–26.

103. I have more to say about this realism of appearances in the next chapter.

104. To paraphrase Immanuel Kant, though a capitalist society begins with individual choices, it does not follow that it all arises out of these choices. The institutions of the nation-state, the market and civil society do all in their power to ensure that we have no choice but to choose who and what we are as human beings (Immanuel Kant, *Critique of Pure Reason*, B1, trans. Norman Kemp Smith [New York: St. Martin's, 1965], 41).

order is therefore judged to be both natural and reasonable insofar as it comports with the rational choices of individuals qua consumers. Local and global markets, together with the states that both support and regulate them (the two swords of liberal capitalism), thus have conferred on them the appearance of being necessary, and any opposition to them should be dismissed as romantic nonsense or madness. Any association that lies outside the orbit of these sorts of transactions between abstract consumers that are contractually linked solely by the authority of the state, by definition, fails to qualify as rational and potentially represents a disruptive or obstructionist practice that must therefore be confined within strict boundaries.[105]

The identification of what currently exists with what is real and rational repeats a tragic pattern that recurs repeatedly in the history of Christian thought. Beginning with Eusebius's praise of Constantine as a type of messianic figure in the fourth century, and extending to Max Stackhouse's panegyric to the institutions of liberal capitalism,[106] what we hear are variations on a familiar theme. What previously obtained in the world is vilified as heretical, irrational, oppressive, or superstitious, while the present social arrangement is lauded as the arrival of what God had intended from the foundation of the world.

At the heart of this marketplace metaphysics is the working hypothesis of the formally equivalent (and therefore abstract) individual, whose identity no longer derives from the people, place, and time into which it was born. This peculiar notion of the unencumbered individual makes sense only in the context of the larger myth of modernity, the story of which was initially told not by economists, but by the pioneers of modern political science: Thomas Hobbes, John Locke, and Jean-Jacques Rousseau. "Man was born free," as Rousseau puts it in *The Social Contract*, "but is everywhere in bondage."[107] This stands in marked contrast to the Christian story, which states that humankind was created with a natural unity that was subsequently disrupted by the secondary intrusion of violence and death into the created order. The modern epic proclaims instead the essential individuality of the human race, with each individual set against all others in what Hobbes calls the natural state of *bellum omnis contra omnem*, the war of all against all.[108] The crucial distinction between creation and fall is thus elided, and evil with all its attendant ills is no longer understood as privation, a lack, but becomes substantial and made co-natural with the good.[109] Individuals come together on the basis of

105. Budde, *(Magic) Kingdom of God*, 81; Boyle, *Who Are We Now?* 29.

106. Eusebius of Caesarea, *In Praise of Constantine* (NPNF² 1); Stackhouse, "Public Theology and Political Theology in a Globalizing Era," 179.

107. Jean-Jacques Rousseau, *The Social Contract*, I.1, trans. Willmoore Kendall (South Bend, IN: Gateway, 1954).

108. Thomas Hobbes, *Leviathan*, I. 13, ed. Edwin Curley (Indianapolis: Hackett, 1994).

109. Milbank contends that this concept of positive evil, which he associates with Kant's moral philosophy, underwrites the radical evil that was manifested in such horrors as the Sho'ah. See John Milbank, *Being Reconciled: Ontology and Pardon* (New York: Routledge, 2003), 1–25.

a social contract, not because they are naturally social beings bound together by a common good, but to protect person and property. Near-absolute sovereignty over private property is thus woven into the fabric of reality.[110]

Hobbes, Locke, and Rousseau drew heavily on theological categories that had developed in the latter Middle Ages in their depiction of the human being as essentially individual. As I have noted, late medieval theology set aside trinitarian construals of divine will and understanding, and replaced them with a monarchic conception of God as "a radical divine simplicity without real or formal differentiation, in which . . . a proposing 'will' is taken to stand for the substantial identity of will, essence and understanding." In addition, the patristic concept of participation in the divine life and unity as the normative understanding of the relationship between God and human beings was set aside in the late Middle Ages in favor of the language of legal covenants, thereby instituting a conception of human interaction as essentially voluntarist and "contractual."[111]

The fundamental "fact" of this secular metaphysics is a novel conception of human freedom. The construction and regulation of this power, however, is not predicated on the traditional understanding of the will as rational appetite, ordered by means of the intellect by the objects of its desire.[112] It is instead, in the words of Iris Murdoch, the outward movement of the lonely will.[113] This conception of will involves the autonomous and self-determined self, its choices for either good or evil unconstrained and unmoved by anything outside the self, and thus it is essentially unrelated to the contingencies of the material world or to a prior understanding of the good. As Immanuel Kant puts it, "every evil action must be so considered, whenever we seek its rational origin, as if the human being had fallen into it directly from the state of innocence. For whatever his previous behavior may have been, whatever the natural causes influencing him, whether they are inside or outside them, his action is yet free and not determined through any of these causes; hence the action can and must always be judged as an *original* exercise of his power of choice."[114] Choice as a formal power of movement thus becomes the paradigm of freedom, not its most obvious result, as it was previously understood.[115]

Zygmunt Bauman contends that this definition of freedom leads to a quandary for the body politic between the intrinsic desirability of free decision making and

110. See Cavanaugh, "The City," 187.

111. Milbank, *Theology and Social Theory*, 14–15; cf. Heiko Augustinus Oberman, *The Harvest of Medieval Theology: Gabriel Biel and Late Medieval Nominalism* (Cambridge: Harvard University Press, 1963), 92, 99.

112. See, for example, Thomas Aquinas, *Summa Theologica*, Ia. IIae. 8.1.

113. Iris Murdoch, "The Idea of Perfection," in *The Sovereignty of Good* (New York: Routledge, 2001), 35.

114. Immanuel Kant, *Religion within the Boundaries of Mere Reason*, 6:41, in *Religion within the Boundaries of Mere Reason and Other Writings*, trans. Allen Wood and George Di Giovanni (New York: Cambridge University Press, 1998), 62–63 (emphasis original).

115. Burrell, *Freedom and Creation in Three Traditions*, 92.

the need to limit freedom of those who are presumed to use it to do evil: "You can trust the wise (the code name of the mighty) to do good autonomously; but you cannot trust all people to be wise." Indeed, it is the freedom to choose that "necessitates an external force *coercing* the person to do good 'for his own salvation,' 'for her own welfare,' or 'in her own interest.'" The only practical way to ensure that individual choice will have morally positive consequences is to subject that freedom to "heteronomously set standards; to cede to socially approved agencies the right to decide what is good and submit to their verdicts."[116]

The function of religion and of religious organizations within the composite modern regime of coercion and commerce is contingency management, with sacralizing the present social order as its primary responsibility.[117] This strategy at one time had a Christian veneer to it. The civic responsibility of church was to serve as the moral conscience of the community and to ameliorate human suffering inflicted on those who slipped between the cracks.[118] In such ways Christian communities help state and market accumulate much-needed "social capital," that is, a stock of social relations and shared values without which a liberal capitalist order could not function for long, and which underwrite the unconstrained exercise of self-interest.[119]

As we move into the twenty-first century, corporations and governments continue to recognize the need to manage the whims of fortune, which in recent years has played havoc with the self-identity of men and women all around the globe. The demands of state, global market, and workplace have dissolved most if not all of the social relations that traditionally have defined who we are and what we should do. The transvaluation of human beings into individuals has reached the stage where people are little more than interchangeable economic units, integers of production and consumption. In the words of Václav Havel, "individuals confirm the system, fulfil the system, make the system, *are* the system."[120] A workforce kept at optimum flexibility, however, exacts a high price in human terms. Corporate firms are therefore interested in the potential of the church and other established religious institutions to ameliorate these costs, provided that their rituals and beliefs are supportive of the firm's goals, and work to deepen the loyalty and productivity of the employees.[121]

The rulers and authorities of liberal capitalism thus decree that when Christians enter the "public square," they must set aside all things connected to the

---

116. Zygmunt Bauman, *Postmodern Ethics* (Cambridge, MA: Blackwell, 1993), 28–30.

117. See Niklas Luhmann, *Religious Dogmatics and the Evolution of Societies*, trans. Peter Beyer (New York: Mellen, 1984); cf. Clifford Geertz, "Religion as a Cultural System," in *The Interpretation of Cultures* (New York: Basic Books, 1973), 87–125.

118. Anthony B. Robinson, "The Making of a Post-Liberal," in Copenhaver, Robinson, and Willimon, *Good News in Exile*, 16.

119. Michael Budde and Robert Brimlow, *Christianity Incorporated: How Big Business Is Buying the Church* (Grand Rapids: Brazos, 2002), 19.

120. Václav Havel, "The Power of the Powerless," in *Living in Truth*, ed. Jan Vladislav (London: Faber & Faber, 1987), 45.

121. I return to this question in chapter 7.

particularity of the church, most especially its comprehensive doctrines. This in effect means, among other things, that both Christology and ecclesiology must be subsumed under something like a doctrine of creation in which the proper order of things can be known apart from both Christ and the church. The state, rather than the people of God gathered by the Spirit through baptism and the Lord's Supper, then becomes the "city set on a hill," and the new creation that scripture associates with the ministry of Jesus and his followers is instead vested in other institutions, including corporations, which mediate salvation in the form of increased choice. Congregations that want to be players in this order of things must do so as a vendor of "spirituality," the purpose of which is to render life more bearable for those who have become little more than faceless functionaries in a vast system of production and consumption.[122]

The compliment typically paid to this new order of human existence in our time and place is that it is pluralistic and multicultural, but for many this is hollow praise indeed. A silicon web has supplanted Weber's iron cage, reducing those ensnared within it to the status of mere economic units, integers of aimless production and conspicuous consumption.[123] Pluralism is but a facade for the transvaluation of all practices, institutions, dispositions, and relationships into commodities that can be exchanged in the global market.[124] A pluralist regime stipulates that choice per se is the highest good, and therefore it is committed to excluding any way of life that is "postulated upon nonconsumerist conceptions of human fulfillment, and so [favoring] a particular vision of the human good."[125] Virtually everything else is optional with respect to the undifferentiated individuality of the market, where every thing and every body is packaged as a product to be consumed (including marriage, having children, and making friends), and the exchange value of these products is determined by their "market share," that is, their ability to satisfy consumers. In spite of its own best intentions, pluralism cannot help but to regard "particularity as icing on a basically homogeneous cake."[126] Substantive understandings of the human good such as that traditionally embodied in the life and language of the church are summarily dismissed as restrictive practices.[127]

Ecclesiastical authorities and theologians who accede to these demands in order to establish a religious concordat with capitalism in the form of a "public theology" are required to excise those aspects of Christian thought that distinguish it as an identifiable way of life—Christ as the antitype of true humanity, the church as the

122. See Budde and Brimlow, *Christianity Incorporated*, esp. chap. 2, "Putting Jesus to Work: When Corporations Get Religion," 27–54.

123. Wendell Berry, "Economy and Pleasure," in *What Are People For?* (New York: North Point, 1990), 130.

124. Boyle, *Who Are We Now?* 79.

125. Ronald Beiner, *What's the Matter with Liberalism?* (Berkeley: University of California Press, 1992), 8.

126. Stanley Fish, "Boutique Multiculturalism, or Why Liberals Are Incapable of Thinking about Hate Speech," *Critical Inquiry* 23 (Winter 1997): 382.

127. Boyle, *Who Are We Now?* 26.

Christian's true *politeia*, and an eschatologically oriented understanding of history. Such an accord harks back "to the style of the *ancien régime* ... to a society in which the churches regarded themselves as the spiritual form of a material community."[128] The difference is that these churches must now "package" their spiritual "values" in accordance with the dictates of the market, which means that they must effectively vacate the specifically Christian content of their life and language.

Under the terms of this agreement, whatever it means to be a Christian can no longer be tied to practices that constitute the church as a social body visibly, publicly manifesting the intrusion of God's apocalyptic regime into the world, but must be limited to matters of the soul, leaving the body to the authority of the powers and economic principalities of this age. Christian identity and church authority are thus disembodied, relegated to a separate sphere of private life, transvalued into "religion," that is, habits and practices that are useful both for depicting the mysterious and invisible whole that is the body politic of the modern state and global market, and also for conserving social energies in a numinous ether called "values," which at the appropriate time can be put to a "real" social use in the state's behalf.[129]

Where Do We Go from Here?

As I noted in chapter 2, the destruction of Jerusalem and the demise of the Davidic monarchy, which resulted in the exile of many Jews to strange lands where they were compelled to serve other gods, while others bore the brunt of occupation in the Promised Land, did not bring Israel's life with God to an end. God instead folded these events back into the saving story of the chosen people, where they serve as types (*tupoi*) to instruct those who seek to love and serve God. When we ask, then, whether a similar sort of re-membering of the body of Christ can take a stand in our time and place, it is encouraging to discover that not every knee has bowed to the rulers and authorities of this world.

On a Saturday evening in late summer of 1942, an official convoy of police cars, motorcycles, and buses pulled into Le Chambon, a small village of about three thousand people. The police chief for that district, a high official with the Vichy government that had been set up by the Nazis following France's defeat at the hands of the dreaded German *Blitzkrieg* in 1940, summoned the pastor of the local Protestant church to the town hall. When André Trocmé arrived, he was told that the authorities knew that under his leadership the town was engaged in suspect activities and, more specifically, that they were hiding a number of Jews. Trocmé was ordered to hand over a list of these persons and where they were hiding, so

---

128. John H. S. Kent, *The End of the Line? The Development of Christian Theology over the Last Two Centuries* (Philadelphia: Fortress Press, 1982), viii.

129. See Milbank, *Theology and Social Theory*, 109. One thinks here of Robert Putnam's famous article "Bowling Alone: America's Declining Social Capital," *Journal of Democracy* (January 1995): 65–78.

that they could be rounded up and taken to the prefecture for "control," which as we now know was a chilling euphemism for deportation to the extermination camps in the east.

Trocmé refused to cooperate, telling the official (truthfully, as it so happened) that he had no such list. But even if it existed, he continued, these people had sought protection from the church in this region. This meant that he was their pastor, their shepherd, and it was not the role of a shepherd to betray the sheep committed to his keeping. The police chief warned Trocmé that failure to obey would result in his arrest and deportation, and after laying down an ultimatum that set a time limit for voluntary compliance, he let him go. Trocmé immediately went to his office and met with a group of Boy Scouts and Bible class leaders, where they set into motion a plan that had been worked out in the weeks leading up to this fateful day. These *responsables*, as they were called, went to outlying farms where the Jews were staying and warned them to flee into the woods under the cover of darkness. "Under a starlit night," writes one author, "it was as if ghosts were purposefully making their respective ways through the square and the streets while the police waited for their ultimatum to expire, sleeping upon straw."[130]

The next morning Trocmé ascended the high pulpit in the big gray church of Le Chambon and preached to the townspeople gathered there for worship. According to some accounts, he cited a passage in the law code in the book of Deuteronomy that established cities of refuge for safeguarding the innocent in ancient Israel. And then he declared that their village must in like fashion become a city of refuge for all those sought by the Vichy government, again quoting Deuteronomy, "lest innocent blood be shed" (Deut. 19:10). The Chambonnais responded to their pastor's charge, and following the admonition in the Sermon on the Mount that they were to be a city set on a hill as their basic plan of action, they continued to hide Jews (coming eventually from all parts of Europe) and smuggled them to Switzerland. Though the police remained in Le Chambon for three weeks, their net snared few victims. Of the dozens of Jews whom the Chambonnais had secreted in the area at the time, only two were arrested, and one of these was later released because it was determined that he was only "half Jewish," which at the time was sufficient to avoid deportation.

The events that occurred in Le Chambon were not the actions of isolated individuals who demonstrated an uncommon courage for brief moments of time. The entire village was involved to one degree or another in a complex rescue effort that took place over the span of several years. Their involvement, moreover, did not come cheaply. Some in the village were imprisoned in concentration camps, including members of Trocmé's own family, and a few were executed. And though the leadership of *pasteur* Trocmé played a crucial role, many other brave and resourceful women and men searched for, but never found, the kind

---

130. Philip P. Hallie, *Lest Innocent Blood Be Shed: The Story of the Village of Le Chambon and How Goodness Happened There* (New York: Harper & Row, 1979; HarperPerennial, 1994), 108–9.

of communal response that was made by the Christians in Le Chambon. By the end of the war, without firing a shot, the residents of this one village, led by the members of the little Protestant church and an even smaller Plymouth Brethren congregation, saved somewhere between 2,500 and 5,000 Jewish lives, most of them children. After the war the mother of three of those children exclaimed, "The Holocaust was storm, lightning, thunder, wind, rain, yes. And Le Chambon was the rainbow."[131]

The resistance of the Chambonnais did not spring out of a social and historical vacuum but grew out of a distinctive pattern of life together, consisting of an alternative set of habits and relations that had been cultivated by the common life and language of a community over an extended period of time. Trocmé's admonition that their village should transform itself into a city of refuge so that innocent blood would not be shed reveals a sense of who they were and a source of power that, when the crisis came (and who knows beforehand when that time will come?), their life together generated possibilities of life and action that disrupted the designs of a seemingly invincible foe. And they did so during a time when the residents of other villages claimed that they were powerless to do anything about their situation.

Perhaps the important lesson the we should learn from the grotesque drama that was the Holocaust is that both bystanders and rescuers are made, not born, and that they are made for the most part years and even centuries before atrocities begin. The faithfulness and courage displayed in Le Chambon during the Second World War did not generate spontaneously out of thin air. This was demonstrated by the fate of the Confessing Church, a small group of Protestants in Germany who opposed Hitler's policies during the 1930s, particularly those that tried to enlist the churches in support of National Socialism. One of the leaders of this group was Dietrich Bonhoeffer. While still a young man of twenty-nine, Bonhoeffer was selected to head up the Preachers' Seminary, which the Confessing Church established in Finkenwalde, northeast of Berlin, to circumvent the Nazi-controlled universities. Bonhoeffer was as much pastor as he was professor and administrator to the small band of students that gathered around him in this makeshift seminary. The Gestapo closed the school after two years, and attempts to continue the work in underground collective pastorates quickly withered.

The certainty and clarity of judgment and manner that led to the selection of Bonhoeffer to this position cannot, as Eberhard Bethge notes, "be acquired in a single generation. He grew up in a family that believed that the essence of learning lay not in a formal education but in the deeply rooted obligation to be

131. Ibid., xvii. For further information about Trocmé and the work of the churches of Le Chambon on behalf of Jews during World War II, see Armin F. C. Boyens, "The Ecumenical Community and the Holocaust," *Annals of the American Academy of Political and Social Science* 450 (July 1980): 143–47; H. R. Kedward, *Resistance in Vichy France: A Study of Ideas and Motivation in the Southern Zone, 1940–1942* (New York: Oxford University Press, 1978), 180–84; Carol Rittner and Sondra Myers, eds., *The Courage to Care: Rescuers of Jews during the Holocaust* (New York: New York University Press, 1986), 99–119.

guardians of a great historical heritage and intellectual tradition."[132] Unfortunately, what Bonhoeffer's family had bequeathed to him, the church had failed to do for most Christians in Germany. And so with the outbreak of the war, the Confessing Church's impromptu association collapsed due to government pressure and nationalist loyalties. Bonhoeffer quickly found himself isolated, without communal institutions and practices that would have made a distinctively Christian form of action possible. He thus decided to join the conspiracy to assassinate Hitler. His part in the unsuccessful plot was eventually discovered, and he was executed just a few weeks before Germany surrendered to the Allied powers.

Bonhoeffer's death was the culmination of the tragic character of his life, which in turn was but an element in the greater tragedy of the church in Germany leading up to the time of National Socialism. Most Christians in Germany did not possess the habits of both body and mind that were adequate to the crucial need of church and non-church people alike, to say nothing of what the Jews and the other peoples of the world needed. Due in large part to this deficit, there were few structures, practices, and skills of political life in Germany capable of resisting Nazi totalitarianism as Christians. The tragedy of Bonhoeffer's story is more poignant, because he recognized the lack of needed virtues and sought to develop the practices that could have made such resistance possible. "But it is a shared tragedy," James McClendon concludes, "for he could not in any case have met the need alone."[133]

In Le Chambon, by contrast, we discover a leader who, for all his personal affinities with Bonhoeffer,[134] was able to act in ways that were not available to Bonhoeffer. When Trocmé told his congregation that they must create a city of refuge for Jews and all others so that innocent blood would not be shed, his summons did not fall upon deaf ears. These Christians had been formed over the centuries to follow the apocalypse of God in Jesus Christ in their own lives, and thus to heed "what the Spirit is saying to the churches" (Rev. 2:7). A theological tradition forged by generations of French Protestants who suffered through their own persecutions had fashioned a community that did not confuse being members of the body of Christ with being citizens of France, enabling a handful of unarmed people to frustrate the will of a diabolical enemy that others saw as invincible.

As historian G. A. Rothrock points out that, "the real 'crime' for which [French Protestants] were so often and finally so severely persecuted was neither their religious practice nor their occasionally treasonable political activity. It was, rather, their resistance to a national consciousness, emerging not just in France but across

132. Eberhard Bethge, *Dietrich Bonhoeffer: A Biography*, ed. Victoria J. Barnett (Minneapolis: Fortress, 2000), 13.

133. McClendon, *Ethics*, 207.

134. According to one report, "Trocmé toyed with the idea of using his German language facility in order to assassinate [Hitler] before he plunged the world into catastrophe. But Trocmé's fear of 'separating himself from Jesus who rejected armed violence to counteract the crime being prepared against Him' held him back" (Marlin E. Miller, Introduction to *Jesus and the Nonviolent Revolution*, by André Trocmé, 5).

much of western Europe, that demanded conformity and submission."[135] More precisely, it was only due to their "religious" practice (which was obviously not limited to private, "spiritual" matters) that the Chambonnais resisted the idolatry of national consciousness, quarried from deposits of tradition in the church. Laboring in quiet anonymity down through the centuries, a handful of saints developed a nonviolent but nevertheless disruptive form of reasoning and acting that served their descendents in Le Chambon well. It allowed them to stand fast against the demands of an idolatrous regime precisely at the point where Christians in Germany fell prey to false ideas, and especially to flawed interpretations of the Bible.

An important part of what differentiated the Chambonnais from their neighbors had to do with their ability to attend truthfully to the world. We can only choose to act within the world that we can *see*, writes Murdoch, in the sense of "see" that is the product of a well-trained and provisioned imagination: "One is often compelled almost automatically by what one *can* see. If we ignore the prior work of attention and notice only the emptiness of the moment of choice we are likely to identify freedom with the outward movement since there is nothing else to identify it with." We must therefore consider this work of attention, how it goes on continuously, building up with us a framework for interpreting the reality of the world such that at crucial moments of choice "most of the business of choosing is already over."[136] For the members of Christ's body, this work of imaginatively following the rhythms and progressions of a world that stands at the point of intersection between two ages requires forms of reasoning cultivated by the church's constitutive practices, beginning with Bible reading.

135. G. A. Rothrock, *The Huguenots: A Biography of a Minority* (Chicago: Nelson-Hall, 1979), 189–90. Actually, it was only due to their "religious" practice that French Protestants resisted the idolatry of national consciousness. For a concise history of the Reformed church in France, see John T. McNeill, *The History and Character of Calvinism* (New York: Oxford University Press, 1954), 237–54.

136. Murdoch, "Idea of Perfection," 35–36.

PART
TWO

4

Lovers, Madmen, and Pilgrim Poets

Imagination, Memory, and Scriptural Reasoning

If the imagination were obedient, the appetites would give us very little trouble.

C. S. Lewis, *Letters to Malcolm*

> Lovers and madmen have such seething brains,
> Such shaping fantasies, that apprehend
> More than cool reason ever comprehends.
> The lunatic, the lover, and the poet
> Are of imagination all compact:
> One sees more devils than vast hell can hold;
> That is, the madman; the lover, all as frantic,
> Sees Helen's beauty in a brow of Egypt.
> The poet's eye, in a fine frenzy rolling,
> Doth glance from heaven to earth, from earth to heaven;
> And as imagination bodies forth
> The forms of things unknown, the poet's pen
> Turns them to shapes and gives to airy nothing
> A local habitation and a name.
> Such tricks hath strong imagination
> That if it would but apprehend some joy,
> It comprehends some bringer of that joy.
> Or in the night, imagining some fear,
> How easy is a bush supposed a bear![1]

These comments by Theseus in William Shakespeare's *A Midsummer's Night Dream* are offered in response to an incredible story told by a group of young

---

1. William Shakespeare, *A Midsummer Night's Dream*, Act V, sc. 1, 4–22.

lovers. They spoke of a fairy king and queen and a magical flower whose juice, when applied to the closed eyelids of one who is asleep, will make that person fall madly in love with the first living creature he or she sees upon waking. Theseus, who according to some exemplifies the Renaissance conception of a "reasonable man,"[2] dismisses such lovers' tales as being of a piece with the rantings of the insane. He then for good measure throws poets into the mix, linking together their imaginative renderings of the world with the overwrought affections of the suitor and the delusional ramblings of the madman. The claim is that poetic imagination can give rise only to fantasy and pretense, having virtually nothing to do with the sane, sensible, "real" world. Everything else is but "airy nothing."

In a fascinating essay on the use of grotesque ideas and images in Southern fiction, Flannery O'Connor labels such views a dreary "realism of fact," or as I shall refer to it, a realism of appearances. Under the influence of the social sciences, this brand of realism has set up for the novel a kind of literary orthodoxy that associates the only legitimate material for long fiction with the movement of social forces, with the typical, with fidelity to the way things look and happen in what passes for normal life. Readers and critics alike look to "literature as a mirror and guide for society," and seek novelists who will serve as the handmaids of their time. After all, the reader wants to be lifted up, to be reassured that what has fallen is at least offered the chance to be restored. He wants a work that will either torment his senses or raise his spirits, transporting him instantly "either to a mock damnation or a mock innocence."[3] The reader is not wrong to look for this motion, writes O'Connor, "but what he has forgotten is the cost of it. His sense of evil is diluted or lacking altogether and so he has forgotten the price of restoration."[4]

Shakespeare does not, however, allow this dismissal of poetic imagination to go unchallenged. Hippolyta, Theseus's betrothed, comes to the defense of the lovers

2. D'Orsay Pearson contests this characterization of Theseus, calling it a "critical myth" (D'Orsay Pearson, "Unkinde Theseus: A Study in Renaissance Mythography," *English Literary Renaissance* 4 [1974]: 276, cited by Laurie J. Shannon, "Emilia's Argument: Friendship and 'Human Title' in *The Two Noble Kinsmen*," *English Literary History* 64 [1997]: 680).

3. O'Connor here calls to mind Augustine's enchantment with theatrical productions during his student days in Carthage: "In the capacity of spectator one welcomes sad feelings; in fact, the sadness itself is the pleasure. What incredible stupidity! The more a person is buffeted by such passions in his own life, the more he is moved by watching similar scenes on stage, although his state of mind is usually called misery [*miseria*] when is undergoing them himself and mercy [*misericordia*] when he shows compassion for others so afflicted. But how real is the mercy evoked by fictional dramas? The listener is not moved to offer help, but merely invited to feel sorrow; and the more intensely he feels it the more highly he rates the actor in the play" (Augustine, *Confessions*, III.2.2).

4. O'Connor, "Some Aspects of the Grotesque in Southern Fiction," 814, 818–20; cf. Flannery O'Connor, "The Grotesque in Southern Fiction," in *Mystery and Manners: Occasional Prose*, ed. Sally and Robert Fitzgerald (New York: Farrar, Straus & Giroux, 1969), 40–41. For further reflection on this kind of realism, see Phillip Blond, "Introduction: Theology before Philosophy" and "Emmanuel Levinas: God and Phenomenology," in *Post-Secular Philosophy: Between Philosophy and Theology*, ed. Phillip Blond (New York: Routledge, 1998), 1–66, 195–228, and "The Primacy of Theology and the Question of Perception," in *Religion, Modernity and Postmodernity*, ed. Paul Heelas (Malden, MA: Blackwell, 1998), 285–313.

and, by extension, of all those whose understanding of the world is not exhausted by a realism of appearances:

> But all the story of the night told over,
> And all their minds transfigured so together,
> More witnesseth than fancy's images,
> And grows to something of great constancy;
> But, howsoever, strange and admirable.[5]

According to Hippolyta, the story told by the young lovers, though quite strange and peculiar, recounts matters that, though beyond the ken of the limited conception of reason espoused by Theseus, were nonetheless quite real and should be taken to heart. Despite the fact that she does not explicitly defend poets, by implication it would seem that she ascribes to their art a similar ability to discern patterns and possibilities that escape the notice of those whose understanding is confined to what is near at hand.

Hippolyta's views are consistent with what O'Connor calls a realism of distances. A realist of distances believes that life is and will forever remain essentially mysterious, that women and men exist in a created order and respond freely to its laws. What he sees close at hand is of interest insofar as it allows him to traverse the distance to an experience of mystery itself. The realist of distances is interested in what we do not understand rather than in what we do, in possibility rather than in probability. He is interested in characters "who are forced out to meet evil and grace and who act on a trust beyond themselves—whether they know very clearly what it is they act upon or not." For those whose understanding of the world is not impoverished by a realism of appearances, every thing is also a sign, thus combining in itself two points, one in the concrete and the other in "a point not visible to the naked eye, but believed in by him firmly, just as real to him, really, as the one that everybody sees."[6]

The stakes in this debate could not be higher. If imagination delivers up nothing more than pretense, fancy's images, airy nothings, then Christians are of all people truly mad. What could be more delusional than serving a king who is not a discernible part of the world over which he claims to rule, or calling ourselves citizens of a city that does not occupy a specific and specifiable place? To contend that the people, places, and things that make up the world of time and space are vestiges of God, but that to make sense of these signs a certain sort of imagination steeped in the generative memory of scripture is required, is surely sheer insanity.

On the other hand, if a well-trained and adequately provisioned imagination is needed to attend truthfully to the inscrutable mystery from which all things on earth and under heaven originate and to which they will return, then the ability to give "a local habitation and a name" to this mystery is vital to the well-being of

---

5. Shakespeare, *A Midsummer Night's Dream*, Act V, sc. 1, 23–27.
6. O'Connor, "Some Aspects of the Grotesque in Southern Fiction," 816.

creation as a whole. Imagination, in the ways it allows us to name the concrete and the particular, forms the point of exchange between the senses and the intellect,[7] setting both into motion. It governs the ways we follow what is happening around us with our eyes and ears, an activity that tacitly assumes or projects a permanent setting for these events. As this occurs interpretive doubts about the nature of reality in general naturally arise, which the intellect must address with the conceptual resources it has at hand.[8] Without imagination women and men would be unable to interact rationally with the world, in both the speculative sense of the term (contemplating what truly is, and which is therefore genuinely good and beautiful as well) and the practical (deliberating over which habits and activities contribute to human flourishing).

The wellspring of the Christian imagination is the Bible, and thus the practice of reading scripture to cultivate forms of reasoning that enable the members of Christ's body to live faithfully and truthfully before God is one of the constitutive activities of the church. There is no clear consensus, however, concerning how Christians ought to engage in this practice of scriptural reasoning, which at bottom is the ability to go on and go further in the use of the biblical witness. The majority would no doubt agree that the scriptures should stand at the center of the community's life and language. But if we ask what precisely is entailed in that statement, any prior agreement would quickly fall apart.

Before we can proceed, then, I need to examine the kinds of activity that have been put forward as the primary form of interpreting scripture.[9] I shall then relate these matters to the work of imagination and its basis in memory. Finally, I shall propose that the Bible is best read as a kind of travel itinerary for Christians to follow as we go on and go further through history toward the divine commonwealth. The generative memory of scripture recounts the right and wrong steps, detours and false ways taken by Israel and the early church in response to the presence and activity of God in their midst. To move into the future we do not speculate about things to come but look back to what has already happened and learn how to retrace the steps taken in our time and place.[10]

Illustrative Readings of Scripture

What is it that Christians seek to accomplish when reading the Bible? Looking at a road map while driving cross-country is a very different sort of interpretive

7. See John Milbank and Catherine Pickstock, *Truth in Aquinas* (New York: Routledge, 2001), 15.

8. See Brian Wicker, *The Story-Shaped World: Fiction and Metaphysics: Some Variations on a Theme* (Notre Dame, IN: University of Notre Dame Press, 1975), 27; and Milbank, *Theology and Social Theory*, 383.

9. Lash, *Theology on the Way to Emmaus*, 37–38.

10. Lohfink, *Does God Need the Church?* 105.

activity from taking part in a poetry reading. Consulting a manual to learn
how to use a new computer is different from what a judge does with a law
book when deciding how to rule on a particular motion. The primary form of
interpreting a dramatic script or musical score is some kind of performance.
Is the practice of reading the Bible similar to any of these activities, or must
we look elsewhere?

"The Bible is to the theologian," writes Charles Hodge, "what nature is to the
man of science. It is his store-house of facts; and his method of ascertaining what
the Bible teaches, is the same as that which the natural philosopher adopts to ascertain what nature teaches." The duty of the Christian theologian is therefore "to
ascertain, collect, and combine all the facts which God has revealed in the Bible,"
using "the same rules in the collection of facts, as govern the man of science."[11]
Consistent with the thinking of his time, Hodge assumes that the world consists
of a set of "facts," discrete bits of stuff that we then match up with "concepts" or
"meanings," wraithlike entities that ostensibly inhabit both minds and words. From
this perspective, meaning

> is conceived (at least implicitly) as a sort of property with which the text has been
> endued. Further, such meaning can be uncovered through the application of some
> set of interpretive procedures. On this view, the biblical text is seen as a relatively
> stable element in which an author inserts, hides, or dissolves (choose your meta-
> phor) meaning. The task of the interpreter . . . is to dig out, uncover, or distill the
> meaning of the text.[12]

The principal aim of reading scripture, according to Hodge, is to identify, extract,
and codify the facts it contains into a systematic "worldview."

Hodge describes the work of biblical interpretation in terms provided by
what was the canonical expression of intellectual culture in his day, the ninth
edition of the *Encyclopaedia Britannica*. According to Alasdair MacIntyre, the
Encyclopaedia represented a particular moment in the history of nineteenth-
century thought when it appeared that a comprehensive scientific synthesis
was at hand. Within this synthesis the various sciences were distinguished,
not by their methodologies, but by their subject matter alone. The constitutive
elements of every science, according to Robert Adamson's article on "Logic"
in the *Encyclopaedia*, are first, the data or facts; second, the unifying synthetic
conceptions supplied by methodological reflection on the storehouse of facts;
third, the methods so employed that allow the inquirer to move from the data
to the unifying conceptions in theoretical discovery and then back again in the
work of explaining and testing the theories; and finally, continuous progress

---

11. Charles Hodge, *Systematic Theology*, 3 vols. (New York: Scribner's, 1891; Grand Rapids: Eerdmans,
1952), 1:10–11. See also Benjamin B. Warfield, *The Inspiration and Authority of the Bible*, ed. Samuel G.
Craig (Phillipsburg, NJ: Presbyterian and Reformed Publishing Co., 1948).

12. Fowl, *Engaging Scripture*, 33–34.

in supplying ever more adequate unifying conceptions that specify ever more fundamental facts. Indeed, writes MacIntyre, progress is among science's most important unifying concepts.[13]

The chief alternative in the nineteenth century to the approach advocated by Hodge was the so-called liberal or experientialist view, which is commonly linked to the theology of Friedrich Schleiermacher. The experiential mode of reading the Bible is often cast as the polar opposite to Hodge's method of interpreting scripture, but in actuality they share much in common. The experientialist method locates the data that are compiled by theologians into a scientific compendium of factual propositions and moral precepts in something called "religious experience."[14] Schleiermacher contends that theological propositions are properly grounded in a universal feeling or type of awareness that he describes variously as "intuition of the infinite," "sensibility and taste for the infinite," "immediate consciousness of the deity," and most famously, as "the feeling of absolute dependence" and "God consciousness."[15] According to this picture, then, the task of biblical interpretation is to set aside everything that had accumulated around this text during the intervening years "and leave us alone in company with the author,"[16] so that he might, as Schleiermacher puts it, "lead [us] into the region of religion where he is at home and to implant his holy feelings in [us]; he expresses the universe, and the community follows his inspired speech in holy silence."[17]

For Schleiermacher and his theological heirs, the biblical texts are the repository not for historical and metaphysical facts, but for the images and ideas that give symbolic expression to the primal, pre-thematic experience of religion. It is this experience that constitutes the pertinent "datum" of biblical interpretation. Harry Emerson Fosdick, writing in the early part of the twentieth century, describes the Bible as the literary record of the universal religious experience as it manifests itself in the lives of a particular people, and which "when properly arranged on the basis of satisfactory [historical-critical] evidence is a trustworthy record of human experience of God."[18] David Tracy has similarly classified the Bible, describing it as a classic, which is any text in which "that event of understanding proper to finite

13. Alasdair MacIntyre, *Three Rival Versions of Moral Enquiry: Encyclopaedia, Genealogy, and Tradition* (Notre Dame, IN: University of Notre Dame Press, 1990), 20–21.

14. We shall trace the origins of this assumption in chapter 6.

15. See Friedrich Schleiermacher, *On Religion: Speeches to Its Cultured Despisers*, trans. Richard Crouter (New York: Cambridge University Press, 1996), and *The Christian Faith*, ed. H. R. Mackintosh and J. S. Stewart (Philadelphia: Fortress, 1928).

16. Benjamin Jowett, "On the Interpretation of Scripture," in *Essays and Reviews*, 7th ed. (London: Longman, Green, Longman and Roberts, 1861), 384. The complete text is available at www.bible-researcher .com/jowett.html.

17. Schleiermacher, *On Religion*, 75.

18. Harry Emerson Fosdick, *The Modern Use of the Bible* (New York: Macmillan, 1925), 47, cited by Nancey Murphy, *Beyond Liberalism and Fundamentalism: How Modern and Postmodern Philosophy Set the Theological Agenda* (Valley Forge, PA: Trinity Press International, 1996), 24.

human beings" (which includes at bottom a religious dimension) finds adequate expression.[19]

Though these two approaches to the Bible are typically thought of as radically different, they actually share a number of traits. First, the biblical images and narratives stand in an illustrative relation to whatever counts as constituting the principal meaning of the text. This is explicitly the case with the experiential model, but it is also true of those who see the Bible as a storehouse of facts. The interpretive task is to dig out, uncover, or distill these truths about self, world, and God from the scriptural images and narratives with which they have been clad. The unwitting tendency of an illustrative approach, writes Michael Root, is to render the scriptures "only pedagogically necessary and ultimately dispensable."[20] Henri de Lubac rightly criticizes this conception of the scriptures, arguing that the "Christian mystery, because of the magnificent providential Economy which embraces both Testaments and links them together, has not been handed down to us as a collection of timeless definitions, unrelated to any historical situation and demanding only to be clothed, according to our fancy, with biblical images as with just so many illustrations."[21] The people, events, practices, and institutions that produced the Bible are in the end incidental to its meaning.

The factual and the experiential modes of interpreting scripture are also perennially tempted to bypass the crucial question of how the church in each generation learns its distinctive way of speaking and thinking. Hodge, for his part, opts for a conception of revelation that consists of the communication of otherworldly facts in relatively unambiguous propositions, thus sidestepping the difficult process of historical reflection and appropriation of scripture and tradition. For those who embrace an experiential approach, the meaning of the Bible has relatively little to do with discrete historical facts, but everything to do with the state of being in relation to God in the immediacy of individual self-consciousness. Benjamin Jowett was supremely confident that when provided with the proper linguistic and historical tools, the interpreter of the biblical text would be able to distill the timeless and universal meaning of these texts from "the accidents of time and place in which it is involved."[22] Both approaches are impatient with the church's biblical, dogmatic, moral, and liturgical tradition, which may ultimately be "an impatience with debate, conflict, ambivalence, polysemy, paradox. And this is at heart an impatience with learning, and with learning about our learning."[23]

19. David Tracy, *The Analogical Imagination: Christian Theology and the Culture of Pluralism* (New York: Crossroad, 1981), 102. We shall return to this question of experience in chapter 7.

20. Michael Root, "The Narrative Structure of Soteriology," in *Why Narrative?* 265–66.

21. Lubac, *Scripture in the Tradition*, 7.

22. Jowett, "On the Interpretation of Scripture."

23. Williams, *On Christian Theology*, 131–32.

Scripture Absorbing the World

In an attempt to avoid these shortcomings, George Lindbeck proposes an understanding of scripture that has attracted considerable attention in recent years.[24] He contends that the principal aim of biblical interpretation is not to remake scriptural images and ideas into illustrative figures of speech for extrabiblical realities, nor is it to invite men and women to mine the Bible for ways to express their pre-thematic experience of transcendence. It is rather for them to make the story of the Bible the constitutive story of their lives. The cross should therefore not be transformed into a figure of suffering; neither the kingdom of God into a symbol for hope in the future. Lindbeck insists instead "suffering should be cruciform, and hopes for the future messianic." Put more generally, the Christian interpretation of scripture "redescribes reality within the scriptural framework rather than translating scripture into extrabiblical categories. It is the text, so to speak, which absorbs the world, rather than the world the text."[25]

There is much to commend in Lindbeck's so-called postliberal account of scriptural reasoning. In particular, he recognizes that the hermeneutical question revolves principally around the way the book of the world is correlated with the book of scripture. As we have noted previously, for most of Christian history nature and history were considered unfollowable apart from the biblical narrative, and both were finally indecipherable without Christ's ecclesial body as the idiomatic "middle term" that linked the two "books" together. In the seventeenth century, however, what Hans Frei calls "the great reversal" begins to take place across the theological spectrum, as interpretation sought to fit the biblical story into another world with its own story "rather than incorporating that world in the biblical story."[26]

As I noted in chapter 1, the book of "Nature" came to be regarded as the true sphere of God's works, the real text on which God's writing was clearly inscribed. The Bible was regarded as simply the republication of "Natural Religion." Modernity attributed to this new primary "text" its own independent intelligibility, and then invested it with indisputable authority for interpreting the meaning and truthfulness of all sacred texts, written as they were in merely human language.[27] And so it was that, as Norman Sykes puts it, "the Word of God assumed a secondary position to his works as set forth in the created universe. For whereas the testimony of the latter was universal and ubiquitous, the evidence of Revelation was confined

---

24. See, for example, the essays in *The Nature of Confession: Evangelicals and Postliberals in Conversation,* ed. Timothy R. Phillips and Dennis L. Okholm (Downers Grove, IL: InterVarsity Press, 1996).

25. George Lindbeck, *The Nature of Doctrine: Religion and Theology in a Postliberal Age* (Philadelphia: Westminster, 1984), 118. Robert Jenson at times uses similar language to describe our continuing relation to the biblical text: "Not only is Scripture within the church, but we, the church, are within Scripture—that is, our common life is located inside the story Scripture tells" (Robert W. Jenson, "Scripture's Authority in the Church," in *The Art of Reading Scripture,* ed. Ellen F. Davis and Richard B. Hays [Grand Rapids: Eerdmans, 2003], 30).

26. Frei, *Eclipse of Biblical Narrative,* 130.

27. Asad, *Genealogies of Religion,* 41.

to sacred books written in dead languages, whose interpretation was not agreed even amongst professed Christians, and which related moreover to distant events which had occurred in remote times and in places far removed from the centres of learning and civilization."[28]

It is this great reversal that Lindbeck seeks to counteract. Those who believe that the first hermeneutical question the church must ask is, "How one can preach the gospel to a dechristianized world?" are already well down the road to becoming theologians who "identify the modern questions that must be addressed, and then . . . translate the gospel answers into a currently understandable conceptuality." And, as he cogently points out, it is "important to note the direction of interpretation" between the book of scripture and the book of nature.[29] Failure to do so will cede the day to forces that seek to relieve the gospel of its specificity.

And yet there are problems in Lindbeck's account that hinder its usefulness as our primary guide for reading scripture, beginning with his dependence on Clifford Geertz's theory of culture as an interlocked system of construable signs forming a context within which people, events, institutions, behaviors, and processes can be intelligibly described.[30] As with many cultural anthropologies written in the twentieth century, Geertz regards the various elements that comprise a whole way of life or culture as a holistic and homogeneous unit. What makes the idea of culture a unitary whole for anthropologists is its identification with norms, values, beliefs, concepts, and dispositions that contain and communicate meaning for the members of that cultural group. These elements must therefore interrelate in a way that, ideally, coheres in a kind of system, or at the very least in the way that an individual person's mind and emotions generally exhibit consistency and coherence. A culture thus forms an integrated context that is viewed synchronically,[31] that is, as a non-temporal "field" of signs that interact more like the static surface of a picture than the timely movements of a drama or symphony.[32]

Lindbeck treats Christianity in general as a kind of culture in Geertz's sense of the term. The stories of Jesus in particular define the true nature of things and thus constitute a kind of metanarrative, interpreting and regulating all other stories. This schema fails, however, to reckon adequately with the structural complexity of

28. Norman Sykes, "The Religion of Protestants," in *The Cambridge History of the Bible*, vol. 3, ed. S. L. Greenslade (New York: University of Cambridge Press, 1975), 195–96.

29. Lindbeck, *Nature of Doctrine*, 118, 132.

30. Geertz, *Interpretation of Cultures*, 14, 17, 26; Lindbeck, *Nature of Doctrine*, 115. Lindbeck's approach has recently been revised by Kevin J. Vanhoozer, who replaces Lindbeck's dependence on Geertz's theory of culture with Hans Urs von Balthasar's emphasis on the dramatic quality of God's action in the world. Vanhoozer rightly wonders whether Lindbeck's indebtedness to Geertz's cultural anthropology once again raises the question of the extent to which theological prolegomena should be properly theological (Kevin J. Vanhoozer, *The Drama of Doctrine: A Canonical Linguistic Approach to Christian Theology* [Louisville: Westminster/John Knox, 2005], 10n30).

31. Kathryn Tanner, *Theories of Culture: A New Agenda for Theology* (Minneapolis: Augsburg Fortress, 1997), 29–35.

32. Williams, *On Christian Theology*, 45.

narrative interpretation, and more specifically, the ongoing narrative relationship we all have with the original story. As a result, his approach to the interpretation of scripture becomes dangerously ahistorical (a trait it ironically shares with the propositional and experiential models). According to John Milbank, Lindbeck does not sufficiently account for the inherent tension between the assumption of a paradigmatic setting for the narrative that subsumes both the original story and our relationship to it, which is sketched in an inherently cautious, general, approximate, and negative fashion in church teaching, and the continuing unfolding of its syntagmatic development. He tries instead "to graft the paradigmatic function inappropriately onto the narrative structures as such. Thus Christians are seen as living within certain fixed narratives which function as *schemas*, which can organize endlessly different cultural contexts." The biblical stories become "hypostasized," extracted from the coming to be and passing away of history, and reconceived as "a permanent, essentially unproblematic code, which can be described and operated as well by an 'outsider' as by an 'insider.'"[33]

Lindbeck reinforces this impression when he states that the biblical text absorbs, "so to speak," the world of time and space, as people, events, objects, and institutions are "inserted" into the synchronic boundaries of a spatially configured "framework."[34] The combination of spatial imagery and the notion of culture as a relatively fixed semiotic system suggests that the meaning of the biblical text is analogous to the distinctive symbolic representation of space by a modern map. Predicated on principles derived from Euclidean and descriptive geometry, the modern map seeks to establish a definitive and comprehensive knowledge of an order of places, says Michel de Certeau, by plotting what is otherwise heterogeneous space on a uniform grid. In this way the map creates "a formal ensemble of abstract places," forging "a totalizing stage" on which elements of diverse origin and significance are assembled to form a synchronic "tableau of a 'state' of geographical knowledge." Space is thus rendered homogeneous by being divided into identical units, each event, character, and setting assigned to its proper place, carefully situated side by side, with no two things occupying the same space.[35] Within such a representation of space, the Christian life is depicted not as an eschatological expedition into lands as yet unexplored, but as a foray across a well-mapped territory.[36]

The maplike conception of the Bible absorbing the world also fails to address adequately the question of how the church learns its way of speaking and thinking from the scriptures. According to Peter Ochs, what Lindbeck actually describes is the way that languages are learned when they come to learners ready-made. Learning to read the Bible is just like learning a language that already exists as a finished product, by being socialized into the fixed meaning of its grammar, such that "the one who

33. Milbank, *Theology and Social Theory*, 386.

34. Lindbeck, *Nature of Doctrine*, 118.

35. Michel de Certeau, *The Practice of Everyday Life*, trans. Steven Rendall (Berkeley: University of California Press, 1984), 119–21.

36. Williams, *On Christian Theology*, 29–31; see also Buber, "What Is Man?" 153.

learns has to be fully absorbed into what already is." Ochs acknowledges that this way of viewing the matter has a certain heuristic value, in that "learning the Bible means learning to feel a certain way or to think a certain way." Finer distinctions are nonetheless needed: "Learning the Bible requires a degree of literacy whose acquisition is like the acquisition of any language, but that literacy is not *sufficient*."[37]

What Lindbeck's conception of biblical literacy does not account for, Ochs argues, is the transformational or performative dimension of Bible learning, "the way in which the Bible's language implicates the reader in its reading—the reader, that is, in her particularity, which means in her place somewhere outside the Bible as well as in it. As also outside it, she is not asked merely to come to the Bible; the Bible also comes to her: this is the dialogically performative—and thus transformative—dimension of Biblical language." This aspect of learning to reason scripturally cannot be reduced to the terms of a given grammar, Ochs writes, "because it brings some particular grammar into question."[38]

Scriptural Reasoning: Going On and Going Further with the Biblical Texts

What Ochs describes as the performative dimension of biblical language is characterized by MacIntyre as that part of the ability of every language user that is poetic, consisting of the ability to know how to go on and go further in the use of the expressions of a language. (Poets do not have an exclusive claim to this skill but only display it in a preeminent degree.) What cannot be learned, for example, from simply memorizing a set of stock words and phrases such as one might use when traveling in a foreign country is twofold: first, a person who truly knows a language has also learned the basic convictions and structures of authority for the native speakers of that language. These shared beliefs permit competent speakers of a language—those who are able to name something *as* a member of some set *for* a particular group bound together by a shared tradition—to communicate certain other things to their hearers beyond what is explicitly uttered in a way that the unskilled speaker is not able. When a speaker offers one particular explanation (for example, ascribing a particular virtue to someone), he or she is at the same time ruling out a set of alternative explanations (implying in this case that the person in question does not suffer from a certain range of vices).[39]

Second, simply learning stock words and phrases to use in routine situations does not demonstrate a basic linguistic competence, any more than having memorized the official rulebook of baseball certifies that one knows how the

37. Peter Ochs, "Scriptural Logic: Diagrams for a Postcritical Metaphysics," in *Rethinking Metaphysics*, ed. L. Gregory Jones and Stephen E. Fowl (Oxford: Blackwell, 1995), 69–70.

38. Ibid.,70.

39. Alasdair MacIntyre, *Whose Justice? Which Rationality?* (Notre Dame, IN: University of Notre Dame Press, 1988), 381–82.

game is played. The badge of elementary linguistic competence is verified instead by the ability "to move from one kind of use of expression in the context of one sentence to another notably different kind of use of the same expression in the context of another and perhaps then go on to innovate by inventing a third kind of use for that very same expression yet another sentential context." The example that MacIntyre offers has to do with the kind of utterances that would demonstrate that someone has a grasp of the English word *white*. A test that states that the person who knows that it is appropriate to assent to the proposition "Snow is white" if and when snow is white is inadequate to make this determination. Competence would be shown by someone who could say without prompting, "Snow is white, and so are the members of the Ku Klux Klan, and white with fear is what they were in snow-covered Arkansas last Friday." As the foregoing suggests, the ability to innovate with such an expression provides the basis for making distinctions between the plain or typical and the figural uses of a term, between the ironic and the straightforward expression, and in a more theoretical turn, between the univocal, the equivocal, and the analogical use of a term.[40]

Knowing how to go on and go further in the use of the expressions of a language involves a set of skills that are acquired in the course of learning to read texts that supply the paradigmatic uses of key expressions for a particular society. At the same time members of that society are becoming familiar with these texts, they are also learning the model exemplifications of the moral and intellectual virtues, the authorizing genealogies of their community, and its foundational prescription. Learning a language and being initiated into a society's traditions thus happen at the same time. The uses of key expressions are established in part by reference to standard authoritative texts, in the church's case, the canonical scriptures, together with other authors and writings whose authority is recognized by at least some part of the community.[41] We must become apprentices to accomplished teachers of scriptural reasoning who have come before us.[42]

Texts accorded canonical status by a community function as the authoritative point of departure for its distinctive way of life and language, providing its essential points of reference for the investigations, activities, and debates that are always carried out within the moral and intellectual traditions that distinguish it from other communities. Those texts to which this canonical status is assigned are regarded, on the one hand, as having a relatively stable meaning associated with them, and on the other, as always being open to rereading. As a result, "every tradition becomes to some degree a tradition of critical reinterpretation in which one and the same body of texts . . . is put to the question, and to successively different sets of questions, as a tradition unfolds."[43]

40. Ibid., 382–83.
41. Ibid.
42. Robert L. Wilken, *Remembering the Christian Past* (Grand Rapids: Eerdmans, 1995), 174.
43. MacIntyre, *Whose Justice? Which Rationality?* 383.

Ochs's comments about the performative nature of Bible reading and MacIntyre's observations about the badge of linguistic competence being the knowledge of how to go on and go further in the use of the expressions of a language point us in the same direction with respect to our understanding of the nature of biblical interpretation. They stress the way the scriptures are put to the question, and to successively different sets of questions, as times and circumstances unfold. This emphasis brings to the fore the crucial role that imagination plays in the interpretation of the Bible as a constitutive practice of the church. Invoking the idea of imagination does not, however, immediately answer all our questions, for the term itself is fraught with difficulties. In light of these difficulties, Ludwig Wittgenstein wisely recommends that we ought to ask, "not what images are or what happens when one imagines anything, but how the word 'imagination' is used."[44]

Imagination, Naming, and the Culture Industries

We can begin by distinguishing between at least two distinct uses of the term *imagination*. It is perhaps most commonly employed to refer to an ability, shared generally by most human beings, to conjure up weak or shadowy imitations of sensory perception in our heads.[45] If I concentrate, I can "see" the face of my best friend from childhood, "taste" what I might have for dinner this evening, "hear" the first movement of Beethoven's Fifth Symphony, "feel" the cold of winters past, and "smell" the scent of fresh-cut grass of the coming summer. It also names the ability to read silently, to deliberate with oneself, or to perform any number of analogous mental operations.

We also use the idea of imagination to speak about a performative exercise of intellect in relation to activities that involve sense perception, having specifically to do with the particular ways we name the people, things, events, and places that we see, hear, taste, smell, touch, handle, measure, assemble and disassemble, classify, distinguish, etc., up to and including the world as ordered and thus followable. The terms we use to talk about the world around us convey an understanding of how men and women properly fit together within society, how things normally go on between them and their fellows, the social expectations that are normally followed, "and the deeper normative notions and images that underlie these expectations." This self-understanding, because it involves "a wider grasp of our whole predicament" and thus extends beyond the immediate background assumptions

---

44. Ludwig Wittgenstein, *Philosophical Investigations*, trans. G. E. M. Anscombe, 3rd ed. (New York: Macmillan, 1958), para. 370, 116e.

45. See David Hume, *An Enquiry concerning Human Understanding: A Letter from a Gentleman to His Friend in Edinburgh*, 1.II., ed. Eric Steinberg (Indianapolis: Hackett, 1977), 9–10. For a recent study on this use of the idea of imagination, see Edward S. Casey, *Imagining: A Phenomenological Study*, 2nd ed. (Bloomington: Indiana University Press, 2000).

for our particular practices, is typically found in, and communicated by, images, stories, and legends.[46]

As I suggested above, the activity of naming involves two interrelated axes of reference. When someone identifies a person, thing, event, or place, he or she first refers to it in some manner *as* a member of some set.[47] This activity obviously is not something that goes on primarily in an individual's head. Indeed, the images that inform one's comprehensive grasp of how things stand in the world are typically found in narrative recitals and liturgical rites,[48] and thus they are spoken before they are "seen."[49] Though this sense of the term may seem straightforward, it is a far more complex undertaking than it might appear at first glance. Most Christians are familiar with the Old Testament commandment that forbids Jews from doing any labor on the Sabbath. To put this into practice, it was necessary to define what activities are covered by the term *labor*. One could think of any number of ways of specifying the extent of this term: work that involves heavy labor, for example, or for which one is compensated in some fashion. Each definition would reconfigure to one degree or another the sense and significance of the commandment.

The oral tradition of interpretation that would later be codified in the Talmud gradually came to define the idea of labor in connection with the biblical concept of humankind being created in the image of God. Labor was specified as acts of deliberate creation in the physical world, so that as God ceased from labor in creating the world on the seventh day, so should the chosen people refrain from creative work on that day. It was subsequently discovered that no single definition could cover all of the complex questions and dilemmas that had already developed or could do so in connection with this injunction. In response the sages and rabbis over time drew up a list of thirty-nine basic labors or acts of creation that serve as *avodah* or prototypes of the work that cannot be performed on the Sabbath. One of these basic labors is "threshing," which is normally associated with separating grain from chaff in the process of harvesting wheat, barley, or some other cereal. Included under this category is milking a cow, which sounds nonsensical at first to modern ears, but which becomes clear when its internal logic is laid bare. Threshing is therefore any action, including milking a cow, designed to extract the edible content from what is not to be consumed, at least at that time (one of course may later eat the meat of a milk cow).[50]

46. Charles Taylor, *Modern Social Imaginaries* (Durham, NC: Duke University Press, 2004), 23, 25.

47. MacIntyre, *Whose Justice? Which Rationality?* 376.

48. See Casey, *Remembering*, 310; and Paul Connerton, *How Societies Remember* (Cambridge: Cambridge University Press, 1989), 41–71.

49. Paul Ricoeur, "Imagination in Discourse and Action," in *From Text to Action*, trans. Kathleen Blamey and John B. Thompson (Evanston, IL: Northwestern University Press, 1991), 171. For his most extended discussion of the mimetic process, see his *Time and Narrative*, vol. 1, trans. Kathleen McLaughlin and David Pellauer (Chicago: University of Chicago Press, 1984), 52–87.

50. Adin Steinsaltz, *The Essential Talmud*, trans. Chaya Galia (New York: Basic Books, 1976), 108–9.

What this example from the Jewish tradition suggests is that when those who belong to a social and linguistic community name something or somebody, they not only do so *as* a member of some set, but also identify it as such *for* those who share something of the same metaphysical commitments, epistemic convictions, and moral dispositions that are constitutive of and constituted by a dedicated network of social practices.[51] The need for relating threshing grain and milking cows in this fashion is inextricably tied to the commandment to the people of Israel to participate in God's Sabbath rest. The Talmud codifies such utterances and actions in terms of which the concepts that characterize the Jewish intellectual and moral tradition were invented and have been elaborated and modified over the centuries.[52]

Because we know how to name particulars only as a member of some set, everything that happens to us in life, everything that we do, every person and object we encounter, up to and including our grasp of the permanent stage on which the drama of creation is set,[53] is implicated in the imaginative process of figuration, and thus they are "always-already interpreted, always-already a reading of what has gone before."[54] Our use of these figures is so habitual that we are generally unaware of them. Some constellation of images is always already at play, for example, in any conception of time: Newton's homogeneous medium that "flows equably without relation to anything external,"[55] Kant's pure form of sensible intuition,[56] the repeating cycles of nature common to agrarian societies, and the fugue-like cadenzas and cadences of scripture (just to mention a few possibilities). These metaphors and analogies for time make it possible for the members of a community to follow the rhythms and progressions of events as they unfold in the dissonances and resolutions of history, which in turn allows them to figure their relationships with every person and object, place and time they encounter within the world.

It is only under the auspices of some imaginative network, comprised by the linguistic conventions into which we are born and then constantly modify throughout our lives, that we know anything at all, and with respect to the temporal and historical character of our lives, that we can identify anything at all as conveying a certain significance. The repertoire of names that we inherit from our families and the other social groups to which we belong, in terms of which we imagine ourselves, others, and the world in which each and all exist, thus supplies the convictions upon which reason—the human ability to progress from evidence to conclusion, from ends sought to possible means for seeking

51. MacIntyre, *Whose Justice? Which Rationality?* 378–89.

52. Ibid., 373.

53. Milbank, *Theology and Social Theory*, 383.

54. Loughlin, *Telling God's Story*, 112.

55. Sir Isaac Newton, *Mathematical Principles of Natural Philosophy and His System of the World*, trans. Andrew Motte, rev. trans. Florian Cajori (Berkeley: University of California Press, 1960), 6.

56. Kant, *Critique of Pure Reason*, B46–53, 74–78.

them, from accepted principles to ideas being proposed for consideration—has something with which to work.[57]

Because some preexisting field of tropes and analogies always governs how we think about ourselves in relation to the world about us, affecting our sense of who we are in ways that are prior to any choice we might make in a given situation, we do not, indeed we cannot, choose or create de novo our imaginative grasp of the world. Any choice we might make in this regard is predicated on intellectual habits and convictions that are always already informed by some network of tropes and similes. We all thus begin life as novices and apprentices, and we mature our way through life, learning as we go what it means to be human and to cope with the business that occupies us as human beings.[58] Those who fail to recognize this process will inevitably be held captive by the particular picture of the world that, as Wittgenstein describes it, resides in their language, and that language will repeat it to them inexorably.[59]

This is not to suggest that one's habits of naming the world and the convictions that are embedded in these habits can never change, for that would be patently false. All of us, however, were initiated into a particular imaginative grasp on the world by virtue of the time and place of our births, and we spend the rest of our lives renegotiating our take on the nature of things through our ongoing engagements with others and with the world that we share. The pertinent question, then, is not whether imagination informs our interactions with the world, with each other, and with ourselves, but *which* complex of denotative fields does so. Without them women and men could not make a considered judgment whether (and if so, in what sense) the world is followable, its contingencies displaying some kind of coherence and purpose, or hopelessly plural, endlessly disappointing, and "susceptible of interpretation only by our hermetic tricks."[60]

All human endeavors, including the relationships we have to the times and places, people and things around us, are thus situated within a "picture" that generates our convictions, provides content for our moral and intellectual dispositions, and shapes our rational judgments about what is true, good, and beautiful. Imagination forms the basis of our ability to draw rational inferences about the nature of things, including God as the beginning and end of all things, and to assess the inferences of others.[61] Some sort of interpretive picture is therefore

---

57. Rationality is not an attribute of abstract conceptual systems, principles, or worldviews, but of communal practices and social projects for which these systems, principles, and worldviews form the working cross-sections. Put somewhat differently, reason is the name we give to the specifically human discursive power to formulate, criticize, and change the concepts, judgments, and formal systems employed in carrying out the activities that characterize human life. See Stephen Toulmin, *Human Understanding* (Princeton, NJ: Princeton University Press, 1972), 133, 478; and Turner, *Faith, Reason and the Existence of God*, 83.

58. Boyle, *Who Are We Now?* 156.

59. Wittgenstein, *Philosophical Investigations*, para. 115, 48e.

60. Kermode, *Genesis of Secrecy*, 145.

61. Sarah Coakley has argued that there are certain epistemic conditions that must be met, a transformation of a person's actual epistemic apparatus, if we are to account for seeing the risen Christ today

involved in contemplating the order to which all things under heaven and on earth belong, a grasp of our whole predicament that both precedes and is presupposed by "our capacity to oppose ourselves to things taken as objects opposed to a subject."[62]

It is not just in "religious" matters, moreover, that humans rely on this power of imagination to contemplate the world. The Enlightenment conception of human knowledge was made possible by the refiguring of the knowing subject as an individual unencumbered by particular times, places, and traditions. Both the activity of knowing and the justification of knowledge were redefined as a first-person singular project: How can *I* be sure that *my* beliefs, *my* perceptions, *my* experiences connect reliably with the external world?[63] Problems of knowledge were thus conceived under the image of an engineering project, seeking to determine the best way to build a reliable bridge across that "space" that separated the disembodied subject from the "external" world.[64] This figure for the process of knowing depicts this subject over against the rest of the created order in much the same way that Jews and Christians traditionally conceived of God's relationship to a world created ex nihilo, out of nothing. (This picture stands in stark contrast to that developed with the Jewish and Christian traditions, according to which men and women exist *as human* only within contingent webs of space, time, and language that ultimately begin and end with God.)

The ability to name the world is also integral to the practical aspects of human life. Actions (as distinct from mere physical movement or the sentient behavior of animals) are meaningful because they are moves carried out in and for the business of living. We do the things we do—make breakfast, plant a garden, choose a school, mow the lawn, bathe the children, work on an assembly line, talk to other people, write books—to achieve ends we regard in one degree or another, either explicitly or implicitly, as contributing to the business of human flourishing. Taken together these actions, both those that are directly related to the production and reproduction of life and those that are not, constitute tacit interpretations of human existence. As such they involve habits of naming and modes of reasoning that attempt to keep track of the innumerable transactions and exchanges that make up the contingencies of human life, and to deliberate over how we should

---

(Sarah Coakley, *Powers and Submissions: Spirituality, Philosophy and Gender* [Malden, MA: Blackwell, 2002], 130–52).

62. Paul Ricoeur, "Toward a Hermeneutic of the Idea of Revelation," in *Essays on Biblical Interpretation*, ed. Lewis S. Mudge (Philadelphia: Fortress, 1980), 101.

63. Alasdair MacIntyre, *First Principles, Final Ends and Contemporary Philosophical Issues* (Milwaukee: Marquette University Press, 1990), 12.

64. To be sure, the language of interiority has a long pedigree in the Christian tradition, but its sense has changed substantially over the centuries. With Augustine, for example, the boundary between inner and outer does not fall between the mind and the body, but between that part of the mind that is dependent on the body for the exercise of its powers, including imagination, and that part that is not so dependent, viz., reason. See Denys Turner, *The Darkness of God: Negativity in Christian Mysticism* (New York: Cambridge University Press, 1995), 90–92.

act in these exchanges, in short, how we should go on and go further as we pursue a particular way of life. How we learn to name these relationships thus determines to a significant degree how we conduct ourselves, and what we can reasonably expect from others.

In the early years of the American experiment in liberal democracy, for example, it was the epistemological picture of the unencumbered subject that underwrote the supposition that any citizen holding beliefs that had to do with matters of public concern but which could not be justified on the basis of beliefs common to all could safely be asked to sacrifice those beliefs "on the altar of public expediency." There was no perceived tension in making this request, says Richard Rorty, because it was assumed that there was a relation between the ahistorical essence of the human soul and moral truth that ensured that free and open discussion would deliver the one right answer to moral as well as to scientific questions. This theory guaranteed that any moral belief that could not be thusly justified was "irrational" and not a genuine product of our moral faculty. This picture has since been deconstructed, and with it the assumption that anyone anywhere could distinguish between innate rationality and the effects of acculturation, between the permanent truths of reason and temporary truths of facts, and between religion, myth, and tradition and something ahistorical, common to all human beings qua human. It would seem that humans are "historical all the way through."[65]

It is the deconstruction of this picture that has led some to conclude that the universe that is the stage on which all human activity is set is finally unfollowable, its features like random marks on a page or aleatoric bits of sound without discernible meter or harmonics. Not surprisingly, this configuration of things also involves a similar exercise of the intellect. Nietzsche drives this point home in his famous tale "The Madman," where he poignantly describes something of what it would mean to live in a world that is not tethered to any transcendent reference point:

> The mad man jumped into their midst and pierced them with his eyes. "Whither is God?" he cried; "I will tell you. *We have killed him*—you and I. All of us are his murderers! But how did we do this? How could we drink up the sea? Who gave us the sponge to wipe away the entire horizon? What were we doing when we unchained this earth from its sun? Whither is it moving now? Whither are we moving? Away from all suns? Are we not plunging continually? Backward, sideward, forward, in all directions? Is there still any up or down? Are we not straying as through an infinite nothing? Do we not feel the breath of empty space? Has it not become colder? Is not night continually closing in on us? Do we not need to light lanterns in the morning?"[66]

Nietzsche's depiction of a world without horizon or foundation reminds us once again that our lives are inextricably situated in some depiction of how things are, how they should be, and what, if anything, the latter has to do with the former.

65. Rorty, "Priority of Democracy to Philosophy," 257–58.
66. Nietzsche, *Gay Science*, 181–82.

Imagination in the sense we are using the term here is obviously not a habit of mind that all persons and communities possess in similar measure. The ability to conjecture, hypothesize, and invent, to name the world in ways other than what is conventionally assumed by most members of a given society, is a power that is perfected only over time (and considerable lengths of time at that, often spanning generations), and even then nothing is guaranteed. The power of certain traditions and their imaginative construals to account for and adjust to an ever-changing world is, for reasons too numerous to mention, superior to others. Some demonstrate a marked aptitude to calibrate unfolding events within a meaningful pattern of life and thought, while others may persist for a time and then dissipate or are assimilated.

One segment of the earthly city that understands the power residing in imagination is the so-called culture industries.[67] These industries—means of mass communication (movies, television, and popular music), distribution systems (cable and satellite systems such as Disney, telecommunications firms, and of course the Internet), data processing networks (computer software and hardware interests), marketing and advertising firms, and educational institutions—account for the majority of the world's output of shared images, stories, information, news, entertainment, and the like. From their strategic position the corporations that dominate these industries control an ever-expanding network of cultural production. In a globalized political economy they exercise an inordinate influence on how people relate not only to the processes and products of economic and political activity, but also to one another, both the neighbor with a face and the anonymous producer of goods that lives quite literally on the other side of the world.

Marketing and advertising in particular play leading roles in generating the images that presently hold much of the world captive. Advertising has not only become ubiquitous over the last few decades, penetrating into virtually every aspect of our lives, but has also changed its focus. Whereas advertising once focused on product-oriented ads that sought to have an immediate effect (namely, to convince someone to buy a specific product), buyer-centered, image-related approaches now dominate. Advertising seeks to mold attitudes and behaviors by associating products and services with seductive images and ideas, typically by playing on our anxieties about our appearance to, and acceptability among, those in our "focus group," that is, those whom we regard as our peers. We are told that a certain product or service will make us appear more youthful, more feminine or masculine, more powerful or desirable, more provocative, more successful, etc. *ad infinitum*. Long-term advertising continually seeks to re-create lifestyles, identities, and social networks around these images of association.

67. The idea of culture industry was first coined by Max Horkheimer and Theodor W. Adorno, "The Culture Industry: Enlightenment as Mass Deception," in *Dialectic of Enlightenment*, trans. John Cumming (New York: Continuum, 1972), 120–60.

Television in particular, with its titillating combination of sight and sound, evocative appeals to the emotions rather than to the intellect, and never-ending stream of images and ideas, dominates the imaginative ecology of capitalism. Its programming and advertising intrude into nearly every space of everyday life, crowding out other formative influences in the lives of young people, including the practices of the church. Television has an unparalleled ability to captivate our attention for extended periods of time with powerful images, simple narratives, and deceptively subtle messages that take very little effort to understand. These images, stories, and legends tacitly inculcate in their recipients an understanding of how men and women ought to relate to one another, how things should go on between them, and the social expectations that should be followed.

Imagination and a Realism of Distances

All our knowledges and interactions with the world, then, be they speculative or practical, whether grounded in ancient traditions or the latest permutations of the global market, are implicated in the figural process of naming *as* (that is, naming by way of, naming analogically, metaphorically, metonymically, synecdochically, ironically, and the like[68]) and naming *for*. The transactions of human life thus come to us already prefigured as intelligible events and actions by the conventions that inform and accredit our sense of the difference between reality and pretense or fantasy, and they perform this task prior to any attempt to position these transactions within an explicit narrative context. It is also this process of figuration that gives rise to the ability of some to imagine the world differently in significant ways, and thus to challenge the competence of the linguistic conventions of the world as it is presently configured to describe reality truthfully.[69] Knowing how to go on and go further, discovering new possibilities for dealing with the world, is not an ability that is exercised only *within* a particular social configuration, but *between* social configurations as well. This is finally what distinguishes a realism of appearances from a realism of distances.

Three millennia ago, "everyone" knew for a fact that Pharaoh was the preeminent power on earth, for the gods of Egypt (among whom the king was numbered) reigned supreme over all things. Among those accounted as wise and powerful, it was unimaginable that anyone or anything could withstand the might and majesty of Pharaoh and the heavenly powers aligned with his kingdom, and to think otherwise was sure evidence of madness. And then something happened, "howsoever strange and admirable," as an obscure desert deity managed to foil the supposedly invincible will of this earthly sovereign by delivering a group of slaves out of the reach of his military and economic might, and then leading them to a land that he had promised to their ancestors many years before.

68. Ward, *Cultural Transformation and Religious Practice*, 132; cf. McClendon, *Doctrine*, 75–77.
69. Anthony Kenny, *Aquinas on Mind* (New York: Routledge, 1993), 40.

Three thousand years later, "everyone" in the American South (that is, everyone who was white, and almost without exception calling themselves Christian) knew for a fact that people from the "dark continent" were inferior by nature, and that God intended that the white race should rule over them with, of course, all due benevolence. But something unforeseen began to happen in black churches all across the South. In one such meeting, held one evening in August 1962 in the Williams Chapel Missionary Baptist Church in Ruleville, Mississippi, the Reverend James Bevel, a young associate of Dr. Martin Luther King, Jr., preached a short sermon from the Gospel of Matthew. Bevel asked the members of the congregation to ponder the rebuke that Jesus directed toward the Pharisees and Sadducees: "Jesus answered and said unto them, 'When it is evening, ye say, "It will be fair weather today; for the sky is red and lowering." O ye hypocrites, ye can discern the face of the sky; but can ye not discern the signs of the times?'" (Matt. 16:2–3 KJV). He urged the congregation not to neglect the signs of their own time, for surely the hour had come for black men and women to claim their right to vote.[70]

Among those gathered in the congregation who were asked to volunteer to go the courthouse and register to vote—an act that would curry the hatred of those who sought to maintain strict racial segregation in Mississippi—was a woman named Fannie Lou Hamer. As a result of attending this meeting, Mrs. Hamer, who had worked as a poor field hand in Mississippi for over forty years, got caught up in the scriptural reasoning that fueled the struggle for freedom (which did not originate among the learned in the academy, but with the marginalized black churches of the American South that were heirs to a tradition forged in suffering and sacrifice), and she quickly became a storied figure in the civil rights movement. This mode of rationality allowed her to imagine the world that she and her fellow Christians inhabited differently in significant ways, and thus to challenge what white Christians "knew" to be the case.

Mrs. Hamer demonstrated her competence at scriptural reasoning countless times, but none more eloquently than one Sunday morning in July 1964. Increasingly frustrated with the reluctance of the young pastor of a small church to support voter-registration efforts, she took advantage of his invitation to say a few words to the congregation to preach an impromptu sermon on the Bible passage for that morning: "And I will dwell among the children of Israel, and will be their God. And they shall know that I am the Lord their God that brought them forth out of the land of Egypt, that I may dwell among them: I am the Lord their God" (Exod. 29:45–46 KJV). According to one witness, Mrs. Hamer majestically rose to her feet, her voice rolling through the chapel as she enlisted numerous biblical figures in support of the cause of freedom. Her thunderous use of both the Old and New Testaments stunned the audience: "Pharaoh was in Sunflower County!

---

70. As narrated by Charles Marsh, *God's Long Summer: Stories of Faith and Civil Rights* (Princeton, NJ: Princeton University Press, 1997), 10–11.

Israel's children were building bricks without straw—at three dollars a day!" She paused, her voice breaking and tears welling up in her eyes: "They're tired! And they're tired of being tired." Mrs. Hamer fell silent for a moment and then pointed a trembling finger at the shaken minister, and every eye turned to look at the pastor. Her voice was commanding: "And you, Reverend Tyler, must be Moses! Leadin' your flock out of the chains and fetters of Egypt—takin' them yourself to register—*tomorra*—in Indianola!"[71]

Fannie Lou Hamer did not simply provide colorful illustrations for an account of the racial situation in the American South that had previously been formulated in other, strictly conceptual terms. She instead showed herself to be a realist of distances, positing a real connection, grounded in the apocalyptic incursion of God into human history, between her own time and circumstances, and those of the children of Israel in bondage three millennia ago. When she named Jim Crow as Pharaoh, those whom segregation oppressed as the Hebrew children, and the reluctant preacher as the one whom God had chosen to lead them to freedom, she was truthfully naming the reality of the situation. The God of Abraham and Sarah, the God of Moses and Miriam, and the God of Rev. Bevel and Mrs. Hamer had finally "heard their cry on account of their taskmasters" (Exod. 3:7), and was exerting sovereignty over the state of Mississippi, acting to liberate his beloved people from the yoke of bondage that the Egyptians who wore white robes and hoods and organized White Citizens Councils had placed on their necks.

Scriptural reasoning cannot be acquired apart from participation in a community that has learned over countless generations how to reason about their world using biblical images and stories. When Mrs. Hamer stood before that congregation and proclaimed that Pharaoh was in Sunflower County, her words did not magically appear out of vacuum, nor did they fall upon deaf ears, for she and her fellow Christians had been trained over the centuries to follow "what the Spirit is saying to the churches" (Rev. 2:7). In clandestine meetings held throughout the South prior to the abolition of slavery, the displaced children of Africa gathered together to cry out to God in the midst of indescribable oppression and suffering, in the hope that God would hear their groaning and take notice of them (Exod. 2:24–5). These secret assemblies, described by Albert Raboteau as the "invisible institution,"[72]

71. Cited in ibid., 32. We could appeal to other exemplars of scriptural reasoning here. We have already considered the story of André Trocmé and the Huguenot church in Le Chambon. To this we can add the life of Bartolomé de Las Casas, the first priest ordained in the Americas, in 1512, who repudiated the unity of faith and nationalism that underwrote Spanish colonialism. Though many would want to see Las Casas as the first "liberation theologian," Gustavo Gutierrez rightly notes that Las Casas saw it as his task "above all in letting it be known in the Indies that there is a God, and that that God is the God of Abraham, Isaac, Jacob, and Jesus. . . . When Las Casas links salvation and justice, then, he is only responding to this biblical focus, which constitutes, furthermore, a permanent facet of Christian tradition" (Gustavo Gutierrez, *Las Casas: In Search of the Poor of Jesus Christ*, trans. Robert R. Barr [Maryknoll, NY: Orbis, 1993], 10).

72. Albert J. Raboteau, *Slave Religion: The 'Invisible Institution' in the Antebellum South* (New York: Oxford University Press, 1978).

were necessary, in large part due to the legal restrictions against gatherings by slaves without white oversight. As an ex-slave preacher tells it, "They would steal off to the fields and in the thickets and there, with heads together around a kettle to deaden the sound, they called on God out of heavy hearts.[73]"

These meetings were also necessary because of dissatisfaction with the worship and preaching in white churches. "While the great majority of White Christians condoned slavery, saying it was permitted or even ordained by God," writes James Cone, "black slaves contended that God willed their freedom and not their servitude." They thus took every opportunity to steal off into the woods at night, risking serious injury and death, to sing, preach, and pray for their liberation. When the slaves worshiped with their masters, they typically put on a "good front" so that their oppressors would think of them as pious and good. As Cone puts it, the "'real meetin' and 'the real preachin' was held in the swamp, out of the reach of the patrols. An ex-slave, Litt Young, tells of a black preacher who preached 'obey your master' as long as her mistress was present. When the mistress was absent, she said, 'he came out with straight preachin' from the Bible.'"[74]

Cultivated by this "straight preachin,'" encouraged by singing, praying, and eating together, and sustained by a living hope "which is not verified first of all by experience, and therefore cannot be falsified by apparent defeat,"[75] Mrs. Hamer and these other cherished members of Christ's body proved to be well trained in the poetics of scriptural reasoning, able to follow signs of God's love for them in a world that continually degraded and dehumanized them. They were convinced that the God who brought slaves out of Egypt and Jesus out of the grave would one day deliver them as well. They put the lie to the claims that they were naturally inferior, and that God intended that the white race should rule over them. Knowing that as with the sons and daughters of Jacob, God had prepared a better country for them, and thus they were not destined to remain in the land of slavery (Heb. 11:16), they were able to imagine new possibilities for dealing faithfully with the present darkness.

Realists of appearances would of course dismiss as either sheer madness or misplaced sentimentality the suggestion that stories about Moses and cities to come have any real bearing on the world in which we now live. Realists of distances such as O'Connor (whose use of the grotesque in her fiction is carefully crafted to expose the banality of what passes for sanity in our world) contend instead that the poetic insights of Fannie Lou Hamer are essential to a truthful take on the world. They preserve and perpetuate the prophetic vision of the Bible, which at bottom has to do with "seeing near things in their extensions of meaning and thus of seeing far things close up." From this standpoint, the meaning of every person, place, and thing does not reside in itself, but in relation to its beginning and end in

---

73. Cited by George P. Rawick in *From Sundown to Sunup* (Westport, CT: Greenwood, 1972), 40.

74. James H. Cone, *Speaking the Truth: Ecumenism, Liberation, and Black Theology* (Grand Rapids: Eerdmans, 1986), 88.

75. Yoder, *For the Nations*, 136.

mystery.[76] Apart from the prophetic imagination, then, the apocalyptic incursion of God into the world would be unintelligible.[77]

Imagination and Memory

The poetic imagination that allowed Mrs. Hamer to follow the enigmatic events of the civil rights movement in their extensions of meaning in God's eschatological intentions for all the families of the earth is bound up with memory.[78] In Book X of *Confessions* Augustine tells us that memory is critical to the formation and integrity of the self: "Great is the power of memory! An awesome thing, my God, deep and boundless and manifold in being! And this thing is the mind, and this am I myself."[79] What Augustine helps us to see, writes Rowan Williams, is that memory is the "self," that it is "my presence to myself, the way in which I constitute myself and understand myself as a subject with a continuous history of experience." Because of memory we are not trapped and confined in the present moment but can see it as the product of contingent processes and choices, and thereby transcend the limitations the here and now would impose on us. Without the understanding of the past that is supplied by memory, our bondage to the present is complete, our sense of ourselves firmly in the hands of those who control the present order of things.[80]

Who we are, and how we are to live our lives, is therefore a product of the past, or as Jacques Derrida puts it, "the *being* of what we are *is* first of all inheritance, whether we like it or know it or not."[81] Our interactions with other persons or things, the nearly countless transactions and exchanges that make up our day-to-day existence, all our comings and goings, actions and affections, desires and decisions, are linked together within an imaginative framework that is generated by memory.[82] Where there is not a living past, and thus no moral, intellectual, and spiritual birthright that we inherit from those who went before us, which we draw from in the present and then pass on to the future, what remains is "the present

76. O'Connor, "Some Aspects of the Grotesque in Southern Fiction," 817.

77. See Dawson, *Christian Figural Reading and the Fashioning of Identity*, 5–6, 134.

78. This stress on memory as the font of imagination runs counter to the Romantic concept of individual creativity as the source of our poetic engagement with the world.

79. St. Augustine, *The Confessions*, X.17, in *The Confessions of St. Augustine*, trans. John K. Ryan (Garden City, NY: Image Books, 1960).

80. Rowan Williams, *Resurrection*, 29–31. This self-presence, adds Edmund Hill, "is perpetually actual, but not perpetually active . . . it represents the mind's perpetually actual potential, which is only intermittently activated. This actual potential is memory in one sense. Yet it does not cease to be memory when it is activated by an active thought to generate a mental word . . . it then becomes active memory, or an act of remembering, recollecting, or calling to mind . . . " (Edmund Hill, OP, Foreword to Books IX–XIV of *The Trinity*, by Augustine [New York: New City Press, 1991], 266).

81. Jacques Derrida, *Specters of Marx: The State of the Debt, the Work of Mourning, and the New International*, trans. Peggy Kamuf (New York: Routledge, 1994), 54.

82. See Connerton, *How Societies Remember*.

moment rescued from nothingness and the desire to grasp the next moment."[83] Regardless of the number of choices that either state or market manages to set before men and women, those whose past has been denied them, and who have no future beyond what already is in place, will never be free.

Among the many insidious effects of marketing and advertising, especially on television, is the undercutting of memory through the ceaseless flow of disconnected images. In a process known as fragmentation, images, ideas, and personalities are extricated from their conventional referents and then reshuffled and recombined to confer novel meanings to products and opportunities for consumption. Commercial television programming, taking features of a past or concurrent culture (its music, dance, dress, language, stories, images) and recycling them with those extracted from other cultures to form disjointed images and impressions with no purpose other than to entice viewers and pitch products, is so prevalent in our culture that our ability to name the world truthfully has been significantly impoverished.[84]

A vital and coherent memory such as that evidenced by Mrs. Hamer thus represents a real threat to the current regime of political and economic power. The powers and principalities of Wall Street, Madison Avenue, and Hollywood understand this all too well, and they work diligently to dissect all received knowledge of the past. They recycle and reassemble these fragments in evernew combinations, creating "spectacles (war, famine, urban violence) without history or memory . . . disconnected images, sounds, and representations following one another, or occurring simultaneously, with no evident coherence of purpose, meaning, or interrelation (save for enticing and intriguing viewers)."[85] Without memory the past no longer has a bearing on our lives, and the future is only an extension and expansion of the present and, for the denizens of a global economy, an endlessly repeated moment of consumption. This is of course precisely the state of affairs sought by the culture industries, and it is what must be recognized and resisted by the church if it is to be re-membered as the body of Christ.

As the foregoing suggests, the generative function of memory within scriptural reasoning is not the mere psychological recall of isolated events and characters that are receding into an ever more remote past. To remember is to call something to mind for the purpose of acting upon it. Christians remember in order to go on and go further toward the future that God has set before us, prepared to meet evil and grace, and to act on a trust beyond ourselves, whether or not we know very clearly at the time what we act upon.[86] In the body of Christ memory is, as John Zizioulas so incisively describes it, the memory of the future.[87]

83. Bonhoeffer, *Ethics*, 128.
84. Budde, *(Magic) Kingdom of God*, 82.
85. Ibid., 80–81.
86. O'Connor, "Some Aspects of the Grotesque in Southern Fiction," 816–17.
87. Zizioulas, *Being as Communion*, 180.

As we get caught up in the church's generative memory, we learn to follow the things that characterize everyday human life in all its routine, wonder, and dread under the sign of past events, personalities, and expectations in the history of the chosen people. Scriptural reasoning is thus not confined to a sphere of "religious" concerns but has to do with birth and death, marrying and giving in marriage, prosperity and hardship, ruling and being ruled, buying and selling, love and enmity, generosity and avarice, hoarding and squandering, hospitality and envy, wisdom and folly, triumph and devastation. These occurrences in the lives of those who came before us, which so disrupted the established order of things that they could only be attributed to an agency that was unencumbered by the conditions of historical causality, are thus connected to those of present and the future, not temporally or causally, nor by external resemblance alone, but as part of a pattern of divine activity and design to which this carefully codified memory bears witness.[88]

This generative memory that was handed down to succeeding generations of God's chosen people, first in oral traditions and then through the developing canon of scripture, was therefore a constitutive part of God's self-disclosure. God acted without and within, revealing himself both through the situation with which he engaged the Israelites and through the imagination, in terms of which he led them "to see and hear the voices and sights surrounding them."[89] The generative memory inscribed in the Bible was therefore not only constituted by, but also constituted, the events it revealed. "The relation between situation and imagination, event and text," writes Gerard Loughlin, "is inter-constitutive of both. Describing the events of revelation and the testimony of Scripture as inter-constitutive reminds us that the Church is at least in part a socio-textual reality, shaping the texts by which it is shaped."[90] There was an intrinsic relationship between the situations described in the text and the imagination at work in those descriptions.

The process of refiguring the present under the form of the biblical past and prophetic future was especially crucial in the formation of Jesus's own identity, and thus to our understanding of the incarnation. Loughlin writes: "Precisely as the one who is figured in the gospels, Jesus the Christ is already prefigured in the Hebrew Scriptures. Jesus is in part a textually constituted reality." Christ consciously understood himself and his life and ministry in terms of his reading of the Jewish scriptures: "Christ clothed himself in scriptural images, and in the clothing constituted the character and identity of God's Messiah." Together this man and these images constituted the self-disclosure of God in Christ. The Bible was not simply the record of or a response to God's self-revelation; it was inextricably a part of it.[91]

---

88. Erich Auerbach, *Mimesis: The Representation of Reality in Western Literature*, trans. Willard R. Trask (Princeton, NJ: Princeton University Press, 1953), 17–18, 73–74; Lubac, *Scripture in the Tradition*, 37.

89. Austin Farrer, *Interpretation and Belief*, ed. C. C. Conti (London: SPCK, 1976), 44, cited by Loughlin, *Telling God's Story*, 111.

90. Ibid., 111–12.

91. Ibid., 112–13.

In his life, death, and resurrection, then, Jesus fulfills the people and events narrated in the Bible, "not by supplying a general meaning . . . but by supplying himself."[92] As the one who shared all things with us, but without sin (Heb. 2:14; 4:15), he does not merely continue the story of God's covenant with Israel but performs a decisive and unsurpassable reconfiguration of that foundational narrative, bringing to fruition the promise to bless all the families of the earth (Gen. 12:3; cf. Matt. 25:31–46). God identifies the risen Christ as the center of all things, the one in whom all things in heaven and earth are to be gathered up.[93] The movement of time—the complex rhythms, harmonies, and recapitulations of history—can therefore be comprehended only in relation to this center, from which all things have their being, and toward which all things tend.[94]

As the preceding suggests, the employment of imagination in the practice of scriptural reasoning has a profound effect on our understanding of the biblical texts as well as on the world we seek to interpret by means of them. Seeing the present under figures and types provided by scripture's generative memory thus reconfigures the sense and significance of the Bible to one extent or another. In most cases the impact on the text is rather minimal; there are times, however, when the transformations are substantial. The Bible itself bears witness to several significant reconfigurations over the course of Israel's history. The advent of the monarchy in ancient Israel, for example, represented a considerable reworking of the covenant as it had developed according to tribal traditions, as indicated in the prophet Samuel's response to Israel's request to have a king like all the other nations: "Listen to the voice of the people in all that they say to you; for they have not rejected you, but they have rejected me from being king over them" (1 Sam. 8:7).

The exile and resulting dispersion had a similar effect on the way the stories of kings and prophets were narrated. On the one hand, the Jews were painfully aware that they now lived under the dominion of other rulers and nations, even within the Promised Land: "Here we are, slaves to this day—slaves in the land that you gave to our ancestors to enjoy its fruit and its good gifts" (Neh. 9:36). On the other hand, God's kingly rule over Israel was now explicitly extended to the whole creation, that even mighty kings such as Cyrus of Persia unwittingly did the Lord's bidding (Isa. 44:28–45:4). And in the New Testament the story of Jesus and his immediate group of followers in Galilee, which is set firmly in first-century Palestinian Judaism, is considerably reconfigured by the rapid spread of the gospel to Gentiles.

It is not a question, then, of whether this process of reconfiguring the generative memory of scripture takes place in the history of Israel, the ministry of Jesus, and the life and witness of the church, but of whether it is the same story that has been renarrated or whether it has become a substantially different

---

92. John David Dawson, "Figural Reading and the Fashioning of Christian Identity in Boyarin, Auerbach and Frei," in *Theology and Scriptural Imagination*, ed. L. Gregory Jones and James J. Buckley (Malden, MA: Blackwell, 1998), 30.

93. See Eph. 1:10.

94. Bonhoeffer, *Ethics*, 58.

story.[95] This difference is crucial, though exceedingly resistant to theoretical expression.[96] There are, of course, lesser distinctions that can and should be made on a regular basis. If the church at a particular time and place judges a certain retelling of the story to be consistent with those told by the body of Christ over the centuries, it can and should go on to ask whether it is a more or less happy rendering of that story, assisted by the word care provided by theologians.

By learning to attend to the happenings of the present under the figure of the biblical past and its rendering of a future that is configured around Christ, the church in every generation gets caught up in this generative memory, and thus into the constitutive relationship between event and imagination. The past impinges on the present, and the future on the present seen in light of the past, so that all three dimensions are read as movements within the one history of divine providence. The divine mystery disclosed in Christ does not therefore exist in idea, ahistorical truth, or object of detached speculation, says Lubac, for it is entirely concrete: "This mystery is a reality in act, the realization of a Grand Design; it is therefore, in the strongest sense, even something historical, in which personal beings are engaged."[97]

Imagination and Apocalypse

Though the connection between past, present, and future is achieved by a variety of rhetorical means in scripture, some that make it explicit, others leaving it implicit, one of the most important, particularly where the apocalypse of God is concerned, takes place through the literary technique of foreshortening. This procedure compresses the time between what is near at hand and the last things, in order to show the coming of God's everlasting rule impinging on events in the present. "Without such foreshortening," McClendon writes, "what comes last might be perspectively projected into the far future and thus into insignificance."[98] As I already noted in chapter 3, the projection of the *eschata* into the distant future is a tendency that was realized in the past. Increasingly in the church's self-understanding, the interval between the present and the consummation of all things began to expand in a process that seemed to have no end.[99] Only with the rediscovery of the significance of apocalyptic language in the latter parts of the Old Testament and virtually the entirety of the New Testament has foreshortening been recognized by many as vital to a faithful proclamation of the gospel.[100]

95. It is this question that is at the heart of the disagreement between Jews and Christians over the meaning of the biblical texts they share.

96. Lash, *Theology on the Way to Emmaus*, 183.

97. Henri de Lubac, *Medieval Exegesis: The Four Senses of Scripture*, vol. 2, trans. E. M. Macierowski (Grand Rapids: Eerdmans, 2000), 93–94.

98. McClendon, *Doctrine*, 90.

99. Trocmé, *Jesus and the Nonviolent Revolution*, 151–55.

100. Refer to chapter two for a fuller discussion of the language of foreshortening.

This technique is further refined in the medieval church's tradition of spiritual exegesis. This way of reading the Jewish scriptures began with its plain or literal sense as its dominant meaning,[101] then sought to discern both present and future as continuous with it, giving rise to the spiritual sense, which was the christological point of the plain sense. The spiritual meaning of the Old Testament was then subdivided into three senses: allegorical (what is signified about Christ and the church), tropological (pertaining to the moral sense of scripture, grounded in our participation in Christ), and anagogical (having to do with the *eschata* and the beatific vision).[102] In the words of McClendon, "Spiritual sense meant, not an abandonment or discarding of the plain sense, but its appropriation into the whole story of divine and human relations; it meant the way the plain words bore upon readers' lives in relation to all that God had done and would do in their regard." The result is again an understanding of the world in which the past was interpreted figurally, and the future was arrayed "in terms of that present and past so joined."[103]

The dual process of assessing past construals of the sense and significance of the biblical testimony and of developing new ones is a never-ending endeavor. The latter point is crucial, for as I noted in the first chapter, the Christian hope for the future that is grounded in the life, death, and resurrection of Christ has been grafted onto other ideas and images to form what is typically called the American dream. The potent idea of intellectual, moral, and technological progress combines with the apparent success of the continental takeover by Western European immigrants to reconfigure the basic meaning of the story of Jesus. The Constantinian and Carolingian transformations of the church, detailed in chapter 3, also raise this question of what constitutes a faithful reading of the biblical text.

Scripture as Itinerary

Given the claim that scriptural reasoning establishes a real connection between events and characters in the Bible and in our own time, we thus return to the question of what Christians should seek to accomplish when they read the scriptures. What kind of activity properly counts as the primary form of interpreting Holy Writ? I have already argued that Hodge's storehouse of facts, Schleiermacher's repertoire of expressions for articulating religious experience, and Lindbeck's implicit map analogy are inadequate. Other possibilities have of course been put forward.

---

101. The literal, straightforward or "storybook" sense of the biblical text is not to be confused with what modern biblical criticism calls the historical sense. As Loughlin notes, this latter sense of the text is only recoverable when one steps "from the story to a critically reconstructed narrative, which in turn leads to the past. The historical sense is found not in the biblical stories, but in the narratives of critical historians" (Loughlin, *Telling God's Story*, 127).

102. For further details, see John J. O'Keefe and R. R. Reno, *Sanctified Vision: An Introduction to Early Christian Interpretation of the Bible* (Baltimore: Johns Hopkins University Press, 2005).

103. McClendon, *Doctrine*, 36, 40, 92–94.

Keven Vanhoozer, N. T. Wright, Francesca Aran Murphy, and Samuel Wells have proposed dramatic paradigms for the activity of interpreting the Bible. Wright, for example, speculates about what it would take to perform a heretofore unknown play of Shakespeare, and then extends his conclusions to the interpretation of scripture. Such models help to make explicit the dramatic nature of the biblical story and also highlight in an insightful and cogent way the improvisational nature of the interpretive task, which can be undertaken only by a skilled company of performers.[104]

Performative analogies such as these remind us that the decisive poles of the Christian interpretation of the scriptures are finally not written texts: the Bible on the one hand, and on the other the various forms of writing—sermons, commentaries, theology manuals, study guides, and even fictional works—that preachers, exegetes, theologians, and novelists produce, seemingly by the truckload. (This is not to say that these secondary texts are unimportant, only that they are complementary to and not constitutive of the fundamental form of scriptural reasoning within the body of Christ.) These poles are instead constituted by historical patterns of human action and passion: what was said, done, and suffered by those in ancient Israel, culminating with the incarnation and the founding of the early church, and what is said, done, and suffered by those who by faith have similarly been caught up in this apocalyptic mission with God.[105]

The "world of scripture" is not a clearly demarcated territory to be occupied, an esoteric code to be deciphered, a set of facts to be systematically arranged, or an alternative to life in the "real" world, but a historical world of action and encounter, the meaning of which is discovered and recovered in analogous patterns in our own times and circumstances.[106] The figural connection between past, present, and future—between, for example, the sacrifice of the Paschal Lamb and Jesus's crucifixion, or the exodus from Egypt and the end of slavery in the United States— is not grounded in extrinsic resemblance alone, but in an "inherent continuity" and "ontological bond" that is attributed to "the same divine will that is active in both situations and which, from stage to stage, is pursuing a single Design—the Design which is the real object of the Bible."[107] How, then, should we construe our reading of scripture so that these patterns and this design can best be discerned for our own lives?

In their respective discussions of what it means to interpret canonical texts, both Ochs and MacIntyre state that it involves bringing them into question. Whether explicitly or implicitly, the fact that we put the question to the Bible in our efforts to

104. Vanhoozer, *Drama of Doctrine*, 115–86; Wright, *The New Testament and the People of God*, 140–42; Francesca Aran Murphy, *The Comedy of Revelation: Paradise Lost and Regained in Biblical Narrative* (Edinburgh: T & T Clark, 2000); Samuel Wells, *Improvisation: The Drama of Christian Ethics* (Grand Rapids: Brazos, 2004), 52–53.

105. Lash, *Theology on the Way to Emmaus*, 42.

106. Williams, *On Christian Theology*, 30.

107. Lubac, *Scripture in the Tradition*, 37.

interpret it seems evident; the real issue is which questions we put to it. Williams, for example, uses a domestic analogy to generate questions, asking about the capacity of the gospel for being "at home" in more than one cultural setting, or, to use the same image in a slightly different, sports-oriented context, whether it is capable of "playing away from home." He contends that the capacity of scriptural reasoning to "play away from home" in different historical, linguistic, and cultural settings, to engage them both critically and constructively, cannot be assumed. It must instead constantly be shown "with all the varying enterprises of giving meaning to the human condition. . . . For the event of Christ to be authentically revelatory, it must be capable of both 'fitting' and 'extending' any human circumstance; it must be re-presentable, and the form and character of its re-presentation are not necessarily describable in advance."[108] The figure of "home" offers one insightful way of dealing with the need to read the church's scripture and its dogmatic and moral traditions in ever-changing situations.

We may also use to good effect the questions with which we began this book, and which seek to unpack the eschatological and apocalyptic vision that unites the various practices of the church: Where do we, members of Christ's body, stand? How did things happen in the past that gave rise to the way they are presently? In what ways should we take our bearings from the words and deeds of those who, relying on the grace and mercy of God, have gone before us? What is at hand in this time and place that we can use as we continue to make our way toward the New Jerusalem, cooperating as best we can with the earthly city in pursuit of those goods that are essential to human life now?

Given the eschatological trajectory of the apocalypse of God, it seems clear (certain dispensationalist readings notwithstanding) that the Bible provides nothing like a map that charts the precise path for us to follow into the future. What it does give us is the *travel itinerary* of God's people, that is, the story of their pilgrimage as strangers and foreigners through this world toward the kingdom of God. An itinerary is a distinctive type of narrative, involving a different symbolic representation of space and time from that of a modern map. As we have already noted, the map plots space on a uniform grid, collating heterogeneous places onto a homogeneous plane to form a synchronic picture of geographical knowledge. An itinerary, by contrast, consists of a series of performative descriptions designed to organize our movements through space: "to get to the shrine you go past the old fort and then turn right at the fork in the path." Of course these two ways of representing space need not be mutually exclusive. In narrations concerning streets, for example, narrative manipulations are dominant, and when the map form intervenes, it is typically conditioned by the narrative: "'If you turn to the right, there is . . . ,' or the closely related form, 'If you go straight ahead, you'll see . . .' In both cases, an action permits one to see something."[109]

108. Williams, *On Christian Theology*, xiv, 39, 142–43.
109. Certeau, *Practice of Everyday Life*, 119–20.

There are also cases in which a narrative itinerary assumes a place indication: "'There, there's a door, you take the next one'—an element of mapping in the presupposition of a certain itinerary." Early medieval maps were in actuality the rectilinear marking out of itineraries, providing performative markers (often in connection with pilgrimages) indicating cities along the route, places to stop and spend the night or pray, etc., and distances calculated in terms of the time it would take to cover the ground on foot. Certeau notes in particular a fifteenth-century Aztec map showing the exodus of the Totomihuacas that was in effect the log of their journey on foot, "an outline marked out by footprints with regular gaps between them and by pictures of the successive events that took place in the course of the journey (meals, battles, crossings of rivers or mountains, etc.): not a 'geographical map' but 'history book.'" To comprehend an itinerary adequately would ultimately require that we retrace its steps.[110]

Retracing the journey of those who have gone before us is an apt figure for describing the way scripture (the New Testament) reads scripture (the Old Testament). At times the figural reading of the Old Testament is subtle, for example, when a righteous man named Joseph is warned in a dream of impending and imminent danger, and he acts in a timely fashion to save his family from harm (Gen. 41:1–49; 45:4–5; 50:15–21; Matt. 2:13–15). At other times the reference to past events is far more explicit. In his first letter to the church at Corinth, Paul recalls certain events from the story of the exodus from Egypt, not as an academic exercise in historical reconstruction, but, as he says, "to instruct us, on whom the ends of the ages have met" (10:11). And in the Epistle to the Hebrews, the author recounts stories of the "cloud of witnesses" in the Old Testament as they obeyed God in faith, again not to offer a historical narrative that could be verified by the latest historiographical methods, but to provide "assurance of things hoped for, the conviction of things not seen" (11:1; cf. 12:1).

As the eleventh chapter in Hebrews unfolds, it becomes obvious that more than just simple assurance is being offered. In the extended discussion of Abraham and Sarah the author states,

> By faith Abraham obeyed when he was called to set out for a place that he was to receive as an inheritance; and he set out, not knowing where he was going. By faith he stayed for a time in the land he had been promised, as in a foreign land, living in tents, as did Isaac and Jacob, who were heirs with him of the same promise. For he looked forward to the city that has foundations, whose architect and builder is God (11:8–10).

Abraham, Sarah, and their offspring are then described as strangers and foreigners on the earth, seeking a homeland, not the land they left behind, but "a better country . . . a heavenly one. Therefore God is not ashamed to be called their God; indeed, he has prepared a city for them" (11:13–16).

110. Ibid.

What stands out in this renarration of the story of Abraham, Isaac, and Jacob, first, is the assertion that these nomads and herdsmen were looking for a "city." There is no mention in Genesis that they had ever intended to found or capture a city, leading us to suspect that the figure of "city" functions here, as it does throughout the New Testament, as a synecdoche for a political association of some kind. Our suspicions are confirmed when the author later states that we "have come to Mount Zion and to the city of the living God, the heavenly Jerusalem, and to innumerable angels in festal gathering," and that in this age "we have no lasting city, but we are looking for the city that is to come" (12:22; 13:14). Second, these ancestors of God's chosen nation are described as strangers and foreigners, not just in Canaan, but also "on the earth," again something that is not in the original account. The narration of the events that happened to Abraham and his immediate offspring as they made their way toward the Promised Land are not intended to be descriptive only of their adventure, for the author concludes with the statement that all those who make up this great cloud of witnesses are a reminder of the race that is set before us, with Jesus as "the pioneer and perfecter of our faith" (11:1–2).

As a kind of travel diary (whose author is ultimately God), the Bible recounts what patriarchs, priests, kings, prophets, apostles, saints, and sinners of Israel and the early church learned down through the centuries under the tutelage of the Holy Spirit about God, themselves, and the world. Initially, the journey was to the land promised to Abraham, Sarah, and their offspring, but as the story progresses toward the life, death, and resurrection of Christ, we learn that this is only the penultimate destination. In retrospect it becomes clear that God's people have been making their way to nothing less than a new heaven and a new earth, where God will wipe every tear from our eyes, and death will be no more, because the first things have passed away (Rev. 21:4).

For those of us who have been summoned by the Spirit to undertake the same journey as members of Christ's earthly-historical body, the account of previous generations serves as our guide. They traveled the way before us, and we are able to recognize in their stories something of the setting, characters, and plot of our own time and place (provided, of course, that we have been trained to see the world about us in this fashion). Though some of the features of the temporal landscape have changed to an extent or have been erased altogether, when taken together it is, nonetheless, still recognizably the same place: a fallen world awaiting the revelation of the daughters and sons of God. These stories, when taken together, provide us with a living and generative memory that guides us on our pilgrimage through the present age toward that eternal commonwealth whose founder and sovereign is the Triune God.

Scripture thus hands on (*traditio*) to us the cumulative wisdom and experience of past generations of prophets, apostles, and saints who embarked on a pilgrimage, not through space but through time, to receive as an inheritance a place, identified in the Sermon on the Mount as the earth itself (Matt. 5:5), all the while never knowing precisely what lay "behind" them as they made their way to the city that is to come. Our situation is no different, formally considered, from theirs. We too are summoned by the Triune God to set out for a place that we are to receive as an inheritance, and we must go out in faith to meet evil and grace, all the while not knowing what lies behind us as we join with this great cloud of witnesses making its way to the city of our God.

The generative memory recorded in the Bible is our itinerary, providing the imaginative figures and analogies that inform our reasoning and keep us moving in the right direction. When Fannie Lou Hamer said with authority that *this*—the state of affairs in Sunflower County, Mississippi, in July 1964—was *that*—the time of Israel's bondage in Egypt—she was using scripture to follow the path that God had set before Moses and was now setting before her and her sisters and brothers in Jesus throughout the South. When André Trocmé ascended his high pulpit and declared that the small village of Le Chambon must become a city of refuge for all those sought by the Vichy government, "lest innocent blood be shed" (Deut 19:10), he too understood what needed to be done, for he had taken his bearings from the great cloud of witnesses who had previously "trod the ground" on which he and his congregation now stood.

Scriptural reasoning is indeed foundational for the body of Christ, but it does not operate alone. The appearance of God's messianic regime in the midst of history proved so disruptive to established regimes of life and language, to the very being of humanity itself, that it took Jesus's followers centuries to develop adequate ways of saying what needed to be said about the significance of this event in relation to different times and places. New and contested uses were put to words such as *God* and *transcendence*, giving rise to complex questions that could not be resolved strictly within the scope of biblical imagery and narration. A tradition of doctrinal theology thus emerged as a constitutive practice of the church.

5

Doctrinally Speaking

Since as Jerome remarks . . . a heresy arises from words wrongly used, when we speak of the Trinity we must proceed with care and with befitting modesty.

Thomas Aquinas, *Summa Theologica*

In 1934 a church group in Germany, exuberant at Adolf Hitler's rise to power, promulgated the "Guiding Principles of the German Christian Church Movement (National Church Movement) in Thüringen," in which they declared that, among other things, there were two sources of revelation for "German Christians." One was "God's revelation in the Bible and the Fathers' testimony of faith." The New Testament is portrayed rather straightforwardly as "the holy testament of the Savior, our Lord, and of his Father's kingdom." The Old Testament is at first glance described rather oddly as "an example of the divine education of a people." With the next few sentences, however, the reason for doing so becomes clear: "As He has for every people, the eternal God has also created a unique law for our people. It has taken form in the Führer Adolf Hitler and in the National Socialist State formed by him. This law speaks to us in the history of our people, which arises from blood and soil. Fidelity to this law demands from us the struggle for honor and freedom."[1]

---

1. "Richtlinien der Kirchenbewegung 'Deutsche Christen' in Thüringen (vom 11 Dezember 1933) über die 'Deutsche Christliche Nationalkirche,'" in *Der Nationalsozialismus: Dokumente 1933–1945*, ed. Walther Hofer (Frankfurt am Main: Fischer, 1962), 131.

As shocking and scandalous as this sounds to our ears, standing as we do in the aftermath of the Shoah, the identification of an earthly social, political, or economic order with the will of God is actually part of an unfortunate yet consistent pattern in the history of Christian thought. In the fourth century, Eusebius of Caesarea wrote lavish orations in praise of Constantine, stating that God was "pleased to honor the author and cause of their obedience through a lengthened period of time; and, far from limiting his reign to three decennial circles of years, he extends it to the remotest period, even to far distant eternity."[2] He also reconfigured several Old Testament passages that had traditionally been read as messianic prophecies, so that with the emperor's conversion, "the ancient oracles and predictions of the prophets were fulfilled, more numerous than we can at present cite, and those especially which speak as follows concerning the saving Word. 'He shall have dominion from sea to sea, and from the river to the ends of the earth.' And again, 'In his days shall righteousness spring up; and abundance of peace.' 'And they shall beat their swords into plough-shares, and their spears into sickles: and nation shall not take up sword against nation, neither shall they learn to war any more'"[3]

Unfortunately, this tendency is not a matter of ancient history, safely tucked away in the past, for as I noted in the first chapter, several prominent theologians in the modern age have asserted that the institutions of liberal democracy and global capitalism have their source in the heavenly realms. Walter Rauschenbusch declared that the spread of democracy was a divinely inspired, supernatural phenomenon.[4] E. Y. Mullins stated in a similar vein that American political society was formed from the life-giving stream of water that flows from the throne of God down to all humankind.[5] And more recently Max Stackhouse unabashedly asserted that globalization is the direct work of God in history, a fulfillment of the prophetic oracles.[6]

Though Rauschenbusch's, Mullins's, and Stackhouse's ways of identifying the activity of God with the domain of the earthly city are a good deal less malevolent than that advocated by the German Christians, they all seek to commandeer the church's teaching, its doctrine, to further the interests and aims of their respective states. In the case of the German Christian movement, this abuse of the language of the faith did not go unchallenged. In May 1934 a dissenting group of pastors and theologians held a synod in the city of Barmen. Calling themselves the Confessing Church, these church leaders issued a declaration repudiating the kind of claims made by German Christian Church movement. At the forefront of what came to be called the Barmen Declaration was the assertion that "Jesus Christ, as he is attested to us in Holy Scripture, is the one Word of God whom we have to hear, and

2. Eusebius, *In Praise of Constantine* VI.2 (*NPNF²* 1.587).

3. Ibid. XVI.7, 606–7; cf. *History of the Church*, X.1.3, 6 (*NPNF²* 1.369). The biblical citations are from Ps. 72:7–8; Is. 2:4.

4. Rauschenbusch, *Christianizing the Social Order*, 23.

5. Mullins, *Axioms of Religion*, 274.

6. Stackhouse, "Public Theology and Political Theology in a Globalizing Era," 179.

whom we have to trust and obey in life and in death. We reject the false doctrine that the Church could and should recognize as a source of its proclamation, beyond and besides this one Word of God, yet other events, powers, historic figures and truths as God's revelation."[7] According to the Confessing Church, God has spoken no other word to the church, in Germany or anywhere else, that commands the faithfulness and obedience of the members of Christ's body.

The fact that the Confessing Church's repudiation of the German Christians took a doctrinal form provides an important clue to the principal role that doctrine properly plays in the body of Christ. Barmen, by invoking the traditional teaching of the church to reject one false confession explicitly (and the others by implication), reminds us that Christian doctrines are not a set of abstract beliefs from which individuals may pick and choose according to their predetermined tastes and prejudices to fashion personalized worldviews, indisputable propositions that must be accepted without question, or the deliverance of disinterested, speculative metaphysical inquiry. To borrow N. T. Wright's trenchant description of the nature of Jewish convictions in the first century CE, the trinitarian and christological affirmations of Barmen constitute a battle cry, "a polemical statement directed outwards against the pagan nations,"[8] or rather, in this case, the pagans who had colonized the Christian community. As the struggles of the Diaspora Jewish community and the church struggle in Nazi Germany demonstrate, doctrine has a crucial role to play in the church's mission to be "a people who find in Christ their center, in the Spirit their communion, in God's reign their rule of life."[9]

In the modern and postmodern eras, however, the synod at Barmen has proven to be the exception. Christian doctrine has fallen on hard times, a fact that in and of itself is symptomatic of the fragmented state of the body of Christ. In generations past the mere suggestion that sound teaching about God and all that is God's was incidental to the mission of the church or to the viability of the gospel would have been dismissed as the babbling of a confused or demented mind. Over the last few centuries, however, the credibility and relevance of the church's doctrinal heritage has been under assault from multiple directions. Seventeenth-century Pietism associated doctrine with a moribund scholasticism (which regrettably was all too true) and concluded that it had little or nothing to do with the cultivation of a genuine personal piety (which, even more regrettably, is false).[10] Enlightenment philosophers, historians, and textual critics placed traditional Christian teaching alongside their newly developed standards of

---

7. "The Barmen Declaration," in *Creeds of the Churches*, ed. John H. Leith (Atlanta: John Knox, 1963, 1973), 518–22.

8. Wright, *Who Was Jesus?* 49.

9. McClendon, *Doctrine*, 21.

10. According to Count Nicolas Ludwig von Zinzendorf, for example, "Religion can be grasped without the conclusions of reason; otherwise no one could have religion except the person with intelligence. . . . Religion must be a matter which is able to be grasped through experience alone without any concepts"

reason and found them wanting (it would take several centuries for postmodern authors to demonstrate that by these same standards modern conceptions of reason were nothing more than manifestations of the will to power). In recent years many Christians see doctrine solely as a source of division within their communities (though as Dietrich Bonhoeffer points out, in the United States, "where the question of truth is not the criterion of church communion and church division, disintegration is greater than anywhere else"[11]). And with the increasing popularity of therapeutic and consumerist forms of religion, intellectual rigor concerning questions of truth, goodness, and beauty strikes others as somehow beside the point.

As a people caught up in the apocalypse of Jesus Christ, seeking to define itself over against false and indecorous teaching so that it might be a distinct witness to a world under the dominion of death,[12] the Christian community must recognize and recover the proper role of doctrine in its life together. Without these shared convictions (which do not eliminate disagreement and debate but locate them within an intelligible context), the church cannot be the church, cannot have a distinctive identity in a fallen world as the body of Christ, and without a healthy church body the existence of its members will invariably be assimilated into the body politic of the earthly city. When the church abandons the struggle for the rectitude of doctrine, for the adequacy of its convictions, it gives up the quest for truth (together with beauty and goodness) as hopeless, and in the process gives up on hope itself. When this happens, the body of Christ is completely at the mercy of the rulers and authorities and their seductive power.

The work of doctrinal theologians is not to supplant the traditional language of the church against those who challenge its sense and veracity in a misguided effort to resuscitate Christian practice (which in any case is something that only the Spirit can do), nor is it to undertake "a series of salvage operations . . . to show how one can still believe in Jesus Christ, and not violate an ideal of intellectual integrity."[13] Indeed, when Christian speech about God depends on theological performance for its vitality and verisimilitude, writes Mark McIntosh, we shall likely talk about a deity other than the God of Israel.[14] The church does itself no favors when it expects theologians to shelter claims to the truthfulness of its convictions from the unrelenting dialectic of intellectual inquiry. If the truth claims of Christ's

---

(Count Nicolas Ludwig von Zinzendorf, "Thoughts for the Learned and Yet Good-Willed Students of Truth," 1–2, in *Pietists: Selected Writings*, ed. Peter C. Erb [New York: Paulist, 1983], 291).

11. He goes on to argue that "precisely where the struggle for the right creed is not the factor which governs everything, the unity of the church is more distant than where the creed alone unites and divides the churches" (Dietrich Bonhoeffer, *Collected Works of Dietrich Bonhoeffer*, vol. 1, ed. Edwin H. Robinson, *No Rusty Swords: Letters, Lectures and Notes 1928–1936* [New York: Harper & Row, 1965], 96–97).

12. Ibid., 324.

13. Van Austin Harvey, *The Historian and the Believer: The Morality of Historical Knowledge and Christian Belief* (Toronto: Macmillan, 1966), 104.

14. McIntosh, *Mystical Theology*, 15.

ecclesial body cannot hold their own in the *agon* of critical disputation, then we should have the courage to discard them forever.[15]

This is not to say that Christians must hold hat in hand and wait meekly upon the judgment of secular skeptics to validate their witness. The truthfulness of Christian convictions (truth, as the good of the mind, is the product first of all of imagination) cannot be conclusively demonstrated or discredited theoretically. The job of the doctrinal theologian is instead to identify and explicate the grammar that informs these truth claims. The verisimilitude of the claims themselves, however, can be manifested only in the laboratory of history, for only there do we have the opportunity to see the goodness, truthfulness, and beauty of human life and language adequately tested. It is in the coming to be and the passing away of human existence that truthfulness can "be practically, imperfectly, partially and provisionally *shown* by the character and quality of Christian engagement in patterns of action and suffering, praise and endurance, that refuse to short-cut the quest by the erection of conceptual or institutional absolutes."[16]

The purpose of church doctrine, then, is not to tell us of God, Jesus, the Spirit, the world we presently inhabit and the world that is to come. That is the work of scriptural reasoning. It is instead to tell us of the significance of these matters, both with respect to its own internal coherence and in relation to competing accounts of what is finally true, good, and beautiful. What follows in this chapter obviously cannot provide a comprehensive account of the nature of doctrine as such. Indeed, it is not self-evident that what is needed at this point in time is some such account. Instead, I shall attempt to sketch the role that doctrine plays in relationship to the other practices, in particular to scriptural reasoning, which when taken together are needed to reconstitute and reinvigorate the church as the body of Christ.

Doctrine, Experience, and Convictions

Christian convictions about God, the world, and the relationship between them, which were painstakingly cultivated over several centuries, once formed an integral aspect of the hermeneutical practice that constituted the body of Christ. Over the past few centuries, however, these doctrines gradually became deracinated systems of belief divorced from the other practices and virtues of the church. The shared beliefs of the Christian community were no longer tied to the church's public worship and work but were transformed into free-floating, interchangeable sets of ideas from which individuals could pick and choose according to their personal tastes.

15. This, I take it, is the burden of Denys Turner's superb book *Faith, Reason and the Existence of God*. With the pronouncement of the First Vatican Council that God can be known with certainty by the natural power of human reason as his point of departure, Turner contends that Christians should think, as a matter of faith, that the existence of God is rationally demonstrable.

16. Lash, *Theology on the Way to Emmaus*, 116.

Theologians have labored diligently to stem this trend and reclaim the proper role of doctrine within the communal formation of Christian life and witness, with varying degrees of success. Some tried to insulate the church's core convictions from the messiness of language, history, and politics by describing them as a set of timeless propositions unrelated to particular times and places, "like truth-functions in a computer."[17] Thus understood, it is not surprising that many both within and outside the church regard these claims as extrinsic appeals to an unchallengeable authority revealed from some elusive "beyond."[18] The usual suspects in this regard are theologians of a conservative bent, but efforts to circumvent the difficult learning curve that comes with the process of disagreement, debate, ambiguity, and puzzlement that constitutes a living tradition cannot be limited to fundamentalists, with their compendia of infallible propositions, and neo-scholastics with their dogmatic manuals. It also holds true of those who formulate doctrinal propositions around one of the most widely used, yet ambiguous concepts in the working vocabulary of classic liberal theology: experience.

At one time this notion of experience typically referred to what a woman or man had lived through and lived out in company with others, and how she or he was shaped and transformed by what happened over the course of time. It involved the acquisition of a certain set of convictions and virtues, particularly that of prudence, and thus its most distinctive and enduring feature had to do with what we *learned* about the timely character of our lives within the communal narratives that encompass our practices of life and language.[19] This public conception of experience designated "the enduring or timely aspect of our lives in relation to God and one another; as plot and character in some setting, it is the stuff of narrative."[20] As a theological notion it properly pertained to "the *ecclesial experience* of being drawn into the pattern of Jesus' life and his relationship with the One he called 'Abba.'"[21] In this sense of the term, *experience* was always "textual," always embodied, always embedded in some form of community, always part of a learning process, and always part of an interpreting and interpreted process, capable of critically examining its theoretical presuppositions. References to experience were regularly made in the first-person plural voice: here is how things seem to us.[22]

When modern theologians use the notion of experience, however, they often put into play a very different set of meanings. In keeping with the turn to the

17. James Wm. McClendon Jr., *Biography as Theology: How Life Stories Can Remake Today's Theology* (Nashville: Abingdon, 1974), 37.

18. For a trenchant critique of the use of revelation as an appeal to an unchallengeable authority from some elusive beyond, see Leo Strauss, *The Rebirth of Classical Political Rationalism: An Introduction to the Thought of Leo Strauss*, particularly part 3, "The Dialogue between Reason and Revelation" (Chicago: University of Chicago Press, 1989), 185–270.

19. Lash, *Easter in Ordinary*, 91.

20. McClendon, *Ethics*, 37.

21. McIntosh, *Mystical Theology*, 41, my emphasis.

22. One thinks of the "vision" that Augustine shared with his mother, Monica, at Ostia in *Confessions* IX.10.

subject, the concept is used to refer to something that ostensibly happens to an individual apart from her or his participation in social networks of communication, production and exchange. This ostensive happening is masterfully summarized by Rowan Williams as "some isolable core of encounter, unmediated awareness of the transcendent, buried beneath the accidental forms of historical givenness, a trans-cultural, pre-linguistic, inter-religious phenomenon."[23] Whatever this something is, then, it occurs to individuals in their solitude and prior to their bodily engagement with others: discrete inner sensations, momentary states of ecstasy, heightened awareness, or emotional intensity. These "conscious mental goings-on," as Richard Swinburne calls them,[24] are theoretically bracketed from the complex polysemy of the events and encounters that form the temporal nexus of human life and language and are treated as "spontaneous," pre-thematized givens. In this sense of the term, appeals to "experience" as the rational warrants for doctrine are of a piece with propositional accounts of revelation that claim to deliver "non-worldly truths to human beings in pretty well unambiguous terms."[25]

Over against these attempts to reduce church doctrine to a collection of timeless truth-functions delivered in a nonworldly fashion or as a set of symbols giving expression to private states of ecstatic intensity, I would argue that doctrinal teaching partakes of a process that, in conjunction with the imagination, serves to orchestrate our bodily actions and affections as members joined to one another in the body of Christ as in a natural body. Doctrine consists of first-order convictions that are unintelligible apart from the ecclesial practices that mediate our story-shaped interactions with the world wherein we live, move, and have our being. Convictions are always situated in medias res, in the middle of things, as part of a distinctive practice of life and language that is already always there, a practice that *is* a shared interpretation of human life lived in the world as it is presently ordered, and only as such is it lived before God.

The vital function of doctrine as a first-order discourse is to give shape and definition to the way the members of Christ's body inhabit and interact with the world. There is no believing without informed reasoning on the part of disciples about what is believed, that is, without the ability to follow the signs revealed in the events of nature and history back to their *arche* and *telos* in the triune life of God. The ascent of the mind to God, however, is neither a private experience nor an end in itself, but an integral aspect of the pilgrimage of the gathered church through the material and social world of the present age to the city that is to come. Doctrine's primary context is therefore the ever-unfolding life and witness of the Christian community, having essentially to do with what

23. Williams, *On Christian Theology*, 131. Peter Hodgson states, for example, "The *radical, root* character of [religious] experience is usually concealed in the mundaneness of everyday existence, as is the potentially revelatory power of experience" (Hodgson, *Winds of the Spirit*, 11).

24. Richard Swinburne, *The Existence of God* (Oxford: Oxford University Press, 1979), 244.

25. Williams, *On Christian Theology*, 131.

the church must teach to be the body of Christ now. The loss or neglect of key Christian convictions can therefore "seriously impair, even defeat, the very existence of a church."[26]

The function of church doctrine should be distinguished from the work of doctrinal theology as a second-order discourse, which is to exercise word care over the convictional utterances Christians make in the course of living and working together before God and in the company of our non-Christian neighbors.[27] Within the church there are some formally recognized as theologians, who come to the fore as distinct and identifiable figures in situations of disagreement and confusion, when "meanings have become entangled with one another, when there is a felt tension between images or practices, when a shape has to be drawn out so that the community's practice can be effectively communicated."[28] Their job is therefore to make explicit the hidden assumptions and unstated inferences embedded in our convictions, untangle the many confusions and inconsistencies in which the church can frequently become ensnared, assess various claims and assertions over against the church's other constitutive practices so as to guard against stereotypical drift, and unmask convenient but misleading impressions and generalizations.[29]

Doctrines, Convictions, and Character

If we are rightly to understand the respective roles that doctrine and doctrinal theology play in the ongoing life of the church, we must first attend to the nature of convictional belief and utterance. According to James McClendon and James Smith, convictions are those persistent beliefs that a person or community will not easily relinquish, indeed which cannot be relinquished without that person or that community coming to have a significantly different character than before.[30] Our convictions define who we are and what we do as human beings, both individually and corporately. In contrast to opinions, which are occasional habits of mind, convictions comprise a constituent and enduring feature of our character. As such they are marked by a delicate play between continuity and change. They not only persist over long periods of time but also have the capacity to resist challenges to their rectitude. To be shaped by a set of convictions is to be *convinced*, such that those so persuaded will consider changing one or more of them only after a good deal of debate and persuasion.

26. McClendon, *Doctrine*, 24.

27. On this notion of word care, see Nicholas Lash, "Ministry of the Word or Comedy and Philology," *New Blackfriars* 68 (1987): 472–83.

28. Williams, *On Christian Theology*, xii.

29. David B. Burrell, CSC, *Aquinas: God and Action* (London: Routledge & Kegan Paul, 1979), 178n17.

30. McClendon and Smith, *Convictions*, 87; cf. McClendon, *Ethics*, 22–23, and *Doctrine*, 29.

Beliefs that rise to the level of convictions are therefore also significant, giving distinctive and characteristic shape to the sense and direction of our lives. I may believe with utter and intense fervor that my favorite college basketball team will win the national championship this year or that my preferred political party will prevail in an upcoming election, but if it turns out that I was mistaken about such matters, who I am and what I do will probably not change substantially. Unlike idle musings, casual observations, or offhand conjectures, then, convictions govern a wide scope of thought and conduct on the part of those convinced by them. To believe in the God of Israel in this sense, for example, is not merely to assent to the proposition that there is such a deity or that the God Christians are called to worship and serve is the only real God. As scripture points out, even the demons believe that.[31] It is rather, says Augustine, "in believing to love, in believing to delight, in believing to walk towards him, and be incorporated amongst the limbs or members of his body."[32]

Convictions are relatively stable beliefs (as is the intellectual and moral character of most people most of the time), but they can and do change over time (as people also tend to do over the course of their lifetime). When our convictions are modified in a substantial way, so are we. Conversely, when we realize later on in life that we are not the same persons we once were, it is almost always because our convictions have changed to some degree, if only in our understanding of their scope and significance. Convictions therefore do not constitute a hermetically sealed system of concepts or symbols that subsists in some sort of timeless stasis. They instead develop over time "in a constant process of adjustment to external as well as internal pressure . . . Convictions make us what we are, but what we are does itself change."[33]

Men and women initially form their convictions (and with them their identities, their loves, and their fears) within those contingent networks of social relationships into which they were born, and then they continue to refine them, in more or less implicit ways, throughout their lives. At birth we inherit a set of beliefs along with the roles we will play at various points in our lives—sibling, cousin, child, and grandchild within a household or clan, member of a village and tribe, citizen of a nation-state, and consumer in the global market. In addition to the informal webs of beliefs that subsist within the common life of a community, there are also formal practices that cultivate in more explicit ways these shared convictions. These can be as simple as schoolchildren singing the national anthem every morning, or as elaborate as the processes of catechesis and spiritual formation practiced by Christian communities. These relationships and convictions are integral to our identities as persons and communities, defining

---

31. James 2:19.

32. Augustine, *Commentary on John*, xxix, trans. Lash, *Believing Three Ways in One God*, 20. Note that in this statement the cognitive dimension of faith is not isolated from either its affective or the communal facets.

33. McClendon and Smith, *Convictions*, 108.

partially at least and sometimes wholly our obligations and duties, challenges and opportunities. To be a person is "to find oneself placed at a certain point on a journey with set goals; to move through life is to make progress—or to fail to make progress—toward a given end."[34]

Because convictions define not only who we are but also what we love and fear, the notion that somebody "holds" or "has" convictions can be misleading. As an idiomatic convention this expression is relatively benign, and perhaps in certain respects even necessary. It can, however, imply that an identifiable ego or self exists apart from some social network of relationships and language and is able to pick and choose which beliefs to include in its own personal worldview. It may also suggest that the mere holding of convictions is an end in itself, rather than seeing them as correlates of intellectual and moral character that constantly come into play as we make our way through this world toward the age to come. It is therefore more precise to say that we *are* our convictions, both individually and corporately, and therefore the concept of a human person or community is empty apart from "the sort of persistence through time that convictions alone provide."[35] It is only because we partake of a particular set of convictions (among other things) that we persist though time and inhabit certain places with a coherent identity, or, to put it somewhat differently, it is due to our convictions we exist *as* persons and *as* communities. To "have" a set of convictions, then, is simply to be persons or a community that displays some form of intellectual and moral character, in terms of which we are engaged over time with the world in all its complexity.[36]

We do not therefore choose our convictions, because there is no identifiable self, no person existing prior to our inhabiting some complex of beliefs and dispositions. The picture of a being that is essentially unencumbered by such things as convictions and yet somehow capable of evaluating competing claims to her or his assent is a metaphysical illusion. It is only on the basis of convictions that already in some way compel our assent that we are even capable of recognizing and assessing competing claims. We therefore evaluate these claims on the basis of convictions we already inhabit, and if we modify or change our beliefs, it will be because something—for example, a series of events or a influential person—has made a compelling case that finally persuades us. What counts as evidence for a conviction, and which procedures we use to evaluate what we have thereby certified as evidence, are matters that are always already shaped by convictions. Because these are persistent and significant beliefs, we do not readily revise them or find ourselves persuaded by new beliefs. But in the exchanges that take place in the arena of contested convictions that is the world we inhabit, our convictions can and often do change in ways both large and small, and for good and for evil.[37]

34. MacIntyre, *After Virtue*, 33–34.
35. McClendon and Smith, *Convictions*, 87, 105–6.
36. Ibid., 176.
37. Ibid., 176, 178, 183.

There is, simply put, no surplus of self- or communal identity over and above our convictions. This does not mean that women and men never entertain doubts about who they are or what they love or fear, or that once acquired they never modify their convictions. Those who are no longer sure what their convictions are, or who rebel against the conventions of their community, are who they are because of the communal web of convictions about which they are confused or against which they strive. Without a coherent set of convictions it becomes increasingly difficult to act consistently and coherently in the business of living in the untidy world of everyday existence. People may sporadically perform particular acts of kindness, stumble from time to time across some flash of insight, or on occasion name the things they encounter in the world truthfully, but "these will be only reactions to particular circumstances, not expressions of settled or identifiable character. One is thus, in a way, the victim of these circumstances, just as a boat having freeboard but no sail or anchor is the victim of every chance wind."[38] A community without convictional coherence and stability over time will similarly dissolve under the pressure of its immediate social environment.[39]

Incidentally, the need to give our assent to some set of convictions is clearly not confined to those whose stance in the world is generally regarded as "religious."[40] Those who believe the good life is to be obtained through the pursuit of material wealth can truthfully be said to love, delight, and participate in the social institutions that make such a pursuit possible. And when the authors of the *Humanist Manifesto 2000* assert that the methods of science, though not infallible, are "on balance . . . the most reliable methods we have for expanding knowledge and solving human problems,"[41] they are giving voice to intellectual and moral beliefs that form the basis of their involvement in everyday life. In both cases a claim is being made in the arena of contested convictions about ourselves and about the world. And just like all other claims to our assent, the truth of these must in some way be justified.

Convictions thus function as counterparts to the virtues in the formation and transformation of character; indeed, they presuppose each other.[42] Our convictions are always already vested in the cultivation of the moral and intellectual (and for Christians, the theological) virtues, while these traits, to the extent that we have acquired them, are always already shaped and directed by our convictions. To rework a Kantian motto, without convictions the virtues are empty,

38. Ibid., 106.

39. Ibid., 108. On the other hand, "a totally ossified community is a contradiction in terms: in a changing world, an unchanging community acquires a new environment, natural and human, thus a new set of relations to the world" (ibid.).

40. To say that we "give" our assent to a set of convictions can lead to the same kind of misconceptions that saying we "have" convictions does. We give our assent to our convictions in the act of existing as temporal creatures, an "act" that may or may not be consciously articulated in particular speech acts.

41. Paul Kurtz, "Humanist Manifesto 2000: A Call for a New Planetary Humanism," *Free Inquiry* 19, vol. 4 (Fall 1999): 8.

42. See McClendon, *Biography as Theology*, 34.

and without the virtues convictions are blind.[43] Hope in and for the future, for example, is a virtue that is necessary to sustain life over time, yet it is never unformed. It always has some content, some sense of how things will go, however inchoate that content may be.[44] In similar fashion, courage or fortitude, which Aristotle associated with the warrior, finds its exemplar within the Christian tradition in the martyr.[45]

The convictional set of a person or community, working in concert with the practical and intellectual virtues, thus forms the cross-section of mind at a particular point in the life's story of that person or community. *Mind* here does not refer to some sort of interior substance, the "real me" that stands in sharp juxtaposition to the "external" material world. It has to do instead with the working capacity human beings have for performing complex operations with signs (intellect, intelligence, or reason) and for pursuing rational goals (will).[46] Through these discursive transactions and volitional pursuits, we interact with the world about us in a variety of ways: identifying, reidentifying, relating, collecting, separating, classifying, and naming. We do not perform these speech acts sporadically or arbitrarily, but in the course of touching, grasping, pointing, breaking down, building up, calling to, answering to, communing with, and, of particular interest to our present concerns, stance-taking and bearing witness with respect to the intrusion of God's messianic regime into the world.[47]

By "stance-taking" McClendon and Smith mean, among other things, the taking up of certain patterns of behavior (including use of language) in relation to the human situation, an act of interpretation that occurs in connection with the exercise of certain roles within the community, first of all as worshiper. The stance of someone who testifies that "God led Israel across the Sea of Reeds" is thus that "of one who remembers and is heir to the storied crossing of the Sea of Reeds and who therein is committed to God and to his fellow-heirs."[48] One learns what it means to take up this stance through catechesis, where the activity of handing over, explanation, and repetition of the creed (*traditio, explanatio, redditio symboli*) locates the baptismal candidate within the world of time and space before God.[49] Subsequent liturgical acts serve, then, to remind the faithful of the stance that was instituted by their baptism.

---

43. The line in Kant is, "Thoughts without content are empty, intuitions without concepts are blind," which is sometimes rendered as, "Concepts without percepts are empty, percepts without concepts are blind" (Kant, *Critique of Pure Reason*, B75, 93).

44. See in this regard McClendon, *Ethics*, 106.

45. Aristotle, *Nicomachean Ethics* III.8; Aquinas, *Summa Theologica*, IIa. IIae. 124.

46. See Kenny, *Aquinas On Mind*, 15.

47. MacIntyre, *Whose Justice? Which Rationality?* 356. The conventions that govern these activities form the primary condition of a followable speech act (McClendon and Smith, *Convictions*, 57–56).

48. McClendon and Smith, *Convictions*, 63.

49. Cheslyn Jones, Geoffrey Wainwright, Edward Yarnold, SJ, and Paul Bradshaw, eds., *The Study of Liturgy*, rev. ed. (New York: Oxford University Press, 1992), 133.

The interpretive activity of witnessing pertains to the sign quality attending the act of stance-taking. "The witness is called," write McClendon and Smith, "not to lecture or to argue, but to testify. She tells us not so much what she thinks as where she is, where she finds herself." The witness sets out to show all who would listen where she finds herself in time and space, and on the basis of what she shows us, "we can infer something about the way things are, the way the world is."[50] Her testimony arises from what has happened to her and what she has done in the course of engaging the natural and social world, and thus it discloses in a dramatic way the sort of world she inhabits along with the rest of us. Her witness is offered to all as a sign of the way the world now is *and will be*. To testify, therefore, is to display something of the way things are and the ways they are being worked out. Her testimony shows us the person in action, and gives an account of all that shapes and directs her in that time and place.[51]

If we are then to understand the convictions of others that determine who they are, what they love and what they fear, we must do so in relation to the associations within which they routinely occupy a number of social (i.e., political, cultural, and economic) roles, and which routinely change to some extent over time. Conversely, the convictions shared by a community over time manifest themselves only in the words, deeds, and relationships of those that are its members and therefore formed by its common life and language. The sense and coherence of these actions are in turn articulated in terms of a narrative history that those who share this understanding of human life tell and retell, and in the telling become characters within it. The narrative of a community "is the glue that binds its convictions into one set."[52] (As we shall see shortly, the appeal to narrative as that which holds the convictions of a community together can itself become a contested matter.)

It is only as we are caught up in these story-formed communities, cultivating shared (and from time to time contested) convictions about human life as lived in relation to some set of goods, that we learn what it means "to make a move in the human situation in which we along with others are engaged."[53] As the dispositional cross-section of character that develops over time, these beliefs are both consequence and cause of our unfolding engagements within the particular situations in which we find ourselves. Convictions come into play as we enact an almost infinite variety of moves in the dramatic setting in which we along with others are cast, mostly directly, in particular expressions of speech. These convictional utterances, however, can be finally understood only with reference to "the full range of actions of the person or community that is convinced by them."[54]

---

50. McClendon and Smith, *Convictions*, 64.

51. Ibid., 64–65. For Christians, these matters are worked out in fear and trembling, for we are convinced that it is God who is at work in and through our engagement in the human situation (Phil. 2:28).

52. McClendon and Smith, *Convictions*, 176.

53. McClendon, *Ethics*, 335.

54. McClendon and Smith, *Convictions*, 17.

Finally, the convictions that define our identities, our loves, and our fears are embedded in relations of power, that is, the ability to pursue some end. Though we often speak of power as though it were a property or substance that could be held or possessed, such notions are misleading.[55] In the domain of human affairs power is mediated as the effect of an entire set of motivated practices that are dispersed and heterogeneous, constantly circulating through a complex array of overlapping institutional alignments that inscribe their movements and orientations on the people who inhabit them.[56] These overlapping configurations form a field of social power within which men and women carry out their daily tasks and exchanges with one another.[57]

Because convictions are so central to our identities as human beings, it comes as no surprise that the question of which doctrines a community should espouse and teach is frequently contested. The church is not exempt from this rule. Over the course of its history interpretive questions have regularly emerged that have resisted easy resolution, and our time is no different. Such disputes give rise to the need for explicit word care in the form of doctrinal theology, a second-order discourse that attends to these questions. What constitutes doctrinal theology has also become a contested issue that must be addressed, a task to which we now turn.

Convictions and Doctrinal Theology

From the beginning the teaching of prophets, apostles, and elders (and of course, Jesus) has played an integral role within the gathered church as it makes its way to the city of God. It is from these teachings that Christian doctrines subsequently developed. Not that doctrinal development came easily or quickly, for as Williams points out, the conviction that Jesus is the Word of God in a decisive sense does not make a dimly apprehended God in Jewish teaching clear to us.[58] As we have noted, the appearance of God's messianic regime in the midst of history proved so disruptive to established regimes of life and language, to the very being of humanity itself, that it took Jesus's followers centuries to develop adequate ways of saying what needed to be said about the significance of this event in relation to different times and places. New uses had to be put to such words as *God* and *transcendence*, so that they could speak clearly and persuasively about the One whom all human beings had to hear, and whom they must trust and obey in life and death.

They discovered, for example, that the ensemble of ideas and images from the Bible, which testify among other things that God delivered the people of Israel

55. Once again we need to recall how difficult it is to get outside of the pictures that hold us captive because they reside in our language, which then seems to repeat them to us "inexorably" (Wittgenstein, *Philosophical Investigations*, para. 115, 48e).

56. Asad, *Genealogies of Religion*, 35.

57. See Clegg, *Frameworks of Power*.

58. Williams, *On Christian Theology*, 138.

from their bondage in Egypt and raised the Israelite Jesus of Nazareth from the dead, presupposes a conception of how the world came into being, how it now is, and how it will finally turn out. They recognized that scriptural reasoning about God revolved around the creation question inherited from their Jewish forebears, and to lose sight of it was "to settle for worshipping an inhabitant of the world, to betray the biblical inheritance and to regress to a worship of the gods; it is a form of idolatry."[59] The abiding sense and significance of this question within the overall scheme of life lived in relation to the God of Israel, however, was not self-evident. Scripture only gestures to the paradigmatic setting within which the events it depicts, together with every creature involved in the hopes and struggles of nature and history, take place. Since that setting is not fully specified, the church puts the biblical texts to a series of questions that must be answered if the story is to be faithfully explicated. As a result of this process of inquiry, a theoretical level emerges from the level of narrative as a distinctive discourse. Once the interpretive grammar for this story has been put to the question, the theoretical process cannot be recalled.[60]

This process is already under way in the texts of the New Testament. We see it at work, for example, in Paul's declaration that "in Christ God was reconciling the world to himself" (2 Cor. 5:19). But this assertion only raises further questions. How was God "in" Christ? Did it differ from the way God was in the people of Israel? Was it analogous to the way God is in the processes of the physical universe, or in the person and rule of the emperor? Is it possible that something similar to the recapitulation in Christ of all things in heaven and on earth (Eph. 1:10) might occur in other persons, events or communities? Can we anticipate similar acts of God in others, or did God's reconciling activity in Christ differ qualitatively from all other occasions past or future, forming a "middle point" of history in relation to which all other events, persons, and communities are ultimately judged? The prologue to the Gospel of John sought to answer such questions by identifying Christ with the Logos of God, but even this move, though invaluable to later doctrinal construction, did not by itself prove sufficient. Was this Word of God made flesh in Christ merely a contingent expression of God's will, as Arius appears to have thought, or is it somehow constitutive of the inner life of God?

In a process that would eventually take centuries to work out in its details, the church addressed the interpretive questions about the paradigmatic setting for the story of Jesus through the doctrines of the Trinity and the incarnation. They do not tell us of Jesus's life, "but of the significance of his life."[61] The doctrine of the Trinity specifies that the words and deeds of Christ are of unsurpassable significance, because in this man the One who calls all things into being and into communion was working in a unique and definitive manner, establishing a concrete point of

59. McCabe, *God Matters*, 43–44.
60. Milbank, *Theology and Social Theory*, 383. I am indebted to Milbank for much of what follows.
61. McCabe, *God Matters*, 58.

reference for assessing all other words and deeds, regardless of whether they come before or after the historical existence of Jesus of Nazareth. Without denying the mystery, simplicity, and oneness of the God of Israel, they determined after years of deliberation that the only way to do justice to all that Jesus did and suffered was to speak of the incarnate Word as both very God and very human. In the words of Ignatius of Antioch, Christ "is the mouth . . . by which the Father has truly spoken."[62] The doctrine of the incarnation states that God joined the divine nature to the day-to-day realities of human existence in Jesus of Nazareth in order to re-create its shattered bone and torn sinew, so that women and men might share in the life-giving activity of God. Without effacing the difference between the speaker and the word spoken, the church taught that it was *God* who appeared in the particular events and circumstances of this man's life and work to gather together what had been dispersed and corrupted by humankind's disobedience.

The church's take on the nature of the world and of humankind in particular is inextricably tied up with a sustained engagement with the divine Logos made flesh that only takes place in the power of the Spirit within the body of Christ. The Christian concern with truth thus has less to do with technical questions involving the nature of knowledge or being as such that occupy professional philosophers,[63] and more with "the need to preserve the possibility of the kind of encounter with the truth-telling Christ that stands at the source of the Church's identity."[64] Church teaching that attends to our knowledge *about* God is properly grounded in the community's encounter with the living mystery, that is, the knowledge *of* the Triune God that participates in his own self-knowledge in Christ. Theoretical concepts are never ends in themselves, but always "at the service of a deeper immersion in the *res,* the thing itself, the mystery of Christ and of the practice of the Christian life."[65] This is why for Aquinas the formal object of *sacra doctrina* is not church doctrine as such, but all that is revealed to us in Jesus Christ under the aspect of God, *sub ratione Dei,* "either because they are God Himself; or because they refer to God as their beginning and end."[66]

Such doctrines are so crucial for the ongoing life of a community that they rise to a high level of generality. McClendon and Smith refer to such generality as a presiding conviction. Another example of a presiding conviction is the belief that, "(This) God exists."[67] The parenthetical demonstrative pronoun modifies the

62. Ignatius of Antioch, *Epistle to the Romans* 8 (*ANF* 1:77). Williams paraphrases Ignatius's statement here as "he is himself 'what the Father says'" (Williams, *Wound of Knowledge,* 19).

63. Turner observes that there is a discernible trend, even in Aquinas's time, to identify *intellectus* with *ratio* or the power of ratiocination or philosophical argument, thus associating "both 'intellect' and 'reason' with the dry impotence of the 'academic,'" and setting up the unfavorable contrast between sterile theological knowledge of the "schoolmen" and the warmth of the pietists (Turner, *Faith, Reason and the Existence of God,* 77).

64. Williams, *On Christian Theology,* 82.

65. Robert Louis Wilken, *The Spirit of Early Christian Thought: Seeking the Face of God* (New Haven, CT: Yale University Press, 2003), xviii.

66. Aquinas, *Summa Theologica* Ia.1.7., 5; cf. Turner, *Faith, Reason and the Existence of God,* 39.

67. McClendon and Smith, *Convictions,* 95–96.

claim of divine existence by specifying that this conviction refers, not to a generic concept of deity, but to the one who delivered Israel from Egypt and raised Jesus from the dead, that is, the Trinity. Without these presiding convictions, which each new generation of believers must reclaim, the identity of the church as the body of Christ would change radically. The church must therefore teach these doctrines to the members of each new generation, and they must understand the significance of these doctrines, if they are to be the church in their time and place.[68]

Presiding convictions thus have to do with the much-misunderstood concept of dogma. Robert Jenson writes in this regard, "Every theological proposition states a historic choice: 'To be speaking the gospel, let us henceforward say 'F' rather than that other possibility 'G.' A dogmatic choice is one by which the church so decisively determines her own future that if the choice is wrongly made, the community determined by that choice is no longer in fact the community of the gospel; thus no church thereafter exists to reverse the decision." This is why there are few dogmas, "for there have been few occasions on which the church has found it both necessary and possible to speak to her members in the ultimately committed fashion."[69]

In the course of explicating scripture's testimony to Jesus's ministry, passion, and triumph through the development of its doctrines, the early church was compelled to come to terms with the pagan rites and philosophies of ancient Greece and Rome. From at least the middle of the second century, then, the church was in constant conversation with classical modes of thought. In these engagements Christian authors accomplished two distinct yet related goals. First, they sought to demonstrate that the gospel was not limited to its original Jewish ethos but could be successfully communicated within a variety of social settings. If the church's claim that what God accomplishes in Christ was good news for all people everywhere was to be credible, theologians needed to show that it was capable of adopting and adapting the ideas, images, and modes of reasoning of other societies.

In the process, however, they also discovered that pagan philosophies offered resources for addressing the difficult problems and questions within the church's own life and language that finally could not be adequately addressed in biblical images and ideas alone. Far from "Hellenizing" the gospel with the supposedly static concepts of Greek philosophy intruding on the dynamic nature of Hebraic revelation, the church fathers plundered concepts and modes of thought developed by the Platonists, Stoics, and Aristotelians, and used this "Egyptian gold" to explicate the testimony of Israel, Jesus, and the apostles.[70] The notion that Greek philosophical categories were intrusions on the purity of the Bible's Hebraic frame-

---

68. McClendon, *Doctrine*, 21.

69. Jenson, *Triune God*, 17. Again, dogmas or presiding doctrines are not limited to religious communities. In any social project or research program there are always convictions that form a heuristic core. See in this regard the splendid insights of Nancey Murphy, *Theology in the Age of Scientific Reasoning* (Ithaca, NY: Cornell University Press, 1990), especially 58–79.

70. Augustine, *Teaching Christianity*, II. 40.

work has thus outlived any usefulness it might have had. A more apt expression, Robert Wilken writes, "would be the Christianization of Hellenism, though that phrase does not capture the originality of Christian thought nor the debt owed to Jewish ways of thinking and to the Jewish Bible. Neither does it acknowledge the good and right qualities of Hellenic thinking that Christians recognized as valuable, for example, moral life understood in terms of the virtues."[71] Christian thought so profoundly transformed the concepts and categories that it borrowed from the world of antiquity that something quite new and extraordinary had emerged on the scene.

The use of pagan conceptions of rationality by Christian thinkers, however, creates its own set of problems. One has to do with the relationship between the various logics that govern the different modes of discourse. There is on the one hand the more concrete and diachronically oriented imagination of scripture, and on the other the more abstract and synchronically aligned propositions that characterize church doctrine. The logic of biblical narrative, for example, the articulated form of which makes sense of the manifold relationships between contingent events and actions in the history of Israel and the church, cannot be assimilated to other logical forms without remainder. The logic of the one is heterogeneous with those of the others, and some coherent way must therefore be found to relate them.

One significant effort to think through this relationship in recent years is offered by George Lindbeck in *The Nature of Doctrine*. As I noted in passing in chapter 4, he proposes what he calls a cultural-linguistic model for conceptualizing religion and doctrine. The essence of religious discourse, according to Lindbeck, resides neither in an abstract list of propositions describing a world of discrete facts nor in postulations derived from some type of pre-thematic religious sensibility or universal moral value. Instead "religions resemble languages together with their correlative forms of life and thus are similar to cultures (insofar as these are understood semiotically as reality and value systems—that is, as idioms for the construing of reality and the living of life)." A religion and its teachings form a distinct culture of sorts, that is, an "interlocked system of construable signs . . . a context within which social events, behaviors, institutions, and processes may be intelligibly described." It is the entire system, and not individual utterances articulated within it, that can be said to correspond to reality.[72]

As with his description of biblical interpretation, there are many elements in Lindbeck's account of doctrine that are noteworthy. He contends, for example, that "experience" is not a prior category for theological reflection (though unfortunately he still associates it with intense states of subjective awareness or emotion): "First come the objectivities of the religion, its language, doctrines, liturgies, and modes of action, and it is through these that passions are shaped into various kinds of

71. Wilken, *Spirit of Early Christian Thought*, xvi–xvii.
72. Lindbeck, *Nature of Doctrine*, 18, 65, 115.

what is called religious experience."[73] He also eschews for the most part any sort of picture-theory of propositions to describe the proper work of doctrine. Finally, Lindbeck agrees that the truth of an utterance is closely bound to its meaning, which in turn is tied to its performative setting with the Christian community. There are other elements in his account of the nature of doctrine, however, that are more problematic.

These elements arise in his conception of the relationship between the different discourses and logics in Christian speech, and especially in his assertion that doctrine does not function as objective truth claims (which he labels a cognitive-propositionalist theory of doctrine) or as expressions of religious consciousness (experiential-expressivist), but as "communally authoritative rules of discourse, attitude, and action."[74] He contends that doctrines are second-order rules of speech that operate strictly as regulative principles, serving only to exclude certain readings of the biblical story and encourage others, and thus they do not exercise a referential or descriptive function. The ancient creeds thus provide three basic regulative principles in relation to the details of the biblical story, which alone have cognitive import: the monotheistic principle (there is one God), the principle of historical specificity (the stories of Jesus refer to an actual historical person), and the principle of christological maximalism (every possible importance is to be ascribed to Jesus consistent with the first two principles). The consubstantiality of the Father and the Son set forth in the Nicene Creed is therefore not "a first-order proposition with ontological reference, but . . . a second-order rule of speech."[75]

Like many other theologians (myself included), Lindbeck uses the categories of first- and second-order speech to differentiate between the different logics that operate in Christian discourse. However, by calling doctrines regulative statements, he imports into these categories a Kantian distinction between constative utterances (i.e., statements that are capable of being true or false) and non-constative utterances, such that only first-order statements have cognitive value. This distinction, though it may have a certain heuristic value in certain circumstances, ultimately breaks down. Performative action, if it is followable, must be situated within a "text." For example, when a couple marries, they invoke "'constatively' the institution of marriage, and all its past performances. The participants of the marriage as much assume a theoretical framework for marriage as the reporter of

73. Ibid., 39.

74. Ibid., 18. Kevin Vanhoozer notes that Lindbeck's account of propositional knowledge erroneously equates propositional knowledge with the widespread but misleading notion that there is a correspondence between mental concepts, propositions that express these concepts, and the reality to which they refer, such that the relation between them can somehow be critically examined (Vanhoozer, *The Drama of Doctrine*, 88–89).

75. Lindbeck, *Nature of Doctrine*, 94. But as Terrence Tilley has noted, even on its own ground Lindbeck's proposal does not do justice to the Nicene Creed in particular, since Arianism is consistent with these three principles (Terrence F. Tilley, "Incommensurability, Intratextuality, and Fideism," *Modern Theology* 5 [January 1989]: 87–117). Lindbeck concedes this point in *The Nature of Doctrine*, 95–96.

the events in the local newspaper. Inversely, his report, which helps to establish the event publicly, is a continuation of the performance." Because it is situated within a text, performance "is always also constative. One only imagines the contrary for Kantian reasons, because one thinks there is some sort of 'transparent' performance located in a universal, 'natural' text."[76] In similar fashion, constative utterances are also proposals for a common interpretation and common or continuous activity that is set within some network of human association, and thus amount to a gesture of performance that invites others to go on with or take up from our activity.[77]

All human utterances thus constitute "a series of *acts performed in the world* in which we live, employing the conventions of the language at our disposal . . . in order to make a move in the human situation in which we along with others are engaged."[78] We grasp the meaning of a speech act when we determine the kind of performative move a speaker is attempting: making a request, debating a policy, proposing an explanation, officiating at a wedding, speculating about the future, instructing a player how to pitch to the batter, confessing one's faith, and so forth. And since every one of these moves is addressed to others, how an auditor responds to these utterances, what McClendon and Smith call "uptake," also figures centrally into the meaning of a speech act, that is, the performative role it plays in the manifold transactions of life. Together these two considerations set the primary and the affective conditions that determine whether the move a speaker makes will be a successful or "happy" one. The descriptive adequacy of an utterance to its referent—the representative condition—is established by the purpose of mind that is framed by the primary and affective conditions of a speech act.[79]

Convictional utterances are performative transactions that take place between persons in the course of overlapping engagements within the complex business of human life. As such they derive their meaning, and thus their truth or falsity, from the work they perform within that shared context.[80] Cognitive statements bearing ontological reference are therefore also performative speech acts that work in concert with our other activities to organize our exchanges with one another and with the world that we share in common. *Representing* and *picturing*, as MacIntyre reminds us, are not interchangeable terms: "Pictures are only one mode of re-presenting, and their adequacy or inadequacy in functioning as such is always relative to some specific purpose of mind."[81]

76. Milbank, *Theology and Social Theory*, 250.

77. Rowan Williams, "The Suspicion of Suspicion: Wittgenstein and Bonhoeffer," in Richard Bell, ed. *Grammar of the Heart: New Essays in Moral Philosophy and Theology* (San Francisco: Harper & Row, 1988), 40.

78. McClendon, *Ethics*, 333 (emphasis original).

79. McClendon and Smith, *Convictions*, 56–74.

80. For example, the liberal doctrine of the autonomous self is intelligible and persuasive only in the context of a social order that is constituted by a certain set of social institutions (including linguistic conventions).

81. MacIntyre, *Whose Justice? Which Rationality?* 357.

Much like the biblical images to which they are correlated, then, doctrines order our transactions (i.e., our touching, grasping, pointing, breaking down, building up, calling to, answering to, communing with, stance-taking, and bearing witness) toward their proper ends, in large part by alluding to relations or proportions between the things that occupy our attention in day-to-day life by way of reference to "an altogether unknown mode of active being."[82] Doctrines function as concrete signs (*signa*) that imply substantial relations between things (*res*) as they participate in their Creator—who alone is truly *res,* and yet not actually some thing or some body, but that which is beyond all specification. Through the formation of our moral and intellectual character, then, these linguistic signs regulate our actions and passions with reference to particular goods (and thereby to our highest good).

The Kantian dichotomy between representational and regulative discourse that forms the basis of Lindbeck's cultural-linguistic theory of doctrine does not adequately account for the paradigmatic connotations of the biblical story invoked by the denotations of scripture and liturgy. To be sure, something like the distinction between first- and second-order utterances is necessary to differentiate the relationship between the various logics that comprise these levels of discourse (though some try to graft propositions from one onto the other[83]). This distinction is more adequately construed as the difference between that which is explicitly denoted by the narrative logic in scripture and the propositions that spell out what is connoted by these narrations, with their respective logics ordered by a hierarchal grammar.[84] Doctrines, though they do not refer on their own, but only in their association with first-order utterances, nonetheless "contain an inescapably 'surplus,' propositional element" that becomes interwoven with scriptural reasoning about the mystery of God and his relationship to the world.[85]

The line that distinguishes between biblical depictions and doctrinal explications, though necessary, can therefore not be drawn sharply.[86] One need only think, for example, of Christian poetry that speaks of the infinite becoming incarnate in what is finite, or devotion to a dying God on a Roman cross.[87] Hans Frei notes

---

82. Milbank, *The Word Made Strange,* 99, 105, 179.

83. Milbank argues that several prominent German theologians—Walter Kasper, Eberhard Jüngel, Jürgen Moltmann, and Wolfhart Pannenberg in particular—tend "to confuse 'levels of discourse,' by trying to work certain elements of relatively 'undigested' mythical discourse into the doctrine of the Trinity, which already presupposes a reflective distance from this material" (Milbank, *The Word Made Strange,* 178). This confusion can work the other way as well, as certain formal features or attributes of divinity can be projected back into biblical affirmations about Christ.

84. See William H. Poteat, *Polanyian Meditations: In Search of a Post-Critical Logic* (Durham, NC: Duke University Press, 1985), 153; cf. 12, 101, 131.

85. Milbank, *Theology and Social Theory,* 385.

86. In similar fashion, the distinction between "metaphorical" and "analogical" language for God is inherently vague and proximate. See Richard Swinburne, *Revelation: From Metaphor to Analogy* (Oxford: Clarendon, 1992), 39–51.

87. Milbank, *Theology and Social Theory,* 384.

that on more than one occasion in Karl Barth's *Church Dogmatics* "the second-order talk merged with imaginative restatements, in various modes, of parts of the original narrative to which it is fitly related."[88] This occurs not because Barth was careless in his use of words, but because the two levels of discourse and their respective logics work in concert with each other in the church's work and worship of God. To put the matter thusly nonetheless raises another question: what is the most adequate way of construing the relationship between the diachronic logic of scriptural reasoning and the more synchronically deployed logic of doctrine? In short, what constitutes appropriate word care when speaking of God?

Affirmation and Negation

As the church fathers sought to provide answers to these queries that were firmly rooted in the Jewish question of creation, they recognized that men and women could not adequately conceive of God and God's relationship to the world as if he were yet one more inhabitant of the universe interacting with its other occupants. Such thinking idolatrously assumes that we can properly think the nature of divine transcendence by projecting our usual conceptions of knowledge, power, and greatness to the highest point imaginable, a conception that would make God a part of our world, yet one more particular being, subject to our rules, our power, our means of control, our ways of understanding and manipulating the people, places, and things around us. Our ways of speaking about God's sheer, ineffable difference had to be emptied out and radically reformulated. An adequate grammar was needed for conceiving the relationship of the God of Israel to the created order, particularly in connection with the concept of transcendence.[89]

To this end the church fathers developed an open-ended dialectic that qualifies all positive affirmations or specifications regarding God's nature. Put simply, though Christians can certainly confess and believe *that* the God of Israel and Father of Jesus Christ exists, a carefully developed grammar of divinity precludes them from attempting to specify *what* this God is. David Burrell distinguishes between the "formal" features of divinity and the divine attributes or properties. These formal features—simplicity, immutability, impassibility, eternity, goodness, limitlessness and unity—"are not so much said of a subject, as they are reflected in a subject's very mode of existing, and govern the way in which anything whatsoever might be said of that subject." These features specify *how* the divine attributes—wisdom,

---

88. Frei, *Types of Christian Theology*, 162.

89. The figure of doctrine as grammar was posed most forcefully by Ludwig Wittgenstein in a terse, almost cryptic observation he makes in *Philosophical Investigations*: "Grammar tells what kind of object anything is. (Theology as grammar)" (Wittgenstein, *Philosophical Investigations*, 373, 116e). This notion was later picked up and developed further by theologians connected with Yale University. See, for example, Paul L. Holmer, *The Grammar of Faith* (San Francisco: Harper & Row, 1978); and Theodore W. Jennings, *Beyond Theism: A Grammar of God-Language* (New York: Oxford University Press, 1985).

beauty, mercy, justice—can be predicated literally of God.[90] What we can know of God, says Denys Turner, "is that we cannot know the meaning of that which we must say of him."[91] Put somewhat more parochially, to know what we cannot know of God is to know something quite important about God.

Negations do not, however, have the final word in our speech about God. We must not conclude that "negative language is somehow superior to affirmative in the mind's ascent to God." Language can lead us to the reality of God "when, by a process simultaneously of affirming and denying all things to God, by, as it were in one breath, both affirming what God is and denying . . . 'that there is any kind of thing that God is,' we step off the very boundary of language itself, beyond every assertion and every denial, into the 'negation of the negation' and the 'brilliant darkness' of God."[92] The *via negativa*, the way of negation, in church doctrine is thus folded into an ascending hierarchy of differentiated affirmations and denials culminating with the negation of negation. This ascent begins with the metaphorical names for God generated by the biblical imagination, and which are derived from perceivable material objects—God is a "fortress," a "king," or a "lion"—and moves upward by the twofold path of negation and analogy to "proper" or conceptual names—God is "wise and wisdom," "good and goodness," and "beautiful and beauty" (to name just a few of these attributes). Both kinds of names are cataphatic or affirmative statements about God, and their use in this capacity is warranted by the fact that God is the creator of all things.[93] In the words of Pseudo-Dionysius, "since [God] is the underpinning of goodness, and by merely being there is the cause of everything, to praise this divinely beneficent Providence you must turn to all of creation. It is there at the center of everything and everything has it for a destiny."[94] By means of these names we come to know God, both diachronically (who God is, namely, the One who delivered the tribes of Israel from Egypt and raised the man Jesus from the dead) and synchronically (what God is, or rather, what he is not).

Perceptual images and conceptual notions thus provide us with legitimate ways of naming God, but at the same time they invariably fall infinitely short of what God is. In the words of Pseudo-Dionysius, "with regard to the supra-essential being of God—transcendent Goodness transcendently there—no lover of the truth which is above all truth will seek to praise it as word or power or mind or life or being. No. It is at a total remove from every condition, movement, life, imagination, conjecture, name, discourse, thought, conception, being, rest, dwelling,

90. David B. Burrell, CSC, *Knowing the Unknowable God: Ibn-Sina, Maimonides, Aquinas* (Notre Dame, IN: University of Notre Dame Press, 1986), 47; cf. Burrell, *Aquinas* and *Freedom and Creation in Three Traditions*.

91. Turner, *Faith, Reason and the Existence of God*, 58.

92. Ibid., 156.

93. Ibid., 155–56.

94. Pseudo-Dionysius, *The Divine Names*, 593C–D, in *Pseudo-Dionysius: The Complete Works*, trans. Colm Luibheid (New York: Paulist, 1987).

unity, limit, infinity, the totality of existence."[95] We therefore cannot privilege either the negations or the affirmations in this open-ended dialectic, for God is beyond both assertion and denial.[96] As we go along we negate not only the affirmations, but the negations as well.

This differentiated grammar of divinity that allows us to speak coherently about the existence and the ineffability of God also makes it possible for us to say something intelligible about the mystery of the incarnation. "It is only when one knows the unutterability of the name of God," writes Bonhoeffer, "that one can utter the name of Jesus Christ."[97] Located at the summit of our inability to fathom the incomprehensible, writes Bonaventure, is Jesus, in whom are united "the first and the last, the highest and the lowest, the circumference and the circle, the *Alpha* and the *Omega*, the caused and the cause, the Creator and the creature."[98] If God and creatures are joint occupants of the universe, however, they necessarily occupy mutually exclusive standpoints within that common space. All affirmations of the sort that Bonaventure makes about Christ would then be blatant contradictions. As John Hick puts it, "to say, without explanation, that the historical Jesus of Nazareth was also God is as devoid of meaning as to say that this circle drawn with a pencil on paper is also a square."[99] But because we know that we do not and cannot know what God is, only what God is not, we can then say of Christ that he is both human and divine without fear of uttering a logical contradiction. "Because, and only if, God is unknowable to us," Turner concludes, "is the Chalcedonian doctrine of Christ possible."[100]

Knowing what God is not is thus not limited to abstract metaphysical questions, for it allows us to differentiate the reality and reign of God from the idolatrous claims to our allegiance made by state, market, race, class, or gender.[101] Because God utterly transcends the world, the peace of the city that is to come can show up in the midst of the earthly city in the most unexpected of places, even in a crucified messiah and his fallible followers. Far from defining God as distant from, indifferent to, and uninvolved in the joys and sufferings of the world, the church's distinctive grammar acknowledges the radical freedom of God *from*, and therefore *for* creation, and especially for our salvation. As the creator of the world, and not an occupant of it existing alongside others, God is not bound by the categories, the powers, the ways, and the institutions of this world, nor is he hampered or overwhelmed by its manifold sufferings. God

95. Ibid., 593C.

96. Pseudo-Dionysius, *Mystical Theology*, 1048B.

97. Bonhoeffer, *Letters and Papers from Prison*, 157.

98. Bonaventure, *The Journey of the Mind to God*, 6.7, trans. Philotheus Boehner, OFM (Indianapolis: Hackett, 1956).

99. John Hick, "Jesus and the World Religions," in *The Myth of God Incarnate*, ed. John Hick (Philadelphia: Westminster, 1977), 178.

100. Turner, *Faith, Reason and the Existence of God*, 59.

101. See D. Brent Laytham, ed., *God Is Not—: Religious, Nice, "One of Us," an American, a Capitalist* (Grand Rapids: Brazos, 2004).

does not change or suffer, and that is a good thing.[102] God is at the same time more intimately related to the world (as its creator and sustainer) than the world is to itself, *and* uniquely free (as utterly distinct from every who and what in the world) to act in its behalf. God's transcendence "meets us, and surprises us, when we are shown simply that the way of this world is not the final and exclusive truth."[103]

When the church's grammar for speaking well about God is neglected, then, the results can be catastrophic. In chapter 3, for example, we took note of the fact that late medieval theology had replaced traditional trinitarian construals of divine will and understanding with a monarchic conception of God, consisting of a radical simplicity that lacked any real differentiation, with a deliberative or proposing will representing the substantial identity of the divine essence, will, and intellect. This innovation set aside the patristic doctrine of participation in the mystery of the triune life and unity as the normative understanding of relationships between God and human beings, and replaced it with the notion of a legal covenant. Among the effects of this shift was the notion of the detached, unencumbered self, and with it a new understanding of human interaction as contractual, a conception that underwrites the dehumanizing displacements of liberal capitalism.

The purpose for ascending the hierarchical ladder of differentiated denials to contemplate the "brilliant darkness" that is the mystery of God is not to leave behind permanently the world of time and space and revel in awe and wonder. Through contemplation, writes John of the Cross, the works and faculties of the soul are purged and transformed, "clothed with the new man, who is created according to God . . . in the newness of sense."[104] This transformation of our faculties enables us to set aside understandings of the world "according to the flesh," that we might bear witness to the advent of the new creation in the midst of the present evil age (2 Cor. 5:16–17).[105] We thus descend back down that same ladder to take up again the perceptual names with a more nuanced understanding of, and desire for, God's relationship to creation, and on that basis to re-engage the world into which the apocalypse of God has intruded. In so doing we learn, as Bonhoeffer puts it, that "God's 'beyond' is not the beyond of our cognitive faculties," for such matters have "nothing to do with the transcendence of God." Instead, "God is beyond in the midst of our life. The

102. See in this regard two insightful books by Thomas G. Weinandy, OFM Cap., *Does God Change?* and *Does God Suffer?* (Notre Dame, IN: University of Notre Dame Press, 2000).

103. Rowan Williams, *Christ on Trial: How the Gospel Unsettles Our Judgment* (Grand Rapids: Eerdmans, 2000), 15.

104. Saint John of the Cross, *Dark Night of the Soul*, II.iii.3, trans. E. Allison Peers (Garden City, NY: Image, 1959).

105. Sarah Coakley, for example, argues that Gregory of Nyssa thought it necessary in some way to use the language of sexuality and gender to ascend to intellectual intimacy with the Triune God, but in the process reverses, undermines, and transcends accepted gender stereotypes (Coakley, *Powers and Submissions*, 128).

church stands, not at the boundaries where human powers give out, but in the middle of the village."[106]

Atonement

Foremost among these matters that have to do with our life here in the middle of the human village, and which we must therefore consider *sub ratione Dei*, is that of our salvation. The traditional theories of the atonement were attempts to answer the questions posed in a variety of ways by the New Testament texts: Why did God become human? Why the cross? The obvious answer to these questions is, the story of Jesus rightly told. But by itself this response only begs the question. We must indicate something of what it means to tell this story rightly—a tale of one Jewish man who was executed in the first part of the first century CE in Roman-occupied Judea—to the diverse sorts of people who live in our time and place.[107] This doctrine articulates what Nicholas Lash calls the "crucial difference . . . between telling a story differently and telling a different story."[108]

According to McClendon, there are parallels between the classic theories of the atonement that exhibit either an implicit or an explicit narrative structure, and Jewish strategies for articulating the continuing import of the biblical story. He borrows the idea of *midrash* from Jewish interpretive practice to clarify the narrative relationship between the biblical depictions of the significance of Jesus's crucifixion and later accounts of the atonement. Rabbinic commentary on scripture is typically divided into two categories: *Halakhah*, which sought to clarify the scope of the legal material in the Bible, and *Aggadah*, which exposited the narrative material of scripture. Together these interpretations formed the *midrashim*, a principal purpose of which was to enlarge the biblical story, and in particular to show the contemporary relevance of scripture.[109]

Probably the best known, but often misconstrued, of these *midrashim* is Anselm's theory of the atonement in his treatise *Cur Deus Homo*, which is predicated on the beauty of sacrifice in the form of a life lived in the mode of donation and gift.[110] As Anselm puts it, it was "fitting that the devil, who conquered man by tempting him to taste of the fruit of a tree, should be conquered by a man through suffering he endured on the wood of a tree. There are also many other things which, carefully considered, show a certain indescribable beauty in this manner of accomplishing

---

106. Bonhoeffer, *Letters and Papers from Prison*, 282.

107. McClendon, *Doctrine*, 230.

108. Lash, *Theology on the Way to Emmaus*, 183.

109. McClendon, *Doctrine*, 231.

110. In what follows I am indebted to D. Bentley Hart, "A Gift Exceeding Every Debt: An Eastern Orthodox Appreciation of Anselm's *Cur Deus Homo*," *Pro Ecclesia* 7 (1993): 333–49. See also Hans Urs von Balthasar, *The Glory of the Lord, Volume 2* (San Francisco: Ignatius Press, 1984); John McIntyre, *Anselm and His Critics* (Edinburgh: Oliver & Boyd, 1954); and Daniel M. Bell Jr., "Sacrifice and Suffering: Beyond Justice, Human Rights, and Capitalism," *Modern Theology* 18 (July 2002): 333–59.

our redemption."[111] God became human, not because God had need of anything, or was compelled by an external standard of justice that is at odds with his internal inclination toward mercy, or demanded bloodshed, or because God's power and dignity were somehow diminished by humankind's rebellion. Atonement for Anselm is *not* about a juridical reckoning on the part of God, nor is it a "purchasing" of anything. Indeed, says David Hart, Anselm's understanding of Jesus's sacrificial death on the cross is "essentially aneconomic (Christ's death purchases nothing, but his obedience to the Father calls forth a blessing)."[112] On the contrary, atonement has everything to do with restoring women and men to happiness in the enjoyment with God.[113]

In line with his patristic predecessors, then, Anselm argues that God became flesh so that, out of the divine abundance and plenitude, women and men might be restored to the place of honor God had always intended for them: participation in the triune life. The injury to God's honor inflicted by human insurrection and attempted usurpation of divine power, position, and dignity does not diminish or in any way wound God himself, as though God could be affected (and thus we find ourselves once again working within the church's grammar of divinity). The harm caused by humankind's rebellion was instead, as Anselm's predecessor Athanasius puts it, the possibility that the goodness of God in creating the world should be brought to nothing through the deceit worked by his creatures:

> For this purpose then, the incorporeal and incorruptible and immaterial Word of God entered our world. In one sense, indeed, He was not far from it before, for no part of creation had ever been without Him Who, while ever abiding in union with the Father, yet fills all things that are. But now He entered the world in a new way, stooping to our level in His love and Self-revealing to us. He saw the reasonable race, the race of men that, like Himself, expressed the Father's Mind, wasting out of existence, and death reigning over all in corruption.[114]

From the plenitude of divine charity eternally shared within the divine life, God has always given to humanity, and when we reject the divine gift of fellowship upon which our very being depends, God continues to give in the form of love incarnate, communicating grace to men and women again and again, without ceasing. So to the question of why God assumes human nature in the incarnation, Anselm essentially replies (again in line with his patristic forebears) that humankind might share together in the divine life as citizens of the heavenly city. Jesus came not to die, but to give life (John 10:10), which is communicated to us through the fellowship of sacrifice that is the body of Christ. Again to cite

111. Anselm of Canterbury, *Why God Became Man* and *The Virgin Conception and Original Sin*, I.3, trans. Joseph M. Colleran (Albany, NY: Magi, 1969).

112. Hart, "A Gift Exceeding Every Debt," 345.

113. Anselm, *Why God Became Man*, I.9.

114. Athanasius, *On the Incarnation*, II.§6–8.

Hart: "The newly refashioned human nature established in the Incarnation is found nowhere (this side of the eschaton) but in the social reality of the church, whose practices of love and disciplines of forgiveness already constitute the new life of the sanctified."[115]

Why, then, did love incarnate die on a cross? Certainly Jesus did not want to die. He was not a masochist seeking death, a fact demonstrated by his prayer in the garden of Gethsemane (Mark 14:35–6; cf. Matt. 26:39; Luke 22:42). He came to accept God's will, which entailed his dying, but that is not the outcome he wanted. Nor can we say that the Father wanted Jesus to be crucified. McCabe contends that like any minimally intelligent parent, the Father wanted Jesus to be alive, to be human, to be blessed, and to flourish as had been intended from the beginning. The mission that Jesus had from the Father, and which he understood to be a command from his Father, was to be totally, completely human.[116] Sacrifice rightly conceived thus involves practices that free us from the fear and desire that keep us in bondage to coercive rulers and calculating economics, and lead us into the just regime of God's pilgrim city, with its distinctive patterns of governance and accumulation and its modes of spiritual discipline.[117]

In Jesus, then, we have the beginnings of a recreated humanity, the first human being "who is not the slave of any power, of any law or custom, community or institution, value or theory."[118] Indeed, says McCabe, it was Jesus, not Adam, who in actuality "was the first human being, the first member of the human race in whom humanity came to fulfilment, the first human being for whom to live was simply to love—for this is what human beings are for. The aim of human life is to live in friendship—a friendship amongst ourselves which in fact depends on a friendship, or covenant, that God has established between ourselves and him."[119] Jesus thus offered during his life on our behalf what we, fallen humankind, did not and could not: true worship of, and obedience to, the Father.

Jesus's mission to communicate to women and men their true nature did not take place in a social vacuum but unfolded around the struggle that has taken place since the beginning between the reign of God and the idolatrous usurpations of other powers throughout history, a struggle that has revolved about the chosen people of Israel. As heir to this people's mandate, Jesus waged nonviolent warfare to establish the rule of God once again in the land of Israel. As McClendon puts it,

> God's rule required justice of a sort beyond the rule of law. . . . God's reign prom-
> ised sins sent away and human hurts healed; God's word pierced the injustices
> of military power (Rome) and religious power (Jerusalem); God's Servant and

115. Hart, "A Gift Exceeding Every Debt," 345.
116. McCabe, *God Matters*, 93.
117. Augustine, *City of God*, X.6, XIX.23.
118. Yoder, *Politics of Jesus*, 145.
119. McCabe, *God Matters*, 93.

Son challenged the iniquity of dominating family structure and of ethnic pride; God's Wisdom and Power exorcised the demons that rage within hurt human souls; God's Messiah . . . drew men and women into a new fellowship (the disciple church), ordained a new social order (love of enemies), evoked a new hope (the coming of the Truly Human One and the Age to Come).[120]

The attempt failed, of course, as his disciples doubted and his enemies plotted. He was handed over by his own kinsmen, abandoned by virtually all of his followers, and crucified by the military might of Rome. Jesus died, not because that is what he or the Father wanted, but because we have made a world in which there is no way of being fully and completely human that does not involve suffering.[121] Humanity's answer to God's grace, writes Barth, is a hate-filled *no*: "From Bethlehem to the Cross He was abandoned by the world that surrounded Him, repudiated, persecuted, finally accused, condemned and crucified. Such is man's attack upon Him, upon God Himself. Here there is an unveiling of Man's rebellion against God. God's Son is denied and rejected."[122]

That being human involves suffering and death is not a new disclosure of the gospel. Michael Wyschogrod contends that two antithetical themes coalesce in God's election of Abraham. On the one hand, says Wyschogrod, to be chosen by God is to be reassured by God's power and to share in that power as God secures a future for the people of promise. But on the other hand, "to be near God is to become a friend of death because of the terrible danger that surrounds all human intimacy with God."[123] McCabe puts the matter thusly:

> The gospels . . . insist upon two antithetical truths which express the tragedy of the human condition: the first is that if you do not love you will not be alive; the second is that if you *do* love you will be killed. If you cannot love you remain self-enclosed and sterile, unable to create a future for yourself or others, unable to live. If, however, you do effectively love you will be a threat to the structures of domination upon which our human society rests and you will be killed.[124]

The resurrection denies those who sought victory over God's rule and affirms what had gone before, confirming God's identification by and with Jesus, and vindicating the nonviolent way of the cross as "God's way, God's *only* way. Our story reveals the continuity of the church that came after with the story of Jesus' earthly career." Apostolic Christianity thus marks the continuation of the Jesus story already begun, a continuing revolution initiated by his life, death, and resurrection. Due to Christ's atoning work, the stories of God and humankind—the

120. McClendon, *Doctrine*, 235.
121. McCabe, *God Matters*, 93.
122. Karl Barth, *Dogmatics in Outline*, trans. G. T. Thompson (New York: Harper & Brothers, 1959), 104.
123. Wyschogrod, *Body of Faith*, 22–23.
124. McCabe, *God Matters*, 218.

one a tale of divine self-giving, the other of treachery and failure—"*are at last indivisibly one*."[125] Anselm is thus restating the oldest model of the atonement of all: recapitulation. As Hart puts it:

> Christ takes up the human story and tells it correctly, by giving the correct answer
> to God's summons; in his life and death he renarrates humanity according to its true
> pattern of loving obedience, humility, and charity, thus showing all human stories of
> righteousness, honor, and justice to be tales of violence, falsehood, and death; and
> in allowing all of humanity to be resituated through his death within the retelling of
> their story, Christ restores them to communion with the God of infinite love who
> created them for his pleasure.[126]

Seek His Face Always: Doctrine and Divine Love

As this understanding of the atonement indicates, doctrine is never finally a matter of disinterested epistemological or metaphysical speculation but serves principally to help us know and love God, and in that love, to love and serve our neighbors. This is especially evident in the writings of Augustine. The unity of his theological reflections—those doctrines about which he was so confident, the tensions that drove him on, the puzzles he could not resolve, and even the temptations to which he sometimes succumbed—is inextricably linked to his lifelong quest to love rightly, that is, to find and participate in the love of God that reorients every other possible human love, "and then to convince others to do the same."[127] Nowhere is this interpretive key to his thought better expressed than in the opening paragraphs of *On The Trinity*: "Dear reader, whenever you are as certain about something as I am go forward with me; whenever you hesitate, seek with me; whenever you discover that you have gone wrong come back to me; or if I have gone wrong, call me back to you. In this way we will travel the street of love together as we make our way toward him of whom it is said, 'Seek his face always.'"[128]

According to Gerald Schlabach, Augustine's doctrine of love, in the final analysis, is identical to his doctrine of the Trinity: "Only through the incarnation of Jesus Christ the Mediator do we really know the love of the ungraspable God who created the universe. Only as Christ draws us into his own relationship of mutual love with his Father do we have the power to respond to God's love. The reality of their loving mutuality is for Augustine the very person of the Holy Spirit."[129] The ultimate aim of the doctrine of the Trinity (to which the doctrine of the atonement is inextricably connected) is to explicate the living encounter with the Word through which the Spirit fills the community with the mind of Christ. This sort of

---

125. McClendon, *Doctrine*, 236.
126. Hart, "A Gift Exceeding Every Debt," 348.
127. Schlabach, "Correction of the Augustinians," 56.
128. Augustine, *The Trinity*, I.3.5, translated by Wilken, *Spirit of Early Christian Thought*, 107.
129. Schlabach, "Correction of the Augustinians," 60.

theological reflection, says McIntosh, "takes place by critical analysis of the ecclesial experience of being drawn into the pattern of Jesus' life and his relationship with the One he called 'Abba.'"[130]

Love as a trait of Christian character is not amorphous, however, nor is it strictly private, but is always determined by its object. In *On the Soul and the Resurrection*, Gregory of Nyssa contends that though the principal passions of fallen humanity, desire and fear, can draw us to God, they are in a fallen world driven by our needs and pleasures. But as we come into God's presence the anarchic impulse of desire gives way to love, and what desire once yearned for is now purified and conformed to the properties of the divine nature. As the soul is conformed to God, old habits that once were ordered around the passions give way to the interior disposition of love by which it becomes attached to the beautiful.[131]

We must not, therefore, confuse the divine love that moves the sun and the other stars with mere sentiment. Sin and death are the result of the refusal of divine love; and the church, the recipient and product of the gift of charity, called to embody it before a fallen world, must for the sake of charity distinguish itself from what Hegel rightly called the slaughter-bench of history.[132] As the character of Father Zosima in Dostoevsky's *The Brothers Karamazov* puts it, love is harsh and demanding,[133] particularly in a world that arrogantly seeks to usurp God's power and prestige. Because it rejected the rule of God by condemning Christ to death, this world has "condemned itself to die, to be the world whose form and image 'fade away' so that the Kingdom of God 'is not of this world.' This is the Christian *no* to the world and, from the first day, Christianity proclaimed the end of 'this world' and required from those who believe in Christ and want to partake of his Kingdom that they be 'dead with Christ' and their true life be 'hid with Christ in God.'" At the same time, however, this same creation in rebellion is redeemed and re-created in Christ, in whom all things find their true end: "This means that for those who believe in Christ and are united to Him, this very world—its time and matter, its life, and even death—have become the 'means' of communion with the Kingdom of God, the sacrament, i.e., the mode, of its coming and presence among men."[134]

According to the gospel, then, it is the charity of the Triune God, not death and rebellion, that brings creation into being, that governs the course of history, and that in the world to come will recapitulate all things in the endless inventions

---

130. McIntosh, *Mystical Theology*, 41. I return shortly to this notion of ecclesial experience.

131. Gregory of Nyssa, *On the Soul and the Resurrection*, trans. Catharine Roth (Crestwood, NY: St. Vladimir's Seminary Press, 1993), 77–81. I am indebted to Wilken's treatment of Gregory's discussion of desire and love in his *Spirit of Early Christian Thought*, 299–303.

132. Georg Wilhelm Friedrich Hegel, *The Philosophy of History*, rev. ed., trans. J. Sibree (New York: Willey, 1944), 21.

133. Fyodor Dostoevsky, *The Brothers Karamazov*, trans. Richard Pevear and Larissa Volokhonsky (New York: Vintage, 1991), 58.

134. Schmemann, *Church, World, Mission*, 29–30.

of love. And love is also the form of all the virtues,[135] but only as it "is first and foremost disciplined by the witness of our God who would have us die, yea even our children die, rather than to live unworthily."[136] Bonhoeffer saw clearly the harsh nature of God's cruciform love as the prospect of his own martyrdom at the hands of the Nazis loomed over him: "it is only when God's wrath and vengeance are hanging as grim realities over the heads of one's enemies that something of what it means to love and forgive them can touch our hearts."[137] Like the Jews in the Diaspora, then, Christians are compelled by love to articulate the points of pressure, tension, and conflict between themselves and a world in thrall to death and violence, and this is one of the tasks that fall to doctrine.

As a consequence, just as we must not confuse love with private sentiment, we must also not see it as something that is apolitical. According to Augustine, the character of a political association is best defined as "a multitude of rational creatures bound together by common agreement as to the objects of their love." To discover the moral nature of any such association, one need only examine what it loves. The difference between the earthly city and the city that God is building is not in the material goods that each must use, or the evils each must suffer in this world, but that each does so with a different faith, a different hope, and a different love. Of Rome Augustine thus writes:

> According to this definition of ours, the Roman people is indeed a people, and its "property" is without doubt a commonwealth. As to the objects of that people's love—both in the earliest days and in the times which followed—and the morals of that people as it fell into bloody seditions and thence into social and civil wars, and so ruptured or corrupted that bond of concord which is, as it were, the health of a people: we have the testimony of history for all this . . . It must be understood, however, that what I have said of the Roman people and commonwealth I also say and think of the Athenians and any other Greeks, of the Egyptians, of the ancient Babylon of the Assyrians, and of every other nation, great or small, which has exercised its sway over commonwealths.[138]

Doctrine and Ecclesial Authority

Though church doctrine can never supplant the biblical story, it is vital to scriptural reasoning. It accomplishes this task by helping us locate our lives within the ever-unfolding drama of the apocalypse of God in Jesus Christ. Getting caught up into this ongoing event has many of the qualities of a musical fugue, with the church's performance of the biblical text generating an ongoing series of contrapuntal

135. Aquinas, *Summa Theologica* IIa.IIae.23.8.

136. Stanley Hauerwas, *Dispatches from the Front: Theological Engagements with the Secular* (Durham, NC: Duke University Press, 1994), 166.

137. Bonhoeffer, *Letters and Papers from Prison*, 157.

138. Augustine, *City of God*, XVIII.54, XIX.24.

variations and inventions down through the centuries. The contingent circumstances, events, and characters that make up our particular stories thus extend and deepen the rich and complex fabric of the biblical narratives. Doctrine renders explicit the assumed dramatic setting within which the eschatological significance of our lives is displayed by scriptural reasoning, doing so in terms that are always general, proximate, open to revision, and thus subject to the grammar of Christian language that governs the relationship between the different logics that constitute that language. The denotative and the connotative functions of sound teaching come together into an account of convictions that revolves around "the intrinsic winsomeness of Jesus' way displayed in Scripture and history."[139]

There remains one question in connection with the subject of doctrine that we can only mention in passing. Bonhoeffer states that one of the most pressing issues raised by the Confessing Church's struggle with Nazism had to do with the question of whether a teaching authority for the Protestant church could be established that would be grounded in scripture and confession alone. If such authority could not be instituted, Bonhoeffer concludes, then the final possibility of a Protestant church was gone. The only viable alternatives would be a return to Rome, submission to the state church, or the path into isolation, that is, the "protest" of true Protestantism against false authorities.[140] Wendell Berry restates the matter in his inimitable way when he doubts that "one can somehow become righteous by carrying protestantism to the logical conclusion of a one-person church. We all belong, at least, to the problem."[141]

Bonhoeffer and Berry are not the only Protestants drawing our attention to this problem. John Howard Yoder observes that the slide downward to unaccountable individuality was implied in the logic of the Reformers once "the hierarchy as interpreter of Scripture was set aside, and when the universities, consistories, synods, and convictions which were expected to take its place became fragmented."[142] This troublesome question of teaching authority is as old as the Reformation itself, and thus by raising it here I am conjuring up a ghost that "had never been exorcised since its first haunting of Luther in the figures of [Andreas] Carlstadt and the despised *Schwärmerei*."[143] It nonetheless took on new urgency in the twentieth century, as the events of 1933 to 1945 tragically demonstrate. What Bonhoeffer calls the path into isolation failed church and non-church people alike in Germany, not to mention the Jews of Europe and the other peoples of the world.

139. McClendon, *Doctrine*, 8.

140. Dietrich Bonhoeffer, *Dietrich Bonhoeffer Works*, vol. 16, *Conspiracy and Imprisonment, 1940–1945*, trans. Lisa E. Dahill (Minneapolis: Fortress, 2006), 78. I am indebted to Hollerich, "Retrieving a Neglected Critique of Church, Theology and Secularization in Weimar Germany," for bringing this statement by Bonhoeffer to my attention.

141. Berry, *What Are People For?* 101.

142. Yoder, *The Priestly Kingdom*, 24; cf. Wolfhart Pannenberg, *Systematic Theology*, vol. 1, trans. Geoffrey W. Bromiley (Grand Rapids: Eerdmans, 1991), 30.

143. Hollerich, "Retrieving a Neglected Critique," 305.

Diverse voices have discoursed at length about the need for a formally recognized and properly constituted magisterial office within Christian communities (with, of course, many of the now familiar disagreements in their respective accounts[144]). Though we shall not resolve these disagreements to everyone's satisfaction here, we can recall developments in the history of the church that bear upon this question. In particular, I noted in chapter 3 that the church in the later Middle Ages sought to meet the rising power and independence of the nascent state by establishing its own legal status and corporate power. A new distinction in canon law appeared between the sacramental power conferred on priests with their ordination and the power of ecclesiastical jurisdiction. It was decided that the consecration of a new bishop did not have to do primarily with his priestly authority, but instead conferred on him jurisdictional powers to govern the mystical body of the church. Canon lawyers then adapted the concept of the right of property from Roman and feudal law to construct a theory of the absolute and universal jurisdiction of a supreme authority, culminating with the doctrine of the *plenitudo potestatis*, the fullness of power, of the papal office.[145]

In the early church, by contrast, the focus for church authority lay not in formal legal concepts, but in the social idiom embodied in the *koinonia*, the communion of the body of Christ, which was generated by the eucharistic celebration. It was out of this liturgical act that the church's teaching authority, institutionally vested in its fullness in the office of bishop, grew and developed. Questions of apostolic succession, the integrity of local congregations, the role of the historic episcopacy (including the papacy), patterns of doctrinal and ecclesiastical development, and a host of other important topics cannot be faithfully considered in isolation from the larger liturgical and missional context that is the church's life and witness. All proposals for healing the schisms that currently rend the unity of the church must start here and then take up the details of ecclesiastical polity that are so difficult to consider in the best of circumstances. The co-inherence of the liturgical and the pedagogical in matters of ecclesiastical authority forms the essential basis from which all other matters follow.

144. Robert W. Jenson, *Systematic Theology*, vol. 2, *The Works of God* (New York: Oxford University Press, 1999), 228–49; George Lindbeck, "The Church," in *Keeping the Faith: Essays to Mark the Centenary of Lux Mundi*, ed. Geoffrey Wainwright (Philadelphia: Fortress, 1988), 179–208; Yoder, *Priestly Kingdom*, 22–34.

145. Figgis, *Studies of Political Thought from Gerson to Grotius*, 4; cf. O'Donovan, *Desire of the Nations*, 206.

6

Sacramental Sinews

Liturgy and the Remembering of Christ's Body

I knew myself to be far away from you in a region of unlikeness, and I seemed to hear your voice from on high: "I am the food of the mature; grow then, and you will eat me. You will not change me into yourself like bodily food: you will be changed into me."

Augustine, *The Confessions*

I was a college freshman, attending Sunday morning services at my local church as every good Baptist is supposed to do. I spent much of the service sorting through the various thoughts and feelings that were washing over me, trying to decide which of them represented a genuine encounter with Christ. As offspring of seventeenth-century Puritan Pietism and eighteenth-century English political philosophy, most Baptists in North America have long believed that "emotional states had a special spiritual significance and that consequently certain displays of feeling were to be considered as signs of godliness." It is this aspect of our Puritan heritage that survived the collapse of Calvinism as a theological system.[1]

1. Colin Campbell, *The Romantic Ethic and the Spirit of Modern Consumerism* (Cambridge, MA: Blackwell, 1987), 127. Of course, such caricatures ultimately do not do justice to the rich diversity in Baptist life, particularly if we look before the eighteenth century. For a more detailed and nuanced examination of the Baptist tradition, see Curtis Freeman, James Wm. McClendon Jr., and C. Rosalee Velloso da Silva, *Baptist Roots: A Reader in the Theology of a Christian People* (Philadelphia: Judson, 1999); and Steven R.

Today many people refer to these inner movements of the soul in which the divine speech is supposedly heard as "experiences" of God. I now realize that I was trying to discern on that particular Sunday morning what qualifies as one of those experiences. Was it the warm glow in my chest? The exhilarating feelings of certitude that asserted themselves whenever I was with those of like mind? The shiver that occasionally ran up and down my spine? It occurred to me even then that I could not really distinguish what was happening "inside" me at that moment, regardless of how immediate and intense the feelings were, from the way altogether mundane events and relationships affected me. Looking back on that occasion I now see that what I had been told to regard as sure and certain signs of a saving relationship with God were in actuality reliable evidence only of the malleability of the human soul, and in particular its capacity for self-deception. They were also both instrumental to and symptomatic of my captivity to rulers and authorities who wished to keep my Christian identity a private, "spiritual" matter.

The question of what qualifies as an experience of, or relationship with, God is an important one for us to ask. Is it finally some inner movement of mind, will, or affections that marks our communion with the Triune God? If so we must concede this is indeed a curious state of affairs. In what other instance does what goes on strictly within one's head or heart qualify as a personal relationship? You can have a personal relationship only with somebody, because that is what it means to be a creature—to be some *body*. Our desires and affections obviously figure into these relationships, for they are part of bodily existence, such that their absence or excess is surely a cause for concern. But they do not comprise the beginning, end, or substance of any relation.

Another occasion comes to mind in this regard, some fifteen years later. Some fellow graduate students and I were celebrating the Eucharist on a Tuesday morning with brothers of the Order of St. John the Evangelist, an Anglican religious order in Durham, North Carolina. I had been attending services at St. John's House several mornings a week for a few months on the recommendation of those whose insight in matters spiritual and theological I had come to trust. But prior to that morning my experience there had been everything that I had been led to expect. Most Baptists observe the Lord's Supper once every three months or so, for we have been taught that if we observe it too often it will not be as "meaningful." (We never restrict the frequency of hymns, prayers, Bible reading, or sermons for that reason.) And of course, from this standpoint what makes something meaningful is that it produces an intense emotional response "inside" the individual.

It did not take long for me to discover that one could sustain the kind of emotional intensity I had come to associate with communion only for so long. The novelty of participating in the elegant and elaborate liturgy gradually subsided. I soon knew when to stand and when to sit, what to say and what to do, when to

Harmon, *Towards Baptist Catholicity: Essays on Tradition and the Baptist Vision* (Waynesboro, GA: Paternoster, 2006).

sing and when to remain silent, because we celebrated the sacrament basically the same way every day. And sure enough, my initial impression of what had transpired at Eucharist that morning at St. John's House could have become the first entry in the dictionary under the word *perfunctory*. If the day had stopped there, the events of that morning would have confirmed everything that my Puritan heritage had warned me about such "popery."

The day did not end there, of course, and so I went about my business, all of which was routine. I did not think much more about what had happened that morning until late that afternoon, when I realized that what had transpired as a result of my participation in the eucharistic liturgy all those weeks had remained with me all day. The routine transactions of that day had been caught up in the mystery at the Lord's table in a way that I had not experienced before, though at the time I was quite unaware of this process. I had discovered something of what Alexander Schmemann calls the "breakthrough" of Christ the Eucharist and Eucharist the Christ "that brings us to the table in the Kingdom, raises us to heaven, and makes us partakers of the divine food."[2] The everyday exchanges of that Tuesday, in their details quite unremarkable, I now could follow as potent signs of God's beauty and power, rendered intelligible by the social idiom embodied in the eucharistic celebration. My apprenticeship in this idiom, culminating in what the Orthodox tradition calls the "liturgy after the liturgy," had finally borne a small bit of fruit.

On that Tuesday morning, now many years ago, I took an important step on the road to recovery from Gnosticism, that ancient adversary of the church's life and mission, resuscitated in recent times by the social idiom of liberal capitalism, a key player in the dismembering of Christ's ecclesial body. This process of recovering the sinews that hold together the members of Christ's body involves at its heart the sacraments of baptism and Eucharist, but we must take care as we proceed. That which Jesus intended to serve as signs of our unity we, his followers, have all too often used as a club with which to beat each other over the head, sometimes literally cracking skulls wide open over doctrinal differences regarding the font and the Lord's table. Add to this dubious track record the tenacity with which Christians of different traditions hold to a variety of doctrinal views on this subject—transubstantiation, consubstantiation, spiritual presence, "just a symbol," etc. The roots of these differences extend for centuries, secured by the sweat and sometimes the blood of our respective forebears.

Nevertheless, if Christians are to begin to disentangle themselves from those practices and institutions that effectively dismembered Christ's body, we must recover something of what is properly performed by those sacramental signs instituted by Christ. I say this not out of a restorationist bent of mind, nor because I believe that what takes place at, in, and through baptism and Eucharist is either magical or mechanical. Neither holiness nor wholeness can be guaranteed simply

2. Alexander Schmemann, *For the Life of the World: Sacraments and Orthodoxy* (Crestwood, NY: St. Vladimir's Seminary Press, 1963, 1973), 39.

by showing up and going through the motions of any rite. It is still the case that God "cannot endure solemn assemblies with iniquity" (Isa. 1:13). Indeed, if what Paul writes to the Corinthian church about eating and drinking to our own condemnation is still in force (see 1 Cor. 11:20–34), quite the opposite effect occurs whenever we do that. Nor do the sacraments stand alone; only in concert with the other constitutive practices and institutions of the church do they function as signs and seals of all that the Triune God has done, is doing, and will do in and for the world in the name of the one who was crucified on its behalf. Our present concern with the sacraments has to do rather with the distinctive social idiom of the church that is enacted by these mystical signs.

Sacrament as Apocalyptic Action

The raison d'être of the church, writes Schmemann, is "not to exist 'in itself' but to be the 'sacrament,' the *epiphany*, of the new creation." Baptism and Eucharist mark the material point of entry of God's apocalyptic regime into the day-to-day life of this world, gathering together a distinctive social order in the name of Christ. These powerful signs fashion an alternative social grammar or idiom for creaturely existence over against the idiom of the world's body politic. Time and again the sacramental signs introduce this new social dimension into the world, and they are therefore not just the *means* of grace, that is, instrumentally related to grace, but also the *media* of grace, and hence integral to its operation. In and through these liturgical practices "the Church is *informed* of her cosmical and eschatological vocation, *receives* the power to fulfill it and thus truly *becomes* 'what she is': the sacrament, in Christ, of the new creation; the sacrament, in Christ, of the Kingdom."[3]

If we are to understand how liturgy fulfills this function, writes Schmemann, we must see it in line with the apocalyptic motif of a journey into the reality of God's kingdom. To punctuate the *telos* of this journey, the Orthodox liturgy begins with a doxology: "Blessed is the Kingdom of the Father, the Son and the Holy Spirit, now and ever, and unto ages of ages." To bless the kingdom is not simply to commend it, but "to declare it to be the goal, the end of all our desires and interests, of our whole life, the supreme and ultimate value of all that exists." The church is the gathering of those in whom the ultimate destination of all life has been revealed and who, with their "Amen," have cast their lot with it. This little word is the appropriate response to the declaration that the movement toward God has begun, for it is a pledge of solidarity binding us to Christ in his ascension to the Father, a gift of inestimable value that comes only from him, "for only in Him can we say Amen to God, or rather He himself is our Amen to God and the Church is an Amen to Christ."[4]

---

3. Schmemann, *Church, World, Mission*, 136–37, Schmemann's emphasis.
4. Schmemann, *For the Life of the World*, 29; cf. Lash, *Believing Three Ways in One God*, 1–2.

The apocalyptic character of baptism and Eucharist presupposes a correlation between a sacrament and the sign character of the material world, both as a whole and in its constituent differences. Because it is created by God, writes Robert Wilken, "matter has within itself the capacity to become a resting place of God, to become something other while remaining what it is."[5] In its capacity to act as a sign of divine things, then, matter operates at two levels, such that, as Aquinas puts it, "all sensible creatures are [also] signs of sacred things."[6] It is crucial at this point to distinguish between two distinct uses of this term *sign*. We typically speak of signs as signs *of* something, analogous to the way we speak of symptoms and indications, for instance, "red sky at night, sailor's delight; red sky at morning, sailor take warning." When we use *sign* in this capacity, we look for its meaning elsewhere, as we would with a sign on a highway indicating how far it is to the next town. The sign stands in, substitutes for something else, such that to ask for its meaning is to ask what this other thing is. The signified is separate and distinct from the signifier.[7]

It is in this sense of the term that many Christians, particularly from free church traditions, talk about the baptism and Eucharist as "just" a sign or symbol. In this tradition, to say that something is symbolic in nature is to assert that the water, bread, and wine represent Christ's death for our act of remembrance and therefore are simply the outward expression of an interior "spiritual" experience. But one sees this use of *sign* as well in traditions that emphasize sacramental observance. William Cavanaugh notes that in Catholic circles there are numerous attempts to see sacrament as a sign or symbol of something else. As an example he cites the introduction to a volume on politics and liturgy in *Concilium* that frames the relationship between the two in precisely this manner: "Since politics is the control of power in society, the ways in which liturgy uses symbols of power has much to say in forming images and concepts of power which Christian peoples bring to bear on political questions."[8] The problem with such formulations, for all their good intentions, is that they define sacramental signs as something other than, and therefore apart from, the "real world."[9]

The other way to speak of a sign is to say that it is a sign *for* something. When we ask for the meaning of a sign in this sense, writes Herbert McCabe, "we are not asking 'what is it instead of,' what is the extra thing it stands for? We are ask-

5. Wilken, *Spirit of Early Christian Thought*, 248. One of the essential conditions that something must meet to act as a representation or sign, writes C. S. Peirce, is that it must, like any other object, have qualities that are independent of its meaning (C. S. Peirce, *Writings of C. S. Peirce*, vol. 3 [Bloomington: Indiana University Press, 1986], 62).

6. "[O]mnes . . . creaturae sensibiles sunt signa rerum sacrum" (Aquinas, *Summa Theologica*, III.a. 60.2). The distinction between the sacramental character of the world and a sacrament proper is that the latter has been ordained to signify our sanctification (*Summa Theologica*, III.a.60.3).

7. McCabe, *God Matters*, 165–66.

8. David Power and Herman Schmidt, "Editorial," in *Politics and Liturgy*, ed. Herman Schmidt and David Power (New York: Herder & Herder), 9, cited in Cavanaugh, *Torture and Eucharist*, 11.

9. Cavanaugh, *Torture and Eucharist*, 11.

ing 'what is it *for*?' How do we use it?" In this sense we know the meaning of sign—a word, for example—not by asking what the other thing is for which the sign stands proxy, but by learning how to use that word,[10] that is, to go on and go further with this expression. On this reading a sign is not an object or event in which some ethereal property called "meaning" has been deposited, but "a set of relationships between objects or events uniquely brought together as complexes or as concepts."[11] The meaning of a sign in this respect does not subsist in something else, but in the business the sign-user transacts with it within a complex of objects, events, and persons.[12] Signs thus organize practice, enabling us to engage in the world in an almost infinite series of actions: recalling previous encounters that allow us to return to and recover what we had previously encountered, forming expectations for the future, and authorizing abductive inferences that allow us to make metaphysical surmises about the nature of reality.[13]

The ability to use signs, or as Walker Percy calls it, to engage in triadic behavior, pushes us across a threshold marking the difference between an animal existing in an environment and a rational animal having a world, an organized cosmos.[14] Triadic behavior *is* our freedom, the capacity to imagine and pursue a variety of rational ends. We thus can fashion the different ways we live peaceably together within the constraints of the material world (and conversely, of not living together). In this respect human freedom is itself a sign of God's creative activity and, more specifically, its source and goal. Signs also constrain us, in that signifiers function only within established social complexes (hence, they serve as modes of alienation as well as communication).[15] Finally, signifier and signified interpenetrate in such a way that the former is irretrievably transformed by the latter. To know something, then, is to encounter it in and through the auspices of its sign, which becomes the preeminent mode of our habitation of a world as an ordered whole.[16]

The world is an ensemble of signs by virtue of having been spoken into existence by God (regardless of whether at any particular time or place somebody is able to read it as such). For the world to be such belongs to its ontology, the sign being "not only the way to perceive and understand reality, a means of cognition, but also a means of *participation*." The people, places, events, and things we encounter in the world do not cease being what they are in their function as signs for God's creative activity. They retain their distinctive properties, their own integrity and identity. At the same time they are also created by God, and thus they ultimately possess no separate, autonomous existence from the source of their being, that

10. McCabe, *God Matters*, 166.

11. Asad, *Genealogies of Religion*, 31.

12. McCabe, *God Matters*, 166.

13. Milbank, *The Word Made Strange*, 99; MacIntyre, *Whose Justice? Which Rationality?* 356.

14. Walker Percy, *Lost in the Cosmos: The Last Self-Help Book* (New York: Farrar, Straus & Giroux, 1983), 96.

15. McCabe, *God Matters*, 170.

16. Percy, *Lost in the Cosmos*, 103–5.

is, the source of who and what they are. It is this natural sign quality of the world, its tacit "sacramentality" that makes sacrament possible and supplies the hermeneutic key for understanding it as apocalyptic action. "It is the epiphany—in and through Christ—of the 'new creation,' not the creation of something 'new.' And if it reveals the 'continuity' between creation and Christ, it is because there exists, at first, a continuity between Christ and creation whose *logos*, life, and light He is."[17] As Augustine puts it, "the Son was sent where he already was, as he both came into the world and *he was in this world* (John 1:10)."[18]

In the best of circumstances the ability to follow the signs of continuity between creation and the apocalyptic activity of God in Christ takes considerable effort and discipline, requiring time and space free from distraction, and a community dedicated to cultivating the requisite habits and skills. In our time and place this task has only become more difficult. In virtually every corner of the globe, the bodies of men, women, and children are being cunningly formed as "individuals," that is, as interchangeable integers of consumption and production, for whom existence consists almost entirely of making choices from a range of options that are controlled by institutions they cannot see, and managed by people they never meet face-to-face. Effectively sundered from meaningful points of reference beyond their self-defined wants and desires, their identity as persons consists of little more than a series of consumer choices to make and a sequence of jobs from which they will be laid off.

When we are immersed in these patterns of life and thought, it is extremely difficult to recognize the ways that the powers and authorities of this age rule our lives. As scripture itself indicates, something more than simply being in a position to see and hear what is going on around us is needed if men and women are to penetrate the social idiom of a fallen creation. In the Book of Isaiah, for example, we read that King Uzziah of Judah died around the year 742 BCE. (6:1). Under his rule Judah had enjoyed a rare period of stability and prosperity that it had not known since the time of Solomon, and the news of his passing surely would have been seen as a foreboding development, especially with the ascension of Tiglath-Pileser III to the throne in Nineveh. With the Assyrian menace looming on the northern horizon, it would be natural if the people of Judah and Jerusalem lamented, "What shall become of us now that our great king is dead?" Those unable to read the signs would likely see these developments as no different than hundreds of other such events that have occurred throughout history. After all, kings and kingdoms come and go. Such is the way of the world.

According to the prophet, on the other hand, the course of these events could be understood only in terms of figures provided by Israel's past. The death of the son of David became the occasion for belatedly recognizing the One in whom Israel's safety

17. Schmemann, *For the Life of the World*, 139–40, 143. We shall return to the question of the nature of signs below.

18. Augustine, *The Trinity*, III.Pref.3, trans. Edmund Hill, OP (New York: New City, 1991).

and security truly lay: "In the year that King Uzziah died, I saw the Lord sitting on a throne, high and lofty; and the hem of his robe filled the temple." As I have noted on several occasions, the image of God as Israel's only true sovereign is inextricably embedded in Israel's memory, and it is in terms of this imaginative frame of reference that Isaiah recognized his sinfulness and that of his fellow Israelites: "Woe is me! I am lost, for I am a man of unclean lips, and I live among a people of unclean lips; yet my eyes have seen the King, the LORD of hosts!" (6:1, 5).

This text does not explicitly state what had made the lips of Isaiah and his fellow Israelites unclean, but later in the book we read that in a similar situation the people had declared that because of a covenant King Hezekiah of Judah had made with Egypt, "the overwhelming scourge . . . will not come to us." Isaiah responds: "we have made lies our refuge, and in falsehood we have taken shelter" (Isa. 28:15). And in the Book of Hosea we read that the northern tribes had plowed wickedness, reaped injustice, and eaten the fruit of lies because they had trusted in their military power and the multitude of their warriors (10:13). What is clear is that Isaiah links the untimely death of a powerful king to Israel's having turned away from the rule of God, a move that invariably brings with it disastrous consequences. In an ironic pronouncement, God instructs Isaiah to say to the kingdoms of Israel and Judah:

> "Keep listening, but do not comprehend;
> keep looking, but do not understand."
> Make the mind of this people dull,
>   and stop their ears,
>   and shut their eyes,
> so that they may not look with their eyes,
>   and listen with their ears,
> and comprehend with their minds,
>   and turn and be healed.

Isaiah asks, "How long?" and the dreadful reply came back:

> Until cities lie waste
>   without inhabitant,
> and houses without people,
>   and the land is utterly desolate;
> until the LORD sends everyone far away,
>   and vast is the emptiness in the midst of the land (6:9–12).

Lacking Isaiah's ability to recognize the signs of God's impending judgment, the people would not rightly interpret what they saw and heard going on around them until it was too late.

The inability of the inhabitants of Jerusalem in Isaiah's day to comprehend what was happening in their midst was not an isolated event in the history of Israel.

When questioned about his habit of teaching in parables to those outside the inner circle of disciples, Jesus associates his work and ministry with Isaiah's vision of the temple. He says to his followers that the mystery of God's apocalyptic regime had been given to them, but to those outside everything comes in parables, so that

> they may indeed look, but not
>   perceive,
> and may indeed listen, but not
>   understand;
> so that they may not turn again and
>   be forgiven. (Mark 4:12)

Christians need to take care, however, not to see this as a charge laid against Israel alone. The inability to follow the signs of God's incursion into a world in thrall to rulers and authorities bent on establishing their authority, to hear the rhythms, the dissonances, and resolutions of the messianic regime irrupting into the world, has sadly been all too prevalent in the lives of those who have claimed to be Christ's disciples. In Mark's Gospel Jesus castigates his inner circle of followers for being unable to grasp what was going on right in front of their eyes. "Do you still not perceive or understand?" he asks them. "Are your hearts hardened? Do you have eyes, and fail to see?" (8:17–18a). Significantly, the evangelist places this saying immediately before a most peculiar event in the narrative, the story of Jesus restoring the sight of a blind man in the village of Bethsaida (8:22–26). After Jesus laid his hands on the man's eyes the first time, his vision was restored, but only partially. "I can see people," the man tells Jesus, "but they look like trees, walking." Jesus must touch his eyes a second time before he could see everything clearly.

This story is followed immediately in Mark's Gospel by a pivotal event that took place in Caesarea Philippi (8:27–33). While Jesus and his disciples were "on the way," *en te hodo*,[19] he asks them, "Who do people say that I am?" After hearing that most spoke of him as some sort of prophet, he then asks, "But who do you say that I am?" Peter, always the impetuous one, replies, "You are the Messiah." Jesus cautions them not to tell anyone about this and then tells them "quite openly" that the Son of Man must suffer and die at the hands of the authorities in Jerusalem, and then after three days be delivered from the grave. Peter refuses to hear this from Jesus and takes him aside to rebuke him. But Jesus does not listen to Peter. Instead he replies in the hearing of the others, "Get behind me, Satan! For you are setting your mind not on divine things but on human things."

Peter obviously perceived something in Jesus that was noteworthy. Moreover, what he did see he described in apocalyptic and, more specifically, messianic terms.

---

19. As many commentators have noted, this phrase is not merely a rhetorical device linking together otherwise unrelated sayings and deeds of Jesus by means of a travel narrative, but a powerful parabolic image depicting the messianic way of life. Cf. Mark 9:33; 10:17, 32, 52; Acts 9:2; 18:25f.; 19:9, 23; 22:4, 14, 22.

But it is readily apparent from his response to Jesus's passion prediction that Peter did not adequately comprehend the meaning of his confession. Nor was he alone among the disciples in this inability to understand adequately all that was entailed in the life and work of this fellow from Galilee. When it came to discerning the significance of Jesus's life among them, the Twelve were like the blind man in Bethsaida after the first time Jesus touched him. They "saw" something extraordinary happening in and around him, but their "vision" was clouded, out of focus. Something more and other than simply being physically present to see and hear what was going on was needed if they were to overcome their hardness of heart and grasp the import of the people and events that swirled around Jesus.

Everything under Heaven

We too require something more and other than simply being physically present to see and hear if we are to follow the significance of all that Jesus did and suffered in relation to our own time and place. We need new habits of life and language, different ways of assessing the world in which we live our lives to recognize and respond faithfully to the signs that the world cannot decipher. We need practices that nurture the skills that transpose simple seeing into discernment and mere existing into holy habitation. Such habits are cultivated only in a company of friends through a shared participation in a social idiom in terms of which we learn how to identify, reidentify, classify, call, and respond to all the things and persons we encounter. In short, through these activities we learn to name and thereby to deal with the world as *world,* that is, as fallen and yet still cherished by its Creator. Baptism and Eucharist find their occasion and significance, then, in the reconfiguring of life according to the social idiom that God's utterance of the Word in history and breathing forth of the Spirit upon the church establish.

The ability to name the activities, institutions, and events going on around us, like reading marks on a page, is thus inseparable from practices that mediate the exchange of signs between persons, beginning with Christ. The sacraments in particular propel the members of Christ's body beyond the boundaries within which state and market seek to confine us by binding us together in a new political association upon which the ends of the ages have met. Hence, Paul can write, "As many of you as were baptized into Christ have clothed yourselves with Christ. There is no longer Jew or Greek, there is no longer slave or free, there is no longer male and female; for all of you are one in Christ Jesus" (Gal. 3:27–28).[20] In similar fashion he regards the sharing of bread and wine as constitutive of Christ's body: "*Because* there is one bread, we who are many are one body, for we all partake of one bread" (1 Cor. 10:17, my emphasis). In this body, where we are bound to him

---

20. This passage is often cited in defense of liberal egalitarianism but more accurately describes the constitution of a new household, where one's identity is conferred by a gift of the Spirit and not by the conventions of a fallen world.

whose life, death, and resurrection ransomed us from the domain of sin, death, and the devil, the *raison d'être* of the incarnation is disclosed for all creatures.

The effect of these sacramental signs is to take the bodies of women and men out of this world and relocate them in the world to come. In this present age that condemned Christ and in so doing condemned itself, bread and wine cannot become the body and blood of Christ, for nothing that belongs to it can be sacralized: "In this world Christ is crucified, His body broken, and His blood shed. And we must go out of this world . . . in order to become partakers of the world to come." The true identity of the church as the body of Christ is fulfilled in that new eon that Christ inaugurated in his passion, resurrection, and ascension, "and which was given to the Church on the day of Pentecost as its life, as the 'end' toward which it moves."[21]

The world to come in which the participants in the liturgy are caught up is not, however, an "other" world, different from the one God has created in Christ and reveals proleptically to the church: "It is the same world, *already* perfected in Christ, but *not yet* in us. It is our same world, redeemed and restored, in which Christ 'fills all things with Himself.'" The distinctiveness of the sacraments lies not in their being a miraculous exception to the natural order of things in creation. Their absolute newness resides in the specific *res* that it "reveals, manifests, and communicates," which is Christ and his kingdom: "The 'mysterion' of Christ reveals and fulfills the ultimate meaning and destiny of the world itself." And since the world is created and given as food for us by God (Gen. 1:29), who then makes food the medium of our communion with him, "the new life which we receive from God in His Kingdom *is Christ Himself*. He is our bread—because from the very beginning all our hunger was a hunger for Him and all our bread was but a symbol of Him, a symbol that had to become reality."[22] Caught up in the mystery of Christ we become attentive to the beginning and end of our existence as rational creatures, an attentiveness that is both a knowing and a desiring.

When the gathered church disperses from our eucharistic feast, the freedom that is ours in Christ translates into the ability to *follow* the dramatic pattern of events that is the liberating work of God as it unfolds within history, or more precisely, *as history*. Attending to the story of the divine performance in the material world of time and space—getting its plot, setting, and characters straight—is a crucial activity of Christian discipleship steeped in the worship of the one true God, the end of which is to participate in the divine activity and life. By means of our sacramental participation in the life and work of God, we learn how to go on and go further as a pilgrim community making our way toward that city that is to come (Heb. 13:14).

Consider the way the symbols of bread and wine in the eucharistic celebration unfold the sense and significance of the dynamic of continuity and fulfillment

21. Schmemann, *For the Life of the World*, 42.
22. Ibid., 42–43, 140 (emphasis original).

within the body of Christ. When we bring these elements to the Lord's table we first of all name them as the good gifts of God's creation. We can see, smell, touch, and taste what happens when, in the providence of God, seed, soil, water, air, nutrients (which until relatively recently were provided by fellow creatures of the four-legged variety), and sunlight combine in proper proportions and under the right temperatures in due season to produce grain and grapes. Dante was surely inspired when he brought the *Divine Comedy* to a conclusion by praising that love that moves the sun and other stars, for it is the movement of these celestial bodies that, among other things, gives us springtime and harvest.

Loaves of bread and bottles of wine, however, do not spring ready-made from the earth. In these products are embodied the skills of the farmers who plant, cultivate, and harvest the grain and the grapes, the expertise of those who grind the grain into flour and mix it with other ingredients to bake it into bread, and those who crush the grapes and oversee the delicate process of fermentation. And we dare not forget the equipment—tractors, combines, trucks, mill grinders, mixers, ovens, conveyors, packaging—without which there would be no bread or wine, or the energy that runs the equipment and the buildings in which it is used, or the capital goods that produce the equipment, buildings, and energy, or the contributions of scientists, engineers, technicians, roughnecks, secretaries—again without whom there would be no equipment, much less the materials from which that equipment is constructed.

Our litany about the natural world is still not finished. The trucks and trains that transport the bread and wine travel on roads and tracks that must be built and maintained. And if we are to eat and drink, the transport of goods over these thoroughfares must take place with a sufficient degree of safety. And so we commission peace officers who deter bandits, detain criminal suspects, and write speeding tickets, and we establish a massive legal apparatus of jurists, lawyers, clerks, and guards to adjudicate the guilt or innocence of the accused. These products, services, and institutions are themselves predicated on a vast array of skills and techniques that are perpetuated through institutions such as public schools, technical institutes, colleges, and universities. These provisions do not appear out of the blue; they must be provided and paid for by political institutions of some type, which themselves require considerable care and feeding.

We are not done yet. When the trucks that carry the finished products arrive in our neighborhoods, they do not just dump them in the middle of the street. The bread and wine are stocked in stores, where they are neither given away nor obtained by the direct exchange of goods and services, but acquired by persons handing over slips of paper that signify something we call money. This social artifact mediates the exchange of other goods and services (and once again all that is entailed in them) for our daily fare, often between persons separated by vast distances. The workings of the global market are therefore not absent from our feast. And then there are the hands that bake the bread and pour the wine, and the kinds of relationships that seem to form and develop only when family and friends meet around the dinner table. It is not an overstatement to say that there is virtually nothing under heaven or on earth that is not tacitly signified in some way by the bread and wine that is offered to God in the liturgy.

One of the aims of the Eucharist, however, is to help us understand that the significance of these products and relationships is not straightforward. Before the bread and the cup are blessed in remembrance of the crucified and risen one, the liturgy reminds us that we live in a fallen creation, a world ruled by fear, greed, division, and desecration, where access to daily sustenance is a tool of the rulers and authorities who claim for themselves the authority that belongs to God alone. "The crucifixion of Jesus was simply the dramatic manifestation of the sort of world we have made," writes Herbert McCabe, "the showing up of the world, the unmasking of what we call, traditionally, original sin."[23] Implicit in the sacraments, then, is an apocalyptic phenomenology, such that the world we now inhabit shows up or appears to us in very distinctive sorts of ways. The relation of the church's liturgical action to the everyday concerns and activities of human beings is therefore crucial to an adequate understanding of the social idiom presupposed by the gospel. In the words of Rowan Williams, "The eucharist hints at the paradox that material things carry their fullest meaning for human minds and bodies—the meaning of God's grace and of the common life thus formed—when they are the medium of *gift*, not instruments of control or objects for accumulation."[24]

True worship is thus fashioned around an alternative regime of life and language that is the product of the gift economy of the Triune God, the center of which is the crucified and risen Lord, and whose boundary is infinite, universal, *catholic*. The attentiveness of memory, understanding, and will cultivated by this social idiom pervades and defines everything Christians do and say. False worship or idolatry, by contrast, consists in the setting of our mind and heart, loyalty and confidence, hopes and fears, on something other than the mystery revealed in the incarnation of the Son and the breathing forth of the Spirit upon the church. When we are convinced that the present constellation of institutions, events, and persons truthfully exhibits the abiding nature of things, and therefore we have no choice but to act in accordance with it, then idolatry takes it most virulent form as the worship of necessity.[25]

This is not to say that there are no limits to the possibilities open to us as creatures, for that too would be idolatry. To be human is to be constituted in no small measure by the limits that subsist in our relationships with our fellow creatures. In this sense, limits are a sign of grace. Walter Lowe rightly suggests that the modern rejection of limits paved the way for the ironic "dialectic of Enlightenment," in which our attempts to master the world led to the would-be

---

23. McCabe, *God Matters*, 23.
24. Williams, *On Christian Theology*, 218.
25. A phrase I take from Lash, *Believing Three Ways in One God*, 108.

master's undoing. Quoting Theodor Adorno, Lowe contends that "'the principle of human domination, in becoming absolute . . . turned its point against man as the absolute object'. Hence the sense of entrapment, the 'iron cage.'"[26] The idolatrous worship of necessity is to regard ourselves without alternatives when it comes to these limits, thus rendering absolute our impotence before these forces and structures, completely enthralled to an authority at whose throne we have no choice but to kneel.

Convergence on and Divergence from Christ

It is at the baptismal font and the table of the crucified and risen Lord, then, that men and women have most directly and insistently to do "with the realization of the Christ-reality . . . in the contemporary world that it already embraces, owns, and inhabits . . . the whole reality of the world has already been drawn into and is held together in Christ. History moves only from this center and toward this center."[27] God's redemptive work of gathering together the whole of creation reaches its denouement in Christ (Eph. 1:9–10, 20–23; cf. 2:11–20). In this one man's sacrifice God's judgment and re-creation of this world find concrete embodiment, establishing the definitive link between the course of history and its consummation in the messianic kingdom.

As pivotal as the incarnation is to this movement of time around Christ, however, it is not enough to say that the Son entered fully into time and history, and in so doing perfectly fulfilled the will of the Father. The universal efficacy attributed to Christ's concrete historical existence by the gospel must be performatively extended to, and displayed in, every time and place so that it becomes the norm of every human being's singular existence. This is the work of the Holy Spirit, repeating within the ever-changing parameters of this world the social idiom instituted in a particular time and place by Christ. The Spirit gathers together persons from every tribe and language, people and nation, and forges them into the body politic of Christ, the earthly-historical form of the crucified and risen Christ. This pilgrim community in the power of the Spirit universalizes the concrete singularity of this one Jewish man, for "the personal in Christ can only confront the personal in the individual Christian in union with what appears to be impersonal, the church and the sacraments."[28]

The convergence and divergence of all life, all activity in relation to the events of this one man's life unfolds as history in and through the company of disciples that joins

---

26. Walter Lowe, "Prospects for a Postmodern Christian Theology: Apocalyptic without Reserve," *Modern Theology* 15 (January 1999): 21. The quote from Adorno only recapitulates an insight of Augustine in the opening lines of *City of God:* "we must not pass over the earthly city . . . which, when it seeks mastery, is itself mastered by the lust for mastery [*libido dominandi*]" (Augustine, *City of God*, I.Pref).

27. Bonhoeffer, *Ethics*, 58.

28. Von Balthasar, *Theology of History*, 81.

Jesus in his atoning sacrifice. The dynamics and parameters of this twofold movement are specified by the announcement in the Gospels that in his life, death, and resurrection the kingdom of God has drawn near. And though the image of the kingdom does not by itself specifically *denote* a political commonwealth, it does *connote* a distinctive conception of politics, that is, a dedicated network of social practices through which the intrusion into the world of God's apocalyptic regime becomes visible to all. The idiom of divine kingship thus presupposes the actual formation of a people through whom the world is confronted by God's sovereign claim upon it.[29]

Baptism is the sign and seal of one's induction into this new regime, marking the transfer of allegiance from the powers of this world to the kingdom of God, and with it the passage from life to death. Paul's reference to dying and rising with Christ in baptism (Rom. 6:3–4) does not refer to the "inner experience" of an unencumbered individual, but to the real moment of transition from the old society into a new form of life in the company of the crucified. In baptism God creates the body of Christ and continually adds new members to it by incorporating them in Jesus's death and resurrection. The baptized are caught up now in the new world that is manifested with the advent of the messianic reign of God: "So if anyone is in Christ, there is a new creation: everything old has passed away; see, everything has become new!" (2 Cor. 2:17).[30]

Immersion in the baptismal waters divests us of all previous definitions of identity based on class, ethnic or national origin, gender, and family ties: "Because in the new family [of Christ] in which all are equally sons and daughters of God there need be no more national egoisms, no struggles between classes and sexes, the promise to Abraham is fulfilled and there arises in the ancient world a new thing that is fundamentally different from all ways of life in paganism."[31] Baptism strips off the old human being with its practices and clothes the catechumen with Christ's new humanity, "which is being renewed in knowledge according to the image of its creator. In that renewal there is no longer Greek and Jew, circumcised and uncircumcised, barbarian, Scythian, slave and free; but Christ is all and in all!" (Col. 3:10b–11). In this new humanity Christians are joined not only individually to the Head who is Christ, but to one another as members of one body.

As the sign of induction into that people who keep company with the God of Jesus Christ, then, baptism inserts us into the way of being and acting that flows from the triune life of God. We are literally immersed into the overflowing love and genuine freedom that is the divine essence. But as Hazel Sherman points out, participation in the economy of God's work does not equal arrival. We still journey toward the city that is to come even as we share through the activity of the Spirit in its life and aims.[32]

29. Wright, *The New Testament and the People of God*, 307.

30. Lohfink, *Does God Need the Church?* 208–10.

31. Ibid., 211.

32. Hazel Sherman, "Baptized—'in the Name of the Father and of the Son and of the Holy Spirit,'" in *Reflections on the Water: Understanding God and the World through the Baptism of Believers*, ed. Paul S. Fiddes (Macon, GA: Smyth & Helwys, 1996), 113.

Baptism admits one to the eucharistic feast of the pilgrim people, described in patristic and early medieval texts in terms of a threefold articulation of "the body of Christ" in the writings of Paul: the historical body of the man Jesus of Nazareth; the sacramental body (*corpus mysticum*, mystical body); and the ecclesial body (*corpus verum*, true body). The sacramental body and the ecclesial body were closely linked in these early writings, with a temporal caesura or gap between them and the historical body. This caesura separates the originating event (the life, death, and resurrection of Jesus) from the manifestation of its effects, which takes place within the liturgical complex of a visible community and secret action or "mystery."[33] Together the Eucharist and the church constitute the contemporary performance of the historical body, the unique event of Jesus. The *communio* of the gathered community and the invisible action of the sacrament forges the essential unity between past event and present community: "The 'mystical,' then, is that which 'insures the unity between two times,' and brings the Christ event into present historical time in the church body, the *corpus verum*."[34] The eucharistic celebration is the performative medium for communicating the idiom (*communicatio idiomatum*) of God's redemptive work to the followers of Christ, and with it the church's interpretive stance in the world.

The gap between Jesus's historical body and the sacramental and church bodies also serves as a warning to Christians not to see the ecclesial community of which they are a part as a simple continuation or extension of Jesus. According to Williams, "when the Church performs the eucharistic action it *is* what it is called to be: the Easter community, guilty and restored, the gathering of those whose identity is defined by their new relation to Jesus crucified and raised, who identify themselves as forgiven." The church is therefore rightly understood as Christ's body, "the place of his presence," writes Williams, "but it is entered precisely by the ritual encounter with his death and resurrection, by the 'turning around' which stops us struggling to interpret *his* story in the light of *ours* and presses us to interpret ourselves in the light of the Easter event."[35]

The emphasis in the early church was thus on the Eucharist as sacred action; the community performed the mysteries (*mysteria telein*) or did the Eucharist (*eucharistiam facere*). At stake in this performance was the church's participation in Christ's sacrificial offering. As *corpus verum*, the true body of Christ performing his will, "the eucharistic action is necessarily His action of sacrifice, and what is offered must be what he offered. The consequences of His action are what he declared they would be: 'This is My Body' and 'This is My Blood.' They made the sacrament depend upon the sacrifice."[36] Paul's admonition to the Christians at Philippi to have the same mind as Christ Jesus finds its social location in this sacrament qua sacrifice: "work out your own salvation

---

33. Certeau, *Mystic Fable*, 82–83.

34. Cavanaugh, *Torture and Eucharist*, 212. The embedded quotation is from Certeau, *The Mystic Fable*, 83.

35. Williams, *Resurrection*, 58, 84.

36. Dom Gregory Dix, *The Shape of the Liturgy*, with additional notes by Paul V. Marshall (New York: Seabury, 1982), 12, 245–46.

with fear and trembling; for it is God who is at work in you, enabling you both to will and to work for his good pleasure" (Phil. 2:12b–13). This statement emphasizes the social idiom fostered by the dynamic relationship among the community, the liturgy, and the presence of the risen Christ and God's apocalyptic regime.

The mysterious action of the sacraments incorporates the bodies of Jesus's followers into the messianic suffering of God, thereby signifying the end (which is both *telos* and *eschaton*) of all true sacrifice in the atoning death of the righteous one. In the words of Augustine, "the whole of the redeemed City—that is to say, the congregation and fellowship of the saints—is offered to God as a universal sacrifice for us through the great High Priest Who offered even Himself for us in the form of a servant, so that we might be the body of so great a Head."[37] As the dwelling place of God in this age, the members of Christ's commonwealth offer up their own bodies to become the living doorposts and lintels on which the Spirit puts the blood of the Paschal Lamb of God who takes away the sins of the world. Incarnation and atonement, reconciliation and the sharing of burdens are thereby communicated, not as abstract facts, but as the concrete *idiomatum* of individual and communal being, producing "a new kind of efficacious sacrifice of praise, self-sharing and probable attendant suffering which unites us with [Christ] in the heavenly city, and at the same time totally obliterates . . . all the contours of inside and outside which constitute human power."[38]

The performative process of repeating in every time and place the social idiom of the divine kingdom is ordered around the habits and relations of the eucharistic *anamnēsis*: "Do this in memory of me." When Christians remember Jesus around the table, it is not we who recall him through an act of memory. As numerous biblical and liturgical studies have demonstrated, the liturgy brings the sacrifice of Jesus before God in such a way that it is presently operative by its effects within the ecclesial body.[39] Through its act of thanksgiving (the root meaning of "eucharist"), the church "offers its thanks, its communal sacrifice, its giving itself away, its losing control in order to be faithful and obedient to the God 'who so loved the world that he gave his only begotten Son' to the end that all who believe in him should not perish but have everlasting life." This is how Christians are *re-membered* by God to the risen Christ and to one another, and become the true body of Christ.[40] The pattern of friendships that characterizes life together in the company of Jesus's disciples is above all else a eucharistic achievement, for it is in the course of friends sharing the divine food that the Spirit re-members them as the body of Christ.[41]

37. Augustine, *City of God*, X.6.

38. Milbank, *The Word Made Strange*, 151.

39. Dix, *Shape of the Liturgy*, 245; see also Nils Dahl, "Anamnesis: Memory and Commemoration in Early Christianity," in *Jesus in the Memory of the Early Church* (Minneapolis: Augsburg, 1976), 11–29; Joachim Jeremias, *The Eucharistic Words of Jesus*, trans. Norman Perrin (Philadelphia: Fortress, 1966), 237–55; Geoffrey Wainwright, *Eucharist and Eschatology* (New York: Oxford University Press, 1981), 64–68.

40. Harmon L. Smith, *Where Two or Three Are Gathered: Liturgy and the Moral Life* (Cleveland: Pilgrim, 1995), 64–65.

41. Paul L. Lehmann, *Ethics in a Christian Context* (New York: Harper & Row, 1963), 65.

The church so constituted offers to the world the social idiom of the new creation—the peaceable relationships, the reconciling patterns of conduct, *and* the
tribulations—introduced into the midst of the old by the sacrifice of Christ. The
unfolding of history in anticipation and refusal of the reality of God taking flesh in
the world is tangibly manifested through the habits and relations of Christ's ecclesial
body to the rulers and powers of this present age (Eph. 3:10; cf. Gen. 12:3; Matt.
25:31–46). Without the bodily participation of the church in what God has accomplished (and continues to accomplish) in Christ's offering, the meaning of the
incarnation, the enfleshment of God's own self-expression, is effectively reduced to
an anecdote about another time and place.

This work of the Spirit is an ongoing, never-ending endeavor, because times and
circumstances change. New characters, social settings, and historical events are
constantly being incorporated within the ebb and flow of time around its center.
The meaning of this process is therefore never fixed but continues to unfold in the
style of a historical drama, the performance of which is never over and done with.
To cite but one case in point, the ways that the sacramental idiom of Christ's body
incorporates those of African descent in the United States will differ in certain
respects from those operative with other persons and groups.[42] The unity of this
drama's story line resides not in the sameness of its performance, but in timely
transpositions of the patterns of human acting and relating decisively enacted by
the life and passion of Jesus.

The dramatic unity wrought by these practices should therefore not be misread
as uniformity. The Holy Spirit particularizes the universality of the new humanity
in Christ by constituting the church as a community of differences. Incorporated
into this community through the sacraments, women and men receive the gifts of
the Spirit, which determine the distinctive singularity of personal existence in the
body politic of Christ. Within this community neither the whole nor the members
are simply functions of the other, and so collectivism and individualism are ruled
out from the start. Differentiation is not for its own sake, to be consumed as yet
one more commodity, but so that all might share in one calling—to be for the
sake of the world sign, foretaste, and herald of the destiny of all things in God's
new creation.[43]

From Apocalyptic Action to Sacred Spectacle

Baptism and Eucharist bind Christians together with the risen Christ in a distinctive type of political commonwealth, creating the standpoint that enables

42. As noted earlier, the dissonance involved in the struggle of African American Christians finds
no more poignant expression than in a poem by Harlem Renaissance poet Countee Cullen, "The Black
Christ," 67–110).

43. See James J. Buckley, "A Field of Living Fire: Karl Barth on the Spirit and the Church," *Modern
Theology* (January 1994): 91.

us to interpret other social formations through comparisons with its own social idiom.[44] The advent of this other city led many in the Roman empire to look upon the followers of Christ as a subversive presence within their society.[45] They were regarded as self-righteous and fanatical, worshipers of a capricious deity, atheists, the enemy of humankind and a just social order. What was it about the church that so upset the Romans? If the essence of the gospel as understood by the early church consisted principally in a private transaction between God and the individual, and thus had little or nothing to do with the commitments, claims, and corruptions of the public realm, what could possibly have led Rome to classify this new movement as an illicit political society?

Perhaps imperial officials were just mistaken about the message of those early followers of Jesus. That explanation, however, does not stand up to scrutiny. Our ecclesial forebears could have taken refuge under a provision in Roman law that allowed for the establishment of a *cultus privatus* dedicated to the pursuit of personal piety and otherworldly salvation, but they did not do so.[46] Instead they proclaimed allegiance to Christ and his kingdom in a manner that required its members to renounce loyalty to Caesar. It would appear that they deliberately provoked Roman customs and conventions with a social, this-worldly alternative to the empire that incorporated elements of its host culture while remaining a distinct people. It was this fact that led Rome to label Christianity a seditious and revolutionary movement: "The life and teachings of Jesus led to the formation of a new community of people . . . [that] had begun to look like a separate people or nation, but without its own land or traditions to legitimate its unusual customs."[47]

Rome was suspicious of the early church because the gospel as it was embraced and proclaimed by the first Christians did not primarily have to do with the communication of information on how to experience salvation within the self (more on this Gnostic misconception below), but with the judgment and transfiguration of the world, or as scripture puts it, the recapitulation of all things in heaven and on earth in Christ (Eph. 1:10). To be sure, the very notion of gospel, of good news, denoted a message, but it was always a message about "what we have heard, what we have seen with our eyes, what we have looked at and touched with our hands" (1 John 1:1). The gospel as it was understood by the early church had to do with the beginning and end of all things, and of human beings especially, *taking flesh, becoming embodied.*

44. Milbank, *Theology and Social Theory*, 388.

45. N. T. Wright, *Christian Origins and the Question of God*, vol. 1, *The New Testament and the People of God* (Minneapolis: Fortress, 1992), 350.

46. John H. Westerhoff, "Fashioning Christians in Our Day," in *Schooling Christians: "Holy Experiments" in American Education*, ed. Stanley Hauerwas and John H. Westerhoff (Grand Rapids: Eerdmans, 1992), 280; Wright, *The New Testament and the People of God*, 350, 355.

47. Robert L. Wilken, *The Christians as the Romans Saw Them* (New Haven: Yale University Press, 1984), 119. I deal with these developments in greater detail in *Another City*.

In our time, however, the sacramental sinews that bind the members of Christ's ecclesial body together have largely been supplanted by the institutions and practices regulating the transactions of a state-centered, market-driven society. Comfortable in the well-worn ruts of conspicuous consumption, comparatively few Christians see their faith as anything other than a private, inward matter that makes their lives more fulfilling. They have been trained to regard the church as another vendor of goods and services, providing for their spiritual consumption and enjoyment, and thus are incapable of mounting a serious challenge to the sway of the global market's cult of productivity and consumption. For the most part the church has acquiesced in this matter, relegating "spiritual" questions to a realm beyond the everyday world where goods are bought and sold, rewards and punishments are meted out, and the young are raised and the elderly cared for, and in the process it has supplied religious justification for the global republic of production and consumption. Ecclesial practices have been reformatted to underwrite the individual in the role of consumer, encouraging each to choose from a vast inventory of religious symbols and doctrines, to select those that best express his or her private tastes and sentiments. Some like white bread while others prefer whole wheat; some like the majesty of the Orthodox liturgy, while others are partial to the informality of Baptist services; some are drawn to the orderliness of the Reformed tradition, others the ecstasy of Pentecostal revivals; some prefer the wide range of spiritual goods and services offered by the suburban megachurch, yet others the eclectic mixture of ancient and postmodern in the so-called emerging church.

Changes in sacramental practice and theory in the late medieval and modern contexts helped to prepare the way for the consumptive habits of modern piety. In the early church, the notion of liturgy was not limited to cultic activity that is separate from the so-called profane areas of life. In the original Greek, *leitourgia* designated a "public work,"[48] that is, "an action by which a group of people become something corporately which they had not been as a mere collection of individuals—a whole greater than the sum of its parts." Starting with the Carolingian Renaissance in the ninth and tenth centuries, however, standard treatments of the concept of sacrament isolated it from its liturgical context, attempting to define as precisely as possible its *essence*, that is, "that which distinguishes it from the 'non-sacrament.'" Such debates posited for the first time a basic discontinuity between "symbol" and "reality," between what is "sacred" and what is "profane."[49]

---

48. The notion of public work has reemerged in recent years in Christian circles, but significantly not in connection with the Eucharist. Harry Boyte and Nancy Kari resurrect the term in connection with the construal of "civil society" as distinct from, yet engaged with, government and economic activity. Over against those who see civil society as a refuge from the coercive power of the state and consumerism, Boyte and Kari seek to reclaim labor as a public space that can challenge political and economic institutions (Harry C. Boyte and Nancy N. Kari, *Building America: The Democratic Promise of Public Work* [Philadelphia: Temple University Press, 1996]); cf. Cavanaugh, *Theopolitical Imagination*, 66–69.

49. Schmemann, *For the Life of the World*, 25, 137.

Medieval debates concerning real presence in the Eucharist thus exhibit a gradual inversion of meaning that culminated in the late twelfth century. As I noted above, patristic and early medieval texts, in their threefold articulation of Paul's image of Christ's body, link together the sacramental body and the ecclesial body, and posit a temporal gap between them and the historical body of Jesus, thereby constituting the contemporary performance of Christ's historical body making its journey toward the kingdom of God. In the later medieval period, however, it is the historical and sacramental bodies that were conjoined, and a synchronic gap opened between them and the ecclesial body. The consecrated bread and wine became the true body of Christ, and the liturgical emphasis shifted from historical incorporation into Christ's body and mission to awed contemplation of a sacred object venerated in the midst of grand spectacle. The visibility of the church as the performative locus of Christ's continued presence in the world was exchanged for the visibility of what took place on the altar.[50]

The intimate connection made by the patristic and early medieval church between the sacramental body (*corpus mysticum*) and the ecclesial body (*corpus verum*) was thus obscured by the dramatic reversal that took place between the meaning of sacrament and of sacrifice. Formerly the liturgical emphasis was on the active participation of the church—the true body of Christ performing his will—in the apocalyptic action of his sacrificial offering. Beginning in the late twelfth century, however, the meaning of sacrifice was made dependent on the sacerdotal consecration of the bread and wine, with the actions performed by the cleric becoming the dominant (and sometimes the sole) role in the proceedings. Since the words of consecration in some sense turn the bread and wine into the body and blood of Christ, what the church did in the Eucharist must be what Christ did with his body and blood, namely, offer them in sacrifice.[51]

As a result of these changes, the Eucharist came to be described not as liturgical action linking the church visibly to the sacrifice of Christ, but as object, with a concentration on the miracle produced in the symbols of bread and wine rather than on the transformation of the church by the presence of Christ in the liturgy. At the same time the redesignation of the church as *corpus mysticum* rendered its essence invisible: "The visibility of the church in the communal performance of the sacrament is replaced by the visibility of the Eucharistic object. Signified and signifier have exchanged places, such that the sacramental body is the visible signifier of the hidden signified, which is the social body of Christ."[52] Whereas in the patristic formula the historical body was manifested in its effects in the liturgical combination of a visible community or people and a secret (mystical) action, in later conceptualizations the visibility of the Eucharistic symbols replaced the communal celebration and served as the visible indicator of the proliferation of

50. Cavanaugh, *Torture and Eucharist*, 213.
51. Dix, *Shape of the Liturgy*, 245–46.
52. Cavanaugh, *Torture and Eucharist*, 213.

the secret effects of grace and salvation that made up the real life of the church, which was now hidden.[53]

Severing the connection between the Eucharist and the church's offering of itself as the true body of Christ resulted in "a greatly diminished sense of the essentially social implications of the Christ's eucharistic presence."[54] With the eclipse of the corporate and social implications, combined with the introduction of new practices such as the elevation of the host, the celebration of the Eucharist was redirected toward the subjective devotional life of the individual in the isolation of his own thoughts and affections.[55] "The emphasis," writes Sarah Beckwith, "was increasingly on watching Christ's body rather than being incorporated in it."[56] According to Dom Gregory Dix, it did not stop with mere watching: "The part of the individual layman . . . had long ago been reduced from 'doing' to 'seeing' and 'hearing'. Now it is retreating within himself to 'thinking' and 'feeling'. He is even beginning to think that over-much 'seeing' (ceremonial) and 'hearing' (music) are detrimental to proper 'thinking' and 'feeling.'"[57] Nothing "inessential" could be allowed to intrude upon an individual's private encounter with the divine, a proscription that could conceivably extend to the sacramental elements themselves.

Churches that do not emphasize eucharistic observance are not immune to the privatization of Christian life by means of a reinterpretation of the sacraments. In the Baptist tradition, for example, the old habits of establishmentarianism—the advocacy of a state-established church (which would have been inconceivable prior to the Reformation)—have proven to be far more difficult to break than anyone ever imagined. The first generation of Baptists regarded the rulers of earthly regimes with a wary eye, because they invariably laid stake to an authority over the church that belonged to Christ alone. In particular, they claimed that the king had exceeded temporal powers granted to him by God when he claimed authority over the church in England. King Charles I, for example, declared in 1628,

> Being by God's ordinance . . . Defender of the Faith and Supreme Governor of the Church within these our dominions, we hold it most agreeable to this our kingly office and our own religious zeal, to conserve and maintain the Church committed to our charge in unity of true religion and the bond of peace; and not to suffer

53. Certeau, *Mystic Fable*, 83–84.

54. David L. Schindler, Introduction to Lubac, *Mystery of the Supernatural*, xiii.

55. Morris, *Discovery of the Individual, 1050–1200*, 12.

56. Sarah Beckwith, *Christ's Body: Identity, Culture, and Society in Late Medieval Writings* (New York: Routledge, 1993), 36.

57. Dix, *Shape of the Liturgy*, 599. Late medieval shifts in eucharistic practice did not occur in a vacuum but were part of a series of changes within the church that helped pave the way for the republic of commerce and consumption. Among crucial social changes that had an impact on the liturgical life of the church were the centralization of clerical administration, elevation of the priestly role in the institution of the sacrament, and a rationalization of ecclesiastical power in terms of formal right and contract that reached its apex in the eleventh century during the papacy of Gregory VII.

unnecessary disputations, altercations or questions to be raised which may nourish factionalism both in the Church and commonwealth.[58]

Baptists rejected such claims as idolatrous, insisting that the church alone was the visible sign of the rule of Christ over all power in heaven and earth, and thus earthly powers had no authority over Christ's body, nor were the king's decrees numbered among the divine ordinances. As the London Confession of 1644 puts it, Christ had established here in this age

> a spirituall Kingdome, which is the Church, which he hath purchased and redeemed unto himselfe, as a peculiar inheritance: which Church, as it is visible to us, is a company of visible Saints, called & separated from the world, by the word and Spirit of God, to the visible profession of the faith of the Gospel, being baptized into that faith, and joyned to the Lord, and each other, by mutuall agreement, in the practical injoyment of the Ordinances, commanded by Christ their head and King.[59]

Because Baptists believed that the rule of Christ claimed the whole of their lives, the church was, as Philip Thompson has put it, "the earthly arena in which the reign of Christ was embodied, and as such was an interruption and delegitimization of the false politics of the state."[60] The existence of Christ's "mystical body" (by this time the standard term designating the church as Christ's body), made visible to all by believer's baptism, intruded upon and called into question the authority of every other ruler and principality.

Early Baptists regarded their participation in the body of Christ as a visible sign of God's presence and activity before the rulers and authorities of the present age, gathered together by what they called Christ's ordinances—prayer, preaching, the devotional reading of scripture, works of mercy, and the pastoral office— but especially by those ordinances explicitly called sacraments, viz., baptism and Eucharist. Their understanding of these practices, and in particular their critique of and resistance to the Church of England, was rooted in their conviction that God's work of salvation could not be constrained by any human institution such as a temporal state. Idolatry, not liberty of conscience, was the principal sin of the crown's attempt to usurp divine authority over the church. The attention they gave

58. "The King's Declaration," *Documents of the English Reformation*, 481.

59. William L. Lumpkin, *Baptist Confessions of Faith*, rev. ed. (Valley Forge, PA: Judson, 1969), 165. The notion of "spirituall" here does not mean "nonworldly," as clearly indicated in an earlier article of the *Confession*: "Touching his Kingdome, Christ being risen from the dead, ascended into heaven, sat on the right hand of God the Father, having all power in heaven and earth, given unto him, he doth spiritually govern his Church, exercising his power over all Angels and Men, good and bad, to the preservation and salvation of the elect, to the overruling and destruction of his enemies" (Lumpkin, *Baptist Confessions of Faith*, 161).

60. Philip E. Thompson, "Sacraments and Religious Liberty: From Critical Practice to Rejected Infringement," in *Baptist Scaramentalism*, ed. Anthony R. Cross and Philip E. Thompson (Waynesboro, GA: Paternoster, 2003), 46.

to what constitutes the faithful practice of baptism reflects this concern. Baptism was for them the sacrament that conferred the proper significance on all bodies—communal as well as individual—and thus it relativized all other political expressions by locating true politics within the church. They were therefore concerned when the Church of England used infant baptism, in the words of Thomas Grantham, to bring persons "by the lump into the Name of Christian Churches."[61]

Once baptism had incorporated these early Baptists into the church's body politic, their day-to-day lives were not merely surveyed, categorized, inventoried, and supplemented by some sort of "spiritual" (i.e., "therapeutic") benefit but were radically transfigured in a way that touched on every aspect of their existence, body as well as soul. They would have agreed with Dietrich Bonhoeffer's contention that repentance and faith are "not in the first place thinking about one's own needs, problems, sins, and fears, but allowing oneself to be caught up into the way of Jesus Christ, into the messianic event."[62] And as they learned from firsthand experience, their participation in the apocalyptic event of Christ's life and passion brought them into conflict with those who actively sought to usurp the place and power of God.

There was a close link between the Baptist tradition of social and political dissent and their understanding of the sacraments.[63] They were persuaded that Word and Spirit did not address the human heart directly but required ecclesial mediation. According to the *Orthodox Creed* of 1679:

> There is one holy catholick church . . . gathered, in one body under Christ, the only head thereof; which church is gathered by special grace, and the powerful and internal work of the spirit; and are effectually united unto Christ their head. . . .
>
> [W]e believe the visible church of Christ on earth, is made up of several distinct congregations, which make up that one catholick church, or mystical body of Christ. And the marks by which she is known to be the true spouse of Christ, are these, viz.,

---

61. Thomas Grantham, *The Prisoner Against the Prelate, or A Dialogue Between the Common Goal [sic] and Cathedral of Lincoln, Wherein the True Faith and Church of Christ are briefly discovered and vindicated By Authority of Scripture, Suffrages of Antiquity, Concessions and Confessions of the Chief Oppressors of the same Church and Faith* (np:no, ca. 1662), cited by Thompson, "Sacraments and Religious Liberty," 46–47.

62. Bonhoeffer, *Letters and Papers from Prison*, 361–62.

63. In the sense I am using it here, dissent is not an expression of unconstrained individuals, but a peculiar form of involvement in and witness to the social structures of a given time and place on the part of the members of Christ's body (one thinks here of the civil rights movement in the United States during the 1960s, led by the Baptist pastor Martin Luther King, Jr.). Meaningful disagreement on particular issues makes sense only against the backdrop of a wider frame of reference in a shared set of practices and body of judgments. Apart from such a backdrop, dissent cannot help but to deteriorate into the misguided notion that our convictions are but expressions of taste and personal preference, having no real connection to the structures that order the world of time and space. Any community that desires to be in good working order requires well-formed dissent, not only for its own sake, but finally for truth's sake, and insofar as the church is concerned, on behalf of a creation, fallen and yet still cherished by its Creator. Dissent is part of a cooperative practice, a form of participation in an ongoing communal endeavor. The point of argument within a tradition is not ultimately to "win," which would locate it instead in the context of a competitive *agon* and not that of a *polis* seeking to bear witness to the Triune God. Its aim must always be to persuade and to be persuaded as the community seeks to come to one mind with respect to the truth.

where the word of God is rightly preached, and the sacraments truly administered, according to Christ's institution, and the practice of the primitive church . . . ; to which church and not elsewhere, all persons that seek for eternal life, should gladly join themselves."[64]

According to these early Baptists, then, the church that challenges the authority of the king does not assemble at the initiative of its members but instead is gathered together by the working of God, which requires, among other things, a more theologically refined sense of remembrance. When Christians gather around the table, it is not we who recall Jesus to mind. As numerous biblical and liturgical studies have demonstrated, it is instead an epicletic appeal to God that he would remember the new covenant enacted by his sacrifice,[65] for this is how we are joined to Christ and to one another as members of his body.

Early Baptists thus recovered for the circumstances of their time and place something of the sense and sensibility that characterized the early church, which was that the gospel was not at bottom a worldview, but a people gathered together, not by their own will or decision, but by the power of the Spirit, to be for the world the earthly-historical form of the crucified and risen Christ. As Wilken describes the self-understanding of the nascent Christian community, "Christianity enters history not only as a message but also as a communal life, a society or city," that was constituted by "inner discipline and practices, rituals and creeds, and institutions and traditions."[66] The initial trajectory plotted by the seventeenth-century Baptists was not, however, generally sustained by later generations. As their external circumstances improved—toleration in England, the institutionalization of religious liberty in the New World, and advances in social standing—the heirs of John Bunyan and Muriel Lester, Anne Hutchinson and Roger Williams made their peace with the earthly city. Baptist churches (together with other Christian communities) increasingly settled for the care of "souls," ceding virtually all claims on the bodies of their members to the civil authorities.[67] And as salvation was reconceived as a private transaction between solitary individuals and God, even this limited jurisdiction was stripped from their purview. Baptism no longer

64. Lumpkin, *Baptist Confessions of Faith*, 318–19.

65. In addition to the writings of Jeremias and Wainwright, see Fritz Chenderlin, SJ, *"Do This as My Memorial": The Semantic and Conceptual Background and Value of* Anamnēsis *in 1 Corinthians 11:24–25* (Rome: Biblical Institute Press, 1982); and David B. Capes, "The Lord's Table: Divine or Human Remembrance? *Perspectives in Religious Studies* 30 (Summer 2003): 199–209.

66. Wilken, *Spirit of Early Christian Thought*, xv.

67. Mark Bell documents how Baptists moved gradually toward cultural establishment during the Interregnum, particularly among the leadership in London who "pushed radicalism to the perimeters, both geographically and theologically." He states that "during the seventeenth century, a number of the leading Baptists eager for accommodation with society had gained considerable wealth. This increase in wealth was frequently accompanied by a change in social position, which gave many Baptists a greater incentive to accommodate with society" (Mark R. Bell, *Apocalypse How? Baptist Movements during the English Revolution* [Macon, GA: Mercer University Press, 2000], 129–30).

accomplished anything concrete but only expressed what had occurred in the experience of the individual. Abdication from the public realm effectively made the church incidental to salvation, reducing it to a *collegium pietatis*, a social club for the cultivation of a privatized spirituality.[68]

As a result of these and other changes, many Baptists, particularly in North America, embraced the division of spheres implemented under the auspices of the modern idea of religion, which they regarded as the liberation of faith from all political entanglements. One of the most prominent names in this retrenchment in the eighteenth and nineteenth centuries was that of John Leland of Virginia (1754–1841). Leland adopted Lockean and Madisonian theories about natural rights and voluntary associations to reconfigure historic Baptist convictions regarding liberty of conscience and the disestablishment of the church from the state. Liberty of conscience became "the inalienable right that each individual has, of worshipping his God according to the dictates of his conscience, without being prohibited, directed, or controlled therein by human law, either in time, place, or manner."[69]

Unfortunately, no world is free of regulatory modes of one sort or another. The position of Leland and his supporters unwittingly reestablished the church socially and politically, in a new form to be sure, but one that nonetheless fit perfectly into the world they thought they were challenging. The institutional disestablishment of "religion" they sought took place under the auspices of a social arrangement that sanctioned a moral identity of the church with the state and its commercial republic.[70] Cast now in the role of "autonomous individuals," women and men are required to render to "Caesar" (the political consortium of managerial government and the global market) their unconditional loyalty. This new emperor in his sovereign benevolence then permitted, or rather *guaranteed*, these newly minted individuals the right to "religious beliefs," which are perfectly free as long as they are perfectly private ("in the closet" of one's mind or heart, so to speak).

The Return of Gnosticism

These shifts in sacramental practice were instrumental to the development of a kind of spirituality that is commensurate with a solitary career of self-determination, which is the highest good in liberal social orders. Such an aspiration presupposes the existence of a realm of nonhistorical freedom, where autonomous selves are not bound by the corporeal presence of other selves or

---

68. Bonhoeffer, *Life Together and Prayerbook of the Bible*, 45.

69. Leland, "A Blow at the Root," 239. See Curtis W. Freeman, "Can Baptist Theology Be Revisioned?" *Perspectives in Religious Studies* 24 (Fall 1997): 271–302.

70. See Nathan O. Hatch, *The Democratization of American Christianity* (New Haven: Yale University Press, 1989).

the created world.[71] In the process an ancient adversary of the church's distinctive social idiom has found opportunity once again to make a determined claim for the members of Christ's body. With the canonization of the myth of the unencumbered self by liberal capitalist social orders, religious piety and polity invariably tend toward Gnosticism, an age-old practice that teaches that faith and salvation are essentially private matters, with no real connection to history or social existence. Indeed, says Philip Lee, such tendencies represent "an attempt to escape from everything except the self."[72]

Harold Bloom, elaborating on Lee's insights, contends that the modern form of Gnosticism is so pervasive that even self-professed secularists and atheists tacitly embrace its view of the human self. Believer and nonbeliever join together to form "a religiously mad culture, furiously searching for the spirit," because "each of us is subject and object of the one quest, which must be for the original self, a spark of breath in us that we are convinced goes back to before the Creation." This gnosticized form of the Christian confession has for the most part kept the figure of Jesus, but it is "a very solitary and personal American Jesus, who is also the resurrected Jesus rather than the crucified Jesus or the Jesus who ascended again to the Father."[73] Indeed, North Americans might not really want a Jesus rooted in history, for as Rodney Clapp observes, "that would be a particular Jesus who might reveal a particular God with a character and purpose different from our own."[74]

Bloom oversimplifies the convoluted genealogy of modern religiosity, overlooking, for example, its Stoic elements.[75] He nevertheless makes explicit the role that Gnostic notions have played in shaping the myth of a self that haunts a ghostly realm of ahistorical freedom, unencumbered by the bodily presence of other selves and by everything that inhabits the physical world.[76] Consider the popular interpretation of the Protestant doctrine of justification by grace through faith that has become axiomatic in many churches. In the Bible divine forgiveness and reconciliation constituted a visible sign of the new creation, an eschatological reality proleptically

71. More will be said in chapter 7 about the invention of the unencumbered individual.

72. Philip J. Lee, *Against the Protestant Gnostics* (New York: Oxford University Press, 1987), 9–10.

73. Harold Bloom, *The American Religion*, 22, 32.

74. Rodney Clapp, *A Peculiar People: The Church as Culture in a Post-Christian World* (Downers Grove, IL: InterVarsity Press, 1996), 35.

75. Daniel Hardy and David Ford rightly observe that a stoicized Christianity can count on many allies in this culture: "The nation state is delighted to welcome a religion that is so timid and orderly, leaving the passions free for economics, war and collective sport" (Daniel W. Hardy and David F. Ford, *Praising and Knowing God* [Philadelphia: Westminster, 1985], 144; cf. 94–99); cf. MacIntyre, *After Virtue*, 168–70, 234–37; and Walker Percy, "Stoicism in the South," *Sign-Posts in a Strange Land*, ed. Patrick Samway (New York: Farrar, Straus & Giroux, 1991), 83–88.

76. As I noted in chapter 4, the early fathers generally had a more sophisticated understanding of interiority. In particular, the distinction they drew between "inner" and "outer" was not that of a gnostic body/soul polarity, but between that part of the mind that is dependent on the body for the exercise of its powers, and that which is not.

realized within this age, and made known to its rulers and authorities by the body politic of Christ. Within the modern regime, however, forgiveness and reconciliation become a private transaction between God and an individual, abstracted from its apocalyptic context and unmindful of any consequences for the internal life of the church or its relationships with other forms of social life.[77]

The privatizing of salvation in terms of the individual's standing *coram deo,* before God alone, unwittingly contributed to the dubious conclusion that the essence of the gospel "is a knowing, by and of an uncreated self, or self-within-the-self, and the knowledge leads to freedom . . . from nature, community, other selves." This freedom exacts a very high price from those who embrace it, "because of what it is obliged to leave out: society, temporality, the other. What remains, for it, is solitude and the abyss."[78] By contrast the sacraments, as they were originally performed, are public actions, incorporating women and men into the visible body of Christ, involving them in a communal and public disciplining of bodies that of necessity is political in nature, confronting the authorities and rulers of this world with a radically different constitution of human life within the apocalyptic action of the Triune God.

Given the state of the world we now inhabit, the allure of Gnosticism is in some ways understandable. We see at virtually every turn the triumph of consumerism, the withering away of local associations that once bound people together in patterns of mutual obligation and enjoyment, the proliferation of individual rights without due regard for the goods that constitute the common welfare, and the expansion of technological networks devoted almost exclusively to means rather than ends. The natural and social world has become "nothing but a meeting place for individual wills, each with its own set of attitudes and preferences and who understand that world solely as an arena for the achievement of their own satisfaction, who interpret reality as a series of opportunities for their enjoyment and for whom the last enemy is boredom."[79] Finally, seemingly intractable racial and ethnic divisions and senseless violence place additional strain on the ability of liberal democracy and its commercial republic to manage the task of achieving and sustaining a truly human form of life.

In the final analysis, however, Gnosticism has no redeeming power for this world. When men and women seek to be free from other selves and from the created world, they only exacerbate their fragmented situation. In the words of Martin Buber, "caprice and doom, the spook of the soul and the nightmare of the world" are bound inextricably together. They "get along with each other, living next door and avoiding each other, without connection and friction, at home in meaninglessness—until in one instant eye meets eye, madly, and the confession erupts from both that they are unredeemed."[80] It was precisely into this world that God sent the Son, not to

77. See L. Gregory Jones, *Embodying Forgiveness: A Theological Analysis* (Grand Rapids: Eerdmans, 1995), 38

78. Bloom, *American Religion,* 37, 49.

79. MacIntyre, *After Virtue,* 25.

80. Martin Buber, *I and Thou,* trans. Walter Kaufmann (New York: Scribner's, 1970), 108.

condemn it, but that it might be saved through him. It is into this same world that God now sends the church in the power of the Spirit to be salt and light, to continue Christ's mission of reconciliation and redemption,[81] a public work that takes shape around sacramental action.

Telling the Little Narratives: Sacramental Performance in a Postmodern World

Many in recent years have argued that in the postmodern world the grand narrative of human development in the style of Hegel and Marx has reached an end, and that from now on only little narratives that try to make sense only of local and contingent events can be told.[82] During this same time global capitalism has effectively established its presence and power as the most "rapacious grand narrative in the history of the West."[83] The regulatory schemes enforced by the combined efforts of the nation-state and the global market have radically reconfigured what it means to be human beings. The everyday activities and relationships of virtually every man, woman, and child on this planet are no longer attuned to the rhythms of nature, the changing of the seasons, the patterns of other life-forms, the peculiarities of particular places and times, or the institutions, crafts, and habits that once mediated human interaction with the rest of creation. These realities no longer serve as signs of the beginning and end of all things, and of reasoning creatures especially. Once every human being was sister, brother, cousin, parent, grandchild, a member of this household, that village, this tribe. Now every human is groomed from birth to be an "individual" whose identity is determined not by being particular persons inhabiting particular places, but by the undifferentiated role of producer and consumer in a global system of governance, accumulation, and exchange. These regulatory mechanisms have uprooted social relationships and personal identities that were once embedded in local associations, and redistributed them via technological networks that extend across vast distances in time and space.

If the body of Christ is to help its members resist complete assimilation to the ways of this regime of coercion and commerce while at the same time fully engaging it at both the institutional and the practical levels, writes Nicholas Boyle, the church will "need to draw its moral strength not from its international presence but from its claim to represent people as they are locally and distinct from the worldwide ramifications of their existence as participants in the global market." In its efforts to embody the social idiom of God's apocalyptic regime, then, the Christian community must learn how to tell "the little narratives of the victims of the grand process,

81. Cf. Rev. 2:26; 2 Cor. 5:18–19.

82. See, for example, Jean-François Lyotard, *The Postmodern Condition: A Report on Knowledge*, trans. Geoff Bennington and Brian Massumi (Minneapolis: University of Minnesota Press, 1984), 37–41, 60.

83. Coakley, *Powers and Submissions*, xiv.

the stories of what the big new world is squeezing out or ignoring . . . full of details which the new world will dismiss as superficial and inessential."[84]

These little narratives find their interpretive context in the journey of the church to God's kingdom, orchestrated in this age through the sacraments. When men and women pass through the waters of baptism and partake of the bread of life and the cup of salvation at the Lord's table, they submit themselves to the all-encompassing claim of Jesus on their lives disclosed in the service of the Word. The dramatic encounters with his contemporaries recorded in scripture—often set in the context of table fellowship—become figures for our own encounters with Christ through reading the Bible in community. When this occurs the solid line that modern methods of interpretation typically draw between the "world of the Bible" and the "real world out there," between what the Bible "meant" and what it "means,"[85] begins to dissipate. The canonical texts provide the performative images in terms of which the members of Christ's body may discern their present circumstances and decide among alternative courses of action in ways that will allow them in the future to remain faithful to the *anamnēsis* of Jesus.

"From the standpoint of the Church," writes Williams, "the events around Jesus make possible those new modes of human being spoken of, symbolized and enacted in the Church, and the appropriation and transformation of Jewish paradigms in a radically different context. To explore the continuities of Christian patterns of holiness is to explore the *effect* of Jesus, living, dying and rising."[86] As we follow Jesus in baptism and then take our seats at the last meal that he shared with his closest friends, we discover patterns of actions and encounters that make up the timely process of creation's convergence and divergence in relation to its center. Meeting Jesus once again around the table of disciples plunges us back into the world precisely as it teeters on the threshold between two ages. As we partake of his board of fare, each of us is given new roles to play, unfamiliar points on which to stand and speak, and perhaps most importantly, a new company of actors with which to perform, gathered "from every tribe and language and people and nation" (Rev. 5:9). The aim of baptism and Eucharist in our circumstances, then, is to take isolated producer-consumers and produce martyrs, witnesses to the apocalyptic activity of God in Christ.

This road company of the messianic kingdom thus does not merely mark the passage of time. Her members are instead "drawn into a share in the vulnerability of God, into a new kind of life and a new identity. They do not receive an additional item called faith; their ordinary existence is not reorganized, found wanting in specific respects and supplemented: it is transfigured as a whole."[87] By enacting

---

84. Boyle, *Who Are We Now?* 91–92.

85. See Krister Stendahl, "Biblical Theology, Contemporary," in *The Interpreter's Dictionary of the Bible*, vol. 1, ed. George Arthur Buttrick (Nashville: Abingdon, 1962), 418–32.

86. Rowan Williams, "The Unity of Christian Truth," *New Blackfriars* 70 (February 1989): 92.

87. Williams, "Postmodern Theology and the Judgement of the World," 138.

in our bodies the social idiom by which human beings are drawn into the vulnerability of God, the Eucharist transposes into our circumstances the confrontation between the present world and the age to come inaugurated by Jesus's life and ministry. The social practices and institutions that bound the members of the early church together in a new style of public life continue to serve as a definitive sign to the world that this new creation has dawned. Through our confession of Christ's Lordship—sealed by baptism, celebrated in the eucharistic feast, and lived out daily in a holy life of service and fellowship—we announce to the world in both word and deed that the end toward which history is moving is not determined by those whom this age calls powerful, but by the one who gathers together all things in heaven and on earth in the crucified Messiah of Israel.

The irruption of the messianic reign of God establishes the goal toward which all things tend, and it also sets the limits for the exercise of power by all worldly authorities. In and through the commonwealth of the church, everything in the created order, all life, is "now, at once, immediately confronted with a claim that is non-negotiable in the sense that in the end God will irrefutably be—God."[88] To be re-membered in Christ is to be caught up in Christ's mission to and for the world, the end of which is to glorify God and to gather up or recapitulate the whole of creation in the great activity of delighting in the beauty of God manifested in every aspect of the cosmos.[89] Because the whole of our existence as human beings is claimed and transfigured by the drawing near of the reign of God to this fallen world, Christ's followers must attend in particular to the cares and concerns that make up the business of everyday life: building houses, tending gardens, buying and selling, marrying and giving in marriage, and raising children. As Christians engage in these public activities, our goal is not simply to survive in what can at times be a hostile environment.[90] The primary task is rather to glorify God in the world (John 17:20–24), which takes place in the generative interaction between the liturgy of the Eucharist and in the liturgy, that is, the public work of mission.

The connection between the two forms of the liturgy is exemplified in the relationship between the Eucharist and the practice of hospitality.[91] The sharing of bread around the Lord's table invokes the common life and purse of the first disciples, whom Jesus formed into a new household that relativized the claims of their "biological" or "ethnic" families on their material resources (cf. Mark 10:29–31). Following Christ's ascension they continued their pattern of eating together, considering it "the right way both to remember his death and his res-

88. McClendon, *Doctrine*, 66.

89. See David L. Schindler, "Christology and the *Imago Dei:* Interpreting *Gaudium et Spes*," *Communio* 23 (Spring 1996): 176–77.

90. For a community to render any kind of useful service to the world, it must survive with its identity intact. From this standpoint survival and servanthood are not antitheses, but dialectically connected.

91. For an excellent discussion of hospitality in relation to the Eucharist, see Elizabeth Newman, *Untamed Hospitality: Welcoming God and Other Strangers* (Grand Rapids: Brazos, 2007), 147–72.

urrection appearances and to affirm their hope of his return."[92] As noted above, before the bread is blessed at Christ's table, it is a sign of a fallen creation, a world in rebellion, dominated by fear, greed, and division. But when it is blessed, it becomes a sign of God's new creation, a realm where perfect love casts out fear, generosity reaches out to the stranger in the gate, and reconciliation heals the world's divisions. John Chrysostom thus exhorts Christians to practice hospitality on the basis of the eucharistic feast:

> Do you wish to honor the Body of Christ? Do not despise him when he is naked. Do not honor him here in the church building with silks, only to neglect him outside, when he is suffering from cold and from nakedness. For he who said, "This is my Body," is the same who said, "You saw me, a hungry man, and you did not give me to eat." Of what use is it to load the table of Christ? Feed the hungry and then come and decorate the table. You are making a golden chalice and you do not give a cup of cold water? The Temple of your afflicted brother's body is more precious than this Temple. The Body of Christ becomes for you an altar. It is more holy than the altar of stone on which you celebrate the holy sacrifice. You are able to contemplate this altar everywhere, in the street and in the open squares.[93]

This shared meal prefigures the hope of the messianic age, when—as Mary's song magnifying the Lord puts it—the rich will give up what we now call their capital, and the poor will be well fed (Luke 1:53).

As these actions suggest, the encounter with Jesus at his table never leaves us as we are but "force[s] to light hidden directions and dispositions that would otherwise never come to view, and thus make[s] the conflicts of goals and interests between people a *public* affair." Those who engage the risen Christ in this manner thus discover that they have perpetually become a question to themselves. All that they had formerly assumed was true, everything that had once appeared good and right and proper in their world, whatever they said or did, is constantly exposed to a new and unexpected light. There are, of course, no guarantees about these engagements. With some, as with the figure of the rich ruler (Luke 18:18–25), the inability to grasp their status as a cherished creature of God "becomes visible and utterable in the form of complicity in rejecting Jesus." With others, as with the Zacchaeus (Luke 19:1–10), the "readiness to come to judgment and to recognize the possibility of truth and meaning becomes visible and utterable in the form of discipleship, abiding in the community created by God's love."[94]

As I noted in the previous chapter, the love that creates the disciple community should not be confused with cheap sentiment. The sacramental re-membering of Christ's body in its social and personal aspects takes place according to well-

92. Yoder, *For The Nations*, 44.

93. John Chrysostom, *Homilies on the Gospel of St. Matthew*, 50.4–5, trans. Tissa Balasuriya, *The Eucharist and Human Liberation* (Maryknoll, NY: Orbis Books, 1979), 26.

94. Williams, "Postmodern Theology and the Judgment of the World," 96.

established patterns attested to in the New Testament. Our baptism is a baptism into the death of Christ (Rom. 6:3–4; cf. Mark 8:34), and the celebration of the Lord's table "always and necessarily operates between the two poles of Maundy Thursday and Easter Sunday, between Gethsemane and Emmaus, between the Upper Room before the crucifixion and the Upper Room to which the risen Jesus comes." Our participation in the life of God in the world occurs in the apocalyptic interval made actual by the eucharistic feast. This gathering continually signifies the restoration of a fellowship broken time and again by human infidelity, including our own. The communal practice of discernment, forgiveness, and reconciliation is thus presupposed by this meal. In this meal "the wounded body and the shed blood are inescapably present."[95]

It is the obligation of each member of Christ's body to make her or his own the intrusion of the wounded body of Jesus into a world that is ordered around a very different set of practices and dispositions. As vital as scriptural reasoning, doctrine, baptism, and Eucharist are in this regard, they do not by themselves cultivate the habits of life and language that reveal to the world God's messianic regime. The practices of spiritual formation—prayer, confession, the giving and receiving of counsel, forgiveness and reconciliation, fasting, hospitality, and the works of mercy—are a necessary complement to the work of these other constitutive activities of the church, enabling Jesus's followers to embody in their daily lives the ultimate meaning and destiny of creation. It is to these practices of spiritual formation, and especially their interaction with the modes of regulating human conduct promoted by the state and market, that we now turn.

95. Williams, *Resurrection*, 40.

7

Holy Vulnerable

Spiritual Formation and the Politics of the Spirit

You should love God unspiritually, that is, your soul should be unspiritual and
stripped of all spirituality.

Meister Eckhart, *Sermon 83*

In an address to the ecumenical conference held in Fanø, Denmark, in August
1934, Dietrich Bonhoeffer poses a key question to the conferees: How does
peace come about? Is it the result of international peace treaties, economic investment in developing countries, or universal peaceful rearmament? According to
Bonhoeffer, it is through none of these, for they confuse peace with safety: "There
is no way to peace along the way of safety. For peace must be dared. It is the great
venture. It can never be safe. Peace is the opposite of security." In the end, "Peace
means to give oneself altogether to the law of God, wanting no security, but in
faith and obedience laying the destiny of the nations in the hand of Almighty God,
not trying to direct it for selfish purposes. Battles are won, not with weapons, but
with God. They are won where the way leads to the cross."[1]

The great venture of peace is part and parcel of the church's interpretive surmise
about human existence as lived in relation to God. As members of Christ's body,

---

1. Dietrich Bonhoeffer, *Dietrich Bonhoeffer Works*, vol. 13, *London: 1933–1935*, trans. Hans Goedeking,
Martin Heimbucher, and Hans-Walter Schleicher (Minneapolis: Fortress, 2007), 307–8.

Christians are gathered together by the Spirit as a sign to all that in the end peace rather than conflict will have the final say, and that vulnerability, not security, forms the path leading to that which alone truly deserves the name of peace: "a perfectly ordered and perfectly harmonious fellowship in the enjoyment of God, and of one another in God."[2] Practices that cultivate women and men capable of leading such extraordinary lives while "living unreservedly in life's duties, problems, successes and failures, experiences and perplexities,"[3] are among the constitutive activities that establish the Christian community as a distinctive body politic that promotes "its own laws and its own patterns of behavior,"[4] a form of life I shall refer to as the politics of the Spirit.

In the first few centuries of the church, those who wished to transfer their allegiance to this new body politic were required to submit to a lengthy and rigorous process lasting three years or more.[5] The extent of their participation in the life of community was carefully circumscribed at the outset, to protect the mystery of the community from profanation. Those who were not yet baptized were allowed to attend the first part of the liturgy, consisting of readings from scripture, singing, prayer, and proclamation, but were often dismissed before the Eucharist was celebrated. As the catechumens made progress in practices of reading the Bible, learning the creeds, prayer, hospitality, forgiveness, and reconciliation, which they learned through imitation from those more experienced in the life of virtue, their level of involvement gradually increased. The whole process was taken very seriously, such that men and women could, if their apprenticeship in the catechetical process was deemed insufficient, be denied membership.[6]

Contrast the profundity, rigor, and seriousness of the early church's modes of spiritual formation with what regularly passes for spirituality in our time and place. One popular trend is a custom-designed deity for discriminating modern consumers, most often one that is "a gentle twin of the one they grew up with. He is wise but soft-spoken, cheers them up when they're sad, laughs at their quirks. He is, most essentially, validating, like the greatest of friends. . . . the God they choose is more like a best friend who has endless time for their needs, no matter how trivial."[7] And at bookstores and discount malls across North America, one can find countless self-help books that claim to help individuals discover their own, true spiritual identity.[8] What these discriminating shoppers of spiritual goods and

---

2. Augustine, *City of God*, XIX.17.

3. Bonhoeffer, *Letters and Papers from Prison*, 370.

4. Wilken, *Christians as the Romans Saw Them*, 118–19.

5. Hippolytus, *The Treatise on the Apostolic Tradition*, XVII, 28,

6. John Navone, SJ, *Seeking God in Story* (Collegeville, MN: Liturgical Press, 1990), 14; Budde, *(Magic) Kingdom of God*, 67–68.

7. Hanna Rosin, "Beyond 2000: Many Shape Unique Religions at Home," *Washington Post*, Jan 17, 2000 (http://www.washingtonpost.com/wp-dyn/A58347-2000Jan17.html): A1.

8. See, for example, *Who Is My God? An Innovative Guide to Finding Your Spiritual Identity*, by the editors at SkyLight Paths (Woodstock, VT: SkyLight Paths, 2000). Such personalized descriptions call

services finally want to know is, How will believing in this spiritual path improve my quality of life? Bottom line, what does this deity (or whatever constitutes the object of spiritual attention) do for me?[9]

Both types of spiritual formation are inextricably linked with very different habits, appetites, affections, and relationships that specify and enact radically divergent interpretations of what human life is all about. Each presupposes a distinctive hermeneutical stance that must be examined in connection with the respective regimes of power that constitute and regulate the social bodies within which each is set. Any discussion of the nature of spiritual formation that fails to take into account the institutions and practices that constitute these competing regimes will invariably provide an incomplete and misleading picture.[10]

It lies beyond the scope of the present work to discuss in detail the rich variety of practices of Christian spiritual formation—prayer, confession, fasting, hospitality, the giving and receiving of counsel, rites of forgiveness and reconciliation, and the works of mercy. I shall concentrate instead on some of the ways these activities, working in concert with the other constitutive practices of the church, help Jesus's followers make the social idiom of the messianic regime of God their own. Within this mode of life our everyday existence begins with the acknowledgment of our vulnerability as creatures, or as the Bible refers to it, the fear of God. This vulnerability is sanctified, made holy, in the incarnation, where the exchange of love between the first two persons of the Trinity opens itself through the activity of the Spirit to all creation. As we are caught up in this exchange, we learn to embrace our contingent existence as given to us by the Creator of all, whom we also learn to love as the one who first loved us. The love of God for creation manifested through the incarnation of the Word and the sending forth of the Spirit, in turn, defines the aim of spirituality as *holy vulnerability*. In the politics of the Spirit, then, vulnerability is scripted, not as a stereotypically female weakness, but as "a (special sort of) 'human' strength."[11]

---

to mind the principal trait of bystanders during the Nazi era in Germany and occupied Europe, namely, men and women whose lives were centered around their own needs; thus, they averted their gaze from the evil going on about them.

9. Robert Jenson points out that the maxim beloved by most Protestants, that to know God is to know God's benefits, makes sense only when God's identity is already well established. In our context, says Jenson, this maxim "is plainly false and has been a disaster for the church" (Jenson, *Triune God*, 51n68).

10. That matters normally listed under the category of spirituality are directly related (though often implicitly and perhaps even unwittingly) to the dispositions, motives, and exchanges that regulate everyday life is not, of course, a new discovery. Alexis de Tocqueville called attention to it early in the nineteenth century: "Religion, which never interferes directly in the government of Americans, should ... be regarded as the first of their political institutions, for, if it does not give them a taste for liberty, it enables them to take unusual advantage of it. . . . I do not know whether all Americans put faith in their religion, for who can read into men's hearts? But I am sure that they believe it necessary for the maintenance of republican institutions" (Alexis de Toqueville, *Democracy in America*, trans. Gerald E. Bevan [New York: Penguin, 2003], 342).

11. Coakley, *Powers and Submissions*, 25. Coakley adds that "Jesus may be the male messenger to *empty* 'patriarchal' values" (emphasis original).

Conversely, if Christian formation is divorced from the social idiom of God's apocalyptic action in Christ, it is stripped of its integrity and purpose, and converts into a virulent and idolatrous form of impiety according to which we become both "subject and object of our own quest."[12] Picturing ourselves as the subject and object of our own individual spiritual quests does not mean, however, that our lives have become our own. Who we are and what we do, in public *and* in private, are instead caught up in an economy of desire that is no longer related to any shared set of goods. This social idiom of the earthly city determines, not particular acts, but the range of possible acts available to us as individuals, that is, as producers and consumers. The control this malformation of the self exercises over us is therefore anonymous and indirect, more akin to seduction than coercion, but precisely for this reason all the more sweeping.

Consumption, Production, and Spiritual Formation

The church of late antiquity knew that if the distinctiveness of its spiritual disciplines from the formative influences of pagan society were compromised, the social space that the body of Christ needed to reproduce itself as a distinctive body politic would at some point collapse in on itself. Just such a contraction gradually occurred in the decades and centuries following the church's accommodation with Rome. Rigorous spiritual formation that once was expected of everyone was increasingly restricted to those entering religious orders, with the catechumenate for lay men and women truncated and eventually abandoned. A dual ethic emerged, with the more demanding "evangelical counsels" reserved for members of religious orders and the less demanding "precepts" for everybody else,[13] the latter, writes John Howard Yoder, being little more than "respectable unbelief."[14]

The dual ethic not only fostered the misconception that religious orders formed an ascetic elite that achieved perfection through self-denial, but paradoxically made promoting a way of life consistent with the status and mission of the church as the body of Christ more remote when monasticism was called into question during the age of Reformation. Bonhoeffer argues in this regard that Martin Luther, though an unrelenting critic of this dual standard, unwittingly confirmed Constantine's covenant with the church. He acknowledges that this was of course not what Luther wanted, that with his doctrine of grace he sought a complete ethic for everyone, not just for the religious orders. But when Luther proclaimed the costly grace of the gospel, he had two decades behind him in which he sought to live under the law: "Luther could cry 'grace alone' because he knew Christ as the one who calls to discipleship. What is true as a final consequence is false as a presupposition,

12. Bloom, *American Religion*, 217.
13. See, for example, Aquinas, *Summa Theologica*, Ia IIae.108.4.
14. Yoder, *The Royal Priesthood*, 57.

and what is obedience as a final consequence is disobedience as a presupposition." As a result, writes Bonhoeffer, "a minimal ethic prevailed," with the existence of the Christian becoming indistinguishable from that of the secular citizen. "The nature of the church vanished into the invisible realm. But in this way the New Testament message was fundamentally misunderstood, [and] inner-worldliness became a principle."[15]

A similar situation exists in our time and place, with the existence of the Christian virtually indistinguishable from that of the conspicuous consumer. The formation of members of Christ's body, always a fluid, dynamic, and precarious process centered in the life and worship of the church, has largely been eviscerated by determined competition from powerful institutions and processes of formation that are also interested in shaping human affections, dispositions, and appetites, but around habits of consumption and the gratification of desire that directly challenge the formation of Christian practices. The aim of these habits is to make people fit for unfettered consumption, and the extent to which they succeed will at the same time make them unfit for discipleship. The two regimes of moral and intellectual formation, because they seek to form persons to act in accordance with certain social ends, are fundamentally incommensurable.[16]

Many in the affluent areas of the world would no doubt find it difficult even to imagine a way of life that does not have as its primary purpose making consumer choices that will guarantee their personal welfare and satisfy their private interests in every sphere allotted to them by the commercial institutions of the earthly city. To be sure, women and men are finite, mortal beings, and we must eat, drink, clothe ourselves, find or build shelter, till the land, and fashion instruments of all sorts, just to mention a few things. We must, in other words, consume in order to live (and thus we must produce). Far too many of us, however, live instead to consume. The current regime carefully orchestrates day-to-day existence around habits of consumption that no longer serve any higher purpose but have become ends in themselves, to be desired for their own sake. Not only are these habits out of proportion to what human beings need to flourish as creatures made in the image of God, they have largely transformed the nature of our most intimate relationships with other people. Friendship and marriage are routinely spoken of as yet another good to enhance an individual's preferred lifestyle.

The unchecked ability of capitalism to prescribe what is valuable, innovative, normal, pleasing, and repulsive erects imposing barriers to the formation of habits and convictions that are intrinsic to the body of Christ. At the heart of this capability is a new economy of desire. In times past certain modes of public demeanor were considered either desirable or not because they were related to accepted standards regulating the common good, and therefore there were

---

15. Bonhoeffer, *No Rusty Swords*, 324. I return to Luther's place in this narrative below.
16. Budde and Brimlow, *Christianity Incorporated*, 61.

"proper" and "improper" objects of desire. Communities large and small promoted (if not always achieved) a harmonious polyphony of desire, orchestrated around an accepted hierarchy of goods. In the new economy of capitalism, on the other hand, a revised discipline of desire has been introduced. Unconstrained appetite is emphasized, together with the manipulation and control of this process, forming women and men to see themselves almost exclusively as "consumers."[17] A new spiritual order has thus been promoted, or rather the lack of rational order—a cacophony of appetite.

In this mode of regulating day-to-day life, to be a person is to be a consumer; virtually everything else is optional to this identity. These options (including making friends, getting married, and having children) are configured as products to be consumed, and the value of every product is determined by its "market share," that is, its ability to please the consumer.

We should not be surprised in such circumstances to see spirituality marketed as yet one more commodity, or the selling of commodities as a form of spirituality. It has become a private and inward matter, a type of therapy designed to make one's life more fulfilling, a "diet plan" for one's "soul" as it were, complete with "before" and "after" testimonies.[18] It is now altogether natural to talk about a relationship with God as another good or service for one's personal enjoyment, an effective way to be in harmony with the universe, cope with the stress and confusion of twenty-first century life, overcome substance abuse, fashion more stable families, enhance one's self-esteem, and in general live more satisfying lives. It is a product, furthermore, that does not require any sort of communal mediation (indeed, that is often explicitly rejected as antithetical to true spirituality) but may be enjoyed in the privacy of one's own home, head, and heart.[19]

Spirituality is not only a commodity or service in a global economy, nor are human beings merely consumers. The capitalist formation of identity and desire also serves an important role in shaping human beings into compliant and efficient producers. The demands of capitalist regimes have always caused a considerable amount of havoc in the lives of women and men, and globalization, with the dispersal of production, finance, and commerce beyond local and national borders, has only intensified these tendencies. Most if not all of the social relations that traditionally defined who they were and what they should do, and which mediated their relationship to governing authorities and their neighbors, are quickly dissolving. Men and women have been reduced to the status of "individuals," performing

17. Milbank, *Theology and Social Theory*, 33.

18. A good example of the marketing of spirituality is Thomas Moore's best-seller *Care of the Soul: A Guide for Cultivating Depth and Sacredness in Everyday Life* (New York: HarperCollins, 1992).

19. Business consultant Laurie Beth Jones, author of *Jesus, CEO: Using Ancient Wisdom for Visionary Leadership* (New York: Hyperion, 1995) and *Jesus in Blue Jeans: A Practical Guide to Everyday Spirituality* (New York: Hyperion, 1997), states in a 1995 interview that "religion" is necessarily manmade and therefore highly fallible," while "spiritual principles are universal; they can and should be applied everywhere" (Tom Brown, "Jesus CEO," *Industry Week* 244 [March 6, 1995]: 16).

a series of functions in accordance with the expectations of the market and under the watchful eye of the sovereign state. Maintaining these units of production is expensive, and thus their time must be kept at an optimum flexibility. Any group or community that might impact upon their availability—family, neighborhood, ethnic group, church, synagogue, or mosque—represents a potentially disruptive practice, and all ties to them must be loosened or, if possible, severed altogether.

A flexible workforce fit for a global regime, however, exacts a high price in human terms. The employees that remain after repeated downsizings and outsourcings are often overworked, alienated from management, and cynical about their prospects for the future. Corporate firms are thus interested in the potential of spirituality to implant a shared vision and sense of excitement and purpose in the office and on the shop floor. At the same time, however, they are suspicious of anything as particular and as potentially disruptive as the church. They are willing to work with established religious institutions, provided that their rituals and beliefs are supportive of the firm's goals and work to deepen the loyalty and productivity of the employees. And though many in the corporate spirituality movement claim that their ideas are independent of historic Christian faith, they are nevertheless quite willing to engage in the widespread exploitation of "a variety of Christian concepts, values, and symbols that have been detached and separated from the contexts of believing communities. Notions of transcendence, vocation, and covenant—which for most people in the United States and many Western capitalist countries make little sense apart from the Christian experience—now exist as free-standing but empty categories, to be filled according to the profit and efficiency strategies of corporate managers."[20]

The reconfiguration of spirituality to help make consumers and producers fit for a global market represents a natural extension of civil religion, the purpose of which, as I noted in chapter 3, is contingency management, that is, sacralizing the present social order as divinely sanctioned. For centuries in Europe and the Americas, the church provided beliefs, values, ceremonies, and symbols that gave sacred meaning to the body politic of the earthly city, providing a thin Christian veneer that conferred an abiding sense of unity and purpose on it, and which transcended all internal conflicts and differences while relating its practices and institutions to the realm of ultimate reality.[21] The church's civic responsibility was twofold: to serve as moral conscience, and to ameliorate the suffering incurred by those who slipped between the cracks. "The church, in this understanding," says Anthony Robinson, "is a center of civic life, one that provides an avenue by which the most fortunate and powerful can be of help to the less fortunate and least powerful."[22] Concentrating the practice of charity in the hands of the

20. Budde and Brimlow, *Christianity Incorporated*, 47–48.

21. See Robert D. Linder, "Universal Pastor: President Bill Clinton's Civil Religion," *Journal of Church and State* 38 (Autumn 1996): 734.

22. Anthony B. Robinson, "The Making of a Post-Liberal," in Copenhaver, Robinson, and Willimon, *Good News in Exile*, 16.

fortunate and powerful is not an accidental feature of modern civil religion, for it grants to the wealthy and influential few the privilege of defining and providing for the common good.[23]

The acute social and economic dislocation associated with global capitalism has only intensified this quandary and acts as a catalyst for political fragmentation. These circumstances have diminished the capacity of states to secure social order, giving rise to ethnic, nationalist, and religious groups that undermine the prerogatives and primacy of the state. Though we typically associate these trends with certain "hotspots" in the world (Africa, the Middle East, Central and South America), they produce a considerable amount of anxiety among the oligarchs in Europe and North America. "With capitalism rendering whole segments of American society economically unnecessary," write Michael Budde and Robert Brimlow, citing African American men as a prime example, "politicians and opinion leaders worry about the 'dis-uniting of America,' the collapse of 'public spiritedness,' and the decline of civic virtue as manifested in voting and support for elected officials."[24]

According to Budde and Brimlow, the traditional form of civil religion in the United States, with its recognizable Puritan republican heritage and biblical imagery (city set on a hill, the New Jerusalem, God's chosen people), no longer provides the sort of religious legitimation needed in a globalized setting that is "sufficient, in the words of Voltaire, to keep the servants from stealing the silver, but not the type likely to encourage religious practices and norms at odds with capitalism, patriotism, or the essentials of the system as presently constituted." The standard reason given is that it could no longer account for the experiences of society's excluded—women, minorities, dissenting voices.[25] In other words, a "thick" account of what constitutes a good life, one that is embedded in particular forms of life and contingent social practices, is supposedly too wedded to these particularities to encompass the vast diversity of convictions and values that human beings embrace in today's global village. What is needed is a spirituality that is divorced from social practices that might disrupt attention and take allegiance away from one's loyalty and obligation to the state and market. A personalized piety that is internalized in beliefs, attitudes, and feelings, and not one that is tied to "outward observance,"[26] will help the pow-

23. See Long, *Goodness of God*, 249–50. According to Milbank, James Stewart (sometimes spelled "Steuart") argued over against Adam Smith that wage-labor was a mode of *discipline*, not freedom. He thus denounces the Catholic practice of distributing surplus public wealth to the needy. This practice is like the miracle of manna from heaven, not the regular and predictable management needed by society: "'the regulation of need,, and not charity, is a more reliable means of social control and increasing the population" (Milbank, *Theology and Social Theory*, 32). See in this regard S. R. Sen, *The Economics of Sir James Steuart* (Cambridge: Harvard University Press, 1957), especially chapter 9, "Steuart's Economics of Control," 130–54.

24. Budde and Brimlow, *Christianity Incorporated*, 14–15.

25. Ibid., 16.

26. See in this regard Patrick Fagan, "Why Religion Matters: The Impact of Religious Practice on Social Stability," published by the Heritage Foundation (www.heritage.org/Research/Religion/BG1064 .cfm). I am indebted to Budde and Brimlow for bringing Fagan's essay to my attention.

ers that be accumulate the social capital, "the stock of social relations and shared values,"[27] that underwrites the unconstrained exercise of self-interest.

Piety, Power, and the Earthly City

The modern sense of spirituality, emphasizing the inner goings-on of the individual divorced from material issues of the production and reproduction of life, represents a radical shift in meaning from its standard usage in the church until the twelfth century. Beginning with the Pauline correspondence in the New Testament, the Greek adjective *pneumatikos* was associated with the *pneuma,* the Spirit whom the early Christians proclaimed was in Jesus and who was also the gift of the risen Christ to his followers. A spiritual person was someone whose whole way of acting in and relating to the world was under the influence of the Holy Spirit, and thus one who manifested the presence of the Spirit in the world. He or she was therefore not somebody who shunned the material world of time and space, but one in whom the Spirit dwelt, the one who was engendered and empowered by God. Spirituality accordingly did not refer to a property that one possessed or a discrete facet of one's private inner life, but to a pattern of personal growth and maturation that took place within the community of those who had been gathered together by the risen Lord "to be a kingdom and priests serving our God" (Rev. 5:10a). It was associated with the active presence of Christ through the work of Spirit as the source and power of the Christian life, and not with the cultivation of extraordinary inner experiences, though of course it involves a range of affections, desires, and loves.[28]

Spiritual formation in the early church thus found its occasion and significance in the radical restructuring of bodily life and language brought about by the apocalypse of God's messianic regime intruding into a fallen world. The task set before each believer by this intrusion, writes Williams, is to make "his or her own that engagement with the questioning at the heart of faith which is so evident in the classical documents of Christian belief." This process of interrogation has little in common with fashionable notions about the relative nature of all human endeavors, nor does it encourage romantic sentiments about the person who, while half-believing, withholds assent from all commitments in order to preserve her moral and intellectual autonomy. "The question involved here," Williams insists,

> is not our interrogation of the data, but its interrogation of us. It is the *strangeness* of the ground of belief that must constantly be allowed to challenge the fixed

27. Budde and Brimlow, *Christianity Incorporated,* 19. Regarding the invention and reinvention of this curious notion of social capital, see Robert D. Putnam, *Bowling Alone: The Collapse and Revival of American Community* (New York: Simon & Schuster, 2000).

28. Philip Sheldrake, *Spirituality and History: Questions of Interpretation and Method,* rev. ed. (London: SPCK, 1995), 42–43.

assumptions of religiosity; it is a *given*, whose question to each succeeding age is fundamentally one and the same. And the greatness of the great Christian saints lies in their readiness to be questioned, judged, stripped naked and left speechless by that which lies at the center of their faith.[29]

The *telos* of this life-long process of spiritual allocution and interpellation, of "being unmade to be remade,"[30] is to be fully and wholly incorporated into the mystery of God's will, hidden from the foundation of the world but now revealed in Christ (Eph. 1:9–10), gathering together all things, and inaugurating in the midst of the conflict and violence of the present age an alternative history for all creation that is reestablished through redemptive suffering.[31] When considered from this standpoint, Jesus's faithfulness brings about the inbreaking of the long-awaited reign of God, and with it the initial rhythms and harmonies of a new creation and new humanity manifested in the polyphony of life that is the church. In and through the ecclesial practices of prayer, fasting, confession, and the like, the Spirit draws women and men from every tribe, nation, language, and people into the orbit of Christ's body, a process that culminates with their participation in his dying and, in the age to come, in his rising.

In this ecclesial context, prayer and contemplation are not divorced from theological reflection. In the words of Evagrius of Pontus, "if you are a theologian, you will pray truly; and if you pray truly, you will be a theologian."[32] Research, study, argument, and reflection on God and his ways with the world thus "find their source and their completion only in prayer."[33] Rigorous theological inquiry, rightly conceived, comprises "an aspect of the mystical journey by means of which God is leading creatures back into unity with the divine life. Theology is the attempt to notice how this is happening, to articulate the stages of the community's journey, to point ahead to the One who alone could mystically arouse the uplifting ecstasy that always leads beyond." Spirituality, if we wish to retain this term at all (and it may be beyond rehabilitation), pertains properly to the impression made by the encounter with God that takes place within the new network of communal relationship and perception that is provided by the church as the fellowship of the Spirit.[34]

The erosion of this configuration of what it means to be spiritual may be traced to the convergence of a number of factors that emerged over a period of several hundred years, and which began to coalesce during the high Middle Ages. According

---

29. Williams, *Wound of Knowledge*, 1.

30. Ibid., 8, 13.

31. See John Milbank, "The Second Difference: For a Trinitarianism without Reserve," *Modern Theology* 2 (1986): 227.

32. Robert E. Sinkewicz, trans. and ed., *Evagrius of Pontus: The Greek Ascetic Corpus* (New York: Oxford University Press, 2003), 199.

33. Jean-Pierre Torrell, OP, *Saint Thomas Aquinas*, vol. 1, *The Person and His Work*, trans. Robert Royal (Washington, DC: Catholic University of America Press, 1996), 157.

34. McIntosh, *Mystical Theology*, 6–7, 56.

to Colin Morris's classic account, eucharistic practice shifted during the eleventh and twelfth centuries from a communal emphasis to a mode of devotion focused on the inner experience of the individual. Confessional practices began to emphasize the importance of self-examination, with a growing distinction between public penance and the inner sorrow that marked true repentance, the latter being that which God most valued. A new interest in and study of the inner workings of the soul emerged during this time, with an awareness of the degree to which a variety of motivations, affections, and appetites were involved in an individual's spiritual progress. Pronounced shifts in the doctrines of salvation and eschatology also exerted an influence, as patristic descriptions of Christ's cosmic triumph over death, the devil, and sin were supplanted by a preoccupation with the pains of Christ in his passion. Finally, the hope of the Christian shifted from the gathering together of all things in Christ to a concern with the fate of the individual after death.[35]

It is not surprising, then, that beginning around the twelfth century the idea of *spiritualitas* began to have new connotations. Leading the way was a new philosophical trend among medieval scholastic theologians, who began to use this term to refer to what pertains to the soul as contrasted with the body, which was part of a sharper distinction between "spirit" and "matter" or "body." The adjective *spiritualis* was increasingly applied to intelligent creatures (that is, human beings) as opposed to nonrational beings, with the effect of vacating its Pauline moral sense and taking on a meaning "more radically opposed to corporeality."[36] Though for a time this new sense stood side by side with its former meaning, says Bernard McGinn, there is little doubt that scholasticism helped to give birth to "conceptions of spirituality which willy-nilly used it as the reason for giving the physical world and especially the human body a largely negative role in what they conceived of as authentic Christian life."[37] Thus began a privatizing tendency in the history of spirituality in the church, with increasing emphasis placed the interior state of the soul, and especially on how one achieved ever more refined stages of inner purity and exaltation.[38]

As *spiritualitas* became restricted to a person's private, interior life, it also was divorced from the intellectual concerns of theology, such that fewer and fewer were competent to integrate spirituality and the other aspects of theology in their own lives.[39] "How few of them are saints," complains Denys the Carthusian in the fifteenth century, "Thomas [Aquinas] and but few others."[40] This stands in

35. Morris, *The Discovery of the Individual, 1050–1200*, 12, 47, 70–79, 139–52; see also McIntosh, *Mystical Theology*, 64–65; and Bernard McGinn, "Love, Knowledge, and Mystical Union in Western Christianity: Twelfth to Sixteenth Centuries," *Church History* 56 (March 1987): 7–24.

36. Sheldrake, *Spirituality and History*, 43.

37. McGinn, "Letter and the Spirit," 3.

38. McIntosh, *Mystical Theology*, 7.

39. Ibid., 63.

40. Denys the Carthusian, *Difficultatum Praecipuarum Absolutiones*, a5, in *Doctor Ecstatici D. Dionysii Cartusiani Opera Omnia XVI* (Tournai: Typis Cartusiae S. M.de Pratis, 1902), 494D, cited by Turner, *Faith, Reason and the Existence of God*, 77.

marked contrast to the church fathers, writes Hans Urs von Balthasar, who had at their disposal

> all the rational methods of distinguishing and defining for the clarification of concepts; they were used in the fierce controversies with heretics, both by individual theologians and by councils. But . . . these methods were not the determining factor in the construction of their theology. Even polemical works such as Irenaeus' *Adversus Haereses*, Athanasius' *Contra Arianos*, Hilary's *De Trinitate*, Gregory of Nyssa's *Contra Eunomium* were embedded in a spiritual, sapiential setting which became more and more pronounced as the decisive element.[41]

A drastic revision of the concept of intellect was thus taking place, one that would drive a deep wedge between the intellective and the affective aspects of the soul. As Denys Turner says of this development, it was widely thought that "if we are to enter into the true 'mystical' darkness of the divine, then the intellectual knowledge of the philosopher has to be set aside in order to leave room for the God of faith, known, it is said, not by intellect, but by love. For *amor ipse notitia est*, love is itself a kind of knowing, of which intellect can know nothing."[42]

The erosion of the ecclesial context that had secured the continuity of theology and spiritual formation did not, however, occur in a social vacuum. It was connected with institutional changes, including a significant shift in the setting for learning, from the monastery to the cathedral school and university. In the monasteries the course of theological study had been concerned with the preparation of students for discerning the hidden depth of the Bible. According to Jean Leclercq, the purpose of reading the classical texts of Greek and Roman antiquity was "to educate young Christians, future monks, to 'introduce' them to Sacred Scripture and guide them toward heaven by way of *grammatica*. To put them in contact with the best models would, at one and the same time, develop their taste for the beautiful, their literary subtlety, as well as their moral sense."[43]

In the cathedral schools and universities, by contrast, there was a revival of interest in the liberal arts in the ninth and eleventh centuries, and these arts were applied directly to the interpretation of sacred scripture.[44] The relationship between the study of scripture and the liberal arts was gradually reversed, initiating a movement that, when combined with the rise to prominence of dialectical inquiry and

41. Hans Urs von Balthasar, *Explorations in Theology*, vol. 1, *The Word Made Flesh* (San Francisco: Ignatius, 1989), 214. It is this sapiential element that Ellen Charry is trying to recover in her work with Christian doctrine. See Ellen T. Charry, *By the Renewing of Your Minds: The Pastoral Function of Christian Doctrine* (New York: Oxford University Press, 1997).

42. Turner, *Faith, Reason and the Existence of God*, 77–78; see also Turner, *Darkness of God*, 186–273; and Coakley, *Powers and Submissions*, 78–82.

43. Jean Leclercq, OSB, *The Love of Learning and the Desire for God*, 2nd ed., trans. Catharine Misrahi (New York: Fordham University Press, 1974), 149.

44. See G. R. Evans, *Old Arts and New Theology: The Beginnings of Theology as an Academic Discipline* (Oxford: Clarendon, 1980).

scholastic disputation, diverted attention away from the monastic maintenance of spiritual life in the company of friends, and toward more technical inquiries and secular applications involving the "literature" and "history" of the past.[45] Though not yet a situation in which rational inquiry was completely severed from a concern for the spiritual life, a gradual dissociation took place as new "masters of the divine books" and "doctors of the sacred page" began to exercise a magisterial authority over the reading of scripture that became more and more desacralized.

According to Henri de Lubac, these learned scholars became "professors of Sacred Scripture" and "university men" before their time. Students crowded around their mentors, not as monks did after their work to hear the *collatio* of their abbot, a practice set within the liturgical framework of the daily office, but as those eager to see who would triumph in whatever *disputatio* was taking place. And though they did manage to accumulate more scientific knowledge, they were also prone to a greater spirit of disquiet: "How many of them seek to be taught only with a view to making a career and have already begun their drive to achieve honors! . . . It is the rising tide of 'science' in the almost modern sense of the word that pushes aside humble spiritual commentary as belonging to inferior stages of growth."[46] The seeds that later blossomed into the divorce of theological inquiry from the work of spiritual formation began to be sown in these new educational institutions as early as the ninth century.

The shift from "humble spiritual commentary" to "scientific" approaches to scripture exemplifies the altered relationship between spirituality and theology in the late medieval setting. It played a significant role in the general demise of the kind of theological hermeneutics practiced by the church fathers, who sought to catch a glimpse of the beauty of truth itself in a world spoken by God. As this tradition of reading scripture and the world was replaced by more "modern" forms of interpretation in medieval academies, the close relationship between the *signa* of the world and the *signa* of scripture also began to unravel, imperceptibly at first, and then more quickly as the world moved into the sixteenth century.[47] Together

45. Lubac, *Medieval Exegesis*, 55; Sheldrake, *Spirituality and Theology*, 39–40.

46. Lubac, *Medieval Exegesis*, 49. Lesley Smith contends that the distinction between monastic and scholastic theology has been overdrawn, at least as it relates to the original circumstances surrounding the establishment of the medieval university (Lesley Smith, "The Use of Scripture in Teaching at the Medieval University," in *Learning Institutionalized: Teaching in the Medieval University*, ed. John Van Engen [Notre Dame, IN: University of Notre Dame Press, 2000], 229–43). Smith is no doubt right, though the effects that interest us here are not those that immediately arose with the university, but those that developed later in conjunction with other intellectual, social, and economic changes.

47. Michael Gillespie contends that modernity arose not in opposition to the medieval world, but out of its rubble: "Superior or more powerful ideas thus did not drive out or overcome medieval ideas, as it often maintained; rather, they toppled the ruins of medieval ideas that had remained standing after the internecine struggle that brought the medieval world to an end. Modern 'reason' was thus able to overcome medieval 'superstition' and 'dogma' only because these were fatally weakened by the destruction of the world in which they made sense." In other words, modernity came into being in response to the crisis engendered by the collapse of the medieval world (Michael Allen Gillespie, "The Theological Origins of Modernity," *Critical Review* 13 [1999]: 3).

with the rise of late medieval nominalism that combined "a highly sophistical analysis of given theological propositions with a deep skepticism about the human mind's capacity to abstract beyond the immediate data of sense experience,"[48] the separation of scholastic and mystical theology was all but secured.

Gender may have also played a role in the redirection of spirituality to the interior lives of individuals. Grace Jantzen notes that when the preeminent representatives of mystical theology were predominantly male, and frequently occupied important ecclesiastical offices (Augustine, Gregory the Great, and Bernard of Clairvaux), spiritual formation was embraced as central to the public life and essential practice of the church. As more and more women become prominent in the field of mystical theology, it came to be thought of as a strictly private matter, something that is susceptible to "hysteria" and thus to be kept separate from the public life of the church, particularly in its role within the political structures of Christendom. "It was only with the development of the secular state," Jantzen writes, "when religious experience was no longer perceived as a source of knowledge and power, that it became safe to allow women to be mystics." With spirituality safely sequestered in the realm of the private and personal, having little or nothing to do with the public realm in general and politics in particular, it was possible to see such matters as "compatible with a woman's role."[49]

In any event, by the time of Teresa of Avila (1515–1582), the movements that made up the interior drama of the soul were elevated to institute a momentous hermeneutical shift within the late medieval church. Michel de Certeau rightly notes that prior to the sixteenth century the world was "perceived as *spoken* by God." A tacit sacramentality to the world thus supplied the hermeneutic key for understanding it in the context of God's apocalyptic action. But by the sixteenth century that perception had largely dissipated, and the material world had "become opacified, objectified, and detached from its supposed speaker." The refined feelings and ecstatic experiences of the inner self became the site for glimpsing the beauty of truth in place of the more public speech of God in the created order. "This *I* who speaks in the place of (and instead of) the Other," says Certeau, "also requires a *space* of expression corresponding to what the world was in relation to the speech of God."[50]

In effect the focus of the doctrine of transubstantiation had shifted from the bread and wine on the altar to the individual's thoughts and feelings. Teresa's

---

48. Williams, *Wound of Knowledge*, 140.

49. Grace M. Jantzen, *Power, Gender and Christian Mysticism* (Cambridge: Cambridge University Press, 1995), 326; cf. McIntosh, *Mystical Theology*, 63–64, and Coakley, *Powers and Submissions*, 50. Though Jantzen alerts us to an important theme here, the situation is much more complex than she realizes. Women were not completely absent from the earlier theological discussions. Gregory of Nyssa, for example, refers to his sister Macrina as his teacher in *On the Soul and the Resurrection*, playing the role of Socrates to his Plato (St. Gregory of Nyssa, *On the Soul and the Resurrection*; see also Gregory, Bishop of Nyssa, *The Life of Saint Macrina*, trans. Kevin Corrigan (Eugene, OR: Wipf & Stock, 2001).

50. Certeau, *Mystic Fable*, 188.

"interior castle," says McIntosh, "becomes the imaginal realm in which the divine speech can still be heard, but now the language of that speech is constituted by the inner movements of the soul. The soul itself is 'but the inarticulable echo of an unknown Subject,' thus it needs a dramatic imaginary inner stage upon which to act out and narrate the mysterious and inexpressible touch of 'Unknownness.'"[51] The inner movements of the soul, its mind, and especially its memory were no longer viewed as *vestigia trinitatis*,[52] but were seen as the last refuge for the divine in a world no longer grounded in mystery. In the process the "contemplative" becomes a solitary figure, a "professional," as it were, in spiritual matters. He or she "recedes, introverts, 'abstracts,' from normal practical reasoning for his [or her] own particular purposes in relation to God."[53]

This new conception of spirituality presupposes the invention of detached personal identity, important elements of which Nicholas Boyle traces to a highly formalized technology of the self developed by the fourteenth-century erotic mysticism known as the *devotio moderna*. The economic relations that were being instituted at that time eventually led to the creation of the bourgeois class in the city-states of Italy, Germany, and the Hanseatic League. Underwriting the development of this new regime of accumulation was the creation of a system of monetary exchange, banking and book-keeping practices that distinguished for the first time between capital and income. "Money is the great leveler," Boyle notes, since "cash from a prince is no better than cash from a pastry cook."[54] The rise of a system of monetary exchange fueled tension between the ideas of the new, politically unemancipated bourgeoisie and the feudal rulers who saw themselves in terms of the great structure of medieval theology and anthropology.

According to Boyle, the creation of a money economy was a necessary step toward forgetting that human beings are of creaturely necessity producers occupying a specific place within a mode of production, and not detached egos, but participants in a larger story. The mystics of the *devotio moderna*, with their systematic methods of prayer and mediation, prompted this self-induced amnesia by conceiving of a detached self-identity as a universal possibility, and by imagining a state of consumption without production that was in principle accessible to all and thus not tied to a particular class in the feudal order: "The mystic has glimpsed a fulfillment of humanity which is outside time, that is, outside the productive nexus, and best imagined as boundless, but personal enjoyment." Under the influence of this picture, women and men learned to imagine themselves, no longer as apprentices who must learn and grow as they make their way through life, but as selves born complete and mature into the world, magically endowed

---

51. McIntosh, *Mystical Theology*, 69; the embedded quotations are from Certeau, *Mystic Fable*, 188–89.

52. Augustine, *The Trinity*, VI.10, 213.

53. Coakley, *Powers and Submissions*, 82.

54. Boyle, *Who Are We Now?* 156; cf. Sheldrake, *Spirituality and History*, 1995, 51–52.

with both economic and intellectual capital, ready to make consumer choices about material and spiritual goods without first having produced something or concerning themselves about those who do produce the product or provide the service to be consumed.[55]

An ironic twist in the plot of this story occurred in the late seventeenth century with the condemnation of the allegedly Quietist teachings of the French spiritual writer Madame Guyon. Her exhortation to radical resignation and disconnection from the external world not only reinforced the drift of spirituality toward a preoccupation with interior states of consciousness, but also gave rise to the suspicion within the Catholic church that the whole topic of spirituality was "too refined, rarified and separated from ordinary Christian life,"[56] most especially the sacraments and the teaching authority of the church. Partly in reaction to Guyon and others, a new theoretical discourse developed that sought to order the individual's struggle for inner perfection in properly orthodox ways. To aid this theorization, inspired in part by the neo-scholastic obsession with good order and detailed classification, a new terminology emerged. The term *mystical theology* was commandeered from Pseudo-Dionysius and pressed into service to describe the transvalued sense of spirituality. According to McIntosh,

> Whereas for [Pseudo-Dionysius] the term referred to the "knowledge" disclosed to Christians as they themselves are known and transformed by the unknowable God, now it comes to be used as a technical term for theoretical teaching about the soul's process of sanctification. Here was a double irony, for just as Madame Guyon's language about the utter *resignation* of the self was in fact an elaborate *rhetoric* of the self, so what might have seemed a turn away from this perspective (to the supposedly more scientific "mystical theology") turns out to be a new and ever more baroque *technology of the self.*[57]

We should not, however, lay blame for the privatization of spirituality solely at the feet of Rome. The Protestant Reformation contributed its fair share to this radical reorientation of spirituality, beginning with Luther's radical division of every human being into an inner and outer person, the former standing solely before God (*coram Deo*) in conscience, and the latter in the historical sequence of particular acts, as one stands before one's fellow human beings (*coram hominibus*). He writes in his famous essay on the freedom of the Christian that human beings have a twofold nature, one spiritual and the other bodily. The spiritual nature is no longer that which has to do with the Spirit, but that which is juxtaposed over against the body, that is, the "spiritual, inner, or new man." The bodily nature is the "carnal, outward, or old man." And though it is true that "in the sight of men a man is made good or evil by his work," we must take care not to think that in

---

55. Ibid., 154, 156–57; cf. Coakley, *Powers and Submissions*, 86.
56. Sheldrake, *Spirituality and History*, 43.
57. McIntosh, *Mystical Theology*, 8.

doing these works we are "justified before God by them, for faith, which alone is righteousness before God, cannot endure that erroneous opinion."[58]

With his division of the human being into two natures, Luther consolidates the late medieval interiorization and individualization of faith. A hard-and-fast dichotomy between faith and works becomes the norm in Protestant spirituality, such that "law" (in virtually any sense of the term) and "works" are by definition outside of grace. Nevertheless, keeping the law and doing good works are necessary to the maintenance of the earthly city if not to true faith. Separate spheres of life are therefore isolated, one for each of the two natures. The temporal world, where goods and services are bought and sold, rewards and punishments are meted out, wars are fought and enemies subjected, and women and men are forced to seek their own individual interests, can now be understood *etsi deus non daretur*, even if God does not exist. The present age does not depend on the apocalypse of God in Jesus Christ for its meaning, nor does the latter add anything of substance to it; the spiritual world of hidden faith has little or nothing to add to the course of the temporal world, save, of course, for the general sentiment that it too is ultimately subject to the sovereignty of God.

The seeds of Luther's division of the human being into two discrete selves germinated in the Puritan piety of the seventeenth and eighteenth centuries. According to Charles Taylor, the English Puritans thoroughly rejected the medieval conception of contemplation, in which matters of the "spirit" are reserved for those in religious communities and thus divorced from everyday life, "i.e., those aspects of human life concerned with production and reproduction."[59] Their rejection of contemplation in favor of everyday life entails a commitment to social leveling and to the belief that the good life is something that everyone can achieve. The virtues of commerce and the knowledges that serve the new regime of capitalist accumulation displace those which attended the medieval hierarchical ordering of society. A new conception of vocation develops that is no longer connected to the priesthood or monastery, but which sanctifies any kind of employment that is deemed useful and imputed to use by God.[60] All such callings are thus equal, and one's participation in them is to be judged not by the activity itself, because the temporal sphere is relatively autonomous, but by "the *spirit* in which one lives what everyone lives, even the most mundane existence."[61]

58. Martin Luther, *The Freedom of a Christian*, in *Three Treatises*, trans. W. A. Lambert (2nd ed.; Philadelphia: Fortress, 1970), 278, 295, 298. Boyle contends that what is commonly thought of as Cartesian dualism is more properly laid at the doorstep of Luther (Boyle, *Who Are We Now?* 158).

59. Charles Taylor, *Sources of the Self: The Making of Modern Identity* (Cambridge: Harvard University Press, 1989), 211.

60. We both trivialize and corrupt the theological concept of vocation—which in scripture pertains solely to Jesus's call to follow him, a calling that never steps out from under the shadow of the cross—when we use it in association with the earthly city's configuration of the common good: security, wealth, and the opportunity to generate more of both.

61. Taylor, *Sources of the Self*, 224. Taylor also argues that the Puritan exaltation of the significance of ordinary life provided a hospitable environment for modern science, understood not as contemplating

Taylor also contends that the Puritans set aside virtually all practices of mediation for the spiritual life, rejecting the traditional view that the power of God is more intensely present in certain holy places, times, and persons and can therefore be properly approached and appropriated by human beings. Now each person "stands alone in relation to God: his or her fate—salvation or damnation—is separately decided." Redemption thus reconceived is the exclusive provenance of God, effectively vacating the traditional role of the church as the mediator of God's salvific work in the world. Personal commitment becomes the sole determining factor: "Salvation by faith thus not only reflected a theological proposition about the inanity of human works but also reflected the new sense of the crucial importance of personal commitment. One no longer belonged to the saved, to the people of God, by one's connection to a wider order sustaining a sacramental life, but by one's wholehearted personal adhesion."[62]

The isolation of one's true, interior life of faith from the life and activity of the body (both individual and ecclesial), perpetuating the fiction of the detached personal identity, produces a sense of the self unfettered by the webs of interlocution embedded in social and geographical ties. The illusion that we can substantially cut ourselves loose from the familial and communal webs of interlocution into which we were born and which nurtured us over the years, and fashion our lives according to self-selected scripts, is one of the most tragic aspects of our present predicament. As poet Micheal O'Siadhail laments,

> Freedom. We sang of freedom
> (travel lightly, anything goes)
> and somehow we became strangers
> to each other, like gabblers
> at cross purposes, builders of Babel.[63]

What the modern world initially promoted as a quest toward freedom turned out instead to have been "an adventure that held the seeds of its own destruction within itself, within its attenuated definition of human nature and its inadequate vision of human destiny. What we got was not self-freedom but self-centeredness, loneliness, superficiality, and harried consumerism."[64] The result of our impiety has not been the freedom from others and from nature that we were promised, but confusion, frustration, cynicism, despair, and alienation. The sweet savor of liberty for which we longed has left the bitter taste of falsehood in our mouths. The more

---

the beauty of the Triune God through the splendor of the created order, but as the means for humans to make good use of God's creation, thus authorizing an instrumentalist stance toward the world.

62. Ibid., 216–17.

63. Michael O'Siadhail, *Hail! Madam Jazz: New and Selected Poems* (Newcastle upon Tyne: Bloodaxe, 1992), 111; cited in Begbie, *Theology, Music and Time*, 218.

64. Stanley Hauerwas and William H. Willimon, *Resident Aliens: Life in the Christian Colony* (Nashville: Abingdon, 1989), 50.

vigorously we sought our freedom, the more thoroughly we enslaved ourselves, our neighbors, and the whole of creation within the techniques, instruments, and structures that we devised to facilitate our emancipation.

The Politics of the Spirit and the Art of Vulnerability

In contrast to the self-centeredness, loneliness, superficiality, and harried consumerism endemic to the modern quest for freedom, the significance of Jesus's activity and passion can be grasped only in the generative context that the Holy Spirit shapes and directs within the body of Christ. The gift of the Spirit, though it cannot be contained by any created thing, takes form within the ecclesial community of faith, creating and sustaining a people who offer to the world a different kind of existence in which relations misshapen by death and sin are transfigured into patterns of life and wholeness. It is in the Spirit that women and men learn that God's address to the world in Christ is ultimately a word of redemption, that life and not death is the goal of creation. Spiritual formation, therefore, is inseparable from the politics of the Spirit.

Though the reference to the Holy Spirit is consistent with the subject of spirituality, linking it with politics might come as a surprise to many, accustomed as most people are to the notion that spirituality is strictly a private matter, having principally to do with their interior lives.[65] When one looks closely at the consistent witness of the scriptures, however, this reaction itself seems curiously out of place, for the formative images that typically describe the activity of God and the response of human beings in both the Old and New Testaments are almost exclusively political images. The fact that many find the predominance of political images in the Bible strange is itself revealing, disclosing more about who we are and how we deal with the world than perhaps any other aspect of modern life.

According to the New Testament, the principal site of the Spirit's activity is not the individual believer, but the gathered community of disciples who form a distinctive form of commonwealth in the world. Salvation does not consist of Christ rescuing isolated souls from life's traumas by recruiting them for an otherworldly existence, but of the Holy Spirit adding to the *koinonia* (a standard term in the political vocabulary of Paul's day) of Christ's body, the church. As a fruit of the Spirit's labors in creation, it is the church (and not heaven as such) that stands over against the world. In short, the church—the community of peace and

65. Though some might contend that this sense of *spiritual* is suggested in the writings of Augustine, Denys Turner persuasively argues that Augustine's understanding of the ascent of the mind to God does not suppose "some incommunicably 'individual' experience." Turner cites in particular the "vision" that Augustine shared with his mother, Monica, at Ostia in *Confessions* IX.10. Augustine reports "an experience shared with Monica, *a dialogue*, itself literally punctuated by the rhythms of their words and silences in the way that what they experience is metaphorically punctuated by them. As the description of a 'mystical' experience, the Ostia passage is altogether out of character with the Plotinian 'flight of the alone to the alone.'" (Turner, *The Darkness of God*, 79).

reconciliation, the city of redemption from the powers and rulers of the present age—is the goal of God's saving work in creation. Who Christians are as individuals, therefore, is the product of their involvement in this communion, this *community*, which is the body politic of Christ.

Politics in this sense, says William Stringfellow, "refers comprehensively to the total configuration of relationships among humans and institutions and other principalities and the rest of created life in this world." It names both the arena of God's mysterious activity in this world, the infinite self-giving that is the Triune Godhead enacted in time and space in Christ's passion and triumph, and the impact of the divine presence and power "upon the fallen existence of this world, including the fallen life of human beings and that of the powers that be. Politics points to the militance of the Word of God incarnate, which pioneers the politics of the Kingdom which is to come." Spiritual formation in this context has to do with "*a reiteration of the act of creation in the Word of God* . . . renewing human life (and all of created life) in the midst of the era of the fall, or during the present darkness, in which the power of death apparently reigns."[66]

Spiritual formation for the members of Christ's earthly-historical body is therefore set firmly in the political context of God's apocalyptic regime. There is of course an intensely personal dimension to this formative discipline, but that it is neither at the outset nor in the end a private matter. Spiritual formation is an ecclesial affair, intersecting with every aspect and every concern of life. No field of human endeavor and inquiry stands outside the purview of spiritual discipline, because our quest for God is not one quest alongside all the others—personal relations, social policies, relations of production, accumulation, and consumption, scientific research, literature, music, and art—which human beings undertake.[67] Spiritual formation impinges on all these areas, not to dictate to them how to go about their business, but to help us follow the concrete ways these activities link together the events that make up the rhythms and harmonies of our day-to-day existence and which direct us toward God.

The politics of the Spirit begins with the fear of God, which takes hold of us, says Martin Buber, when the whole of our existence between birth and death becomes incomprehensible and uncanny.[68] Only when we have accepted deep down ("in our bones," so to speak) that we do not hold the deed to our own lives, nor to anything or anyone else in the world, can the habits and relations of life that echo the harmonies of God's own internal self-giving relations begin to take shape in our lives. The fear of God entails accepting our very existence as *gift*, and to accept this is to come face-to-face with our contingency, our vulnerability as creatures. And from this fact, says Nicholas Lash, "nothing follows. Here we are. This is how

66. William Stringfellow, *The Politics of Spirituality* (Philadelphia: Westminster, 1984), 25–26, 30 (emphasis original).

67. Lash, *Theology on the Way to Emmaus*, 8–12.

68. Martin Buber, *Eclipse of God: Studies in the Relation Between Religion and Philosophy*, trans. intro. Robert M. Seltzer (Atlantic Highlands, NJ: Humanities Press International, 1988), 36.

things are. That's it. No safety belts, no metacosmic maps or guidebooks, no mental cradles for our 'ultimate' security."[69]

At the outset of our apprenticeship in the Spirit's discipline, then, we discover that our existence resides in incomprehensible, ineffable mystery. This is not, writes Buber, "the relative mystery of that which is inaccessible only to the present state of human knowledge and is hence in principle discoverable. It is the essential mystery, the inscrutableness of which belongs to its very nature; it is the unknowable."[70] The mystery eludes all categories of our understanding and shatters every form of security that we devise to protect ourselves from the vulnerability implied in the world's giftedness. Consequently, there are no experts in the knowledge of matters divine, for the God who, according to Scripture, knows us in Jesus Christ is unknowable as such, "the You that in accordance with its nature cannot become an It."[71] There is, however, a spiritual art to living with the mystery, the aim of which is holy vulnerability.

The spiritual art of vulnerability presents a fundamental challenge to the prevailing ethos of state and market, which requires the identification of a discrete and secure "subject" as the proper locus of choice and action. This subject (which can be a person or an institution such as a corporation, an army, or a nation-state) designates "a *place* that can be delimited as its *own* and serve as the base from which relations with an *exteriority* composed of targets or threats . . . can be managed. As in management, every 'strategic' rationalization seeks first of all to distinguish its 'own' place, that is, the place of its own power and will, from an 'environment.'"[72] Scholars give the name of instrumental rationality to this sort of strategic calculation of power. Though it involves very complex forms of reasoning, instrumental rationality is, very simply, a way of coping with the world that continually strives to subject all things, even life itself, to its control. In striving for control, instrumental reasoning recognizes no boundaries, acknowledges no limitations, encounters no mystery, and allows no exemptions from its all-embracing quest for mastery. No *thing* lies outside the scope of its calculating gaze, including the divine.

On the long pilgrimage toward the world to come, by contrast, we must learn that the nature of the mystery that accounts not only for our existence as human beings, but for the world as a whole, is shrouded in impenetrable darkness. God is not an object, a thing or person that we can encounter, identify, categorize, compare, and contrast along with all the other things and persons that make up the world. *What* God is will forever remain unknown to us. In the words of Dante,

69. Lash, *Believing Three Ways in One God*, 39.

70. Buber, *Eclipse of God*, 36.

71. Buber, *I and Thou*, trans., 123. Buber's claim that God is not some thing or some body must be distinguished from the later, Kantian reduction of the concept of mystery in reference to God to a mere passive agnosticism, whereas for theologians who stand in the line of Pseudo-Dionysius it is a knowledgeable unknowing. The difference, says Turner, is that for post-Kantian theologians the apophatic rests in the deficiency of reason; for the Dionysian tradition, it is reason's apotheosis (Turner, *Faith, Reason and the Existence of God*, 79).

72. Certeau, *Practice of Everyday Life*, xix, 35–37 (emphasis original).

For, trusting to man's reason, mad is he
> who hopes to plumb the endless ways of those
> three Persons in substantial unity.

Be satisfied with "*so it is*," O Man,
> for if you could have known the whole design,
> Mary would not have had to bear a son.[73]

Our most adequate analogy for conceiving of our relation to the unknown God is provided by intimate human relationships, which exhibit a mysterious nature in their own right. When we meet people for the first time, we normally begin the process of getting to know them by gathering some standard information about them: where they work, whether they are married, how many children they have, from what part of the world they come, where they went to school, etc. In other words, we treat them, for the most part, as one more object or thing in the world. But as we get to know them better, as we begin to acquire a shared history with each other, as the stories that narrate the plot of our lives become increasingly intertwined, such information, while still a factor in the relationship, moves into the background. As this common history develops, our friends and family can no longer be identified by simply referring to the aforementioned list of facts; they become more complex, harder to describe, possessing a depth not seen at first. The closer we are to people, writes Lash, "and the better we understand them, the more they evade our cognitive 'grasp' and the greater the difficulty that we experience in giving adequate expression to our understanding. Other people become, in their measure, 'mysterious,' not insofar as we *fail* to understand them, but rather in so far as, in lovingly relating to them, we succeed in doing so."[74]

The fear of God is therefore not a permanent dwelling place of postmodern despair to which we are condemned, but as Buber expresses it, a "dark gate" through which we move into the everyday, which is where we address the dilemmas and delights of our existence before God. Once across this threshold, it is the embodied reality of day-to-day life, not the private recesses of the individual heart, that is "henceforth hallowed as the place in which he has to live with the mystery. . . . That the believing man who goes through the gate of dread is directed to the concrete contextual situations of his existence means just this: that he endures in the face of God the reality of lived life, dreadful and incomprehensible though it be. He loves it in the love of God, whom he has learned to love."[75] We human beings must,

---

73. Dante Alighieri, *Purgatory*, III.34–39.

74. Lash, *Easter in Ordinary*, 236. The mysterious character of human relationships also extends to the relation with one's self. The better you get to know yourself, the more complex and mysterious you become, *especially* to yourself. Anybody who has been surprised by how she responded in a moment of stress or crisis knows something of the mystery which is the relationship to oneself. See also Dietrich Bonhoeffer, *Dietrich Bonhoeffer Works*, vol. 2, *Act and Being: Transcendental Philosophy and Ontology in Systematic Theology*, trans. H. Martin Rumscheidt (Minneapolis: Fortress, 1996), 126.

75. Buber, *Eclipse of God*, 36–37.

in other words, begin in the concreteness and vulnerability of our own existence, with all its uncertainty and uncanniness. Only then are we in a position to grasp the divine act of creation and redemption as the overflow of intertrinitarian love, and, as a consequence of being taken up into the divine exchange of love through our communal praise and adoration, are we able to love.[76]

In a fallen and rebellious creation, foreboding evils deepen the darkness that attends the mystery: disease, war, hunger, cruelty, and abuse, the mere threat of which affects our daily lives in innumerable ways. And then for all things comes death, the single most determinative aspect of our creaturely existence. In the words of Pope John Paul II, the "daily experience of suffering—in one's own life and in the lives of others—and the array of facts which seem inexplicable to reason are enough to ensure that a question as dramatic as the question of meaning cannot be evaded. Moreover, the first absolutely certain truth of our life, beyond the fact that we exist, is the inevitability of our death. Given this unsettling fact, the search for a full answer is inescapable."[77] It is not surprising, then, that so many Christians are tempted to bypass this first step and move straight to the comfort afforded by an affirmation of God's love. "The essence of the American," writes Harold Bloom, "is the belief that God loves her or him, a conviction shared by nearly nine out of ten of us, according to a Gallup poll."[78]

As with most forms of temptation, however, this is one we should avoid, for as Buber observes, the one "who begins with the love of God without having previously experienced the fear of God, loves an idol which he himself has made, a god whom it is easy enough to love."[79] Thus we must return often to the Bible's scripting of spiritual maturity as a holy vulnerability, and to the divine love that scripture describes as fierce and all-consuming, which would have us sacrifice our lives and even those of our children, a love which presupposes rather than replaces the fear of God as the point of departure for the polyphony of life in Christ. But without this "gut-level" grasp of just how fragile and besieged, how insecure and out of control human life really is, the wisdom and wholeness that characterize spiritual maturity will lie forever beyond our reach.

This is not to say that the fear of God is somehow in opposition to love for God. The point is rather that it makes sense to speak of loving God only when the relationship between God and ourselves is already well established, when we love God for who God is and not as we might want him to be. "What is needed above all else," says Augustine, "is to be converted by the fear of God to wishing to know his will, what he bids us seek and shun. Now this fear of necessity shakes us with thoughts of our mortality and of our death to come, and so to say nails our flesh and fixes all the stirrings of pride to the wood of the cross." Together with

76. 1 John 4:19.

77. John Paul II, *Fides et Ratio: To the Bishops of the Catholic Church on the Relationship between Faith and Reason* (Boston: Pauline, 1998), 40.

78. Bloom, *American Religion*, 17.

79. Buber, *Eclipse of God*, 36.

the meekness that comes with piety, he writes, the fear of God teaches us to heed the commandment in Scripture that "God is to be loved on God's account, and one's neighbor on God's account."[80]

The fear of God is also a protest against a spirituality without suffering, which assumes that God calls men and women into being and into communion apart from the pain and distress of the world. Spirituality without suffering and conflict has to do with the gods of this world, not the God of Jesus Christ. As I noted in chapter 2, the cross comes about because of the kind of world we have made for ourselves, a world bent not toward God but toward violence and death. Crucifixion is what happens when human beings are faithful to God rather than to the rulers of the present age. Forms of piety that leave us feeling safe, sated, and secure do not share in the messianic suffering of God, but in the deceptions of the present age.

Holy vulnerability, however, should never be confused with a fatalistic acceptance of the status quo. As Buber notes, the fact that in the fear of God "one accepts the concrete situation as given to him does not, in any way, mean that he must be ready to accept that which meets him as 'God-given' in its pure factuality. He may, rather, declare the extremest enmity toward this happening and treat its 'givenness' as only intended to draw forth his own opposing force. But he will not remove himself from the concrete situation as it actually is; he will, instead, enter into it, even if in the form of fighting against it."[81] The hope that is ours in Christ, in other words, does not deny the darkness that casts its shroud over the present order of things, but neither does it succumb to that despair that is finally the worship of necessity.

We must therefore never confuse Christ's acceptance of suffering, nor his insistence that his disciples must follow him down this same path, with passivity in the face of it. Abuse and suffering are endured in hope of the new creation, relying on whatever God may will, "and this," says Williams, "is preeminently the gift of the Spirit." Our suffering is conformed to the pattern of Christ "by the presence of the same Spirit of protest, trust and hope." The follower of Christ "meets pain in acceptance and *hope*; he or she confronts it, identifies with those experiencing it, and then struggles through it to grow into new humanness, more capable both of pain and of love . . . The Spirit is the 'pledge,' the Spirit is that which more and more conforms to Christ; and so the Spirit is that which impels us forward, which creates hope out of our cries of protest in the present. We protest because we have tasted the reality of new life."[82]

The spirituality promoted by state and market, by contrast, seeks constantly to capitalize on our fear of death, so that they might manipulate our creaturely vulnerability and anxiety to consolidate their hold upon our loyalty. Popular piety corrupts the insatiable human longing for wholeness and integrity with the lure of

---

80. Augustine, *Teaching Christianity*, II.7.
81. Buber, *Eclipse of God*, 37–38; see also Lash, *Believing Three Ways in One God*, 108.
82. Williams, *Wound of Knowledge*, 12.

security, safety, stability, and predictability through the eradication of tragedy. The quest for security and its corruption of God's creation manifests itself in a variety of ways. In some the *libido dominandi*, the lust for mastery, runs roughshod over our created solidarity with one another and with all the world, as we are alternatively encouraged, enticed, and threatened to seek safety and stability by taking ownership of the people and things around us. We strive to transform God's gift of communion with other people and things into private property, commodities to be possessed and disposed of as it suits our needs. Others who are "numbed by terror and acknowledged impotence retreat into varieties of personal and moral individualism, places of private feeling and individual 'experience.'"[83] In these persons the quest for security serves to drive them further and further away from the pain and disappointment of day-to-day contact with others, in a vain attempt to carve out an inner world of safety and tranquility within themselves. They flee to the inner garden of the soul to be alone with Jesus.

The fear of God, on the other hand, does not mark the end of our understanding of the divine mystery, but only its point of departure. The art of knowing God as ineffable has been interpreted by Christians down through the centuries in terms of sharing in the paschal mystery of Christ. In the words of Paul, "if we have been united with him in a death like his, we shall certainly be united with him in a resurrection like his" (Rom. 6:5).[84] The idea of mystery, in other words, does not denote simply God's infinite incomprehensibility, though it does presuppose it. When early Christian authors adopt the Greek terminology of what is secret or hidden (*mustikos*) from the Hellenistic mystery cults,[85] they use it principally in relation to what they regarded as the hidden depth of meaning in the Bible. For figures such as Clement and Origen, the story of God's people narrated in scripture has its secret meaning revealed and articulated by Christ, the incarnate Logos of God: "Christ is the hermeneutical key who opens a vast treasury of meaning, giving access to God's eternal will for creation; the exegetical process of arriving at this new knowledge is referred to as mystical, and the knowledge itself comes also (for Origen) to be designated as such."[86]

The Christian invocation of the concept of mystery, with the attendant notions of knowing and loving God, has therefore had a christological focus from the beginning. It does not designate some sort of esoteric inner experience, but the hidden meaning and transformative understanding disclosed in Christ about God's presence and activity in the world. In the movement of self-giving love, the Triune God creates the world, and in the missions of the Word and the Spirit decides not to be God apart from a fallen and lost world. In the end, writes McIntosh, "the mystical is not simply the ineffable incomprehensibility of God (no matter

---

83. Lash, *Easter in Ordinary*, 85.

84. Cf. McIntosh, *Mystical Theology*, 41.

85. Guy G. Stroumsa, *Hidden Wisdom: Esoteric Traditions and the Roots of Christian Mysticism* (New York: E. J. Brill, 1996), 31–45.

86. McIntosh, *Mystical Theology*, 42.

whether that incomprehensibility is thought of in ancient Neoplatonic terms or modern post-Kantian ones); rather what is most *mysterious* is not the divine being per se but precisely the infinite self-giving of God which is the fundamental characteristic of the divine Trinity and is enacted in history in the life, death and resurrection of Jesus."[87]

Only as we come to know the unknown God, then, can we truthfully know ourselves. Augustine was among the first to observe how the knowledge of God and self-knowledge, while distinct, are finally inseparable: "Let me, then, confess what I know about myself, and confess to what I do not know, because what I know of myself I know only because you shed your light on me, and what I do not know I shall remain ignorant about until my darkness becomes like bright noon before your face."[88] The art of vulnerability is, at bottom, a process of self-discovery, made possible by the work of the Spirit within the common venture of discipleship that belongs to the community of Jesus. And this means that at the heart of this shared journey into the mystery of God revealed in Christ is the discipline of unselfing.

Contemplation and the Discipline of Unselfing

Once we have crossed the threshold of the dark gate into the everyday, we are ready to undertake the discipline of unselfing, of being unmade so that we can be remade. This notion will no doubt make some uncomfortable, as it sounds all too similar to the destructive habits of self-abnegation that some in our world have either been persuaded or forced to accept. Unfortunately, many have good reason to be suspicious of such ideas. The biblical notions of repentance, servanthood, and self-sacrifice have routinely been detached from the social practices that made the early church a subversive organization to the Romans, and reinscribed within the habits and relations of the prevailing culture and society, where they are normally reserved for certain people, especially women and minorities.[89]

We should, however, take care not to allow distortions to determine our response to God and the world. Sarah Coakley argues that there is a long-term danger in the repression of all forms of vulnerability and in the failure to regard all questions of fragility, suffering, and self-emptying save in terms of victimization. Such responses tend to presume the very questions they beg about power, gender, and identity, namely, "the alignment of 'males' with achieved, worldly power, and women with the lack of it. The presumption is that women *need* 'power'—but of what sort?"[90] Acting on these impulses would not result in freedom but would continue our captivity within the structures and aims of the modern world in the form of an

---

87. Ibid., 44. (emphasis original).
88. Augustine, *Confessions* X.5.
89. See Jantzen, *Power, Gender and Christian Mysticism;* and Daphne Hampson, *Theology and Feminism* (Cambridge, MA: Blackwell, 1990).
90. Coakley, *Powers and Submission,* 32–33.

antithetical bondage.[91] Both forms of the quest for security—retreating within oneself and striving for mastery of self and others—constitute pathologies that have contributed to the dismembering of Christ's body.

The exhortation to enter into the vulnerability of Christ's ecclesial body, aptly expressed in the hymn of Philippians 2, "Let this same mind be in you that was in Christ Jesus," is "not an invitation to be battered; nor is its silence a silencing." If anything, writes Coakley, it nurtures in us the virtue of courage, that we might speak with a prophetic voice. Through the practice of contemplation we enter into "the subtle but enabling presence of a God who neither shouts nor forces, let alone 'obliterates.'" If we refuse to engage in this practice, we turn away from the grace of God that invites us to enter into this presence. "Thus the 'vulnerability' that is its human condition is not about asking for unnecessary and unjust suffering (though increased self-knowledge can indeed be painful); nor is it . . . a 'self-abnegation.' On the contrary, this special "self-emptying" is not a negation of the self, but the place of the self's transformation and expansion into God."[92]

The spiritual discipline of unselfing interrupts the processes of forming our identity as disembodied consumers and faceless producers in order to cultivate a new self within the community of Jesus, one that is not confined by its "Adamic" past, but liberated for its future in the messianic kingdom. Who we are as persons is not something that already lies within each of us, needing only to be set free from the shackles of other people's expectations. Who each of us is, the name by which each of us will be called (Rev. 2:17), is rather a task to be perfected in grace within the body of Christ, the details of which constitute a complete lifetime's program.[93] Our true identity in Christ can be achieved only over time, signs of which may arise from time to time, but the definitive understanding of which will be revealed only when God will be all in all.[94]

In keeping with its trinitarian context, the process of unselfing takes the form of a story. Not just any story, however, and not a story that each of us gets to write for ourselves according to our own individual tastes. It is instead the account of a journey with a fellow group of travelers that radically reconstructs the sense and direction of our lives. If spiritual formation is truly an engagement with the questioning at the heart of faith that permeates the classical documents of the early church, then the form this interrogation takes is the rewriting of our autobiographies that occurs as we are caught up in the communion, the *community*, of Christ. The politics of the Spirit has basically to do with each member of Christ's body becoming a coauthor of the story of Jesus—a story with a multitude of characters, countless twists in the plot, and numerous confrontations with the present order of things. As we move through the often traumatic process from self-possession

91. Lash, *Theology on the Way to Emmaus*, 55–56.
92. Coakley, *Powers and Submission*, 35–36.
93. Williams, *Wound of Knowledge*, 21; Coakley, *Powers and Submission*, 139.
94. Williams, *On Christian Theology*, 287–89; Ward, *Cultural Transformation and Religious Practice*, 78.

to self-giving, and from unrestrained desire and acquisitiveness to maturity and wholeness, our individual stories find their meaning and purpose in the history of the Spirit with God's people.

Spiritual formation, working in concert with the other practices of the church, has no purpose apart from this story. Baptism begins our involvement in the politics of the Spirit as the sign and seal of our induction into a new society, marking the passage from life to death and the transfer of our citizenship from the realm of darkness to the kingdom of light. Immersion in the baptismal waters relativizes all previous definitions of identity based on class, ethnic or national origin, and gender, so that these matters no longer determine who we are as persons. Together with the Spirit's endowment of every member of the community with her or his own distinctive role (the spiritual *charisma*), baptism establishes a new mode of social relations within the community, a way of relating that, unlike the brand of equality prescribed by liberalism, does not treat us as faceless, interchangeable integers of production and consumption.

The discipline of unselfing divests us of the illusion that "I" exist apart from creation, apart from history, apart from a community and a tradition, apart from the habits and relations that comprise my dealings with others. It is a discipline of demythologizing the working assumptions of contemporary existence, foremost among which is the idea that each of us is free to make up our own story, that our lives belong to us rather than being a gift. A leading motif in the modern myth is the claim that each of us already possesses in the privacy of our inner selves a "fixed point of certainty and unshakable reassurance in our most unstable and insecure world."[95] In short, we have been enchanted by a picture of ourselves as gods, unconstrained by the material forces and historical relations of the created order, "spectators of a distanced spectacle."[96] In the end the effective denial of our creatureliness is the desire to be rid of God so that we might win the right to determine our own identity and destiny.[97]

The consequences of this founding illusion of modernity have been devastating not only for human beings, but for all of God's creatures. The origins of modern science can be traced in no small measure to the desire to subject nature to our instrumental control, so that we might safeguard ourselves from her many menaces and manage her resources for our benefit. When we thus picture ourselves in timeless caprice as lords and masters of the physical world, rather than recognizing our place within it, God's creation "becomes something manipulable for the sake of the values we have chosen. It becomes the stock of resources on hand for the fulfillment we value."[98] As the earth staggers under the weight of pollution, waste, and squandered resources, we cannot ignore the fact that the knowledges we so

95. Lash, *Easter in Ordinary*, 18.

96. Poteat, *Polanyian Meditations*, 267.

97. Cf. Stanley Hauerwas, *Against the Nations: War and Survival in a Liberal Society* (San Francisco: Harper & Row, 1985), 196.

98. Rouse, *Knowledge and Power*, 66.

proudly developed to secure our freedom from nature's menace now enslave us along with the physical world. In effect, we traded away our spiritual birthright for the promise of security and self-determination, and received instead a new and more pervasive form of bondage.

As Luther knew so well, the discipline of unselfing embraces God's judgment: "He who judges himself and confesses his sin justifies God and affirms his truthfulness, because he is saying about himself what God is saying about him."[99] But as with the fear of God, divine judgment is not finally a cause for despair or hopelessness. The Spirit judges us in Christ not by uttering words of condemnation but through complex processes of interaction that "force to the light hidden directions and dispositions that would otherwise never come to view, and thus make the conflicts of goals and interests between people a *public* affair." The Spirit takes Jesus's interactions with the people he encountered during his lifetime, dramatically narrated in scripture as "a series of ritual, quasi-legal disputations," and transforms every new social setting and every historical circumstance into "an event of judgment in that it gives the persons involved definitions, roles to adopt, points on which to stand and speak. They are invited to 'create' themselves in finding a place within this drama—an improvisation in the theater workshop, but one that purports to be about a comprehensive truth affecting one's identity and future."[100]

Judgment is therefore a necessary precondition for conversion, when a person shifts her or his allegiance from one set of powers to another, and from one measure of reality to another, namely, "the reality of God which has become manifest in Christ in the reality of the world."[101] The work of the Spirit is "to make explicit what is at stake in particular human decisions or policies, individual and collective, and in this sense bring in the event of judgment, the revaluation of identities."[102] In contrast, the false piety fostered by liberal capitalism reconfirms the prevailing habits and relations of the world, which constitutes a de facto legitimation of the status quo. Such politics is in the end nonjudgmental, in both the popular and biblical senses of that term, and is therefore incapable of displaying God's love for the world incarnated in the crucified one.

For those who stand before God within the body of Christ, judgment brings not condemnation, but the possibility of genuine freedom joined with a new capacity to participate in the divine exchange of love. As we shed the vanity that is the quest for security, the world's grip upon us also starts to relax. The freedom of a holy vulnerability

takes the form of dispossession, letting go, surrendering the title-deeds we forged. . . . Emancipation, letting things and people go from our grasp . . . is how life in the

99. Martin Luther, *Luther's Works*, ed. Hilton C. Oswald, vol. 11: *First Lectures on the Psalms II: Psalms 76–126* (Saint Louis: Concordia, 1976), 93.
100. Williams, "Postmodern Theology and the Judgment of the World," 96–97 (emphasis original).
101. Bonhoeffer, *Ethics*, 197.
102. Williams, "Postmodern Theology and the Judgment of the World," 97.

Spirit is to be lived; which is to say: it is how we are to die. What occurs in death is, in the last resort, the same for all of us: we are deprived of all possessions, "even of ourselves." To learn to die (which is, of course, the way that finite creatures learn to live) is, therefore, to learn to relate to each and every person, thing, disease, event, delight, that we encounter, neither as enemy nor as possession but as gift, as friend.[103]

The art of vulnerability in the *koinonia* of the Spirit thus conveys a radically distinct articulation of freedom, one that is very different from modern simulacra. Most people, if asked to define freedom, will usually do so as freedom *from* something or someone. Freedom is, essentially, the opportunity (and the right) to be a tyrant over one's own affairs. A few will add that freedom must eventually be the freedom *for* someone or something if it is to persist, and so link it with the idea of responsible choice. Yet neither of these prepositions—*from* or *for*—addresses adequately the freedom that is ours in Christ. Both are still mired in the picture of the self as an individual who in the essence of his being is unfettered by relations with his fellow creatures, and those relations into which such an individual does enter are, and always will be, his choice.

In the church, by contrast, we learn to live—quite literally—out of control, emancipated from the promise of mastery with which the earthly city lures us yet will never allow us to achieve. Contemplation, which is the end of the practice of spiritual formation, is not an esoteric preoccupation, but, as Williams says, "a deeper appropriation of the vulnerability of the self in the midst of the language and transactions of the world."[104] We learn through a contemplative way of life to give back our habits, our relations, our attempts at knowledge, our very lives. As we do so we cultivate the virtue of patience, divesting ourselves of our feeble and vain attempts at security, "sometimes in darkness not unlike Gethsemane."[105] The freedom that is the Spirit (2 Cor. 3.17) is therefore signified by yet a third preposition, the freedom *of*. It is the freedom of our adoption as the daughters and sons of God, the freedom of servanthood within the household of Christ. Within this household, freedom is a gift that can never be possessed and a power that can never become ours, and yet it is a gift and power in which we share in the Spirit through our participation in the *koinonia* of the people of God.

The freedom of the Spirit, therefore, does not have anything to do with that specter which modernity calls the human ego, a Gnostic apparition that only haunts its body but really does not belong to it. Human beings only begin to learn what freedom is when we learn what it means to be some*body*, that is, when we

---

103. Lash, *Believing Three Ways in One God*, 103.
104. Rowan Williams, "Theological Integrity," *New Blackfriars* 72 (1991): 148.
105. Lash, *Believing Three Ways in One God*, 81. Incidentally, this is why the church has long affirmed that martyrdom, taking up one's cross and following Christ, is not an unfortunate accident that some Christians are forced to endure, but the natural outcome of a life of love and service, and a prominent feature of early Christian spirituality.

know *viscerally* that human life is vested in, and is nothing apart from, our bodies, and that our bodies are inextricably woven into the social and material fabric of God's creation. Freedom thus depends upon our interactions and exchanges with others—parents, relatives, neighbors, even the institutions of liberal capitalist society—and with all created things. The freedom of Christ involves even our enemies, for only as the followers of Jesus are liberated to love those who seek to do them harm, do they have assurance that they are making progress on their journey toward that liberty, indeed, that *liberality*, which *is* the reign of God. The life of freedom thus requires intense and rigorous schooling within the context of the messianic community and its distinctive skills and institutions.

The freedom that comes through the politics of the Spirit is itself formed by the other practices of the church. Through our participation in these activities we come to understand that emancipation is the gift and effect of getting caught up in a true story that transfigures our fate as finite, fallen beings into our destiny as redeemed and cherished creatures. But the realization of this destiny does not take place apart from confrontation and conflict. The sacraments always situate themselves in the context of Jesus's death and resurrection, and thus in the context of the faithfulness of Christ being met time after time by the infidelity of friend and foe alike. These practices nurture what Johann Baptist Metz calls the memory of suffering, in the light of which "it is clear that social power and political domination are not simply to be taken for granted but that they continually have to justify themselves in view of actual suffering." The art of vulnerability, in which the victims of suffering and oppression provide contrapuntal dissonance, challenges the world to justify itself in light of the human cost it exacts, but at the same time it also extends the divine offer of new life in the messianic community, the historical sign of God's peaceable kingdom.[106]

To be buried and raised with Christ in baptism, therefore, not only begins the process of accepting our vulnerability before God, but also makes explicit the role of the disciple in the biblical drama. The Bible, together with the church fathers, teaches that the true and perfect disciple of Christ is the martyr, the one who is ready to go with Jesus to the cross.[107] The sharing of bread and the cup within the family of God is likewise never simply a fellowship meal but concretely embodies the divine summons "to share in God's sufferings at the hands of a godless world."[108] As I noted in chapter 6, the origins of this meal are invariably set in the context of Jesus's betrayal by his disciples on the night before his death. The story of the Eucharist, then *and* now, thus does not ignore the tragic suffering associated with everyday life, nor does it cover over our complicity in this tragedy, but incorporates these within its costly solidarity with the world. As with baptism, the Eucharist also

106. Johann Baptist Metz, *Faith in History and Society: Toward a Practical Fundamental Theology*, trans. David Smith (New York: Seabury, 1980), 115.

107. John D. Zizioulas, "The Early Christian Community," in *Christian Spirituality: Origins to the Twelfth Century*, ed. Bernard McGinn, John Meyendorff, and Jean Leclercq (New York: Crossroad, 1997), 39.

108. Bonhoeffer, *Letters and Papers from Prison*, 361.

affirms and proclaims God's vindication of suffering, both Christ's and ours, in the community of the crucified.

Finally, though the practice of spiritual formation rejects the quest for security that holds the world in its grip, Christ's followers are not left adrift in chaotic waters without a sense of direction or assistance. In that community where men and women live by "the conviction of things not seen" (Heb. 11:1), relying on the grace of the one who subjects the world to God's will by his weakness and suffering, we learn to discriminate between the fraudulent offer of certainty and security, which is forever beyond our reach, and the kind of certitude that develops through our continuing faithfulness to Christ, who on the cross accepted our vulnerability as his own.[109] By contrast, the calculating cynicism that is cultivated by many in our culture, as they seek to preserve their autonomy by describing all commitments as self-interested pursuits, is but "the irresponsible dilettantism which we call 'bad faith.'"[110] But for "those who are called, both Jews and Greeks," the discipline of following Christ with one's brothers and sisters is "the power of God and the wisdom of God" (1 Cor. 1:24).

The goal of the politics of the Spirit is the ability to live and work as artisans of the age to come while dwelling in the midst of the present age. To do this we must understand the social idiom of liberal capitalism, its ways of organizing human life and action. In particular, we must attend to its fundamental impulse, the lust for mastery, which drives the quest for security and certainty that lies at the root of postmodern spirituality. We must cooperate with our earthly neighbors in the pursuit of the material goods necessary to mortal life, but without surrendering to the worship of necessity, which insists that we have no alternative but to act in accordance with the limitations this age would impose on us. This will require habits of discernment that allow us to discriminate between uses of these goods that are open to God's apocalyptic activity in Christ and may therefore be rightly directed toward the peace of the heavenly city, and those that are closed to that activity and are incompatible with the church's art of vulnerability.

---

109. My thanks to Dorothee Soelle for drawing my attention to the subtle yet substantial difference between spiritual security and spiritual certitude. See Soelle, *The Window of Vulnerability: A Political Spirituality* (Minneapolis: Fortress, 1990).

110. Lash, *Believing Three Ways in One God*, 19.

8

Living in Tents

Becoming Artisans of the Age to Come

"O people who can rest
    assured to see the light of Heaven someday,
    your desire's only care and only quest.

May grace soon melt the film of sin away,
    that from a conscience finally made clear
    may fall the river of your memory;

Graciously tell me—and I'll hold it dear—
    if any of you hails from Italy.
    My knowing it may bring some good to you."

"My brother, each man is a citizen
    of one true city. What you mean to say
    is, 'who once lived a pilgrim in that land.'"

                Dante Alighieri, *Purgatory*

According to the ancient Egyptians, the society that developed around the fecundity of the Nile River was the place around which all life, including that of the gods, was ordered in perpetuity. Imperial Rome similarly declared itself to be the eternal city, to whose legions the celestial powers set no limits, world or time, but bequeathed the gift of empire without end. In more recent times nation-states have staked their claim to Rome's political mantle as "*the City*, a permanent and 'eternal' City, *Urbs aeterna* . . . an ultimate solution of the human problem."[1] And now the global marketplace proclaims itself to be the privileged site where all reality must henceforth always be strategically conceived and coordinated. The common thread here is the notion that some particular place or institution within this world provides the standpoint from which all things are rightly named, assessed, and pursued.

As citizens of the *civitas peregrina*, the one true city on pilgrimage through this world toward the age to come, Christians do not subscribe to this widely held belief. As with all things that belong to the schema of this present age (1 Cor. 7:31), we are persuaded these places and the institutions they support are destined to pass away. Because our true homeland and commonwealth still lie before us, we do not narrate the unfolding of history in relation to any particular place in this world but privilege instead the polyphony of time orchestrated by the apocalypse of God in Jesus Christ. We see ourselves as nomads, living, as it were, in "tents" in the various places to which God has sent us to serve as a sign and an instrument of his intentions for the world.

Because the two cities are currently mixed together and entangled, Christians must learn to make wise use of the same goods and to endure with patience the same evils as the citizens of the *civitas temporalis* do, all the while bearing witness to the one "who has made peace with God and peace among human beings."[2] Like everyone else, then, we must eat, drink, find clothing, secure shelter, till the land and fashion instruments of all sorts, marry and give in marriage, raise and protect children, bury parents, and cope with natural disasters, debilitating disease, and social upheavals. We are called to do so, however, according to a different faith, a different hope, and a different love, and without succumbing to forms of acting and speaking that domesticate, marginalize, and exploit the church's life, language, and witness.[3]

Knowing how to live and work as citizens of the city that is to come while dwelling in the midst of the present world is a primary aim of the art of vulnerability. An important dimension of our calling as members of Christ's body, then, is to become skilled artisans of the age to come in the middle of a world that is under the rule of sin and death. In particular, we need to acquire those virtues of discernment that allow us to discriminate between uses of goods that are compatible with the apocalyptic action of God in Christ, and those which foreclose on that event. In addition, we must learn to recognize practices and institutions that would have us confess an alien faith, embrace a false hope, and follow a lesser love.

In this last chapter, I discuss some of the recurring tendencies in the social idiom of the earthly city that set the context in which the Christians are called

---

1. Florovsky, "Empire and Desert," 135.
2. Bonhoeffer, *Works*, vol. 5, 33.
3. Augustine, *City of God*, I.35, XVIII.54.

on to practice the art of pilgrimage. In one way or another these tendencies are linked to what Augustine calls the *libido dominandi*, the lust for mastery, which is predicated on the possession, threat, and use of coercive force, and therefore on death and the fear of death. This desire to take charge of our lives, to carve out zones of security for ourselves, permeates every aspect of a fallen world, including those involved in the reproduction of life in all its facets. Of all the manifestations of this desire to dominate the world about us, however, none is more persistent and destructive than war.

War and the *Libido Dominandi*

Though by its very existence the church challenges claims to our allegiance on the part of the state and the market, it does not compete with these temporal authorities for control over geographical space, nor does it seek to determine what are the best means to achieve such control. It is obligated, however, to seek the welfare of the earthly city, which requires that we cooperate with our earthly neighbors in the pursuit of the material goods necessary to life in this age. Indeed, in most cases we cannot avoid some sort of cooperation, because the two cities are mingled together at present. We must make use of the same goods and endure the same evils as the citizens of the earthly city do, but we direct them to different ends.[4]

Our pursuit of these goods, however, must not hinder our worship of the one supreme and true God or injure true faith and godliness. Our cooperation with the earthly city must therefore be aware of the lure of the *libido dominandi*. It is this fundamental desire to control our surroundings that holds the world in its grip, and it is what led the rulers and authorities to rebel against God's apocalyptic intrusion in the world by condemning Christ to death, and in so doing condemned them to be the form of the world that is passing away. By contrast, Christians are called upon to cultivate the kind of holy vulnerability that allows us to use earthly goods without resort to the moral authority of death, so that we might direct their use toward that alone which can truly be called peace, "a perfectly ordered and perfectly harmonious fellowship in the enjoyment of God, and of one another in God."[5]

The lust for mastery is a virulent form of idolatry, that is, the setting of our mind and heart, loyalty and confidence, hopes and fears on something other than the grace and mercy of God. It gives rise to the worship of necessity, which is the affirmation of the present order as the enduring nature of things. Things just *are* as we now find them, and we must therefore work with these "givens." The worship of necessity proclaims that we have no alternative but to act in accordance with the limitations it would impose on us. It thus renders absolute our impotence,

4. Ibid., XIX.17.
5. Ibid., I.Pref., XIX.17.

leaving us completely enthralled to authorities at whose thrones we have no choice but to kneel.[6]

The idolatrous worship of necessity informs the realism of fact that underwrites modern social analysis (including much of what is labeled "Christian social ethics") and literature. Reinhold Niebuhr, for example, gives tacit consent to the givenness of the present order of things when he accepts without protest or qualification the "fact" that "society is in a perpetual state of war."[7] Not only does such an assumption presuppose an understanding of the world markedly at odds with scripture, in that it projects an ontology of original violence (a view advocated by early Gnostics), it also confers upon the bureaucratic politics of the modern state and the ever-expanding market of global capitalism the status of a theodicy.[8] These mechanisms are mythically ordained to manage individual and "tribal" self-interests so as to maintain an optimum balance of relative goods, but in the process they also perpetuate the ancient heroic *agon* celebrated (in somewhat different ways) by both Machiavelli and Nietzsche.

The worship of necessity has many guises, but we encounter it most poignantly in the assertion that war is a regrettable but necessary and just part of human life, and thus we must be prepared as good citizens to sacrifice for our homeland, that is, our nation-state.[9] Though this might seem like a straightforward, reasonable, and dispassionate assertion, the invocation of the concept of sacrifice, drawn from the realm of cultic ritual and observance, links it to the practice of idolatry. From time to time, so the argument goes, blood sacrifice must be offered to the gods, that is, to the powers and principalities that determine the warp and woof of the universe. Granted, most nations and peoples would prefer to offer the lives of the enemy, of "them," and not those of their own youth, but sacrifice in some form must nevertheless be made.

Though some may be scandalized by a cultic description of war, our own speech betrays us, for while the making of offerings to blood-thirsty gods is not generally a part of the working vocabulary of most nations, the language of martyrdom and sacrifice, plundered from the language of the church, most certainly is. Time and again those in the military who have died for their country are extolled as having made "the supreme sacrifice."[10] The question immediately arises: To whom do we

6. Lash, *Believing Three Ways in One God*, 108.

7. Reinhold Niebuhr, *Moral Man and Immoral Society: A Study in Ethics and Politics* (New York: Charles Scribner's Sons, 1932, 1960), 19.

8. See Milbank, *Theology and Social Theory*, 27–48.

9. Cavanaugh points out that the nation-state comes about when the idea of the nation—a people united by some combination of shared ethnicity, language, or history—is fused with the political apparatus of the state. Nationality is not simply "natural" or "objective," since ethnicity, language, and history are all themselves the result of contingent historical construction (William T. Cavanaugh, "Killing for the Telephone Company: Why the Nation-State Is Not the Keeper of the Common Good," *Modern Theology* 20 (April 2004): 246).

10. A good deal of research has recently been done on this theme of blood sacrifice for one's country. From a sociological perspective there is Carolyn Marvin and David W. Ingle, *Blood Sacrifice and the*

offer this sacrifice, if not to the gods? If we respond, to the God of Abraham and Sarah, then it would seem that we are tacitly admitting that Christ's sacrifice was not sufficient for the sins of the world, that he did not "once for all" enter in the eternal Holy of Holies to obtain our redemption (Heb. 9). If we say instead that we offer it to the nation-state of which we are a part, we are granting to a part of the created order what belongs solely to God. And if the answer is, we offer this sacrifice to ourselves, or to our posterity, then we explicitly embrace the sin of Adam, seeking not only to be like the gods, but on our own terms (Gen. 3).[11]

Perhaps some will dismiss the notion of sacrifice as "just a metaphor,"[12] though I doubt that many of those whose world and self-identity have been shaped by war through the ages would accept such a summary dismissal.[13] But even if we are successful in this regard, then other problems arise that are associated with the desire to deny completely the idea and the practice of sacrifice.[14] We who are the twenty-first-century heirs of the Enlightenment have been trained to believe that it is our sacred task to create a world that makes sacrifice a thing of the past. We can achieve this goal by fashioning a world of unencumbered freedom where all our limits are freely chosen, and where our god or gods (should we choose to worship one or more) are little more than cosmic but highly personable therapists who entice each of us to discover ourselves through our individually designed and crafted destinies.

The modern university in particular is an institution supremely dedicated to the creation of a world free of sacrifice, in part, and most ironically, by a commitment to include every voice in a story of progress in which no one should suffer for the actions of anyone else. To this end, it takes special care to invite all the excluded voices to see themselves as characters in the modern story that denies the reality of sacrifice. The problem with what is in many respects a noble project is that these excluded voices seem almost always to tell of suffering that makes sense only as a story of sacrifice. Hence, we find it necessary, as we tell this story, to relegate these sacrifices to the past as we attempt to create a common story that no longer is dependent on sacrifice.

Nation: Totem Rituals and the American Flag (New York: Cambridge University Press, 1999); and from a historiographical point of view, Richard M. Gamble, *The War for Righteousness: Progressive Christianity, the Great War, and the Rise of the Messianic Nation* (Wilmington, DE: ISI, 2003).

11. This is a point driven home by Augustine, who notes that "Adam and Eve would have been better fitted to resemble gods if they had clung in obedience to the highest and true ground of their being, and not, in their pride, made themselves their own ground. For created gods are gods not in their own true nature, but by participation in the true God" (Augustine, *City of God*, XIV.13).

12. Those who use this expression, "just a metaphor," are sadly, almost criminally, deficient in their understanding of how theological language works. See Janet Martin Soskice, *Metaphor and Religious Language* (Oxford: Oxford University Press, 1985).

13. See, for example, Tom Brokaw, *The Greatest Generation* (New York: Random, 1998).

14. I am indebted to Stanley Hauerwas for what follows. See his "The Liturgical Shape of the Christian Life: Teaching Christian Ethics as Worship," in *In Good Company: The Church as Polis* (Notre Dame, IN: University of Notre Dame Press, 1995), 165–68.

From the standpoint of the gospel, however, the story that men and women can by their own wits live without sacrifice, at least from now on, is a lie. It is a lie because it creates false memories that instigate more sacrifices that are even more damnable, because these stories prevent us from acknowledging the suffering and death of the past as sacrifice. No doubt most people in the United States feel terrible about the suffering that has taken place in the past, particularly by excluded peoples—African Americans, other people of color, Native Americans, women, Jews, the poor, etc. We hope that our recognition of prejudice, slavery, segregation, and genocide in the past is a sign of our goodwill and essential righteousness. And so we deceive ourselves by saying that now that we have acknowledged our guilt about the sweat and blood of past generations offered up to idols against their wills, we just need to try to be and to do better. Though such measures are implemented from the most sincere of motives, what is often overlooked by the inclusion of these stories within the metanarrative of liberal capitalist society is that these excluded peoples become victims all over again, involuntarily inscribed into a history narrated by those who profited either directly or indirectly by their suffering.

And yet at the end of the day, sacrifice never comes to an end in the earthly city. Hegel reminds us that history, when lived "according to the flesh," that is, apart from cross and resurrection, is a slaughter-bench.[15] From this standpoint time unfolds in response to the offering of blood to the gods of war, who constantly renew their demand for the lives of human beings, and we have no choice but to obey meekly, hoping against all rational expectation that this will be the last time that we shall have to bloody our hands. All the while we seek new scapegoats to explain our past aggressions and take comfort in the illusion that since we have diagnosed the cause and thereby remedied it we shall soon have no reason to offer sacrifice. The particular scapegoat that the Enlightenment identified as the catalyst for war was "religion," and so it narrated history as the past violence of warring religious parties to justify the sovereignty of the nation-state. This prejudice was immortalized in the catchy tune "Imagine," in which the late John Lennon encouraged us to imagine a world in which, among other things, there is no religion. "It's easy if you try," he assured us.[16]

---

15. Hegel, *Philosophy of History*, 21. In his 2002 State of the Union speech, President George W. Bush explicitly affirmed this understanding of history: "History has called America and our allies to action, and it is both our responsibility and our privilege to fight freedom's fight. . . . In the sacrifice of soldiers, the fierce brotherhood of firefighters, and the bravery and generosity of ordinary citizens, we have glimpsed what a new culture of responsibility could look like. We want to be a nation that serves goals larger than self. We've been offered a unique opportunity, and we must not let this moment pass" (www.whitehouse .gov/news/releases/2002/01/20020129-11.html). Augustine wisely points out that a nation cannot make such a claim without unwittingly celebrating the iniquity of the unjust who give them this "unique opportunity." Augustine suggests, surely with tongue planted firmly in cheek, "should they not worship even Foreign Iniquity as a goddess?" After all, if a nation's neighbors were just, then the empire could not avail itself of this opportunity and broaden the scope of its rule (Augustine, *City of God*, IV.15). I am indebted to Michael Hanby for bringing this passage to my attention.

16. ©Bag Productions Inc.

This view has recently been reaffirmed in Charles Kimball's widely acclaimed book, *When Religion Becomes Evil*. As the title suggests, Kimball is highly critical of the evil and violence done in the name of religion, asserting (without offering any evidence to back up his claim) that "more wars have been waged, more people killed, and these days more evil perpetrated in the name of religion than by any other institutional force in human history."[17] The only problem, unfortunately, is that careful historiography demonstrates that the so-called Wars of Religion in Europe, the paradigmatic test case in these matters, were not fought over religion, though heads of state to rally the masses to their respective sides invoked religious rhetoric.[18] Kimball also conveniently ignores the fact that wars have been getting more frequent and more deadly with the secularization of the modern world, and that the twentieth century, the most "nonreligious" in history, was also the bloodiest on record.[19]

The events of September 2001 have resuscitated the practice of scapegoating religion, now in the demonized form of "fundamentalist" or "radical" religion, which is then linked immediately with that most dreaded of concepts: terrorism. This way of describing the current state of affairs is part of a larger narrative, according to which there is a dichotomy between the religious and the secular, and that the former is irrational and dangerous, and must be constantly reined in by "reason," instantiated in secular political power. Delimiting the human condition in this manner establishes an other who is essentially irrational, fanatical, and violent, which in turn authorizes coercive measures against this other. In our time and place, writes William Cavanaugh, "the Muslim world especially plays the role of religious Other. *They* have not yet learned to remove the dangerous influence of religion from political life. *Their* violence is therefore irrational and fanatical. *Our* violence, by contrast, is rational and peacemaking, and sometimes regrettably necessary to contain *their* violence."[20] The not-so-subtle message is that the only good religion is one in which everyone acts like good American Protestants, that is, in which no one takes her or his religion seriously.

17. Charles Kimball, *When Religion Becomes Evil* (San Francisco: HarperSan Francisco, 2002), 1. Compared to others, Kimball's view of religion is charitable. For more malevolent accounts, see Daniel C. Dennett, *Breaking the Spell: Religion as a Natural Phenomenon* (New York: Viking, 2006); and Sam Harris, *The End of Faith: Religion, Terror, and the Future of Reason* (New York: Norton, 2004).

18. See in particular Richard S. Dunn, *The Age of Religious Wars: 1559–1715*, 2nd ed. (New York: Norton, 1979); and J. H. Elliott, *Europe Divided: 1559–1598*, 2nd ed. (Malden, MA : Blackwell, 2000).

19. Of course, Kimball is not alone in this view. A virtual cottage industry has blossomed around this prejudice since the eleventh of September 2001. In addition to Dennett and Harris, see R. Scott Appleby, *The Ambivalence of the Sacred: Religion, Violence and Reconciliation* (Lanham, MD: Rowman & Littlefield, 2000); Leo D. Lefebure, *Revelation, the Religions, and Violence* (Maryknoll, NY: Orbis, 2000); Mark Juergensmeyer, *Terror in the Mind of God: The Global Rise of Religious Violence* (Berkeley: University of California Press, 2000); Oliver McTernan, *Violence in God's Name: Religion in an Age of Conflict* (Maryknoll, NY: Orbis 2003); and Charles Selengut, *Sacred Fury: Understanding Religious Violence* (Walnut Creek, CA: Altamira, 2004).

20. William T. Cavanaugh, "Sins of Omission: What 'Religion and Violence' Arguments Ignore," *The Hedgehog Review* 6 (Spring 2004): 35, Cavanaugh's emphasis.

The scapegoating of religion in the United States is frequently justified by the assertion that the attacks on the World Trade Center and the Pentagon changed everything. On the contrary, Christians affirm with Ecclesiastes that there is nothing new under the sun (1:9). The last time a world-transformative event occurred was over a fifty-day span two thousand years ago in the city of Jerusalem, between the Jewish festivals of Passover and Pentecost. What we now call terrorism is but the next stage in the evolution of modern warfare; sadly, we shall probably have to get used to it, at least for the foreseeable future. The only thing of any consequence that might possibly have changed since that day is the illusion that if America has enough of the right kind of technology and enough firepower, if "we" can sacrifice enough of "them," we can insulate ourselves from the violence with which most of the peoples of this world have had to contend since the time Adam and Eve were expelled from the garden.

The good news of God's apocalyptic intrusion into the world in Christ and his church is that we are free from the presumption that war is necessary. In the offering of our Passover lamb, sacrifice comes to its proper end, its proper purpose; for in this, the offering of God to God, God refuses to let the never-ending slaughter-bench determine the course of human history. And through our liturgically configured participation in this, the end of sacrifice, we are saved from our illusions concerning what will save us from the bloodshed that has dominated the storyline of history, and thus from the worship of necessity. The God of Jesus Christ is a bloody and bloodied God, and our salvation is equally bloody, because we are called upon, not to offer the other up to death for our security, but to offer ourselves, to be martyrs, to offer testimony to the end of sacrifice in the sacrifice of the Passover lamb. Baptism can therefore never be "just a symbol," for it is the washing that readies our bodies for burial, preparing us to share in the true history of the world as citizens of the one true city and just regime, bearing witness to that time when death will be no more.

Natural and Unnatural Life

Through our participation in God's sacrifice for the welfare of the world, we are made citizens of the commonwealth of the new creation, with a story that is not based on violence or self-deception. Instead, the miraculous sign of the resurrection, God's declaration that in the end life and not death will have the final word, constitutes our history. The refusal to engage in the worship of necessity through the offering of sacrifice in war is thus one of the marks of the church's life and witness to a world in thrall to the lust for mastery. At the same time, however, war is the exceptional case. In most circumstances the church must cooperate in some manner and to some extent with the world and its ways of regulating the necessities of everyday life. How do we determine which uses of material goods cultivate true faith and godliness, allowing the peace of the heavenly city to be manifested in the midst of the earthly city?

To this end Dietrich Bonhoeffer points to the idea of the natural in Catholic moral theology as a helpful way of relating the eschatological trajectory of the church to the use we are to make of earthly goods.[21] He develops it as a mediating concept between the created as such, in order to take into account the fallenness of humankind, and the sinful, in order to include the created. By entering into natural life, Christ transforms it into the realm of the penultimate, that is, that which is directed toward the ultimate—the justification of all things in the messianic reign of God. The concept of the natural denotes a moment of independence and self-development for the created as such, with a relative freedom appropriate to natural life. Within this freedom, however, "there is a difference between its right use and its misuse, and this is the difference between the natural and the unnatural; there is therefore a relative openness and a relative closedness for Christ." The natural is, therefore, that within creation which is directed toward the coming of Christ, while the unnatural is that which has closed itself off against Christ's coming.[22]

The formal determination of the natural is provided by God's intention to preserve the world and direct it toward Christ, and thus what is natural can be discerned only in relation to Christ. Materially, it is the form of preserved life itself, embracing the whole of creation. Reason belongs to the material dimension of the natural as the source of knowledge of itself. It is not a divine principle that can elevate human beings above the natural to the supernatural, but is itself a part of creation that has been graciously preserved by God, participating wholly in the natural. Its function is to "take in" (vernehmen) as a unity that which is whole and universal in reality. The natural and reason are thus correlated with each other, the former as the form of being of the preserved life, the latter as the form of its awareness. Reason thus shares fully in the effects of the fall, perceiving "only what is given in the fallen world, and, indeed, exclusively according to its content."[23]

The categories of natural and unnatural function typologically as anticipations and refusals, respectively, of the apocalyptic regime of God in Jesus Christ. The natural can therefore not be defined or understood apart from the event of grace. On its own, the natural cannot compel the coming of Christ (hence, the grace of God's apocalyptic action is truly unmerited), nor can that which is unnatural make it impossible: "in both cases the real coming is an act of grace."[24] As Aquinas expresses it, human beings are created with a natural desire to see and participate

21. Bonhoeffer is influenced here by Josef Pieper's *Reality and the Good*, though in good Protestant fashion he continues to attribute to the Thomist tradition a belief in the essential integrity of reason in spite of the fall, and also in reason's ability to grasp the formal determination of the natural in the preserving will of God. Bonhoeffer, *Ethics*, 175 note 1. See Josef Pieper, *Living the Truth: The Truth of all Things* and *Reality and the Good*, trans. Lothar Krauth and Stella Lange (San Francisco: Ignatius, 1989).

22. Bonhoeffer, *Ethics*, 173–74.

23. Ibid., 174–75.

24. Ibid., 173–74.

in God, but that desire can be realized only by God's gracious initiative.[25] The church's constitutive practices—scriptural reasoning, doctrine, liturgy, and spiritual formation—provide the means by which Christians recognize as either natural or unnatural the activities and habits that foster our pursuit of the necessities of life within the earthly city.

According to Bonhoeffer, the incarnation can never serve as God's affirmation of the natural in abstraction from the cross and resurrection. The humanity of Jesus does not ratify the established world and human life as it exists in a fallen world. There can be no greater error, says Bonhoeffer, than to separate the three elements of the event of grace: "In becoming human we recognize God's love toward God's creation; in the crucifixion God's judgment on all flesh; and in the resurrection God's purpose for a new world."[26] In Christ, God judges our conceptions of what it takes to make and to keep human life human, and offers in their place the decisive definition in Jesus's life and passion.[27] True creatureliness is only followable in terms of the relationship between the present age and the age to come, or between nature and grace, made visible in this age by the actions and speech of the risen Christ's earthly-historical body.

With this conception of the natural realm we are able to acknowledge and relate what God has created to the coming of the apocalypse of God in Christ. There remains that within the created as such that has not been completely effaced by the fall and thus retains its sacramentality, its character as *signum*, the product of God's speech. It is perfectible in the sense of being capable of being reimagined and recontextualized within the church as markers of God's eternal commonwealth and therefore conducive to the cultivation of virtue and the worship of the one true God. Seen in this light, the natural is "that form of life preserved by God for the fallen world that is directed towards justification, salvation and renewal through Christ."[28]

Bonhoeffer's discussion of the natural provides a point of departure for developing our sense of what is involved in being artisans of the age to come in the midst of the present age, but we must proceed with caution. Because the incarnation does not simply ratify the world as it is presently ordered, there is no reason to assume, for example, that we owe unquestioned allegiance to the state, or that we are obligated to participate in the ever-increasing levels of consumption required to sustain a global economy. Our involvement in the natural realm is a matter of discernment, which requires the use of reason directed toward the peace of God's regime. As artisans of the age to come, then, we must become what Frank Lentricchia calls "connoisseurs of reason,"[29] but never uncritically.

25. Thomas Aquinas, *Summa contra Gentiles*, 3:51–53, trans. Anton C. Pegis, FRSC (Notre Dame, IN: University of Notre Dame Press, 1975).

26. Bonhoeffer, *Ethics*, 157.

27. See Yoder, *The Politics of Jesus*, 99.

28. Bonhoeffer, *Ethics*, 174.

29. See Frank Lentricchia, *Ariel and the Police* (Madison: University of Wisconsin Press, 1988), 133.

Connoisseurs of Reason

As a part of the material dimension of the natural, the ability of human reason to "take in" the world is also subject to the lust for mastery, manifesting itself in what Michel de Certeau calls strategic action. Strategy involves a calculation of power that becomes possible when a "subject of will and power" is identified as the "proper" locus of choice and action. This proper subject—consumers pursuing their individual self-interest, corporations, armies, city governments, scientific laboratories, states, and even Western culture as a whole—designates "a *place* that can be delimited as its *own* and serve as the base from which relations with an *exteriority* composed of targets or threats (customers or competitors, enemies, the country surrounding the city, objectives and objects of research, etc.) can be managed." Every strategic exercise of reason first distinguishes its own place that is determined almost exclusively by its own power and will from its surrounding "environment." Strategic rationality forms the basis for what counts as rational in modern science, politics, military planning, and especially marketing and advertising.[30]

According to Certeau, there are three effects generated by the identification of the proper subject. The first is the triumph of place over time. Privileging place allows it to capitalize on acquired advantages, prepare for future expansions, and secure for itself a certain independence over against the variability of circumstances. The particularity and contingency, the irreducibility and irreversibility of *history* are reconfigured as the manageable pluralism of *historicity*.[31] Events occurring in the past and prospects yet to be realized in the future are assimilated into a homogeneous and fixed present, where they "appear as simultaneously co-present to vision—*as we have*, in this tradition, *described vision*, and as this description *functions* in our reflection."[32]

A second effect is directly related to the role this particular description of vision plays in modernity's construction of natural life. The establishment of a caesura between a place appropriated as the subject's own and that of its "other" generates a mastery of places through sight: "The division of space makes possible a *panoptic practice* proceeding from a place whence the eye can transform foreign forces into objects that can be observed and measured, and thus control and 'include' them within its scope of vision. To be able to see (far into the distance) is also to be able to predict, to run ahead of time by reading a space."[33] Entire traditions and

30. Certeau, *Practice of Everyday Life*, xix, 35–36.

31. Ibid., 36.

32. Poteat, *Philosophical Daybook*, 66.

33. Certeau, *Practice of Everyday Life*, 36. The allusion here is to the Panopticon, Jeremy Bentham's architectural design for the model prison. Michel Foucault uses Bentham's design as a figure for describing the disciplinary sinews that hold the current regime and its regulative modes of "rationality" together. See Michel Foucault, *Discipline and Punish: The Birth of the Prison*, trans. Alan Sheridan (New York: Random House, Inc., 1979), 200.

communities may be identified, kept in confinement and "properly" supervised by a panoptic practice.[34]

As I have noted previously, the practices, habits and teachings of the church have been rationally "taken in" by the panoptic confinement of religion. The grammatical ambiguity of this phrase is deliberate, for it makes explicit both what has happened to Christ's ecclesial body (now reconfigured as a "religion") and how this confinement was achieved (by being so classified). Together the concepts of "religious" and "secular" serve to weave the whole of natural life into the rationalized fabric of modern and now postmodern life. Religion is an intrinsic feature in the strategic containment and surveillance of reality—the differentiation of existence into supposedly autonomous value spheres (science, religion, morality, art, political economy)—where it serves to make productive use of alternative ways of practicing everyday life.

The panoptic confinement of religion has three interrelated objectives which, for the most part, it has successfully pursued since the emergence of the modern world. First, as we have already argued, it stipulates that dispositions, practices, and institutions that once were part and parcel of the conduct of everyday life be confined to a sequestered sphere, where they are configured as private values. The idea of the privatization of religious belief and sentiment, which in recent years has come under intense scrutiny in some quarters, is thus in the strict sense a tautology, since in modernity religion is by definition private. Second, the classification of these habits, practices, and institutions as private values repositions them at the margins of society, where they are effectively precluded from being directly involved in, or interfering with, society's primary modes of discipline and supervision. Finally, the strategy of panoptic confinement also allows society to invoke these "values" at the public level whenever the dominant regime needs "to overcome the antinomy of a purely instrumental and goalless rationality," a rationality that nonetheless "bear[s] the burden of ultimate political purpose."[35]

The third effect of identifying a proper subject is a specific type of knowledge that is the product of these strategic deployments, "one sustained and determined by the power to provide oneself with one's own place. . . . In other words, *a certain power is the precondition of this knowledge* and not merely its effect or its attribute. It makes this knowledge possible and at the same time determines its characteristics. It produces itself in and through this knowledge."[36] To borrow from the vocabulary of classical trinitarian theology, it is the distinctive *perichoresis* of knowledge and power with the regime of governance and accumulation and its modes of regulation that makes the transformation of the uncertainties of history into the followable spaces of historicity possible.

34. Certeau, *Practice of Everyday Life*, 36. The modern map, which we discussed in chapter 4, is predicated on strategic modes of reasoning, assembling elements of various origin and significance into a synchronic tableau that prescribes a set state of geographical knowledge.

35. Milbank, *Theology and Social Theory*, 106.

36. Certeau, *Practice of Everyday Life*, 36.

A single determinative logic is thus embodied within the ensemble of procedures, operations, and techniques that order everyday life within liberal capitalism. This logic posits supposedly objective structures having to do in one way or another with rational choice. The existence of these structures is typically inferred from statistics, which regulate the functioning of these practices in particular situations. It makes effective use of figurative readings of traditional texts (e.g., nineteenth-century lives of Jesus, or twenty-first-century depictions of Jesus as CEO) and proportional analogies to provide the foundation for these procedures, allowing the subject to "'navigate' among the rules, 'play with all the possibilities offered by traditions,' make use of one tradition rather than another, compensate for one by means of another." Ultimately, a strategy guarantees that the desired structures will be faithfully inscribed in these practices: "According to this analysis, structures can change and thus become a principle of social mobility (and even the only one). Achievements cannot. They have no movement of their own. They are the place in which structures are inscribed, the marble on which their history is engraved. Nothing happens in them that is not the result of their exteriority."[37]

Strategic rationality dominates the world in which most women and men now live, embedded in habits, activities, patterns, and institutions designed to keep us in our place, pledging unswerving allegiance to the state (in part by eliminating the church as a body politic in its own right), and make us fit for unfettered consumption in the global market (and unfit for Christian faith, hope, and love). To specify more concretely how this form of reasoning directs us to these ends, I shall draw on insights from the regulationist school of political economy, which is part of a larger approach to international political economy that examines how global processes interact with more localized processes of political and social transformation, especially the complex interactions, dispositions, political structures, and cultural forms that permit highly dynamic and therefore unstable economic systems to achieve for a time a semblance of order and coherence.[38]

Regimes of Accumulation and Modes of Regulation

According to Michael Budde, a principal concern of the regulationist school of political economy is to account for the tension between capitalism's inherent tendency toward instability, disequilibrium, crisis, and change (the spiritual effects discussed in the previous chapter) and its demonstrated ability to foster periods of political and economic stability that coalesce around a set of institutions, rules, and norms. The fit between the often disruptive processes of capital accumulation and the institutionalization of social stability can neither be taken for granted nor effectively manipulated. "Moments of alignment may be relatively brief in historical

37. Ibid., 52–57.
38. Harvey, *The Condition of Postmodernity*, 122.

terms," says Budde, "and do not have within them the seeds of a predetermined successor era." Circumstances are often quite fluid, demanding a great deal of experimentation and improvisation.[39]

Regulation theory accounts for whatever degree of economic stability obtains at any given time and place as the effect of the interaction between a regime of accumulation and its mode of regulation. A regime of accumulation refers to the societal regularities at the macroeconomic level that permit a stable and coherent process of accumulation of capital. It involves, among other things, the promulgation of a series of rights and laws that effectively serve to commodify land, goods, and labor (thus separating what is "mine" from what is "thine"), established routines of production and labor, recognized norms for the relationships and forms of exchange that may be permitted between individuals and groups, uniform patterns of management, rules for sharing in the fruit of production, and standards for consumption.

A mode of regulation refers to rules, habits, and procedures, both formal and informal, that inscribe capitalism's social idiom in individual bodies so that they will engage in conduct that will effectively reinforce and reproduce the regime of accumulation. This regimen seeks to keep men, women, and children in their place as producers and consumers, stripped of the memory and imagination that might question the legitimacy of the dominant regime. This category includes state subsidies for business and international trade, the development of standardized monetary systems and systems of taxation, international treaties, rules of negotiation and collective bargaining, industrial codes, commercial and consumer credit, educational and vocational training institutions, and cultural expectations regarding what counts for a good life.[40]

The fit between a regime of accumulation and a mode of regulation cannot be assumed a priori; "it is often an ad hoc, error-ridden, and historically contingent process."[41] For example, during the so-called Fordist era, dated roughly from the end of World War II until the early 1970s, the regime of accumulation included increasing mechanization, mass production techniques, "scientific" methods of labor management and the use of technology to enhance work output and keep tabs on workers, and growing polarization between skilled mental workers and unskilled manual workers, all contributing to increased productivity per worker. In return for acceding to managerial decisions regulating investment and technological innovation, workers saw a rise in real wages. The mode of

39. Budde, (Magic) Kingdom of God, 21; cf. Alain Lipietz, "New Tendencies in the International Division of Labor: Regimes of Accumulation and Modes of Regulation," in Allen J. Scott and Michael Storper, eds., Production, Work, Territory: The Geographical Anatomy of Industrial Capitalism (Boston: Allen & Unwin, 1986), 19.

40. Ash Amin, "Post-Fordism: Models, Fantasies, and Phantoms of Transition," in Post-Fordism, ed. Ash Amin (Cambridge, MA: Blackwell, 1994), 8; Budde, (Magic) Kingdom of God, 21–22; Cavanaugh, "The City," 192.

41. Budde, (Magic) Kingdom of God, 19, 21; cf. Harvey, Condition of Postmodernity, 121.

regulation included laws governing minimum wages and collective bargaining, state welfare policies that stabilized the consumption of wage earners during periods of unemployment, and the expansion of credit to stimulate the purchase of consumer goods.[42]

These measures were adopted in part as a solution to the crisis of overproduction and underconsumption of material goods that prevailed in the early decades of the twentieth century. Military spending, state welfare, and consumer credit helped to maintain consumption levels during cycles of recession and unemployment. By the late 1970s, however, a different crisis had developed. The problem was no longer that of overproduction and underconsumption, but of reduced profit margins and decreasing returns on investment and accumulation. Declining productivity and increased technology costs, coupled with increased competition from international markets, eroded the capacity to accumulate, leading to lower employment, which in turn disrupted the financing of the welfare state and further destabilized the rhythm of accumulation. This crisis compelled management to revisit the cooperative relationships between capital and labor that had been forged after years of struggle, as corporations looked for ways to speed up production and reduce inventories, reduce real wages and other costs such as medical and retirement benefits, trim overall employment, and alleviate tax burdens. The realization problem (profits cannot be "realized" unless and until someone buys the product), once resolved by a combination of increased real wages, welfare insurance, and consumer credit, is now addressed by expanding into overseas markets.[43]

In a "post-Fordist" world, then, problems of production have largely been superseded by the question of how to increase the overall number of consumers and stimulate the volume of consumption, in large part by promoting it as the solution to an ever-wider set of human needs. As Budde and Robert Brimlow note, "Without the willingness of people to buy, spend, and borrow for an unceasing supply of goods, novelties, and services, the modern market economy would grind to a halt."[44] The new economy of desire (mentioned in the previous chapter), unencumbered by any shared agreements as to a substantial good (or by the reality of one's neighbor), is the order of the day. The construction of consumption around the paradox of infinite desire competing for scarce resources, principally through strategies of marketing and advertising that work diligently to refashion lifestyles, identities, and social networks in ways that make the pursuit of material goods and services the rationale for human life itself, has thus become a central feature of global capitalism's mode of regulation.[45]

42. Ibid., 22; Harvey, *Condition of Postmodernity*, 136–38.

43. Budde, *(Magic) Kingdom of God*, 22–24; cf. James O'Connor, *Accumulation Crisis* (New York: Blackwell, 1984), 24–67.

44. Budde and Brimlow, *Christianity Incorporated*, 14.

45. Budde, *(Magic) Kingdom of God*, 26.

Economy and Gift

Because our lives are entangled with the regime of liberal capitalism and its modes of regulating behavior, Christians cannot avoid the state and its monopoly on the "legitimate" use of force on behalf of capital accumulation (which stipulates that this authority be unlimited and absolute[46]), or the routines of production, forms of exchange, and patterns of consumption that in a global market enable us to acquire the material goods we need. The question for the artisans of the age to come is therefore not whether we shall live in and by the state's sphere of authority or the necessary exchanges of markets, but which uses of the material goods overseen by them are natural and which are not. As a pilgrim people intermingled with the citizens of this world, we have no choice but to participate in this political and economic regime. We must therefore "do business" with the institutions of the state and the global market, and "the first duty of the critic is to understand our position and not succumb to delusions."[47] To acknowledge this is not to capitulate to the demands of either set of institutions, but to identify the starting point for developing a faithful Christian response to it.

What we do have a choice about is the *manner* of our interaction. It belongs to the interpretive art of the church to discern between natural and unnatural uses of the material goods that are necessary to life in the body and which are overseen by the institutions of the earthly regime. These goods are not limited to consumer products and services such as water, sewer, power, and fire protection, but include schools, judicial systems, communication networks, and the professions, trades, and occupations that allow us to provide needed goods for ourselves, our families, and neighbors. Christians may therefore participate in political forums that range from local school boards to national assemblies, from long-established institutions to spontaneous demonstrations, to appeal for the wise use of these goods, for example, when the civil rights movement promoted voter registration as part of its campaign to end Jim Crow segregation.

Since the incarnation does not simply ratify the world as it is, Christians are not obligated to fill all the slots, provide all the services of the earthly regime, or make sure that history comes out right. As Yoder points out, that is not possible with regard to governing the earthly city.[48] Such tendencies are much more typical of Stoicism, a moral and spiritual tradition that is, as Daniel Hardy and David Ford observe, "timid and orderly, leaving the passions free for economics, war and collective sport."[49] In the body of Christ, the Spirit sets us free to engage as a deliberative body in the vital and yet difficult activity of discerning what constitutes a natural mode of consumption, or which among the many trades, occupations,

46. Milbank, *Theology and Social Theory*, 13.
47. Boyle, *Who Are We Now?* 81.
48. Yoder, *Priestly Kingdom*, 161.
49. Hardy and Ford, *Praising and Knowing God*, 144.

and professions within the earthly city are open to the peace of the apocalyptic reign of God, and which are not.

Augustine thus determined (in keeping with church teaching at the time) that with his baptism he would need to resign his position as a teacher of rhetoric, which in classical Roman society put one on the path to civic success. The tools of rhetoric were not devoted to God's law but used as weapons for "lying follies and legal battles." Indeed, he acknowledged that some may judge that he had sinned in this matter "by allowing [himself] to remain even for an hour in a professional chair of lying once [his] heart was fully intent on [God's] service."[50] In other circumstances, good uses may be found for professions not typically associated with Christian ministry. Bankers, for example, could use their skills and position to help low-income families rise above subsistence levels, which in turn would allow them to contribute to the common good.

In addition to the wise use of goods regulated by a liberal capitalist regime, the church also offers alternatives to its patterns of accumulation and forms of managing behavior, thereby providing tangible signs of God's apocalyptic action in Christ, not in its proper "religious" place at the margins of life, but in the midst of the world of production and use. These alternatives will not be part of a social order that humans enact for themselves through contracts between autonomous individuals (a form of exchange that both presupposes and perpetuates strategic forms of reasoning and the *libido dominandi*). As I observed previously, it is the incarnation that is the basis for this alternative ordering of material goods. All things on earth and in heaven, including the use of the things necessary for this life, have been caught up in this ultimate exchange between God and humankind. This *oikonomia* can only be received as divine gift, beginning with baptism and then received ever anew at the feast at the Lord's table, where we learn that, "Because there is one bread, we who are many are one body, for we all partake of one bread" (1 Cor. 10:17). The alternative that takes form around Christ's table undercuts the monopoly that exchange ordered by the lust for mastery holds in the present age.

A different economy, unlike that enacted by the current regime, thus takes form within the pilgrim commonwealth of Christ. In liberal capitalism men and women have been severed from the overlapping relationships that exist within families, churches, guilds, and other local social groupings, their authority usurped by the state. Thus removed from organic communities, women and men are stripped of their identities as daughter, son, Christian, Muslim, etc., and transformed into interchangeable units of production and consumption, that is, individuals. Thus "freed," they are compelled to enter into contractual relationships, the formal nature

50. Augustine, *Confessions* IX.2,. According to Hippolytus, "if a man teach children worldly knowledge, it is indeed well if he desist. But if he has no other trade by which to live, let him have forgiveness" (Hippolytus, *Treatise on the Apostolic Tradition*, 25. For a provocative discussion of the suitability of contemporary professions for Christians, see Robert Brimlow, *Paganism and the Professions* [Eugene, OR: Wipf & Stock, 2002]).

of which stipulates that human beings are essentially unencumbered agents who engage others solely on the basis of self-interest. "Rather than 'cohere' directly to one another," writes Cavanaugh, "we relate to each other through the state by the formal mechanism of contract." Property, including the product of their labor, becomes commodified and thus alienable.[51]

In the community fashioned in the Spirit around the Eucharist, by contrast, a different mode of exchange is established, one that binds us to the risen Christ and to one another by drawing our relationships, including those having to do with earthly goods, into the infinite plenitude of God's triune life. The gift of Christ's body sets aside the primacy of contractual exchange and the marginalization of the gift relationship to the private sphere, where the recipient is rendered passive and the giver experiences giving as an alienation of property. In God's gift of the Son to the world, the Father is not alienated from the gift but goes with the gift, is in the gift.[52] In return an exchange of sorts is expected of the recipient, though not one that presumes to return to God something that might be lacking in the divine life, "since there is nothing extra to God that could return to him."[53]

Within the economy of divine plenitude, the expected return of the gift on the part of the recipient is not one that can be pre-established by contract, for it too must bear the character of the counter-giver. In the alternative economy of Christ's ecclesial body, writes Cavanaugh,

> this type of giving is perfected as the dualism of giver and recipient are collapsed; Christ is the perfect return of God to God. In the Eucharist, we receive the gift of Christ not as mere passive recipients, but by being incorporated into the gift itself, the Body of Christ. As members of the Body, we then become nourishment for others—including those not part of the visible Body—in the unending trinitarian economy of gratuitous giving and joyful reception.[54]

Nourished by God's prevenient gift, artisans of the age to come look for opportunities to cultivate types of associations that in the material realm lend themselves to this mode of gift exchange. Through these relationships we come to share more deeply in the life and goodness of God, and along the way develop rich conceptions of the common good for those outside the body of Christ to contemplate, while at the same time helping to foster the ability of all to contribute to it. These associations do exist, but often on a scale that seems inconsequential in a global economy: Catholic Worker houses of hospitality, Community/Church Supported Agriculture programs,[55] Habitat for Humanity building projects, cooperative stores,

51. Cavanaugh, "The City," 192–93, 195.

52. Ibid., 195.

53. John Milbank, "Can a Gift Be Given? Prolegomena to a Future Trinitarian Metaphysic," *Modern Theology* 11 (January 1995): 133, cited by Cavanaugh, "The City," 195.

54. Cavanaugh, "The City," 195–96.

55. For more information on Community/Church Supported Agriculture, see the Alternative Farming Systems Information Center website at www.nal.usda.gov/afsic/csa/, the National Catholic Rural Life

community development associations,[56] and community gardens and fair trade exchanges.[57] In addition to these forms of exchange there are the corporeal works of mercy: feeding the hungry, clothing the naked, welcoming the stranger, assisting the poor, visiting those who are sick or in prison, and burying the dead.[58] But then again, should scale be a determining factor for an endeavor that began with a handful of fishermen and widows cowering in fear before the most powerful empire the world had to that time ever known?

These gratuitous and joyful relationships of giving and receiving do not treat others as either superfluous or instrumental to one's own appetites, but as occasions for us to love gratuitously, just as God has loved us.[59] These relations are sustained by what Alasdair MacIntyre calls the virtue of just generosity, which issues in actions that in a very real sense are uncalculating, in that there is no strict proportionality of giving and receiving. That is to say, "those from whom I hope to and perhaps do receive are very often, even if not always, not the same people as those to whom I gave. And what I am called upon to give has no predetermined limits and may greatly exceed what I have received. I may not calculate what I owe on the basis of what others have given me."[60]

That said, there is a form of rationality that accompanies just generosity. According to MacIntyre, a prudent calculation is required if one is to have something to give: industriousness in acquiring property, thrift in saving, and discrimination in giving so that the truly needy may receive.[61] Though this linking of just generosity with a modified form of prudential calculus is more natural than a system tethered solely to surplus desire and unconstrained self-interest, it still presupposes the normative standing of an economy of scarcity in which the principle of marginal utility reigns supreme. In the gift economy of God's apocalyptic activity, by contrast, the plenitude of divine charity eternally shared within the Godhead becomes available to all. The unnatural competition for scarce resources that fuels strategic reasoning is overcome, as finitude is no longer conceived as something to be overcome but an opportunity to learn the true significance of creaturely freedom, and the other is not a target or threat to master, but the one we are called to love. Desire is thereby redirected as a

---

Conference at www.ncrlc.com/religiouscongregationsland.html, or the University of Massachusetts's Extension Center website at www.umass.edu/umext/csa/about.html .

56. John M. Perkins, ed., *Restoring At-Risk Communities: Doing It Together and Doing It Right* (Grand Rapids: Baker, 1995).

57. For more information on fair trade opportunities, see www.fairtradefederation.com.

58. As many have noted, the danger in emphasizing these sorts of ventures predicated on charity is that they seem to focus on the symptoms of capitalism's pathologies without addressing the systemic causes, but as Daniel Bell points out, one of the spiritual works of mercy is admonishing sinners ("Sacrifice and Suffering," 358n68).

59. Catherine of Siena, *Dialogue*, para. 64.

60. Alasdair MacIntyre, *Dependent Rational Animals: Why Human Beings Need the Virtues* (Chicago: Open Court, 1999), 126.

61. Ibid.

just (that is to say, a gratuitous) generosity flowing from the reciprocity of gifts within the body of Christ.

Once again it is Certeau who helps us specify the mode of reason utilized by a gift economy in his discussion of what constitutes a tactical logic. A tactic is a calculated action that is specifically determined by the lack of its own place, that is, by its inability (or, for the church, the unwillingness) to designate a proper locus from which the limit of the other is delimited as a strategic target or threat. Without this proper place, women and men lack a necessary condition for realizing that most cherished of objectives in the modern world—autonomy. It is not surprising, then, that while strategy is the typical disposition of modern science, politics, and the military, a tactic is "an art of the weak."[62]

Those who follow a tactical course of action, writes Certeau, do not have the wherewithal to plan a general strategy or to view the adversary as a whole within a distinct space, but must play on and with a terrain imposed on it and organized by a foreign power. A tactic operates in discrete actions, taking advantage of any opportunities that present themselves, but without a place where it can stockpile its winnings for the next encounter. This "nowhere" provides a certain mobility, forgoing the pretense of stability and control, and relying instead on the ability to take advantage of the opportunities that present themselves only at particular times and places.[63]

The identifying characteristic of a tactic, therefore, is that it has no "place" of its own, a secure base of operations from which it can control its relations with the "other." The lack of a base of operations from which to plan and execute a comprehensive hermeneutical strategy does characterize, in certain respects, both the nihilistic tendencies of certain forms of postmodernism and the artisanship required of Christians. Postmodernism, however, regards this absence as the permanent abode of humankind, and thus ironically succumbs to the urge to define for all humanity its "proper place," which in this case is the *nihil*. The difference has to do with how women and men come to terms with the inextricable and inescapable sense of contingency, particularity, and mystery that circumscribes not only the whole of human existence but also our every attempt to deal with it. From at least some postmodern vantage points, the mystery and ineffability of life seems like a cruel trick or devious sleight-of-hand, a fate to which we must ultimately resign ourselves, but only after the effort is made to stake out at least a trace of autonomy, if only in the impoverished mode of "resistance." This disposition, in other words, is still ensnared within the self-deception that has governed modernity since the time of Luther and Descartes, the myth that humans are essentially discarnate gods, only now this illusion subsists in the form of a ghostly afterimage, a surrealistic specter that continues to haunt it. Simply put, those who embrace this way of naming the world seek to transform the nothingness into yet another

62. Certeau, *Practice of Everyday Life*, 37.
63. Ibid.

proper place, while those who seek to prop up the modern project continue in a state of self-deception.

For artisans of the *civitas peregrina*, by contrast, the lack of a proper place is a "dark gate" through which believers step forth into the everyday, which then becomes the gift of time and space to worship truthfully and live faithfully before the ineradicable mystery of our existence. The biblical injunction to fear God is a constant reminder of our fundamental relationship with the mystery, characterized by "unknowing," that is, by the inability to designate a strategic site from which we can determine and manage our relations with the "other," most especially with the other we call God. By faith we step across this threshold of irreducible mystery and into the everyday, where we receive and celebrate our existence but also lament and struggle against all that mocks and afflicts it, before the one who makes our lives possible as both gift and query.[64]

There is another sense in which Certeau's description of a tactical mode of reason bears upon the practice of everyday life from the standpoint of the church and its interpretive art. A tactical engagement with the world, because it does not identify a place upon which it constructs an edifice that would allow it to maintain a panoptic grasp on its neighbors, does not possess an autonomous existence, and therefore it must conduct itself on a terrain imposed on it, a social landscape that is currently occupied and organized by others. It does not have (and in the case of the church, it deliberately eschews) the means to keep to itself, so it must learn how to maneuver within the strategic field of vision established by the identification of a proper place and subject.[65]

The conclusion that Certeau draws from this state of affairs, however, is that "a tactic is determined by the *absence of power* just as a strategy is organized by the postulation of power."[66] The church, in its interactions with liberal capitalism's regime of power and mode of regulation, reasons most faithfully in a tactical mode, and in so doing it should indeed shun the strategic power of the proper place. This does not mean, however, that there is not any other form of power at work in the world that resists the attempt of strategic rationality to reduce the temporal relationship of the body of Christ to the present age to spatial dimensions, and more specifically, to the private sphere of "religion." The validity and viability of the church's constitutive practices presuppose the power of the Spirit, who as "the pledge of our inheritance toward redemption as God's own people" (Eph. 1:14; cf. 2 Cor. 1:22; 5:5) enables us to make good use of time and the opportunities it presents.[67]

The body of Christ, then, is not without its own source of power for dealing with the liberal capitalist regime, particularly as the powers and principalities of this age seek under the influence of the *libido dominandi* to confine all things within their

64. Buber, *Eclipse of God*, 36.
65. Certeau, *Practice of Everyday Life*, 36–37.
66. Ibid., 38.
67. Ibid.

own panoptic brand of universality, their own ersatz "catholicity," as it were. The church challenges this idolatrous pretension to express and exhaust the human world to the extent that it attends to the lives of people as they are locally, distinct from the implications of their fragmentary existence as interchangeable producers and consumers in the global market. The body of Christ needs to replot on a human scale the stories of those who are but ciphers within the predatory strategic narrative of the state and the global market, within the face-to-face exchanges that can take place only at the level of local forms of ecclesial association—congregation or parish, diocese and the like.[68] To those deprived of houses, lands, siblings, and parents, the church offers "houses, brothers and sisters, mothers and children, and fields with persecutions—and in the age to come eternal life" (Mark 10:30).

Where, Then, Does The Church Stand Now?

It is fitting that we conclude by returning to the question with which we began: Where, then, do we stand? Insofar as the ecclesial body of Christ is concerned, we stand where we have always stood since Pentecost (though at times we have lost our sense of direction): on pilgrimage toward the city whose architect and builder is God, serving the places in which we now find ourselves as both sign of the age to come and vehicle of passage for this world through time. As we have seen, this form of life requires new habits of life and language, new ways of assessing the world in which we live, new practices binding us to the body of Christ that is our salvation. If in this particular place we are to be weaned from the myth that the state is our true homeland, and unconstrained consumption our highest good, we will need to be formed according to a different faith, a different hope and a different love.

We dare not confuse these theological virtues with value judgments that have principally to do with individuals in isolation from their material relations with their neighbors and with the world about them. They are instead dispositions of character that transpose simple seeing into discernment and mere existing into holy habitation, and they are formed only in the company of friends through participation in a shared network of constitutive practices. These sorts of friendships are cultivated as women and men from every tribe, language, people, and nation pass through the baptismal waters, admitting them to the eucharistic feast, where around the table of the risen Lord we are caught up in the power of the Spirit into the way of Jesus Christ and the vulnerability of God's pilgrim city.

Flannery O'Connor warns us, however, not in the end to place too much stock in our virtues, as important as they are for the journey. In her short story "Revelation," O'Connor describes a vision that came just after sundown one day to Mrs. Turpin as she was washing down her hogs. Mrs. Turpin was someone who had always

68. Boyle, *Who Are We Now?* 92.

prided herself on being a respectable person, working hard every day, doing for the church, having a little of everything and "the God-given wit to use it right," including hogs that were "cleaner than some children." In her vision she saw "a vast horde of souls" making their way to their true homeland. As she looked at the company of saints rumbling toward heaven on a bridge of light extending upward from the earth "through a field of living fire," Mrs. Turpin was astonished to see that people like her were not leading the procession. Instead there were "white trash, clean for the first time in their lives," black folks in white robes, "and battalions of freaks and lunatics shouting and clapping and leaping like frogs." Her kind was bringing up the rear, "marching behind the others with great dignity, accountable as they had always been for good order and common sense and respectable behavior. They alone were on key. Yet she could see by their shocked and altered faces that even their virtues were being burned away." For a time Mrs. Turpin did not move but kept her eyes fixed "on what lay ahead." She eventually turned to make her way up the darkening path to the house. "In the woods around her the invisible cricket choruses had struck up, but what she heard were the voices of the souls climbing upward into the starry field and shouting hallelujahs."[69]

69. Flannery O'Connor, "Revelation," in *Collected Works*, 654.

Works Cited

Alighieri, Dante. *Paradise*. Translated by Anthony Esolen. New York: Modern Library, 2004.

———. *Purgatory*. Translated by Anthony Esolen. New York: Modern Library, 2004.

Amin, Ash, editor. *Post-Fordism*. Cambridge, MA: Blackwell, 1994.

Anderson, Benedict. *Imagined Communities: Reflections on the Origin and Spread of Nationalism*. Revised ed. New York: Verso, 1991.

Anselm. *Prologion, with the Replies of Gaunilo and Anselm*. Translated by Thomas Williams. Indianapolis: Hackett, 1995.

———. *Why God Became Man* and *The Virgin Conception and Original Sin*. Translated by Joseph M. Colleran. Albany, NY: Magi, 1969.

Appleby, R. Scott. *The Ambivalence of the Sacred: Religion, Violence and Reconciliation*. Lanham, MD: Rowman & Littlefield, 2000.

Aquinas, Thomas. *Summa contra Gentiles*. Translated by Anton C. Pegis, FRSC. Notre Dame, IN: University of Notre Dame Press, 1975.

———. *Summa Theologica*. Revised ed. Translated by Fathers of the English Dominican Province. New York: Benziger, 1948.

Arac, Jonathan, editor. *Postmodernism and Politics*. Minneapolis: University of Minnesota Press, 1986.

Aristotle, *Nicomachean Ethics*. 2nd ed. Translated by Terence Irwin. Indianapolis: Hackett, 1999.

———. *The Politics*. Translated by Carnes Lord. Chicago: University of Chicago Press, 1984.

Asad, Talal. *Genealogies of Religion: Discipline and Reasons of Power in Christianity and Islam*. Baltimore, MD: Johns Hopkins University Press, 1993.

St. Athanasius, *On the Incarnation: The Treatise De Incarnatione Verbi Dei*. Translated and edited by a religious of CSMV. Crestwood, NY: St. Vladimir's Seminary Press, 2000.

Auerbach, Erich. *Mimesis: The Representation of Reality in Western Literature*. Translated by Willard R. Trask. Princeton, NJ: Princeton University Press, 1953.

Augustine, *The City of God against the Pagans*. Edited by R. W. Dyson. New York: Cambridge University Press, 1998.

———. *The Confessions*. Translated by Maria Boulding. Hyde Park, NY: New City, 1997.

———. *The Confessions of St. Augustine*. Translated by John K. Ryan. Garden City, NY: Image Books, 1960.

———. *Teaching Christianity: De Doctrina Christiana*. Translated by Edmund Hill, OP. Hyde Park, NY: New City, 1996.

———. *The Trinity*, III. Pref.3. Translated by Edmund Hill, OP. New York: New City, 1991.

Averroës. *Decisive Treatise and Epistle Dedicatory*. Translated by Charles E. Butterworth. Provo, UT: Brigham Young University Press, 2001.

Bader-Saye, Scott. *Church and Israel after Christendom: The Politics of Election*. Boulder, CO:
Westview, 1999.

Balasuriya, Tissa. *The Eucharist and Human Liberation*. Maryknoll, NY: Orbis Books, 1979.

Balthasar, Hans Urs von. *Studies in Theological
Style*. Vol.2 of *The Glory of the Lord: A Theo-
logical Aesthetics*. San Francisco: Ignatius
Press, 1984.

————. *A Theology of History*. San Francisco:
Ignatius, 1994.

————. *The Word Made Flesh*. Vol. 1 of *Explorations in Theology*. San Francisco: Ignatius,
1989.

Barnett, Victoria J. *Bystanders: Conscience and
Complicity during the Holocaust*. Westport,
CT: Praeger, 1999.

Barth, Karl. *Dogmatics in Outline*. Translated
by G. T. Thompson. New York: Harper &
Brothers, 1959.

Bauerschmidt, Frederick Christian. "Walking in
the Pilgrim City." *New Blackfriars* 77 (No-
vember 1996): 504–18.

Bauman, Zygmunt. *Postmodern Ethics*. Cambridge, MA: Blackwell, 1993.

Baxter, Michael. "'Overall, the First Amendment
Has Been Very Good for Christianity'—
NOT! A Response to Dyson's Rebuke,"
DePaul Law Review 43 (Winter 1994):
423–446.

Beasley-Murray, George R. *Jesus and the Kingdom
of God*. Grand Rapids: Eerdmans, 1986.

Beckwith, Sarah. *Christ's Body: Identity, Culture,
and Society in Late Medieval Writings*. New
York: Routledge, 1993.

Begbie, Jeremy. *Theology, Music and Time*. Cambridge: Cambridge University Press, 2000.

Beiner, Ronald. *What's the Matter with Liberalism?* Berkeley: University of California Press,
1992.

Bell, Daniel M., Jr. *Liberation Theology After the
End of History*. New York: Routledge, 2001.

————. "Sacrifice and Suffering: Beyond Justice, Human Rights, and Capitalism," *Modern
Theology* 18 (July 2002): 333–59.

Bell, Mark R. *Apocalypse How? Baptist Movements
during the English Revolution*. Macon, GA:
Mercer University Press, 2000.

Bell, Richard, editor. *Grammar of the Heart: New
Essays in Moral Philosophy and Theology*. San
Francisco: Harper & Row, 1988.

Benjamin, Walter. *Illuminations*. Translated by
Harry Zohn. New York: Schocken, 1969.

Berger, Peter L. *The Sacred Canopy: Elements of
a Sociological Theory of Religion*. Garden City,
NY: Doubleday, 1967.

Bernstein, Richard J. *Beyond Objectivism and
Relativism*. Philadelphia: University of Pennsylvania Press, 1983.

Berry, Wendell. *What Are People For?* New York:
North Point, 1990.

Bethge, Eberhard. *Dietrich Bonhoeffer: A Biography*. Edited by Victoria J. Barnett. Minneapolis: Fortress, 2000.

Blond, Phillip, editor. *Post-Secular Philosophy:
Between Philosophy and Theology*. New York:
Routledge, 1998.

Bloom, Harold. *The American Religion: The Emergence of the Post-Christian Nation*. New York:
Simon & Schuster, 1992.

Blowers, Paul M. "The *Regula Fidei* and the Narrative Character of Early Christian Faith," *Pro
Ecclesia* 6 (Spring 1997): 199–228.

Bonaventure, *The Journey of the Mind to God*.
Translated by Philotheus Boehner, OFM.
Indianapolis: Hackett, 1956.

Bonhoeffer, Dietrich. *Act and Being: Transcendental Philosophy and Ontology in Systematic
Theology*. Vol. 2 in *Dietrich Bonhoeffer Works*.
Translated by H. Martin Rumscheidt. Minneapolis: Fortress, 1996.

————. *Conspiracy and Imprisonment, 1940–
1945*. Vol. 16 in Dietrich Bonhoeffer Works.
Translated by Lisa E. Dahill. Minneapolis:
Fortress, 2006.

————. *Creation and Fall: A Theological Exposition of Genesis 1–3*. Vol. 3 in *Dietrich Bonhoeffer Works*. Translated by Martin Rüter and
Ilse Tödt. Minneapolis: Fortress, 1997.

————. *Discipleship*. Vol. 4 in *Dietrich Bonhoeffer
Works*. Translated by Martin Kuske and Ilse
Tödt. Minneapolis: Fortress, 2001.

————. *Ethics*. Vol. 6 in Dietrich Bonhoeffer Works. Translated by Reinhard Krauss,
Charles C. West, and Douglas W. Stott. Minneapolis: Fortress, 2005.

————. *Ethik*. Vol. 6 in *Dietrich Bonhoeffer Werke*. Edited by Ilse Tödt, Eduard Tödt, Ernst Feil, and Clifford Green. Munich: Chr. Kaiser, 1992.

————. *Letters and Papers from Prison*. Enl. ed. Translated by R. H. Fuller, J. Bowden, et al. New York: Macmillan, 1971.

————. *Life Together and Prayerbook of the Bible*. Vol. 5 in *Dietrich Bonhoeffer Works*. Translated by Daniel W. Blosch and James H. Burtness. Edited by Geffrey B. Kelley and Albrecht Shonherr. Minneapolis: Fortress, 1996.

————. *London: 1933–1935*. Vol. 13 in Dietrich Bonhoeffer Works. Translated by Hans Goedeking, Martin Heimbucher, and Hans-Walter Schleicher. Minneapolis: Fortress, 2007.

————. *No Rusty Swords: Letters, Lectures and Notes, 1928–1936*. Vol. 1 in Collected Works of Dietrich Bonhoeffer. Edited by Edwin H. Robinson. New York: Harper & Row, 1965.

————. *Sanctorum Communio: A Theological Study of the Church*. Vol. 1 in *Dietrich Bonhoeffer Works*. Translated by Reinhard Krauss and Nancy Lukens. Minneapolis: Fortress, 1998.

Bottum, Joseph. "Christians and Postmoderns." *First Things* 40 (February 1994): 28–32.

Boyarin, Daniel. *A Radical Jew: Paul and the Politics of Identity*. Berkeley: University of California Press, 1994.

Boyens, Armin F. C. "The Ecumenical Community and the Holocaust." *Annals of the American Academy of Political and Social Science* 450 (July 1980): 143–47.

Boyle, Nicholas. *Who Are We Now? Christian Humanism and the Global Market from Hegel to Heaney*. Notre Dame, IN: University of Notre Dame Press, 1998.

Boyte, Harry C., and Nancy N. Kari, *Building America: The Democratic Promise of Public Work*. Philadelphia: Temple University Press, 1996.

Braaten, Carl. *Mother Church: Ecclesiology and Ecumenism*. Minneapolis: Fortress, 1998.

Bray, Gerald, editor. *Documents of the English Reformation*. Minneapolis: Fortress, 1994.

Brimlow, Robert. *Paganism and the Professions*. Eugene, OR: Wipf and Stock, 2002.

Brokaw, Tom. *The Greatest Generation*. New York: Random, 1998.

Brown, Tom. "Jesus CEO." *Industry Week* (March 6, 1995): 14–20.

Brueggemann, Walter. *The Land: Place as Gift, Promise, and Challenge in Biblical Faith*. 2nd ed. Minneapolis: Fortress, 2002.

Buber, Martin. *Between Man and Man*. Translated by Ronald Gregor-Smith. New York: Routledge, 2002.

————. *The Eclipse of God: Studies in the Relation Between Religion and Philosophy*. Translated by Maurice S. Friedman, Eugene Kamenka, Norbert Guterman, and I. M. Lask. Atlantic Highlands, NJ: Humanities Press International, 1988.

————. *I and Thou*. Translated by Walter Kaufmann. New York: Scribner's, 1970.

————. *Kingship of God*. 3rd. ed. Translated by Richard Scheimann. New York: Harper & Row, 1967; Atlantic Highlands, NJ: Humanities Press International, 1990.

Buckley, James J. "A Field of Living Fire: Karl Barth on the Spirit and the Church." *Modern Theology* 10 (January 1994): 81–102.

Budde, Michael. *The. (Magic) Kingdom of God: Christianity and Global Culture Industries*. Boulder, CO: Westview, 1997.

Budde, Michael, and Robert Brimlow. *Christianity Incorporated: How Big Business Is Buying the Church*. Grand Rapids: Brazos, 2002.

Burnaby, John, editor. *Augustine: Later Works*. Philadelphia: Fortress, 1955.

Burnham, Frederic B., editor. *Postmodern Theology*. San Francisco: Harper & Row, 1989.

Burrell, David B., CSC. *Aquinas: God and Action*. London: Routledge & Kegan Paul, 1979.

————. *Faith and Freedom: An Interfaith Perspective*. Malden, MA: Blackwell, 2004.

————. *Freedom and Creation in Three Traditions*. Notre Dame, IN: University of Notre Dame Press, 1993.

————. *Knowing the Unknowable God: Ibn-Sina, Maimonides, Aquinas*. Notre Dame, IN: University of Notre Dame Press, 1986.

Burrell, David B., CSC, and Elena Malits, CSC. *Original Peace: Restoring God's Creation*. New York: Paulist, 1997.

Calvin, John. *Institutes of the Christian Religion*. Translated by Ford Lewis Battles. Philadelphia: Westminster, 1960.

Cameron, Averil. *Christianity and the Rhetoric of Empire: The Development of Christian Discourse*. Berkeley: University of California Press, 1991.

Campbell, Colin. *The Romantic Ethic and the Spirit of Modern Consumerism*. Cambridge, MA: Blackwell, 1987.

Capes, David B. "The Lord's Table: Divine or Human Remembrance?" *Perspectives in Religious Studies* 30 (Summer 2003): 199–209.

Cartwright, Michael G., and Peter Ochs. Editors' introduction to *The Jewish-Christian Schism Revisited*, by John Howard Yoder. Grand Rapids: Eerdmans, 2003.

Casey, Edward S. *Imagining: A Phenomenological Study*. 2nd ed. Bloomington: Indiana University Press, 2000.

———. *Remembering: A Phenomenological Study*. 2nd ed. Bloomington: Indiana University Press, 2000.

Catherine of Siena. *Dialogue*. Translated by Suzanne Noffke, OP, New York: Paulist, 1980.

Cavanaugh, William T. "'A Fire Strong Enough to Consume the House': The Wars of Religion and the Rise of the State." *Modern Theology* 11 (October 1995): 397–420.

———. "Killing for the Telephone Company: Why the Nation-State Is not the Keeper of the Common Good." *Modern Theology* 20 (April 2004): 243–74.

———. "Sins of Omission: What 'Religion and Violence' Arguments Ignore." *The Hedgehog Reiview* 6 (Spring 2004): 34–50.

———. *Theopolitical Imagination: Discovering the Liturgy as a Political Act in an Age of Global Consumerism*. New York: T & T Clark, 2002.

———. *Torture and Eucharist: Theology, Politics, and the Body of Christ*. Malden, MA: Blackwell, 1998.

Certeau, Michel de. *The Mystic Fable*. Vol. 1. Translated by Michael B. Smith. Chicago: University of Chicago Press, 1992.

———. *The Practice of Everyday Life*. Translated by Steven Rendall. Berkeley: University of California Press, 1984.

Charry, Ellen T. *By the Renewing of Your Minds: The Pastoral Function of Christian Doctrine*. New York: Oxford University Press, 1997.

Chenderlin, Fritz, SJ. *"Do This As My Memorial": The Semantic and Conceptual Background and Value of* Anamnēsis *in 1 Corinthians 11:24–25*. Rome: Biblical Institute Press, 1982.

Childs, Brevard S. *Biblical Theology of the Old and New Testaments: Theological Reflection on the Christian Bible*. Minneapolis: Fortress, 1992.

Chrysostom, John. *Homilies on the Gospel of St. Matthew*. Translated by Tissa Balasuriya. Maryknoll, NY: Orbis Books, 1979.

Cicero, *De Re Publica de Legibus*. Translated by Clinton Walker Keyes. Cambridge, MA: Harvard University Press, 1951.

Clapp, Rodney. *Border Crossings: Christian Trespasses on Popular Culture and Public Affairs*. Grand Rapids: Brazos, 2000.

———. *A Peculiar People: The Church as Culture in a Post-Christian World*. Downers Grove, IL: InterVarsity Press, 1996.

Clegg, Stewart R. *Frameworks of Power*. London: Sage, 1989.

Clement of Alexandria. *Protrepticus*. In vol. 2 of *The Ante-Nicene Fathers*. Edited by Alexander Roberts and James Donaldson. 1885–1887. 10 vols. Repr. Peabody, MA.: Hendrickson, 1994.

Coakley, Sarah. *Powers and Submissions: Spirituality, Philosophy and Gender*. Malden, MA: Blackwell, 2002.

Cochrane, Charles Norris. *Christianity and Classical Culture: A Study of Thought and Action from Augustus to Augustine*. London: Oxford University Press, 1940.

Cone, James H. *Speaking the Truth: Ecumenism, Liberation, and Black Theology*. Grand Rapids: Eerdmans, 1986.

Connerton, Paul. *How Societies Remember*. Cambridge: Cambridge University Press, 1989.

Copenhaver, Martin B., Anthony B. Robinson, and William H. Willimon. *Good News in Exile: Three Pastors Offer a Hopeful Vision for the Church.* Grand Rapids: Eerdmans, 1999.

Cousins, Ewert H., editor. *Process Theology.* New York: Newman, 1971.

Cross, Anthony R., and Philip E. Thompson, editors. *Baptist Scaramentalism.* Waynesboro, GA: Paternoster, 2003.

Cullen, C. *The Black Christ and Other Poems.* New York: Harper & Brothers, 1929.

Curran, Charles E. *Catholic Social Teaching, 1891–Present: A Historical, Theological, and Ethical Analysis.* Washington, DC: Georgetown University Press, 2002.

Dahl, Nils. *Jesus in the Memory of the Early Church.* Minneapolis: Augsburg, 1976.

Davis, Ellen F., and Richard B. Hays, editors. *The Art of Reading Scripture.* Grand Rapids: Eerdmans, 2003.

Dawson, John David. *Christian Figural Reading and the Fashioning of Identity.* Berkeley, CA: University of California Press, 2002.

Dennett, Daniel C. *Breaking the Spell: Religion as a Natural Phenomenon.* New York: Viking, 2006.

Derrida, Jacques. *Specters of Marx: The State of the Debt, the Work of Mourning, and the New International.* Translated by Peggy Kamuf. New York: Routledge, 1994.

Dix, Dom Gregory. *The Shape of the Liturgy,* with additional notes by Paul V. Marshall. New York: Seabury, 1982.

Donnelly, Dorothy F., editor. *The City of God: A Collection of Critical Essays.* New York: Peter Lang, 1995.

Dostoyevsky, Fyodor. *The Best Short Stories of Dostoevsky.* Translated by David Magarshack. New York: Modern Library, 1955.

———. *The Brothers Karamazov.* Translated by Richard Pevear and Larissa Volokhonsky. New York: Vintage, 1991.

Dunn, Richard S. *The Age of Religious Wars: 1559–1715.* 2nd ed. New York: Norton, 1979.

Eagleton, Terry. *The Illusions of Postmodernism.* Cambridge, MA: Blackwell, 1996.

Elliott, J. H. *Europe Divided: 1559–1598.* 2nd ed. Malden, MA: Blackwell, 2000.

Elshtain, Jean Bethke. *Augustine and the Limits of Politics.* Notre Dame, IN: University of Notre Dame Press, 1995.

Erb, Peter C., editor. *Pietists: Selected Writings.* New York: Paulist, 1983.

Eusebius. *The History of the Church.* In vol. 1 of *The Nicene and Post-Nicene Fathers.* Series 2. Edited by Philip Schaff. 1886–1889. 14 vols. Repr. Peabody, MA: Hendrickson, 1994.

———. *Life of Constantine.* In vol. 1 of *The Nicene and Post-Nicene Fathers.* Series 2. Edited by Philip Schaff. 1886–1889. 14 vols. Repr. Peabody, MA.: Hendrickson, 1994.

Evagrius of Pontus. *Evagrius of Pontus: the Greek Ascetic Corpus.* Translated and edited by Robert E. Sinkewicz. New York: Oxford University Press, 2003.

Evans, G. R. *Old Arts and New Theology: The Beginnings of Theology as an Academic Discipline.* Oxford: Clarendon, 1980.

Fagan, Patrick. "Why Religion Matters: The Impact of Religious Practice on Social Stability." No pages. Cited 21 May 2006. Online: www.heritage.org/Research/Religion/BG1064.cfm.

Fiddes, Paul S., editor. *Reflections on the Water: Understanding God and the World through the Baptism of Believers.* Macon, GA: Smyth & Helwys, 1996.

Field, Lester L., Jr. *Liberty, Dominion, and the Two Swords: On the Origins of Western Political Theology (180–398).* Notre Dame, IN: University of Notre Dame Press, 1998.

Figgis, John Neville. *Studies of Political Thought from Gerson to Grotius, 1414–1625.* Cambridge: University Press, 1956.

Fish, Stanley. "Boutique Multiculturalism, or Why Liberals Are Incapable of Thinking about Hate Speech." *Critical Inquiry* 23 (Winter 1997): 378–95.

Flannery, Austin, OP, editor. *Vatican Council II: The Conciliar and Post Conciliar Documents.* New revised ed. Northport, NY: Costello Publishing Company, 1992.

Florovsky, The Very Rev. Georges. "Empire and Desert: Antinomies of Christian History." *The Greek Orthodox Theological Review* 3 (Winter 1957): 133–59.

Foucault, Michel. *Discipline and Punish: The Birth of the Prison*. Translated by Alan Sheridan. New York: Random House, 1979.

Fowl, Stephen E. *Engaging Scripture: A Model for Theological Interpretation*. Malden, MA: Blackwell, 1998.

Fox, Richard Wightman. *Reinhold Niebuhr: A Biography*. San Francisco: Harper, 1987.

Freeman, Curtis W. "Can Baptist Theology Be Revisioned?" *Perspectives in Religious Studies* 24 (Fall 1997): 271–302.

Freeman, Curtis, James Wm. McClendon Jr., and C. Rosalee Velloso da Silva. *Baptist Roots: A Reader in the Theology of a Christian People*. Philadelphia: Judson, 1999.

Frei, Hans. *The Eclipse of Biblical Narrative: A Study in Eighteenth and Nineteenth Century Hermeneutics*. New Haven: Yale University Press, 1974.

———. *Types of Christian Theology*. Edited by George Hunsinger and William C. Placher. New Haven: Yale University Press, 1992.

Fukuyama, Francis. "The End of History?" *The National Interest* 16 (Summer 1989): 3–18.

———. *The End of History and the Last Man*. New York: Free Press, 1992.

Gadamer, Hans-Georg. "Hermeneutics and Social Science." *Cultural Hermeneutics* 2 (1975): 307–16.

Gallie, W. B. *Philosophy and the Historical Understanding*. New York: Schocken, 1964.

Gamble, Richard M. *The War for Righteousness: Progressive Christianity, the Great War, and the Rise of the Messianic Nation*. Wilmington, DE: ISI, 2003.

Geertz, Clifford. *The Interpretation of Cultures*. New York: Basic Books, 1973.

Gewirth, Alan. *The Community of Rights*. Chicago: University of Chicago Press, 1996.

———. *Reason and Morality*. Chicago: University of Chicago Press, 1978.

Gierke, Otto. *Associations and Law: The Classical and Early Christian Stages*. Translated by George Heiman. Toronto: University of Toronto Press, 1977.

Gillespie, Michael Allen. *Nihilism before Nietzsche*. Chicago: University of Chicago Press, 1995.

———. "The Theological Origins of Modernity." *Critical Review* 13 (1999): 1–30.

Grant, George. *Time as History*. Toronto: University of Toronto Press, 1995.

Greene, Graham. *The Power and the Glory*. New York: Viking, 1946; New York: Penguin, 1991.

S. L. Greenslade, editor. *The Cambridge History of the Bible*. Vol. 3. New York: University of Cambridge Press, 1975.

Gregory of Nyssa. *On the Soul and the Resurrection*. Translated by Catharine Roth. Crestood, NY: St. Vladimir's Seminary Press, 1993.

Gregory, Bishop of Nyssa. *The Life of Saint Macrina*. Translated by Kevin Corrigan. Eugene, OR: Wipf & Stock, 2001.

Guroian, Vigen. *Incarnate Love: Essays in Orthodox Ethics*. 2nd ed. Notre Dame, IN: University of Notre Dame Press, 2002.

Gutierrez, Gustavo. *Las Casas: In Search of the Poor of Jesus Christ*. Translated by Robert R. Barr. Maryknoll, NY: Orbis, 1993.

Hallie, Philip P. *Lest Innocent Blood Be Shed: The Story of the Village of Le Chambon and How Goodness Happened There*. New York: Harper & Row, 1979; HarperPerennial, 1994.

Hampson, Daphne. *Theology and Feminism*. Cambridge, MA: Blackwell, 1990.

Hanby, Michael. "Creation without Creationism: Toward a Theological Critique of Darwinism." *Communio* 30 (Winter 2003): 654–94.

Hardy, Daniel W., and David F. Ford. *Praising and Knowing God*. Philadelphia: Westminster, 1985.

Harink, Douglas. *Paul among the Postliberals: Pauline Theology beyond Christendom and Modernity*. Grand Rapids: Brazos, 2003.

Harmon, Steven R. *Towards Baptist Catholicity: Essays on Tradition and the Baptist Vision*. Waynesboro, GA: Paternoster, 2006.

Harnack, Adolf von. *What is Christianity?* Translated by Thomas Bailey Saunders. New York: Harper & Brothers, 1957.

Harris, Sam. *The End of Faith: Religion, Terror, and the Future of Reason*. New York: Norton, 2004.

Harrison, Peter. *"Religion" and the Religion in the English Enlightenment.* New York: Cambridge University Press, 1990.

Hart, D. Bentley. "A Gift Exceeding Every Debt: An Eastern Orthodox Appreciation of Anselm's *Cur Deus Homo.*" *Pro Ecclesia* 7 (1993): 333–49.

Harvey, Barry. *Another City: An Ecclesiological Primer for a Post-Christian World.* Valley Forge, PA: Trinity Press International, 1999.

Harvey, David. *The Condition of Postmodernity: An Enquiry into the Origins of Cultural Change.* Cambridge, MA: Blackwell, 1990.

Harvey, Van Austin. *The Historian and the Believer: The Morality of Historical Knowledge and Christian Belief.* Toronto: Macmillan, 1966.

Hatch, Nathan O. *The Democratization of American Christianity.* New Haven: Yale University Press, 1989.

Hauerwas, Stanley. *Against the Nations: War and Survival in a Liberal Society.* San Francisco: Harper & Row, 1985.

———. *Dispatches from the Front: Theological Engagements with the Secular.* Durham, NC: Duke University Press, 1994.

———. *In Good Company: The Church as Polis.* Notre Dame, IN: University of Notre Dame Press, 1995.

Hauerwas, Stanley, and L. Gregory Jones, editors. *Why Narrative?* Grand Rapids: Eerdmans, 1989.

Hauerwas, Stanley, and John H. Westerhoff, editors. *Schooling Christians: "Holy Experiments" in American Education.* Grand Rapids: Eerdmans, 1992.

Hauerwas, Stanley, and William H. Willimon, *Resident Aliens: Life in the Christian Colony.* Nashville: Abingdon, 1989.

Havel, Václav. *Living in Truth.* Edited by Jan Vladislav. London: Faber and Faber, 1987.

Heelas, Paul, editor. *Religion, Modernity and Postmodernity.* Malden, MA: Blackwell, 1998.

Hegel, Georg Wilhelm Friedrich. *The Philosophy of History.* Revised ed. Translated by J. Sibree. New York: Willey, 1944.

Heschel, Abraham. *Sabbath: Its Meaning for Modern Man.* New York: Farrar, Straus, 1952.

Heyking, John von. *Augustine and Politics as Longing in the World.* Columbia: University of Missouri Press, 2001.

Hick, John, editor. *The Myth of God Incarnate.* Philadelphia: Westminster, 1977.

Hippolytus. *The Treatise on the Apostolic Tradition.* Edited by Gregory Dix and Henry Chadwick. Ridgefield, CT: Morehouse, 1937, 1968, 1992.

Hobbes, Thomas. *Leviathan.* Edited by Edwin Curley. Indianapolis: Hackett, 1994.

Hodge, Charles. *Systematic Theology.* Vol. 1. New York: Scribner's, 1891; Grand Rapids: Eerdmans, 1999.

Hodgson, Peter C. *Winds of the Spirit: A Constructive Christian Theology.* Louisville: Westminster/John Knox, 1994.

Hofer, Walther, editor. *Der Nationalsozialismus: Dokumente 1933–1945.* Frankfurt am Main: Fischer, 1962.

Hollerich, Michael J. "Retrieving a Neglected Critique of Church, Theology and Secularization in Weimar Germany." *Pro Ecclesia* 2 (Summer 1993): 305–32.

Holmer, Paul L. *The Grammar of Faith.* San Francisco: Harper & Row, 1978.

Homer, *Iliad.* Translated by Stanley Lombardo. Indianapolis: Hackett, 1997.

Horkheimer, Max, and Theodor W. Adorno. *Dialectic of Enlightenment.* Translated by John Cumming. New York: Continuum, 1972.

Houtepen, Anton. *God: An Open Question.* Translated by John Bowden. New York: Continuum, 2002.

Hume, David. *An Enquiry concerning Human Understanding: A Letter from a Gentleman to His Friend in Edinburgh.* Edited by Eric Steinberg. Indianapolis: Hackett, 1977.

Hütter, Reinhard. *Bound to Be Free: Evangelical Catholic Engagements in Ecclesiology, Ethics, and Ecumenism.* Grand Rapids: Eerdmans, 2004.

Ignatius of Antioch. *Epistle to the Romans.* In vol. 1 of *The Ante-Nicene Fathers.* Edited by Alexander Roberts and James Donaldson.

1885–1887. 10 vols. Repr. Peabody, MA.: Hendrickson, 1994.

Jantzen, Grace M. *Power, Gender and Christian Mysticism*. Cambridge: Cambridge University Press, 1995.

Jefferson, Thomas. *The Writings of Thomas Jefferson*. Edited by William Peden. Chapel Hill: University of North Carolina Press, 1954.

Jeffrey, David Lyle. *People of the Book: Christian Identity and Literary Culture*. Grand Rapids: Eerdmans, 1996.

Jenkins, Philip. *The Next Christendom: The Rise of Global Christianity*. New York: Oxford University Press, 2002.

Jennings, Theodore W. *Beyond Theism: A Grammar of God-Language*. New York: Oxford University Press, 1985.

Jenson, Robert. "How the World Lost Its Story." *First Things* 36 (October 1993): 19–24.

———. *Systematic Theology*. Vol. 1: *The Triune God*. Vol. 2: *The Works of God*. New York: Oxford University Press, 1997–1999.

Jeremias, Joachim. *The Eucharistic Words of Jesus*. Translated by Norman Perrin. Philadelphia: Fortress, 1966.

Saint John of the Cross, *Dark Night of the Soul*. Translated by E. Allison Peers. Garden City, NY: Image, 1959.

John Paul II. *Fides et Ratio: To the Bishops of the Catholic Church on the Relationship between Faith and Reason*. Boston: Pauline, 1998.

Jones, Cheslyn, Geoffrey Wainwright, Edward Yarnold SJ, and Paul Bradshaw, editors. *The Study of Liturgy*. Revised ed. New York: Oxford University Press, 1992.

Jones, Laurie Beth. *Jesus, CEO: Using Ancient Wisdom for Visionary Leadership*. New York: Hyperion, 1995.

———. *Jesus in Blue Jeans: A Practical Guide to Everyday Spirituality*. New York: Hyperion, 1997.

Jones, L. Gregory. *Embodying Forgiveness: A Theological Analysis*. Grand Rapids: Eerdmans, 1995.

Jones, L. Gregory, and James J. Buckley, editors. *Theology and Scriptural Imagination*. Malden, MA: Blackwell, 1998.

Jones, L. Gregory, and Stephen E. Fowl, editors. *Rethinking Metaphysics*. Oxford: Blackwell, 1995.

Jowett, Benjamin. *Essays and Reviews*. 7th ed. London: Longman, Green, Longman and Roberts, 1861.

Juergensmeyer, Mark. *Terror in the Mind of God: The Global Rise of Religious Violence*. Berkeley: University of California Press, 2000.

Kant, Immanuel. *Critique of Pure Reason*. Translated by Norman Kemp Smith. New York: St. Martin's, 1965.

———. *Religion within the Boundaries of Mere Reason and Other Writings*. Translated by Allen Wood and George Di Giovanni. New York: Cambridge University Press, 1998.

Kantorowicz, Ernst H. *The King's Two Bodies: A Study in Mediaeval Political Theology*. Princeton, NJ: Princeton University Press, 1957, 1985.

Kedward, H. R. *Resistance in Vichy France: A Study of Ideas and Motivation in the Southern Zone, 1940–1942*. New York: Oxford University Press, 1978.

Kenny, Anthony. *Aquinas on Mind*. New York: Routledge, 1993.

Kent, John H. S. *The End of the Line?: The Development of Christian Theology over the Last Two Centuries*. Philadelphia: Fortress, 1982.

Kepnes, Steven. "A Handbook for Scriptural Reasoning." *Modern Theology* 22 (July 2006): 367–83.

Kermode, Frank. *The Genesis of Secrecy: On the Interpretation of Narrative*. Cambridge: Harvard University Press, 1979.

Kimball, Charles. *When Religion Becomes Evil*. San Francisco: HarperSanFrancisco, 2002.

Klinghoffer, David. *Why the Jews Rejected Jesus: The Turning Point in Western History*. New York: Doubleday, 2005.

Kurtz, Paul. "Humanist Manifesto: A Call for a New Planetary Humanism," *Free Inquiry* 19:4 (Fall 1999): 4–20.

Ladner, Gerhart B. "Aspects of Medieval Thought on Church and State," *Review of Politics* 9 (1947): 403–9.

Lash, Nicholas. *Believing Three Ways in One God: A Reading of the Apostles' Creed.* Notre Dame, IN: University of Notre Dame Press, 1993.

————. *Easter in Ordinary: Reflections on Human Experience and the Knowledge of God.* Charlottesville: University Press of Virginia, 1988.

————. "Ministry of the Word or Comedy and Philology." *New Blackfriars* 68 (1987): 472–83.

————. *Theology on the Way to Emmaus.* London: SCM, 1986.

Laytham, D. Brent, editor. *God Is Not—: Religious, Nice, "One of Us," an American, a Capitalist.* Grand Rapids: Brazos, 2004.

Leclercq, Jean, OSB. *The Love of Learning and the Desire for God.* 2nd ed. Translated by Catharine Misrahi. New York: Fordham University Press, 1974.

Lee, Philip J. *Against the Protestant Gnostics.* New York: Oxford University Press, 1987.

Lefebure, Leo D. *Revelation, the Religions, and Violence.* Maryknoll, NY: Orbis, 2000.

Lehmann, Paul L. *Ethics in a Christian Context.* New York: Harper & Row, 1963.

Leith, John H., editor. *Creeds of the Churches.* Atlanta: John Knox, 1963, 1973.

Leland, John. *The Writings of John Leland.* Edited by L. F. Greene. New York: Arno, 1969.

Lentricchia, Frank. *Ariel and the Police.* Madison: University of Wisconsin Press, 1988.

Lewis, C. S. *Mere Christianity.* New York: Macmillan, 1952, 1960.

Lindbeck, George A. *The Nature of Doctrine: Religion and Theology in a Postliberal Age.* Philadelphia: Westminster, 1984.

Linder, Robert D. "Universal Pastor: President Bill Clinton's Civil Religion." *Journal of Church and State* 38 (Autumn 1996): 733–49.

Locke, John. *A Letter concerning Toleration.* Edited by James H. Tully. Indianapolis: Hackett, 1983.

Lohfink, Gerhard. *Does God Need the Church? Toward a Theology of the People of God.* Translated by Linda M. Maloney. Collegeville, MN: Liturgical Press, 1999.

Long, D. Stephen. *The Divine Economy: Theology and the Market.* New York: Routledge, 2000.

————. *The Goodness of God: Theology, the Church, and Social Order.* Grand Rapids: Brazos, 2001.

Loughlin, Gerard. *Telling God's Story: Bible, Church and Narrative Theology.* New York: Cambridge University Press, 1996.

Lowe, Walter. "Prospects for a Postmodern Christian Theology: Apocalyptic without Reserve." *Modern Theology* 15 (January 1999): 17–24.

Lubac, Henri de, SJ, *Augustinianism and Modern Theology.* Translated by Lancelot Sheppard. New York: Crossroad, 2000.

————. *Catholicism: Christ and the Common Destiny of Man.* Translated by Lancelot C. Sheppard and Elizabeth Englund, OCD. San Francisco: Ignatius, 1988.

————. *Medieval Exegesis: The Four Senses of Scripture.* Vol. 1. Translated by Mark Sebanc. Grand Rapids: Eerdmans, 1998.

————. *Medieval Exegesis: The Four Senses of Scripture.* Vol. 2. Translated by E. M. Macierowski. Grand Rapids: Eerdmans, 2000.

————. *The Mystery of the Supernatural.* Translated by Rosemary Sheed. New York: Crossroad, 1998.

————. *Scripture in the Tradition.* Translated by Luke O'Neill. New York: Herder & Herder, 1968, 2000.

Luhmann, Niklas. *Religious Dogmatics and the Evolution of Societies.* Translated by Peter Beyer. New York: Mellen, 1984.

Lukes, Steven, editor. *Power.* New York: New York University Press, 1986.

Lumpkin, William L. *Baptist Confessions of Faith.* Revised ed. Valley Forge, PA: Judson, 1969.

Luther, Martin. *First Lectures on the Psalms II: Psalms 76–126.* Vol. 11 in *Luther's Works.* Edited by Hilton C. Oswald. Saint Louis: Concordia, 1976.

————. *Three Treatises.* Translated by W. A. Lambert. 2nd ed. Philadelphia: Fortress, 1970.

Lyotard, Jean-François. *The Postmodern Condition: A Report on Knowledge.* Translated by Geoff Bennington and Brian Massumi. Minneapolis: University of Minnesota Press, 1984.

MacIntyre, Alasdair. *After Virtue*. 2nd. ed. Notre Dame, IN: University of Notre Dame Press, 1984.

———. *Dependent Rational Animals: Why Human Beings Need the Virtues*. Chicago: Open Court, 1999.

———. *First Principles, Final Ends and Contemporary Philosophical Issues*. Milwaukee: Marquette University Press, 1990.

———. *Three Rival Versions of Moral Enquiry: Encyclopaedia, Genealogy, and Tradition*. Notre Dame, IN: University of Notre Dame Press, 1990.

———. *Whose Justice? Which Rationality*. Notre Dame, IN: University of Notre Dame Press, 1988.

Markus, R. A. *Saeculum: History and Society in the Theology of St Augustine*. Revised ed. Cambridge: Cambridge University Press, 1988.

Marsh, Charles. *God's Long Summer: Stories of Faith and Civil Rights*. Princeton, NJ: Princeton University Press, 1997.

Marvin, Carolyn, and David W. Ingle. *Blood Sacrifice and the Nation: Totem Rituals and the American Flag*. New York: Cambridge University Press, 1999.

McCabe, Herbert. *God Matters*. London: Geoffrey Chapman, 1987.

McClendon, James Wm, Jr. *Biography as Theology: How Life Stories Can Remake Today's Theology*. Nashville: Abingdon, 1974.

———. *Systematic Theology*. Vol. 1: *Ethics*. Rev. ed. Vol. 2: *Doctrine*. Vol. 3: *Witness*. Nashville: Abingdon, 1986-2000.

McClendon, James Wm. , Jr., and James M. Smith, *Convictions: Defusing Religious Relativism*. Revised ed. Valley Forge, PA: Trinity Press International, 1994.

McGinn, Bernard. "The Letter and the Spirit: Spirituality as an Academic Discipline." *Christian Spirituality Bulletin* 1 (Fall 1993): 1, 3–9.

———. "Love, Knowledge, and Mystical Union in Western Christianity: Twelfth to Sixteenth Centuries." *Church History* 56 (March 1987): 7–24.

McGinn, Bernard, John Meyendorff, and Jean Leclercq, editors. *Christian Spirituality: Origins to the Twelfth Century*. New York: Crossroad, 1997.

McIntosh, Mark A. *Mystical Theology: The Integrity of Spirituality and Theology*. Malden, MA: Blackwell, 1998.

McIntyre, John. *Anselm and His Critics*. Edinburgh: Oliver & Boyd, 1954.

McNeill, John T. *The History and Character of Calvinism*. New York: Oxford University Press, 1954.

McTernan, Oliver. *Violence in God's Name: Religion in an Age of Conflict*. Maryknoll, NY: Orbis 2003.

Metz, Johann Baptist. *Faith in History and Society: Toward a Practical Fundamental Theology*. Translated by David Smith. New York: Seabury, 1980.

Meyer, Ben F. *The Early Christians: Their World Mission and Self-Discovery*. Wilmington, DE: Michael Glazier, 1986.

Milbank, John. *Being Reconciled: Ontology and Pardon*. New York: Routledge, 2003.

———. "'Postmodern Critical Augustinianism': A Short *Summa* in Forty-two Responses to Unasked Questions." *Modern Theology* 7 (April 1991): 225–37.

———. "The Second Difference: For a Trinitarianism without Reserve." *Modern Theology* 2 (1986): 213–34.

———. *Theology and Social Theory: Beyond Secular Reason*. Cambridge, MA: Blackwell, 1990.

———. *The Word Made Strange: Theology, Language, Culture*. Cambridge, MA: Blackwell, 1997.

Milbank, John, and Catherine Pickstock, *Truth in Aquinas*. New York: Routledge, 2001.

Milbank, John, Catherine Pickstock, and Graham Ward, editors. *Radical Orthodoxy: A New Theology*. New York: Routledge, 1999.

Moore, Thomas. *Care of the Soul: A Guide for Cultivating Depth and Sacredness in Everyday Life*. New York: HarperCollins, 1992.

Morris, Colin. *The Discovery of the Individual, 1050–1200*. New York: Harper & Row, 1972.

Mullins, E. Y. *The Axioms of Religion: A New Interpretation of the Baptist Faith*. Philadelphia:

American Baptist Publication Society, 1908.

Murdoch, Iris. *The Sovereignty of Good*. New York: Routledge, 2001.

Murphy, Francesca Aran. *The Comedy of Revelation: Paradise Lost and Regained in Biblical Narrative*. Edinburge: T & T Clark, 2000.

Murphy, Nancey. *Beyond Liberalism and Fundamentalism: How Modern and Postmodern Philosophy Set the Theological Agenda*. Valley Forge, PA: Trinity Press International, 1996.

———. *Theology in the Age of Scientific Reasoning*. Ithaca, NY: Cornell University Press, 1990.

Murray, John Courtney, SJ. *We Hold These Truths: Catholic Reflections on the American Proposition*. Lanham, MD: Sheed and Ward, 2005.

Navone, John, SJ, *Seeking God in Story*. Collegeville, MN: Liturgical Press, 1990.

Nederman, Cary J. and Kate Langdon Forhan, editors. *Readings in Medieval Political Theory: 1100–1400*. Indianapolis: Hackett, 1993.

Neuhaus, Richard John. "Three Constellations of American Religion." *First Things* 111 (March 2001): 71–77.

Newman, Elizabeth. *Untamed Hospitality: Welcoming God and Other Strangers*. Grand Rapids: Brazos, 2007.

Newman, John Henry. *Fifteen Sermons Preached before the University of Oxford between A.D. 1826 and 1843*. Notre Dame, IN: University of Notre Dame Press, 1997.

Newton, Sir Isaac. *Mathematical Principles of Natural Philosophy and His System of the World*. Translated by Andrew Motte. Rev. trans. Florian Cajori. Berkeley: University of California Press, 1960.

Niebuhr, Reinhold. *Moral Man and Immoral Society: A Study in Ethics and Politics*. New York: Charles Scribner's Sons, 1932, 1960.

Nietzsche, Friedrich. *The Gay Science*. Translated by Walter Kaufmann. New York: Vintage, 1974.

———. *The Portable Nietzsche*. Translated by Walter Kaufmann. New York: Penguin, 1954.

Nisbet, Robert A. *The Quest for Community: A Study in the Ethics of Order and Freedom*. New York: Oxford University Press, 1953.

Novak, David. "Edith Stein, Apostate Saint." *First Things* 96 (October 1999): 15–17.

Nussbaum, Martha C. *Cultivating Humanity: A Classical Defense of Reform in Liberal Education*. Cambridge: Harvard University Press, 1997.

Oberman, Heiko Augustinus. *The Harvest of Medieval Theology: Gabriel Biel and Late Medieval Nominalism*. Cambridge: Harvard University Press, 1963.

O'Connor, Flannery. *Collected Works*. New York: The Library of America, 1988.

———. *Mystery and Manners: Occasional Prose*. Edited by Sally and Robert Fitzgerald. New York: Farrar, Straus & Giroux, 1969.

O'Connor, James. *Accumulation Crisis*. New York: Blackwell, 1984.

O'Donovan, Oliver. *The Desire of the Nations: Rediscovering the Roots of Political Theology*. Cambridge: Cambridge University Press, 1996.

O'Keefe, John J., and R. R. Reno. *Sanctified Vision: An Introduction to Early Christian Interpretation of the Bible*. Baltimore: Johns Hopkins University Press, 2005.

Origen. *Contra Celsus*. In vol. 4 of *The Ante-Nicene Fathers*. Edited by Alexander Roberts and James Donaldson. 1885–1887. 10 vols. Repr. Peabody, MA.: Hendrickson, 1994.

———. "Dialogue of Origen with Heraclides and His Fellow Bishops on the Father, the Son, and the Soul." Translated by Robert J. Daly, SJ *Ancient Christian Writers: The Works of the Fathers in Translation*, no. 54. Edited by Walter J. Burghardt, Thomas Comerford Lawler, and John J. Dillon. New York: Paulist, 1992.

Pannenberg, Wolfhart. *Systematic Theology*. Vol. 1. Translated by Geoffrey W. Bromiley. Grand Rapids: Eerdmans, 1991.

Peirce, C. S. *Writings of C. S. Peirce*. Vol. 3. Bloomington: Indiana University Press, 1986.

Percy, Walker. *Lost in the Cosmos: The Last Self-Help Book*. New York: Farrar, Straus & Giroux, 1983.

———. *Sign-Posts in a Strange Land*. Edited by Patrick Samway. New York: Farrar, Straus & Giroux, 1991.

Perkins, John M., editor. *Restoring At-Risk Communities: Doing It Together and Doing It Right*. Grand Rapids: Baker, 1995.

Peterson, Merrill D., and Robert C. Vaughan, editors. *The Virginia Statute for Religious Freedom*. New York: Cambridge University Press, 1988.

Petry, Ray C., editor. *Late Medieval Mysticism*. Philadelphia: Westminster, 1957.

Phillips, Timothy R., and Dennis L. Okholm, editors. *The Nature of Confession: Evangelicals and Postliberals in Conversation*. Downers Grove, IL: InterVarsity, 1996.

Pieper, Josef. *Living the Truth: The Truth of all Things and Reality and the Good*. Translated by Lothar Krauth and Stella Lange. San Francisco: Ignatius, 1989.

Plato. *The Republic*. 2nd ed. Translated by Allan Bloom. New York: Basic, 1991.

Porter, Bruce D. *War and the Rise of the State: The Military Foundations of Modern Politics*. New York: Free Press, 1994.

Poteat, William H. *A Philosophical Daybook: Post-Critical Investigations*. Columbia: University of Missouri Press, 1990.

———. *Polanyian Meditations: In Search of a Post-Critical Logic*. Durham, NC: Duke University Press, 1985.

Pseudo-Dionysius, *Pseudo-Dionysius: The Complete Works*. Translated by Colm Luibheid. New York: Paulist, 1987.

Putnam, Robert. "Bowling Alone: America's Declining Social Capital." *Journal of Democracy* 6 (January 1995): 65–78.

———. *Bowling Alone: The Collapse and Revival of American Community*. New York: Simon & Schuster, 2000.

Raboteau, Albert J. *Slave Religion: The 'Invisible Institution' in the Antebellum South*. New York: Oxford University Press, 1978.

Radner, Ephraim. *The End of the Church: A Pneumatology of Christian Division in the West*. Grand Rapids: Eerdmans, 1998.

Rahner, Hugo, SJ. *Church and State in Early Christianity*. Translated by Leo Donald Davis, SJ. San Francisco: Ignatius, 1992.

Rauschenbusch, Walter. *Christianizing the Social Order*. New York: Macmillan, 1912.

Rawick, George P. *From Sundown to Sunup*. Westport, CT: Greenwood, 1972.

Rawls, John. *Political Liberalism*. New York: Columbia University Press, 1993.

Ricoeur, Paul. *Essays on Biblical Interpretation*. Edited by Lewis S. Mudge. Philadelphia: Fortress, 1980.

———. *From Text to Action*. Translated by Kathleen Blamey and John B. Thompson. Evanston, IL: Northwestern University Press, 1991.

———. *On Paul Ricoeur: Narrative and Interpretation*. Edited by David Wood. New York: Routledge, 1991.

———. *Time and Narrative*. Vol. 1. Translated by Kathleen McLaughlin and David Pellauer. Chicago, The University of Chicago Press, 1984.

Ritschl, Dietrich. *The Logic of Theology: A Brief Account of the Relationship between Basic Concepts in Theology*. Philadelphia: Fortress, 1987.

Rittner, Carol, and Sondra Myers, editors. *The Courage to Care: Rescuers of Jews During the Holocaust*. New York: New York University Press, 1986.

Rorty, Richard. *Achieving Our Country: Leftist Thought in Twentieth-Century America*. Cambridge: Harvard University Press, 1998.

Rosin, Hanna. "Beyond 2000: Many Shape Unique Religions at Home." *Washington Post*, Jan 17, 2000: A1.

Rothrock, G. A. *The Huguenots: A Biography of a Minority*. Chicago: Nelson-Hall, 1979.

Rouse, Joseph. *Knowledge and Power*. Ithaca, NY: Cornell University Press, 1987.

Rousseau, Jean-Jacques. *The Social Contract*. Translated by Willmoore Kendall. South Bend, IN: Gateway, 1954.

Sandel, Michael J. *Democracy's Discontent: America in Search of a Public Philosophy*. Cambridge, MA: Belknap, 1996.

Sanders, E. P. *Judaism: Practice and Belief, 63 BCE–66 CE*. Philadelphia: Trinity Press International, 1992.

Sauter, Gerhard, and John Barton, editors. *Revelation and Story: Narrative Theology and the Centrality of Story*. Burlington, VT: Ashgate, 2000.

Schindler, David L. "Christology and the *Imago Dei*: Interpreting *Gaudium et Spes*." *Communio* 23 (Spring 1996): 156–84.

Schipani, Daniel S., editor. *Freedom and Discipleship: Liberation Theology in Anabaptist Perspective*. Maryknoll, NY: Orbis, 1989.

Schleiermacher, Friedrich. *The Christian Faith*. Edited by H. R. Macintosh and J. S. Stewart. Philadelphia: Fortress, 1928.

———. *On Religion: Speeches to its Cultured Despisers*. Translated by Richard Crouter. New York: Cambridge University Press, 1996.

Schmemann, Alexander. *Church, World, Mission: Reflections on Orthodoxy in the West*. Crestwood, NY: St. Vladimir's Seminary Press, 1979.

———. *For the Life of the World: Sacraments and Orthodoxy*. Crestwood, NY: St. Vladimir's Seminary Press, 1963, 1973.

Scott, Allen J., and Michael Storper, editors. *Production, Work, Territory: The Geographical Anatomy of Industrial Capitalism*. Boston: Allen & Unwin, 1986.

Selengut, Charles. *Sacred Fury: Understanding Religious Violence*. Walnut Creek, CA: Altamira, 2004.

Sen, S. R. *The Economics of Sir James Steuart*. Cambridge: Harvard University Press, 1957.

Shannon, Laurie J. "Emilia's Argument: Friendship and 'Human Title' in *The Two Noble Kinsmen*." *English Literary History* 64 (1997): 680.

Sheldrake, Philip. *Spirituality and History: Questions of Interpretation and Method*. Revised ed. London: SPCK, 1995.

Sinkewicz, Robert E., translator and editor. *Evagrius of Pentus: The Greek Ascetic Corpus*. New York: Oxford University Press, 2003.

Skinner, Quentin. *The Age of Reformation*. Vol. 2 in *The Foundations of Modern Political Thought*. London: Cambridge University Press, 1978.

Editors at SkyLight Paths. *Who Is My God? An Innovative Guide to Finding Your Spiritual Identity*. Woodstock, VT: SkyLight Paths, 2000.

Smith, Harmon L. *Where Two or Three Are Gathered: Liturgy and the Moral Life*. Cleveland: Pilgrim, 1995.

Smith, Wilfred Cantwell. *The Meaning and End of Religion: A New Approach to the Religious Traditions of Mankind*. New York: Macmillan, 1962.

Soelle, Dorothee. *The Window of Vulnerability: A Political Spirituality*. Minneapolis: Fortress, 1990.

Soskice, Janet Martin. *Metaphor and Religious Language*. Oxford: Oxford University Press, 1985.

Soulen, R. Kendall. *The God of Israel and Christian Theology*. Minneapolis: Fortress, 1996.

Southern, Richard William. *Western Society and the Church in the Middle Ages*. Harmondsworth, UK: Penguin, 1985.

Spruyt, Hendrik. *The Sovereign State and Its Competitors*. Princeton, NJ: Princeton University Press, 1994.

Stackhouse, Max L. *Covenant and Commitments: Faith, Family, and Economic Life*. Louisville: Westminster/John Knox, 1997.

———. *Public Theology and Political Economy: Christian Stewardship in Modern Society*. Grand Rapids: Eerdmans, 1987.

Stark, Rodney. *The Rise of Christianity: A Sociologist Reconsiders History*. Princeton: Princeton University Press, 1996.

Steinsaltz, Adin. *The Essential Talmud*. Translated by Chaya Galia. New York: Basic Books, 1976.

Stendahl, Krister. "Biblical Theology, Contemporary." Pages 418–32 in vol. 1 of *The Interpreter's Dictionary of the Bible*. Edited by G. A. Buttrick. 4 vols. Nashville: Abingdon, 1962.

Stevens, Wallace. *Letters*. Edited by Holly Stevens. New York: A. A. Knopf, 1966.

Storrar, William F., and Andrew R. Morton, editors. *Public Theology for the 21st Century*. New York: T & T Clark, 2004.

Strauss, Leo. *The Rebirth of Classical Political Rationalism: An Introduction to the Thought of Leo Strauss*. Chicago: The University of Chicago Press, 1989.

Strayer, Joseph R. "The Laicization of French and English Society in the Thirteenth Century." *Speculum* 15 (1940): 76.

———. *On the Medieval Origins of the Modern State*. Princeton, NJ: Princeton University Press, 1970.

Stringfellow, William. *The Politics of Spirituality*. Philadelphia: Westminster, 1984.

Stroumsa, Guy G. *Hidden Wisdom: Esoteric Traditions and the Roots of Christian Mysticism*. New York: E. J. Brill, 1996.

Swinburne, Richard. *The Existence of God*. Oxford: Oxford University Press, 1979.

———. *Revelation: From Metaphor to Analogy*. Oxford: Clarendon, 1992.

Tanner, Kathryn. *Theories of Culture: A New Agenda for Theology*. Minneapolis: Augsburg Fortress, 1997.

Taylor, Charles. *Modern Social Imaginaries*. Durham, NC: Duke University Press, 2004.

———. *Sources of the Self: The Making of Modern Identity*. Cambridge: Harvard University Press, 1989.

Tertullian, *De Corona*. In vol. 3 of *The Ante-Nicene Fathers*. Edited by Alexander Roberts and James Donaldson. 1885–1887. 10 vols. Repr. Peabody, MA.: Hendrickson, 1994.

Thiselton, Anthony C. *Interpreting God and the Postmodern Self: On Meaning, Manipulation and Promise*. Edinburgh: T & T Clark, 1995.

Tilley, Terrence F. "Incommensurability, Intratextuality, and Fideism." *Modern Theology* 5 (January 1989): 87–117.

Tillich, Paul. *Dynamics of Faith*. New York: Harper & Row, 1957.

Toqueville, Alexis de. *Democracy in America*. Translated by Gerald E. Bevan. New York: Penguin, 2003.

Torrell, Jean-Pierre, OP. *Saint Thomas Aquinas*. Vol.1, *The Person and His Work*. Translated by Robert Royal. Washington, DC: Catholic University of America Press, 1996.

Toulmin, Stephen. *Cosmopolis: The Hidden Agenda of Modernity*. Chicago: University of Chicago Press, 1990.

———. *Human Understanding*. Princeton, NJ: Princeton University Press, 1972.

Tracy, David. *The Analogical Imagination: Christian Theology and the Culture of Pluralism*. New York: Crossroad, 1981.

Trocmé, André. *Jesus and the Nonviolent Revolution*. Translated by Michael H. Shank and Marlin E. Martin. Scottdale, PA: Herald, 1973.

Turner, Denys. *The Darkness of God: Negativity in Christian Mysticism*. New York: Cambridge University Press, 1995.

———. *Faith, Reason and the Existence of God*. Cambridge: Cambridge University Press, 2004.

Van Engen, John, editor. *Learning Institutionalized: Teaching in the Medieval University*. Notre Dame, IN: University of Notre Dame Press, 2000.

Vanhoozer, Kevin J. *The Drama of Doctrine: A Canonical Linguistic Approach to Christian Theology*. Louisville: Westminster John Knox, 2005.

Virgil. *The Aeneid*. Translated by Robert Fagles. New York: Viking, 2006.

Wainwright, Geoffrey. *Eucharist and Eschatology*. New York: Oxford University Press, 1981.

———, editor. *Keeping the Faith: Essays to Mark the Centenary of Lux Mundi*. Philadelphia: Fortress, 1988.

Ward, Graham. *Cultural Transformation and Religious Practice*. New York: Cambridge University Press, 2005.

Warfield, Benjamin B. *The Inspiration and Authority of the Bible*. Edited by Samuel G. Craig. Phillipsburg, NJ: Presbyterian and Reformed Publishing Co., 1948.

Weber, Max. *Politics as Vocation*. Philadelphia: Fortress, 1965.

———. *The Protestant Ethic and the Spirit of Capitalism*. Translated by Talcott Parsons. London: Unwin, 1930.

Weinandy, Thomas G., OFM Cap. *Does God Change? The Word's Becoming in the Incarnation*. Still River, MA: St. Bede's, 1985.

———. *Does God Suffer?* Notre Dame, IN: University of Notre Dame Press, 2000.

Wells, Samuel. *Improvisation: The Drama of Christian Ethics*. Grand Rapids: Brazos, 2004.

Wicker, Brian. *The Story-Shaped World: Fiction and Metaphysics: Some Variations on a Theme*. Notre Dame, IN: University of Notre Dame Press, 1975.

Wilken, Robert L. *The Christians as the Romans Saw Them*. New Haven: Yale University Press, 1984.

———. *John Chrysostom and the Jews: Rhetoric and Reality in the Late 4th Century*. Berkeley: University of California Press, 1983.

———. *Remembering the Christian Past*. Grand Rapids: Eerdmans, 1995.

———. *The Spirit of Early Christian Thought: Seeking the Face of God*. New Haven, CT: Yale University Press, 2003.

William of St. Thierry. *The Mirror of Faith*. Translated by Thomas X. Davis. Kalamazoo, MI: Cistercian, 1979.

Williams, D. H., editor. *The Free Church and the Early Church: Bridging the Historical Divide*. Grand Rapids: Eerdmans, 2002.

Williams, Rowan. *Christ on Trial: How the Gospel Unsettles Our Judgment*. Grand Rapids: Eerdmans, 2000.

———. "Language, Reality and Desire in Augustine's *De Doctrina*." *Literature and Theology* 3 (July 1989): 138–50.

———. *Lost Icons: Reflection on Cultural Bereavement*. Edinburgh: T&T Clark, 2000.

———. *On Christian Theology*. Malden, MA: Blackwell, 2000.

———. "Politics and the Soul: A Reading of the *City of God*." *Milltown Studies* 19/20 (1987): 55–72.

———. *Resurrection: Interpreting the Easter Gospel*. New York: Pilgrim, 1984.

———. "Theological Integrity." *New Blackfriars* 72 (1991): 140–51.

———. "The Unity of Christian Truth." *New Blackfriars* 70 (February 1989): 85–95.

———. *The Wound of Knowledge*, 2nd ed. Boston: Cowley, 1990.

Wittgenstein, Ludwig. *Philosophical Investigations*. Translated by G. E. M. Anscombe. 3rd ed. New York: Macmillan, 1958.

Wolff, Hans Walter. *Joel and Amos: A Commentary on the Books of the Prophets Joel and Amos*. Translated by Waldemar Janzen, S. Dean McBride Jr., and Charles A. Muenchow. Philadelphia: Fortress, 1977.

Wright, N. T. *The Climax of the Covenant*. Minneapolis: Fortress, 1992.

———. *Jesus and the Victory of God*. Vol. 2 in *Christian Origins and the Question of God*. Minneapolis: Fortress, 1996.

———. *The New Testament and the People of God*. Vol. 1 in *Christian Origins and the Question of God*. Minneapolis: Fortress, 1992.

———. *Who Was Jesus?* Grand Rapids: Eerdmans, 1993.

Wyschogrod, Michael. *The Body of Faith: God in the People Israel*. San Francisco: Harper & Row, 1983.

Yoder, John Howard. "Armaments and Eschatology." *Studies in Christian Ethics* 1 (1988): 55–58.

———. *For the Nations: Essays Public and Evangelical*. Grand Rapids: Eerdmans, 1997.

———. *The Politics of Jesus: Vicit Agnus Noster*. 2nd ed. Grand Rapids: Eerdmans, 1994.

———. *Priestly Kingdom: Social Ethics as Gospel*. Notre Dame, IN: University of Notre Dame Press, 1984.

———. *The Royal Priesthood: Essays Ecclesiological and Ecumenical*. Edited by M. G. Cartwright. Grand Rapids: Eerdmans, 1994.

Zizioulas, John D. *Being as Communion*. Crestwood, NY: St. Vladimir's Seminary Press, 1985.

Zwingli, Ulrich. *Commentary on True and False Religion*. Edited by Samuel Macauley Jackson and Clarence Nevin Heller. Durham, NC: Labyrinth, 1981.

Scripture Index

Old Testament

Genesis

Exodus

Leviticus

Deuteronomy

1 Samuel

2 Samuel

Nehemiah

Psalms

Isaiah

Jeremiah

General Index

Abraham, 21, 58, 60–62, 64–65, 71, 75, 78, 85–86, 96, 99, 152, 162–63, 193, 213, 269

Adam, 62–63, 71, 86, 192, 259, 269, 272

Adamson, Robert, 135

Adorno, Theodor W., 149n67

Africa, 45n60, 64, 152, 240

African Americans, 51n81, 85n81, 151–53, 240, 270, 287

age to come, 20, 24, 32, 50, 55, 75, 77n65, 82, 86–87, 89, 106, 174, 193, 229, 242, 264, 266, 274, 280, 282, 286. *See also* present age

Alexander the Great, 79

Alighieri, Dante, 9, 34, 62, 91, 210, 254, 265

America, United States, 36, 39, 40–41, 45, 85n81, 98n12, 160, 168, 216, 222n63, 239, 240, 255, 270n15, 270–72

Amin, Ash, 278n40

Amos, 98

analogy, 23, 38, 142, 145–46, 150, 160, 164, 185n86, 187, 277

Ananias, 82–83

ancien régime, 18, 20, 123

Anderson, Benedict, 118n99, 118n102

another city, another commonwealth, 12, 20, 43, 55, 101, 217. *See also* City of God

Anselm, 33, 190–94

anti-Judaism, anti-Semitism, 60n11

Antiochus IV, 79

apocalypse, apocalyptic, 21, 24–25, 41, 50–51, 54–55, 58–60, 72–83, 86–87, 89–91, 95, 100, 104, 106, 115, 123, 126, 152, 154, 158, 160–61, 168, 189, 196, 202–3, 205, 207, 211, 213, 215,

219, 222, 226–28, 231, 236, 241, 246, 249, 252, 264, 266–67, 272–74, 281, 283

apophatic, 252n71. *See also* cataphatic, negation

Appleby, R. Scott., 271n19

apprentice, apprenticeship, 35, 142, 146, 201, 234, 248, 253

Aquinas, Thomas, 53, 62n15, 63n22, 99n13, 111, 117n96, 120n112, 165, 176n45, 180, 196n135, 203, 236n13, 244, 273–74

arche, 171

Aristotle, 99n13, 102n25, 102n26, 176

Arius, 179

art of pilgrimage, 25, 267

art of the weak, 284

artisans, 25, 33, 264, 266, 274, 280, 282, 285

Asad, Talal, 24n38, 32n6, 34, 36n24, 44n57, 111n62, 138n27, 178n56, 204

Asia, 45n60

Athanasius, 80, 191, 244

atonement, 88–89, 190–91, 194, 215

Auerbach, Erich, 156n88

Augustine, 25, 31n3, 32, 33, 43, 77n46, 84, 90, 101n24, 104–6, 132n3, 147n64, 154, 170n22, 173, 181, 192n117, 194–96, 199, 205, 212n26, 215, 234, 246, 247n52, 251n65, 256, 258, 266n3, 267, 269n11, 270n15, 281

authority, secular, 16, 38, 64, 96, 102, 106, 108, 110, 113–14, 119, 123, 207, 211–12, 220–21, 223, 280–81

authority, divine, 58, 68, 170, 211, 220–21

authority, ecclesiastical, 97, 106, 108–9, 123, 197–98, 248